CALLIOPE'S SISTERS

A Comparative Study of Philosophies of Art

Richard L. Anderson

Kansas City Art Institute

PRENTICE HALL
Englewood Cliffs, New Jersey 07632

Library of Congress Cataloging-in-Publication Data

Anderson, Richard L.
    Calliope's sisters : a comparative study of philosophies of art /
  Richard L. Anderson.
        p.   cm.
    Bibliography: p.
    Includes index.
    ISBN 0-13-155425-5
    1. Aesthetics--Comparative studies.   I. Title.
  BH39.A57 1990
  701'.17--dc20   89-8389
                                                          CIP

Editorial/production supervision
  and interior design: Virginia L. McCarthy
Cover design: Kim Anderson
  and Richard L. Anderson
Cover photo: Wooden mask made by a 19th-century
  Lega carver, from the collection of The Nelson-
  Atkins Museum of Art, Kansas City, Missouri
  (acquired with Nelson Foundation funds)
Manufacturing buyer: Carol Bystrom

 © 1990 by Prentice-Hall, Inc.
A Division of Simon & Schuster
Englewood Cliffs, New Jersey 07632

Printed in the United States of America
10 9 8 7 6 5 4 3 2

ISBN 0-13-155425-5

Prentice-Hall International (UK) Limited, *London*
Prentice-Hall of Australia Pty. Limited, *Sydney*
Prentice-Hall Canada Inc., *Toronto*
Prentice-Hall Hispanoamericana, S.A., *Mexico*
Prentice-Hall of India Private Limited, *New Delhi*
Prentice-Hall of Japan, Inc., *Tokyo*
Simon & Schuster Asia Pte. Ltd., *Singapore*
Editora Prentice-Hall do Brasil, Ltda., *Rio de Janeiro*

To the memory of
Raymond Bragg,
humanist, friend, and exemplar,
and to the future of
William Archer Anderson

CONTENTS

3

ABORIGINAL AUSTRALIAN AESTHETICS: Sacramental Union with ,the Eternal Dreamtime   55

4

AESTHETICS OF THE SEPIK: Powerful Spirits and Phallic Aggression in New Guinea   72

5

NAVAJO AESTHETICS: A Unity of Art and Life   95

6

YORUBA AESTHETICS: Goodness and Beauty in West Africa   *112*

PART TWO

11

INTRODUCTION TO PART TWO

12

COMPARATIVE AESTHETICS: The Many Faces of the Muse

13

ART AS CULTURALLY SIGNIFICANT MEANING

14

STYLE, FEELING, AND SKILL

LIST OF ILLUSTRATIONS

PREFACE

The idea for this book was born ten and a half years ago as I was putting the finishing touches on another book, a textbook that surveyed the major issues in the anthropological study of art, with chapters on such topics as "The Functions of Art," "The Artist's Life and Work," and so on. The last professional colleague to review the manuscript before it went to press was Warren d'Azevedo, whose careful reading caught a number of errors and omissions—mostly minor, but some embarrassingly important. Generally, Warren's remarks were encouraging and supportive, but at one point he remarked that until anthropologists get out of their habit of studying art exclusively as the handmaiden of other subjects and begin taking art on its own terms, we can never hope to gain a fundamental understanding of art *per se.*

I teach at the Kansas City Art Institute, a college where, far from being a "handmaiden" of anything, art is the central focus of concern; and perhaps because of that, d'Azevedo's remark struck me as being absolutely on target. Art does, admittedly, play an interesting role in other realms of human life, but what is the core of art itself? Wouldn't it be worthwhile to examine that question in a number of different societies? From previous reading, I knew that sufficient information was available to undertake such a study. After toying with the idea for a while, a couple hours of jotting down ideas produced a rough outline for this book: I would describe philosophies of art in several diverse, non-Western societies and then examine the similarities and differences among them.

Turning the outline into a book has been a protracted (though satisfying) experience; nevertheless, its results remain tentative for two reasons. First, the body of research and writing about non-Western art has increased so dramatically in recent years that no one can claim total familiarity with all of it; and second, the extant literature continues to have numerous gaps, tantalizing lacunae that only future research and publication will fill. But despite these limitations, there is enough information at hand to undertake a synthetic, cross-cultural study of philosophies of art, and that is what this book sets out to do.

The book's inevitable flaws and shortcomings would have been far greater had it not been for the assistance and support of many individuals and institutions. Extensive and detailed critical suggestions came from Joann W. Keali'inohomoku, to whose scholarship and good judgment I am greatly indebted. Others who read and provided valuable comments on part or all of the manuscript are Valerie Alexander, Elizabeth Anderson, Jack Cashell, Anne Devaney, Evelyn Hatcher, Harvey Hix, Briggita Hauser-Schäublin, John Messenger, Marcella Nesom, Rachel Pennabecker, Paul D. Schaefer, and Robert Farris Thompson. Countless valuable ideas, corrections, and clarifications have been prompted by students in my classes at the Kansas City Art Institute, and I heartily thank them for their help.

I also stand in debt to the staffs of the libraries (and especially the inter-library loan personnel) at the Kansas City Art Institute, the University of Missouri at Kansas City, and the Kansas City Public Library. Mimi Pettigrew and Teddy Graham gave able secretarial assistance, and helpful financial support was provided by numerous grants from the Andrew W. Mellon Fund and the Association of Independent Colleges of Art. At Prentice Hall, the ever-competent Nancy Roberts, Virginia McCarthy, and Vicky Tandler have all been a pleasure to work with.

Finally, I give my heartfelt thanks to Kim Anderson for her sympathetic support, for her discerning insights into art and the human soul, for the many editorial suggestions she made toward clarifying my presentation, and for being an ever stimulating participant in the artist-scientist dialogue that this book represents.

R.L.A.
Kansas City

ACKNOWLEDGMENTS

Grateful acknowledgment is also made to the following for permission to quote from copyrighted material:

From Laurens Van der Post, 1958, *The Lost World of the Kalahari*, p. 247. Reprinted by permission of William Morrow and Company, Inc.

From Knut Rasmussen, 1931, *The Netsilik Eskimos: Social Life and Spiritual Culture. Fifth Thule, Vol. 8.* Reprinted by permission of AMS Press.

From Ronald M. Berndt, 1964, *The World of the First Australians.* Reprinted by permission of the University of Chicago Press and Ure Smith.

From Carl August Schmitz, 1963, *Wantoat: Art and Religion of the Northeast New Guinea Papuans.* Reprinted by permission of Mouton de Gruyter.

From Gary Witherspoon, 1977, *Language and Art in the Navajo Universe.* Reprinted by permission of University of Michigan Press.

From Robert Farris Thompson, 1983, *Flash of the Spirit: African and Afro-American Art and Philosophy.* Reprinted by permission of Random House.

From Miguel León-Portilla, 1971, "Philosophy in Ancient Mexico," in Volume 10 of *The Handbook of Middle American Indians.* Reprinted by permission of University of Texas Press.

From Masaharu Anesaki, 1933, *Art, Life, and Nature in Japan.* Reprinted by permission of Marshall Jones.

From Tom Wolfe, 1975, *The Painted Word.* Reprinted by permission of Farrar, Strauss, & Giroux.

From Eliot Deutsch, 1975, *Studies in Comparative Aesthetics.* (Monograph of the Society for Asian and Comparative Philosophy, No. 2.) Reprinted by permission of University Press of Hawaii.

From Richard Selzer, 1979, *Confessions of a Knife,* p. 196. Reprinted by permission of William Morrow & Company and Hogarth Press.

From George Devereux, 1961, "Art and Mythology," in Bert Kaplan, ed., *Studying Personality Cross-culturally.* Reprinted by permission of Harper and Row.

INTRODUCTION
Calliope's Sisters

When the early Greeks speculated about the fundamental nature of art, they initially thought the matter was fairly simple. The goddess Mnemosyne (memory) bore a daughter of the great god Zeus. The child was called Calliope. When she was grown, she gave to human beings the gift of art, a benefaction that was particularly fitting from one who joined the genius of past experience, as represented by memory, with the awesome and immediate power over the present moment that was Zeus's. But this mythical account of the origin of art soon seemed inadequate. How could a single goddess foster such diverse activities as comedy and tragedy, music and dance, sacred poetry and the lyrics of love? By the eighth century B.C., Hesiod was describing Calliope's enlarged family. Now she was the foremost member of a group of nine sisters, the Muses, each associated with a specific art. Or were the nine led by a tenth Muse, Apollo, the god of light? Other accounts assigned still different duties, names, and numbers to these Olympian patrons of the arts.

But mythology's chief value lies in its ability to give humans an unambiguous understanding of their seemingly contradictory and chaotic lives. The classical poets must have realized this for Calliope's family was soon simplified again by attributing all art to "The Muse." This usage generally remains with us today, reflecting our common assumption that all art derives from a single source, that it is possessed of a unitary nature and purpose, and that it can be evaluated by a single principle of criticism. Of course, on closer reflection, most Westerners concede (as did Hesiod) that things may not be so simple; and even a passing acquaintance with non-Western art complicates the picture even further. But despite such problems, this assumption continues to inform much of our thinking about art.

Thus we still have the ancient dilemma of Calliope's sisters. Are they, and the arts they represent, distinctly different personages with no more than a slight familial resemblance to each other? Or does the Muse have a single identity, capable of donning superficially differing guises depending on time, place, and medium? These questions are at the core of this book, but before we address them some methodological issues must be discussed. We can start by asking why Calliope's family should interest us in the first place.

1

The Role of Art and Aesthetics

The instrumental concerns of our day-to-day lives, such as making a living, the humdrum business of economics, and the practical matters of politics, provide for our needs as biological organisms. Simply put, they keep us alive. But why live at all? For what reason do we exert our minds and bodies so that we will be sustained? One answer lies not in the instrumentalities of our bodily existence but in the affective realm of our minds. We live to perpetuate our own spiritual existence and the lives of our loved ones; we live because of the symbolic value we attach to life itself; and we live to experience the joys and passions of today and tomorrow. Life's gratifications range from the private to the public, the idiosyncratic to the societal, and the sensuous to the intellectual. It is unclear where practical activities leave off and expressive culture begins, but it *is* clear that the Muse makes a very important contribution to the latter. In a word, art can make life worthwhile. And, as Herbert Read has observed, the alienation that plagues the modern Western world can only benefit from a renewed interest in the blessed Muse.

The apparent neglect of the arts in popular Western culture is paralleled by the scant attention they have received from scholars. While everything from moon rocks to Oedipal urges have been examined in minute detail, art has often been ignored. And when art has inspired study, the most common approach has been merely to describe and categorize it according to stylistic features or else to examine it as an adjunct to more concrete activities such as art's economic functions or the training of artists. What has received very little attention is the issue that constitutes the very core of art, namely aesthetics.

Of course *aesthetics,* as the branch of Western philosophy that focuses on the fundamental nature and value of art, has spawned a substantial literature, and the main currents of Western aesthetics will be described in a later chapter. However, a basic assumption of this book is that the Western world does not have a monopoly on wisdom and insight regarding art. To the contrary, an important means to a deeper understanding of any particular endeavor is to examine it in other human cultures in the hope of ferreting out the shared and pan-human.

From this broader, cross-cultural perspective, let us return to Calliope and her family. The question now becomes this: Looking at the world around us, is there a single motivation that prompts works of art in all human cultures; or, if the essence of art is multiple, does Calliope have only a finite number of sisters; or is the situation one of total relativism, with a unique Muse inspiring every culture's characteristic art?

Progress often results from asking questions that are just difficult enough, neither too easy as to be trivial nor too difficult as to produce only frustration. The question of Calliope's sisters most assuredly will not prove to be too easy. The danger, rather, is that the questions are too difficult to be conclusively studied at the present time. However, thanks to work carried out in recent years by scholars interested in non-Western art, I believe that the search for Calliope's sisters may now be undertaken with a hope of some real success. Certainly the current state of our knowledge is such that we may begin to get glimpses of some of the sisters and of the fundamental nature of art.

The Cultural Anthropological Approach

Although I will also draw on the work of art historians, art critics, and phi losophers, the prevailing perspective throughout this book is that of cul tural anthropology. In contrast to *archaeologists,* who learn about societies that no longer exist by examining the materials they left behind, *cultural anthropologists* usually focus their attention on societies that can be studied via the statements of living members of the society. Occasionally these are cultures of the past. The main outlines of early sixteenth-century Aztec soci ety, for example, are known today largely because the Aztecs and their Span ish conquerors left many written descriptions of Aztec life ways. But far more often a cultural anthropologist's goal is to learn about a contemporary culture by living in it for a year or more, learning the language of its people, and participating in their daily activities. The observations and impressions of such fieldwork serve as a basis for the anthropologist's written account of the society, called an *ethnography.*

The ethnographer may focus on any of a number of subjects, but an important distinction that must be made at this point is between "emic" and "etic" culture, either or both of which the anthropologist may describe. Things that have an observable existence and that can be studied through methods that are applicable in any human population have come to be called *etic.* The average number of people in a native household or the num ber of calories they consume daily in their diet are examples of etic data.

By contrast, *emic* culture exists only in the minds of the culture's mem bers, having meaning only in the context of the native conceptual system. Thus, whereas family size is etic, the way family members conceptualize kin ship relations is emic.

The distinction between etic and emic culture will arise continually in this book, and it will be important that the reader appreciate that different kinds of information are conveyed by etic statements (e.g., "masks are carved out of wood from two species of trees") and emic statements ("native critics generally feel that masks carved from one type of wood are more desirable than those carved from the other"). The difference between such statements can be seen, for example, in the fact that they are verified or refuted in different ways. To confirm the etic statement about two kinds of wood being used in masks, one would consult a botanist; to confirm the

emic statement about the relative beauty of the woods, a native art connoisseur. *Information about emic aesthetics in ten societies constitutes the primary data
upon which this book is based.*

Cultural anthropologists have traditionally spent less time examining
the cultures of complex societies such as the United States, China, and India
than they have studying small-scale societies such as those of Native American Indians, the societies of sub-Saharan Africa, and the native peoples of
the Pacific islands. The first cultural anthropologists, writing only a little
more than a century ago, viewed small-scale societies as being altogether
simpler, less developed, and generally inferior to contemporary Western
society. However, after rigorous methods of fieldwork were adopted, this
viewpoint, which would now be called *ethnocentric*, was discarded for both
empirical and ethical reasons. It was largely replaced by the concept of *cultural relativism*, the belief that every traditional society, regardless of the size
of its population and the complexity of its technology, is an integrated
whole, possessed of institutions and beliefs that are typically very well suited
to the needs of the society's members.[1]

The Concerns of Aesthetics

As the term is used here and in much other scholarly writing, *"aesthetics"*
refers to theories about the fundamental nature and value of art. This definition is of course logically contingent upon a definition of art, a thorny
matter that reflective people in the West have failed to satisfactorily resolve
after 2,500 years of continual debate.

Indeed, the American philosopher Morris Weitz (1967; see also Ladd
1973:417–421) has argued that we can never hope to isolate a single quality
that is the definitive feature of all art. Rather, Weitz suggests, art can have
only what Wittgenstein called an "open definition." That is, the best we can
ever do is note the several traits that commonly give a "family resemblance"
to those things that we currently think of as art. When we meet things with

---

[1]Thus when contemporary cultural anthropologists use the term *primitive* to refer to
small-scale societies, they only mean ones that (a) have a relatively small and sparse population,
(b) rely upon a relatively simple technology that lacks metallurgy, ceramics, writing, and such,
and (c) display a relatively low degree of economic specialization. The term is absolutely *not*
meant to suggest that these societies or their members are backward, crude, or otherwise inferior to nonprimitive societies; the intellectual sophistication of the aesthetic systems described
in this book should provide convincing evidence on this score. Inasmuch as many people
nevertheless associate "primitive" with generally negative qualities, it now seems best to avoid
its use altogether.

Also, cultural relativism itself has limitations. For one thing, totally objective relativism
is never possible inasmuch as the study of any phenomenon is inevitably colored by the questions one asks, the theoretical approach one adopts, and so on. And even if objectivity were
possible, thoroughgoing relativism is not always desirable. For example, one should not simply
study cultural or biological genocide relativistically; one is morally responsible for evaluating
its consequences and acting accordingly.

which we are unfamiliar, either because they are new or because they come from alien cultures, they are judged to be art according to the degree to which they share these familial similarities—or else the repertoire of family resemblances will itself evolve.

The tentativeness and unwieldiness of Weitz's approach to defining art may be frustrating, but I feel it to be realistic, if for no other reason than that it does not ignore a pervasive feature in the history of art, namely the unpredictability of art's evolution. The traits that seem to nicely characterize the art of one era always change as artists and their art move creatively into the future. (I have previously discussed [Anderson 1989:8–17] the hazards of attempting to use a closed definition of art cross-culturally, especially if the proffered definitive trait is art's being non-utilitarian or prompting a qualitatively unique affective response in the percipient or person who perceives the art work.)

Aesthetics may also deal with conceptions about beauty, but inasmuch as the grotesque may also play an active role in art, aesthetics is not solely a theory of beauty. On the other hand, although natural things such as sunsets and flowers may also prompt feelings similar to those generated by art, the primary concern here is with art produced by the human mind and body. It is usually the shared beliefs and consistent behaviors of a society that most interest the anthropologist, and the present comparative study of aesthetics will likewise deal primarily with aesthetic values held by a sizable portion of the populace for a significant period of time. However, unanimity of belief is neither expected nor necessary. The aesthetic diversity that exists in all societies is both quantitative (some individuals devote more thought to art than do others) and qualitative (there are differences of opinion as to what art is and isn't).

From the foregoing account of aesthetics, it should be clear that the starting point for the comparative study of aesthetics is ethnographic data. The methods involved in such fieldwork have already been mentioned, but a related factor should be made explicit here, namely that useful information about aesthetics cannot safely be *deduced* simply by looking at another society's art works. Stylistic conventions can be described by examining foreign art works, but since there is no simple, one-to-one correspondence between art work and conceptual motivation, and since aesthetic systems are often complex intellectual constructs, aesthetic values and metaphysical assumptions about art cannot be reconstructed in depth and with certainty based on, say, a carving's appearance or a song's melody.

Organization of the Book

After a few more introductory issues are dealt with in this chapter, the remainder of the book is divided into two sections, the first descriptive and the second analytic. The first, and longer, part delineates aesthetic values in ten societies, supplemented by some brief comments about each society's culture, its art, and the adequacy of the data about these topics. (To avoid falling into a tediously repetitive pattern, and also in response to their particular topics, the chapters do not all follow a single organizational plan. Nevertheless, each does present the philosophy of art of the culture in question, plus the material that I believe to be necessary for placing that philosophy in its proper context.)

I have used two criteria for selecting these ten societies. First, and most obviously, information about the society's aesthetic system must be available. The present state of the literature is such that very few societies meet this requirement. The cultural anthropologist who spends one, two, or more years living in a society and who may eventually write hundreds of pages describing it often makes little or no mention of the society's art, much less the philosophical values that underlie the art—even though he or she dutifully informs students that art is an important universal phenomenon. And since studying a society's aesthetics requires a broad knowledge of its culture plus extensive face-to-face questioning (preferably in the native language) of the makers and users of art, information about native aesthetics is rarely reported by art historians and museum curators, since their chief interest usually lies in collecting and describing art works. Thus the subject of non-Western aesthetics has often remained in the unexplored territory between cultural anthropology and art history. However, at a slow but steady pace, descriptions of non-Western aesthetics have accumulated, and a comparative study is now possible.

The second criterion for selecting societies for Part One is diversity. Within the constraints of the available literature, I have chosen societies that are distributed across every continent, that create art in many media and with varied styles, and that represent distinctly different parts of the continuum of sociocultural complexity: small-scale, nomadic groups that rely upon hunting, gathering, and fishing (the San, Eskimo, and Australian Aborigines); societies that subsist on various forms of horticulture and herding (the Sepik River tribes, Navajo, and Yoruba); and societies that possess complex technologies and large, heterogeneous populations (the Aztecs, India, Japan, and the West).

If Part One is descriptive, Part Two is analytic. In it, I discuss the similarities and differences among the ten aesthetic systems dealt with in Part One. Or to put it differently, after Part One describes Calliope's incarnation in ten societies, Part Two will reveal the traits she seems to have universally, and it will also note why other traits seem to vary systematically from one place to another.

Obviously, our conclusions can only be tentative. Data remain scant, and available information is biased both by the underrepresentation of the hunter-gatherer pattern of living that was the only human option until the comparatively recent past, as well as by the overrepresentation of the complex societies (and their political and intellectual elites) that politically dominate the modern world.

Besides problems stemming from the limited availability of data, a second type of problem hinders our search for the elusive Calliope. Metals are said to be malleable if they are easily shaped, bent, or hammered into a form that meets the smith's needs, and aesthetic systems are by their nature highly malleable intellectual entities, easily twisted and distorted by the heavy-handed treatment of non-natives, especially in efforts at cross-cultural comparison. I have tried to be faithful to the integrity of the aesthetic systems presented in Part One, attempting to describe each one in and of itself, generally avoiding discussing one society's aesthetics as it compares to another's.

A related problem is even more fundamental: Just what is it that we will be describing as "art" in the following chapters? Clearly, if we tacitly accept the Western belief that art is limited to what is on display in galleries and museums, to what one hears in concert halls, or to what is performed on the ballet stage, then the quest for art in non-Western settings can yield only meager results.

If "our" definition of art does not lead to productive results, then perhaps we should use "theirs." But this approach, too, is immediately ruled out by the well-known fact that most languages do not have a word that means the same thing as the English word, "art."[2] This being the case, one of the chores undertaken in the following chapters is the development of a definition of art that avoids these problems.

One might ask, however, do we have to have an explicit and precise definition of "art" before we even begin our comparative study of aesthetics? Fortunately not. Perhaps this can be best understood by considering the way in which anthropologists have gone about studying one of their favorite topics, kinship. Experience has shown that there are two ways that are *not* very fruitful for studying kinship in non-Western societies. In the first place, it is unproductive to describe and analyze a non-Western kinship system by using terms such as "aunt" or "cousin" that come from our own,

---

[2]After extensive fieldwork with the Bala (a Basongye people living in Zaire), Alan P. Merriam (1973:273–274) concluded that to the Bala way of thinking, music differs from non-music in three respects: Music is always the product of human activity, it is always created in accord with some preconceived organizational principles, and it is composed of sounds that have a minimal continuity in time.

Several factors to which Westerners attach importance in their definition of music, such as the "manipulation of sound for its own sake" (Merriam 1973:278) are not verbalized in Bala discussions about music. Therefore Merriam concludes that if one confines oneself to only explicit statements about aesthetics, then "problems arise when we find a culture like the Bala in which what *we* call art, even though separable as objects produced by people whose behavior is special, is merely something else that man does" (Merriam 1973:281). (See also Chapter 13 of Merriam's [1964], important *The Anthropology of Music*, as well as Keil's [1979] response to Merriam's approach.)

Western system of kinship. But it is equally useless to go to another society expecting to find an explicit, native statement of abstract kinship principles: One is likely to find that the people in question do not have a word that can be accurately translated as meaning "kinship," much less "consanguinity" or "patrilineality."

But even though they have had to avoid narrowly using either our or their definitions, scholars have made great strides in understanding the phenomenon of kinship. They have done this by, first, accepting the general and broad assumption that when one speaks of kinship one has in mind patterned social relations within nuclear and extended families, notions of legitimacy regarding offspring, ideas about whom one can or cannot marry, and so on. With this general domain in mind, fieldworkers have gone to other cultures and pursued the question, How do the people in this society think about such issues? Then, after a considerable amount of descriptive information has been accumulated, one can step back from the data and look for any cross-cultural patterns that might exist.

Similarly with art and aesthetics, the best way to proceed seems to be by recognizing that when we use the word "art," we usually have something in mind that is valued beyond its practical contribution to such instrumentalities as subsistence, that is made so as to have some sort of sensuous appeal, and the production of which reflects skills that are more highly developed in the maker than among other members of the society. Then, having in this very broad and tentative way demarcated the area of our concern, we can go to other societies and look for things and activities that generally fall into this domain, asking, How do people here think about their "art"?

And this, in fact, is exactly what the following chapters in Part One do: They describe philosophies of art as they look from "inside" cultures. After this has been done in ten different societies, we can move to a broader level of generality by looking for the patterns of similarities and differences that exist in the "arts" of the societies we have surveyed. This is the business of Part Two.

A comparative study of aesthetics allows us to develop a more appropriate appreciation of the arts of other societies, giving us the means to perceive them in the ways intended by their creators, making them not mere curiosities but sophisticated manifestations of metaphysical, cultural, and emotional meaning.

Also in learning about non-Western aesthetic systems, we begin to gain an appreciation of the rich diversity of human thought as it relates to art. In a study of Far Eastern aesthetics, Thomas Munro has remarked, "If Western aestheticians wish to go on ignoring Oriental art and theory, they might more accurately entitle their books, 'Western Aesthetics,' instead of seeming to make false claims of universal scope" (Munro 1965:7–8).

Cross-cultural aesthetic understanding may also enrich us by stimulating new perspectives on our own philosophies of art, providing us with new ways of looking at the natural, social, and cultural worlds around us—just as the exposure of early twentieth-century Western artists to art objects from Africa and elsewhere stimulated important new directions in Western art styles.

There is, finally, the matter of Calliope and her elusive family. Accounts of non-Western aesthetic systems provide a starting point for a truly comparative aesthetics. After cataloging the ways in which art is conceptualized in a variety of times and places, we can begin to look for commonalities and patterns of variation in these cultural definitions of art. It is unlikely that we shall gain a certain and intimate knowledge of the cunning Calliope the first time out, but the time is ripe to begin the search.

LOCATIONS OF THE NON-WESTERN SOCIETIES
DISCUSSED IN PART ONE

1. Eskimos
2. Navajos
3. Aztecs

4. Yoruba
5. San
6. India

7. Japan
8. Sepik River, New Guinea
9. Arnhem Land, Australia

PART ONE

1

SAN AESTHETICS
The Enhancement of Life
in a Foraging Society

In [Nxou's hands the musical bow] seemed to become a greater
kind of bow, hunting meaning in the wasteland of sound. . . . All
the men could play the instrument but none like Nxou. The
women would sit for hours, the full look of peace upon them,
listening to him. (Van der Post 1958:247)

Thinking about the San, a hunting and gathering society in southwestern
Africa, prompts one to ask some fundamental questions about human consciousness. Are we at one with these people whose material circumstances
differ enormously from our own? How much do we share of their conceptions
of the natural, social, and spiritual worlds? Ultimately, is San consciousness
like your and my own consciousness, so that we feel, think, and exist in terms
that are not qualitatively different from each others'? Or, alternatively, do we
live in different mental worlds, forever shut off and alienated from each other,
at most only able to touch fingertips but never souls, able to understand each
others' meanings in rare moments of insight that result more from accident
than design? Both sides of the argument can be supported to some degree.

On the one hand, an unbreachable distance seems to separate us from
the San. They practice a means of subsistence, hunting and gathering, from
which our own cultural tradition began to diverge some 10,000 years ago with
the gradual adoption of agriculture. They make almost all the things they own,
but they possess no more than they can carry on their backs and in their arms
from one temporary encampment to another. They traditionally live in
groups of twenty to fifty men, women, and children, tendering allegiance to
no larger polity and maintaining only a bare minimum of internal political
organization and economic specialization within the band.

On the other hand, personal accounts of San daily life tell us of individuals who experience the same emotions and concerns that engage us. They
display courage and extreme ingenuity in the face of adversity and hardship.

FIGURE 1-1 San man and child. *(Photo courtesy John K. Marshall, Documentary Educational Resources, Watertown, Massachusetts.)*

They put much effort into finding a good mate, providing for their families, and maintaining supportive and harmonious interactions with relatives and friends. They dearly want others to think well of them, and they accomplish this not through braggadocio but by being both amiable and responsible. And they have a vast capacity for playfulness and good humor (see **Figure 1–1**).

One way of trying to resolve this dilemma is by examining the San's ideas about art. As we shall see, the satisfactions that the San derive from art strongly resemble those that inform popular culture in the contemporary Western world. But before making comparisons, we must look at San culture, art, and aesthetics on their own terms.

The !Kung San

For perhaps 10,000 years, southern Africa has been the home of a genetically, linguistically, and culturally distinctive people (see map, p. 10). Europeans long knew one major group as "Bushmen," a term that has strongly derogatory connotations in Africa today and that has largely been replaced by "San." Even before Europeans began arriving in southern Africa by ship, invasions by other Africans had forced the San's ancestors to withdraw from most of the region. These African newcomers were taller, had darker skin, and spoke Bantu languages. By contrast, the San were short in stature, yellow-brown of skin, and spoke Khoisan languages, distinctive for their use of several "click" sounds.[1] The San did not adopt the invaders' horticultural practices and settle into permanent villages but continued their nomadic lives based on gathering undomesticated plants and hunting wild animals.

In so doing, the San were making a virtue of necessity because the only land not taken from them, first by the Bantu-speakers and later by Europeans, was the Kalahari Desert, an area too dry to support very much agriculture by the San or anyone else. During the twentieth century, the San have drastically declined in numbers so that only about 40,000 remain in Botswana, Namibia, and elsewhere. Most of these survivors have abandoned traditional life ways and now work for White or Bantu farmers. Only a group of northern San, known as the !Kung and numbering about 6,500 individuals, continued to live as hunter-gatherers recently enough for us to accumulate in-depth, fieldwork-based accounts of their culture. (Unless otherwise indicated, subsequent references to the "San" will refer only to the !Kung San who lived during the 1950s and 1960s in the Dobe and Nyae Nyae areas, near the Namibia-Botswana border.)

The Kalahari conforms to Western preconceptions of a desert in that there is little surface water and summer temperatures rise to as high as 50 degrees Celsius (120 degrees Fahrenheit), but it is not a land of barren dunes. Grasses, shrubs, vines, and scattered trees cover much of its sand; and it is this vegetation, along with the wildlife it supports, that allows the San to survive in the Kalahari . Although their existence is somewhat precarious and food is often the major topic of conversation, San rarely die from lack of food or water, a feat that illustrates the San's practical ingenuity. Most of the San's caloric intake and water are provided by the women, who recognize more than fifty species of edible plants. Men, for their part, hunt with bows and poisoned arrows to kill both small game as well as antelopes and other large animals. The San consume every part of the animal, down (we are told) to the "mucous lining of the nostrils and the gristle inside the ears" (Thomas 1959:9).

The San's use of ostrich eggs reveals the economy and elegance of their response to the challenges of the environment. A small hole is pecked in one end of the egg and its contents are poured out, providing an amount

---

[1]English speakers occasionally use "clicks," or sounds made by passing air into, rather than out of, the mouth. Sometimes we show mild displeasure or reproof by using a dental click (spelled "tsk tsk," but linguistically indicated by a single slash mark, /); and a lateral click (//) is used to make horses start moving or go faster. In Khoisan languages, however, instead of being "special purpose" sounds these clicks and three others (an alveolar click, !; a palatal click, ≠; and a bilabial click, ☉.) are normal parts of many words (cf. Marshall 1965:244–245).

of food equivalent to about two dozen chicken eggs. After being rinsed out, the shell makes an ideal container for drinking water. With its hole plugged with grass, such a canteen is sturdy enough to last for years, always keeping its contents deliciously cool as water slowly soaks through the eggshell walls and evaporates. When it finally does break (or when broken shells are found), it provides the raw material for the most prized San jewelry—ostrich eggshell beads (**Figure 1–2**).

Social organization of the San is loosely structured, with only a slight emphasis on the male line. In practice, bands are composed of polygamous and monogamous families who get along well with each other and can hunt and gather effectively together. Usually an older man serves as the minimal leader of the band, but he lacks the authority to compel action. (The !Kung word for "chief," *//kai*, is applied to Bantu headmen—or, in a derisive manner, to the rare San with pretensions of prominence.)

Elizabeth Marshall Thomas (1959) entitled her excellent popular book about the San *The Harmless People*, a phrase that accurately captures the quality of San lifestyle. But the "harmless" San, like many other small-scale, non-Western peoples, have suffered great harm at the hands of those who possess more powerful technologies. With the arrival of the horticultural Bantu-speakers, many San were reduced to serf status, and eighteenth-century Dutch settlers organized vigilante groups called *commandos* that

FIGURE 1–2   San jewelry: three strings of ostrich eggshell beads.   *(Smithsonian Institution, Department of Anthropology, catalogue nos. 407186, 407185, 407184.)*

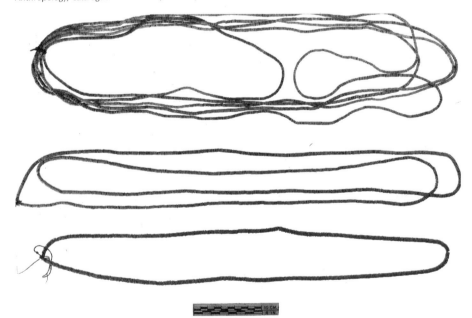

killed San men and carried the women and children into slavery on White farms (Lee 1979:32). Forced labor has continued into the present, and the few remaining San live near the uneasy borders between Namibia, which (contrary to United Nations resolutions) is effectively controlled by White-ruled South Africa; Botswana, an independent republic whose Black leaders have tried to stay on friendly terms with South Africa; and Angola, where Black guerrilla groups have been active since the early 1960s.

Although more has been written about the San than the other no-madic hunter-gatherers of Africa, the literature is uneven. We understand the San's subsistence activities well; their kinship, social structure, and religion, less well; and their art and aesthetics in only piecemeal fashion. Miscellaneous comments on art may be gleaned from early explorers, but the richest source of information derives from a series of expeditions by individuals associated with Harvard University.

This research was not prompted by the academic interests of Harvard anthropologists but was begun by Lawrence Marshall, a retired business executive. Under the sponsorship of Harvard's Peabody Museum, Marshall and his family lived with !Kung San for several years in the 1950s and 1960s, spending most of their time in the Nyae Nyae area. Lorna Marshall and Elizabeth Marshall Thomas systematically collected ethnographic data during these periods, the former publishing several highly professional works on San culture and society and the latter writing a more informal (although highly informative) account of !Kung and Gikwe San life. John Marshall has meanwhile made many movies of San activities, including the well-known feature-length film, "The Hunters." The Marshalls also introduced other scholars to the region, and a growing anthropological interest in the ecological adaptations of hunter-gatherers prompted Richard B. Lee and Irven DeVore to launch the Harvard Bushman (San) Research Project in 1963. Lee's writing, like that of the Marshalls, is exemplary for its clarity and rigor.

Body Decoration and Other Art Activities

The San literature allows us to address an interesting question—namely, in what sense do the San have art? We may begin by describing the artifacts and activities that potentially are art: ornamentation of the body and of household items, music and dance, and a few other miscellaneous activities.

Although an early second-hand report claimed that unacculturated San wore no clothes (Bleek 1928:8), contemporary adult !Kung San are much concerned with what they wear. The minimal essentials are made of leather: a loincloth for men, and for women an apron and a "kaross," or large cape held at the waist by a cord which provides a pouch on the women's backs in which everything from babies to food supplies may be carried.

Karosses are sometimes decorated with colors, and men's loincloths may be worked and fringed, but the greatest decorative effort goes into the younger women's aprons which may be elaborately decorated with ostrich eggshell beads **(Figure 1–3)**.

San, old and young, wear many kinds of jewelry. Leather bracelets are made from strips of hide cut from antelope heads; beaded necklaces are common; leather or wooden rings are worn around arms, waists, and legs; and hair ornaments are made of flowers, fur, and, most commonly, beads. Manufactured beads are sometimes used, as are beads made of native aromatic wood, nuts, and animal teeth; but by far the most cherished beads are those made from ostrich eggshells **(Figure 1–4)**. Marshall, who rarely exaggerates, says that these are "the most prized possessions of the !Kung" (Marshall 1965:257).

The beads, which were worn throughout southern Africa before the San were pushed back into the Kalahari, are made by women. Schapera, paraphrasing Bleek (1928:9), describes the elaborate technique used to produce the beads:

> The eggshell is broken into small pieces which are softened in water and pierced with a small stone or iron borer. They are then threaded on to a strip of sinew and the rough edges chipped off with a horn. Soft bark fibre is next

FIGURE 1–3   !Kung girl's apron, decorated with ostrich eggshell beads. *(Smithsonian Institution, Department of Anthropology, catalogue no. 407166-167.)*

FIGURE 1-4 A group of San girls with ostrich eggshell beads. *(Photo courtesy John K. Marshall, Documentary Educational Resources, Watertown, Massachusetts.)*

twisted between the beads, making the chain very taut, and the edges are finally rubbed smooth with a soft stone. (Shapera 1930:66)

San can never have too many ostrich eggshell beads. Besides their being used to decorate women's pubic aprons, beads are worn in the hair and used to make single or multiple-stranded necklaces, headbands, bracelets, and armlets.

San body decoration does not end with clothing and jewelry. Traditional San also often paint their bodies, using fat, clay, soot, or powdered aromatic herbs (Theal 1910:41; Bleek 1928:12; Marshall 1961:242–43; Kaufmann 1910:140).[2] In some San groups, young men powder their hair with pulverized *//hara*, a sparkling black stone.

A pervasive desire to appear beautiful in the eyes of other San prompts most such body decoration. Occasionally body decoration is done for religious purposes, but even then the rationale is more sensuous than supernatural. For example, Thomas describes a young girl's preparation for her wedding thus: "The bride's mother adorned the bride, washing her, hanging white bead ornaments from her hair, rubbing her clothing with

---

[2]Prehistoric rock paintings and engravings prove that body decoration has a long history in southern Africa.

red, sweet-smelling powder, a symbol to Bushmen of beauty" (Thomas 1959:158). As in the West, being beautifully dressed does not make the marriage bond more hallowed, but using the occasion to show off one's finery seems fitting.

Tattooing serves as another means of body decoration among the San. Girls receive their first scars when they are seven or eight, and later additions may leave them with decorated legs, buttocks, and faces (Marshall 1965:267). And in at least some groups, young men also wear tattoos and scars, typically on their faces, arms, and legs. Sometimes small pieces of animal flesh are placed in the boy's incisions (Werner 1906:256; Fourie 1960/1928).

Haircutting provides a final means of body ornamentation. San hair grows into small, tight tufts that eventually break off, but many younger San cut off some of the tufts to make fanciful patterns. The designs **(Figure 1–5)** have no particular meaning but are only for decoration (Marshall 1976:82).

Body decoration is by far the most important expressive visual medium among contemporary San. Other artistic practices may be listed briefly:

1.   Ostrich eggshell canteens are sometimes marked or engraved with designs. In some places such decorations help the owners identify their own canteens, but elsewhere beauty is their sole purpose (cf. Marshall 1976:77; Lee 1979:122).

FIGURE 1–5   San boy with facial tattoos and decorative haircut. *(Photo courtesy John K. Marshall, Documentary Educational Resources, Watertown, Massachusetts.)*

2.   Stone and bone pipes and wooden utensils are occasionally decorated, the geometric patterns being incised with a heated iron needle. Kaufmann remarks that "the hairline precision of the lines is particularly striking" (1910:194; see also ibid.:152; Bleek 1928:10; Schapera 1930:207).

3.   San women and youths sometimes make elaborate string figures
(Marshall 1976:351), although it is unclear as to whether their motives are
aesthetic, recreational, or both.

4.   Young women sometimes draw geometric designs on the bark of
mangetti and baobab trees (Marshall 1965:275).

5.   Although Europe's ancient cave paintings at sites such as Lascaux
and Altamira are better known to Westerners, the rock paintings and engravings found in southern Africa match the European sites in aesthetic
interest and outstrip them in number. Hundreds of decorated rock shelters
and caves are known in southern Africa, and Pager (1975:9) has estimated
that 150,000 individual figures probably exist, the most ancient being thousands of years old. It is likely that ancestors of the San created most or all
the paintings and engravings. Rock painting continued into the nineteenth
century, when the last known rock painter was shot in a raid by white commandos, probably in the 1860s. He was found wearing a belt with ten small
horns attached, each containing a different color of paint (Stow 1905).
People, their artifacts, and the animals they hunt are the most common
subjects of rock art; and although their purpose is unclear (cf. Pager 1975;
Lewis-Williams 1981), the paintings are interesting for their stylistic realism.
Contemporary San typically have several characteristic anatomical traits including an inward curvature of the lower back (lumbar lordosis) in both
men and women, permanently semierect penes in men, and extremely fatty
buttocks (steatopygia) in some women (Dart 1937:1960–166). All these features are clearly evident in many of the rock paintings and engravings.

6.   Lorna Marshall observes, "The !Kung are a music-loving people.
Most of the time someone in a !Kung encampment is making music. People
sing to the babies to soothe or entertain them. They sing to enliven their
tasks and their games. They sing at the water-hole and in leisure hours by
their fire. Everyone sings, almost everyone plays an instrument" (Marshall
1976:363). Dance, which often accompanies music, is also common in San
encampments.

The technology of San music is minimal (**Figure 1–6**), being produced
by four instruments: (a) a one-stringed bow, either the unmodified bow that
men use for hunting, with the player's open mouth serving as a resonator
at one end of the bow, or else a bow with an attached gourd or tin can

FIGURE 1-6   Group of San boys playing a musical instrument called a *//gwashi*.   *(Photo courtesy John K. Marshall, Documentary Educational Resources, Watertown, Massachusetts.)*

resonator; (b) a one-stringed violin played with a three-inch bow; (c) ankle-rattles worn by dancers; and (d) a four- or five-string lyre-like instrument called *//gwashi* (**Figure 1-7**). According to Thomas, the sound of the *//gwashi* is

> beautiful, sometimes full, sometimes thin, and makes very deep and various music, for Bushmen, their music being by far their greatest art, are not given to whistles or clear, shrill sounds—all their instruments make blurred and vibrant music with a richness in every note. Their compositions, too, are never simple, not even the music of their musical games, but always mixed, always subtle, partly gay but partly sad.   (Thomas 1959:223)

San music is often individualistic and spontaneous, and this is particularly true of "mood songs," whose chief function is the expression of intimate feelings and the personal experiences of the composer-singer (Thomas 1959:119).

Music also occurs as part of the Ritual Healing Dance. This dance begins at nightfall and continues until at least dawn. Its purpose is both to protect the healthy and cure the sick. As women clap and sing, dancers

FIGURE 1-7 San boy playing a //gwashi. *(Photo courtesy John K. Marshall, Documentary Educational Resources, Watertown, Massachusetts.)*

move in a circle around a fire, and the experienced among them begin to feel their spiritual energy, *num* (or *n/um*), begin to warm up. With intense concentration, aided by the rhythm of the music and dance as well as the fire's smoke and heat, their *num* begins to boil, causing a few dancers to pass into a trance-like state of enhanced consciousness called *kia*. A healer in *kia* experiences a heightened sense of reality and can see the otherwise invisible arrows that bring people bad luck, disease, or even death. By interceding with the spirits that send the arrows, the healer protects everybody present at the dance from misfortune (Shostak 1981:291–303; Katz 1982).

Do the San Have "Art"?

Compared to other cultures, the San philosophy of art is unusual for two reasons. As the following chapters will show, in many societies aesthetics is intimately linked to ideas about the realm of the supernatural. By contrast, a large portion of San art is made for secular purposes. This alone makes San aesthetics worth studying.

But in addition to that, the San philosophy of art is somewhat less complex than most of the other groups we will discuss. Using the San as our first case study, then, permits us to ask some questions that are fundamental to a comparative study of aesthetics and that could easily get lost in a denser context. With those factors in mind, let us examine the role of art in San thought.

Anthropologists often claim that all societies have art, but this is generally presented as an article of faith, not a proven fact. Of course, sweeping generalizations of the sort, "All societies have X" can only be conclusively substantiated by evidence that X exists in every single society, a task that, for art, lies far beyond our current capabilities. An easier, if less conclusive, alternative is to examine the least likely cases—cultures about which one might say that if any society is without art, it surely must be this one.

San society is a good candidate for such a statement. If the only evidence on the question were to come from the galleries of non-Western art in Western museums, the answer would be perfectly clear: The San have no art. Even African scholars generally believe that !Kung visual arts have a low degree of development (Wolfe 1969:5).

Ultimately, of course, the question hinges on one's definition of art. As noted earlier, Morris Weitz (1967) has argued convincingly that we should not expect to find a single trait that, once and for all, distinguishes art from non-art. Rather, we can only recognize that those things we have come to call art usually share several characteristics, like the traits that constitute a "family resemblance" among siblings. Other objects are "art" to the degree that they share the traits that we associate with the rest of the "family" of art. Three of the traits most commonly associated in the Western mind with art are its being beautiful, skillfully made, and non-utilitarian. It is interesting to see the extent to which these traits are found in San culture.[3]

Although most contemporary Western artists and aestheticians agree that it is not necessarily present in art, *beauty* has often been associated with art in earlier eras of the Western tradition, and the idea remains popular today. For their part, the San clearly recognize and value beauty. The preceding description of San body decoration clearly shows that they are much concerned with personal appearance, and a closer look reveals that there are several dimensions to native conceptions of "beauty" as it applies to the human body.

First, it is possible to cull from the literature several bodily attributes that San find beautiful. For example, part of a song recorded by Kirby (1936:431) says:

> The Bushman girl with the "pepper corn" head,
> The lice are playing in her hair,
> But she has lovely legs!

---

[3]As will be apparent later, the San produce art not only by the informal definition used here but also by the more widely applicable and rigorous list of traits discussed in Part Two of this book.

Judging from other references (Thomas 1959:184, 227; Marshall 1959:349, 1976:39), a woman's legs are considered "lovely" if they are neither long nor thin.[4]

Besides not being too thin, a beautiful San woman should have light skin, good teeth, youth, and should stand about five feet tall. A handsome man should conform to a different standard of beauty. A group of San young women told Lorna Marshall that a man should be "a good hunter like /Gunda; and they like handsome teeth and a wide smile like Tsamgo's, and straight, slender legs like //Ao's and a fluid, swift walk like /Gao's, and they hate a big black belly" (Marshall 1959:349). (Thomas [1959:86–87, 168–171] recounts two episodes in which young San women humiliated and rejected men with this last trait.)

But "art" and "aesthetics" usually bring to mind not the gifts of nature but the products of human activity, and it is not people's physical attributes but the ways in which they decorate their bodies that are most often mentioned in San discussions of beauty. From the accounts of fieldworkers who have lived with the San, there is no doubt that a desire to improve one's looks and enhance one's beauty is the chief motivation for the San's making and wearing jewely, tattooing and painting their bodies, decorating their clothes, and cutting their hair. When Bleek asked an old San woman why women tattoo themselves, the answer was, "That the men may see us pretty" (1928:11), and when Elizabeth Marshall Thomas wondered if Gikwe San women really felt that being tattooed was justified, a woman said that "in her case it had been worth the pain and trouble because . . . she was extremely ugly and had been made more beautiful" (Thomas 1959:52–53). Also, at least some of the men's tattoos are made for ornamental purposes also.

As will be noted below, supernatural beliefs do prompt some of the San's tattoos and perhaps some San body painting as well, but undoubtedly the most important motivation is the desire to be beautiful, and the San clearly go to great lengths to cultivate beauty through decorating their bodies.[5]

The San also enjoy the beauty of music and dance. Mood songs give

---

[4]Tobias (1961) has hypothesized that the characteristically fatty buttocks and thighs of many San women may result from an interplay between natural and sexual selection. Like the camel's hump, the fat helps the women of the desert sustain themselves and their nursing children through periods of scarce food and water; and development of the trait might have been accelerated by the San's great admiration of steatopygia, thus making a virtue of necessity.

[5]Interestingly, although the San literature frequently mentions personal beauty, the San rarely apply the concept of beauty to things other than people. And when they do, there are often allusions to the desirable qualities found in men and women. For example, Marshall reports that the !Kung distinguish between "male rain," which is violent and destructive, and "female rain," which "beautifies the trees and grasses" and makes wild plant foods grow (1959:232).

pleasure not only to the performer but also to his or her audience. The songs of the Ritual Healing Dance are believed to be potentially powerful because, like healers themselves, they contain *num*. However, Richard Katz, who has studied the Ritual Healing Dance in depth, writes: "The num[6] songs are both spiritual vehicles and beautiful music. The !Kung can appreciate their beauty without the danger of releasing their num because they believe that num is activated only during the dance, especially when it interacts with the dancers' num" (Katz 1982:124).

Another feature of the "family resemblance" of art is that it is made with *skill*. Indeed, in the 800 years of its recorded history in the English language, "art" has usually been used to refer to "skill, its display or application" (*Oxford English Dictionary* 1971:467). Only in the last 300 years has it come to be used more narrowly to apply to "the application of skill to the arts of imitation and design, Painting, Engraving, Sculpture, Architecture" (ibid.).

The skills involved in the creation of art may be manual or conceptual; but in any case, to play a role in art, the skill must be differentially distributed. In essence, if everyone does it equally well (whatever "it" may be), the activity is probably not considered to be art. As Sieber (1979) pointed out regarding more complex African societies, the artist's special skills set him or her apart from non-artists, leading to that hallmark trait of large-scale societies, specialization—and also leading, one might add, to connoisseurship.

But how well does this apply to San culture, where social homogeneity is exceptionally high and where specialization is nearly nonexistent? If art is thought of as those activities in which some people have noticeably greater skill than others, do the San have art?

Regarding music and dance, the answer is an unequivocal "yes." Although the San lack full-time singers, players, or dancers, Marshall states that some San "are more talented as musicians than others, and some take more interest in playing and singing well" (Marshall 1976:363; cf. also ibid.:373; England 1968; and Kaufmann 1910:151). Further, other San definitely appreciate and admire the more accomplished performers. Van der Post describes the playing of the hunting bow by a man named Nxou: "In his hands it seemed to become a greater kind of bow, hunting meaning in the wasteland of sound not with arrows of flint and iron but with . . . ordered notes flying out of the silence. All the men could play the instrument but none like Nxou. The women would sit for hours, the full look of peace upon them, listening to him" (Van der Post 1958:247; cf. also Thomas 1959:73, 131; Marshall 1962:148).

---

[6]It is the practice of some ethnographic writers to underline or italicize foreign words only the first time they occur in a document.

Differential skill among the San is less well documented outside the performing arts. Almost all old people among the San are storytellers, but some are applauded for giving more rousing renderings of folktales than others are capable of (Biesele 1976:307, 310). Indeed, it appears that as long as one is not boastful about it, creative energies may be displayed in any expressive medium (Shostak 1984).

Lastly, art is often defined as being *non-utilitarian*: Art is highly valued despite its making little or no concrete contribution to the practical maintenance of life. The San's ostrich eggshell beads fit this pattern well. For instance, Thomas (1959:156–157) tells of a "tragedy" in which an old couple's hut accidentally caught fire and burned to the ground, injuring no one but destroying all the hut's contents. The greatest cause of the distress felt by the couple and their neighbors was that the old woman had been a prolific bead-maker, and all her beads were destroyed by the fire.

San love ostrich eggshell beads because they make the wearer attractive; but, we might ask, what is it that makes them more beautiful—and more valuable—than beads made from other materials? For one thing, the supply of raw material—ostrich eggs—barely meets the needs of the bead-makers, so scarcity may be a factor. Also, because bead-making is a long, tedious process, a typical ornament, made of several thousand beads, represents an enormous amount of labor.

In any case, the San endow ostrich eggshell beads with special value. Gift-giving plays an important role in San culture, both at rites of passage, such as betrothals and weddings, but gifts are also exchanged spontaneously, to reaffirm the reciprocity that ties members of a San band into a tightly woven social fabric. Ostrich eggshell beads, with their intrinsic attractiveness and labor-intensive nature, make perfect candidates for valuable gifts to symbolize the bonds between people.

In summary, if art is tentatively conceived as referring to things or activities that *either* are of outstanding beauty, are skillfully produced, *or* are non-utilitarian, then the San do have art. San certainly love the beauty of personal appearance and adornment as well as the beauty of the songs of the Ritual Healing Dance. And at least in "mood songs," some San cultivate special skill, and others appreciate their abilities. Further, the San value ostrich eggshell beads beyond their overt contributions to happiness and well-being.

If, however, art is defined as existing in a single medium that is *both* beautiful, skillfully produced *and* non-utilitarian, then the situation is less clear. Whereas each of these qualities exist in different San media, we lack enough information to be certain that any one medium has all three. Regarding San mood music, for example, differences in skill are recognized, and it seems clear that San often make music for the sheer enjoyment of it, rather than for any overtly practical purpose. But although Western visitors among the San have often reported that *they* found great beauty in San music, we can only speculate about the Sans' own feelings about the music. It seems extremely likely that, if asked, a !Kung individual would say, yes, mood songs are indeed beautiful. But the issue cannot be settled until we have more information.

San Aesthetics

No explicit philosophy of art has been reported for the San. For example, Bleek and Lloyd (1911) left us with an enormous compendium of San folk-lore and mythology, but references to art rarely occur in it, and no theory of San aesthetics, latent or explicit, is to be found in its stories.

This is not to say that the San give no thought to art. Clearly, the San spend much time making and enjoying art, especially in the forms of body decoration and music-making. But in the absence of individuals who are full- or part-time specialists in formalizing and verbalizing abstract concepts (i.e., lacking professional philosophers), San aesthetic values are not available to us as an overt, integrated system of thought. Therefore we must reexamine San art and its uses to discover the ideas that are implicit in San culture regarding the fundamental nature and value of art.

First we may dismiss as inapplicable several aesthetic theories that have had some currency in Western culture. Although a founder of formalism, Roger Fry (1910), praised the aesthetic qualities of southern African rock paintings, nothing in the San literature indicates that contemporary San make art in accordance with explicit, formal principles of composition, color usage, and so on. It is also alien to San thought to use art as a status symbol: The San are egalitarian in the extreme, and even if they were inclined to one-upmanship their nomadic way of life obviously rules out the accumulation of property as a means of displaying one's elevated status. Thomas (1959:22) remarks that "a Bushman will go to any lengths to avoid making other Bushmen jealous of him. . . . No one cares to keep a particularly good knife too long, even though he may want it desperately, because he will become the object of envy." The San take pride in having a handsome appearance, but it is inconceivable that art would be used as a symbol of elevated status in such a society.[7]

To a limited extent San aesthetics is linked to religion, although the

---

[7]An early study suggested that San once used artifacts as cultural makers. Lebzelter reported that "female doctors" wore special chains made of aromatic wood and ostrich eggshell beads (1934:38) and that tattoos indicate membership in specific bands (ibid.:31). However, no subsequent researchers have corroborated these claims.

relationship is not a simple one. !Kung do not pray to the sun, moon, or stars; they do not systematically pray for rain or food; and they do not believe that animals, trees, water, or other natural phenomena are inhabited by spirit beings (Marshall 1962). They do believe in the existence of two gods—one greater, one lesser, each with a wife and children. The great god ≠*Gao!la* created all things including people and human knowledge, and he is all-powerful in controlling both nature and humans, often using the spirits of the dead, or *//gauwasi*, as his agents. The *//gauwasi* are not, however, identified with specific ancestors, and there are no San "witches" who try to further their personal interests by influencing the *//gauwasi*.

The San keep ethics and religion separate. They abhor unacceptable conduct, of course, but they believe that after death the bad people as well as the good go to the east to live with ≠*Gao!la*. Preventing or avenging a mortal's wrong-doing is the responsibility of other mortals. There are no priests, but individuals may pray spontaneously and quietly for favors—for example, that *Khwova!na*, the wife of the great god and mother of the bees, will give men good luck as they hunt for honey.

The Ritual Healing Dance is the most significant religious ceremony among the San. During its protracted music and dancing, one or more individuals enter a trance state. The dance, along with the rites of passage performed for young men and women, is intended to induce the supernaturals to look favorably on the participants and aid their well-being.

The visual arts play a limited role in all this. The San do make oracle discs of antelope hide (**Figure 1–8**), and Lee's research shows that some scarification is religiously motivated.[8] After scarifying a young man an older !Kung told Lee, "I cut his chest and put in medicine . . . to lift up his heart and make him *want* to seek meat; I put [medicine] in his arm and wrist to make his arm soft and his aim correct" (Lee 1979:239; cf. also Marshall 1976:41; Werner 1906:255; Lebzelter 1934:41; Schapera 1930:304).

But these activities bear only a tenuous relationship to art. For example, applying the three criteria mentioned above, we find that the accouterments of religion are not esteemed for their beauty, require no special skill in their production, and are considered to be purely utilitarian value.

It is interesting to examine the role of the performing arts in San religion. Music and dance are essential parts of the Ritual Healing Dance—and, for that matter, of female rites of passage as well. A healer named Nisa told Marjorie Shostak, "When the drum[9] starts sounding 'dong . . . dong . . .

---

[8]Sometimes the relative importance of vanity and religion is unclear. For example, the linguist Bleek noted that it was difficult to know if her informants were saying that facial tattoos enhance the wearer's ability to "see well," or that they enhance beauty and make one "look nice" (1928:11).

[9]A drum, played by a man, distinguishes the women's dance, to which Nisa refers, from the Ritual Healing Dance, in which most of the dancers are men. Women are less likely than men to be healers, but some women do go into the trance state of *kia*.

FIGURE 1–8 San oracle discs. *(Smithsonian Institution, Department of Anthropology, catalogue no. 407191.)*

dong . . . dong,' my n/um grabs me. That's when I can cure people and make them better" (Shostak 1981:302); and another healer told Richard Katz, "Rapid shallow breathing draws num up. What I do in my upper body with breathing, I also do in my legs with the dancing. You don't stomp harder, you just keep steady. Then num enters every part of your body" (Katz 1982:42).

But as this quotation suggests, it is *num*, and not the aesthetic qualities of the music or dance, that is the activating agent. It is interesting to quote Katz again in this regard:

> "If many persons kia at a dance," I ask, "is it because the singing is strong?"
> "When the healers fall into kia," Nai says, "it is because of num. We don't congratulate anyone. It is the num which does it."
> In the dancing, emphasis is not on style or aesthetics, though the dance is a beautiful, sensitive art form, which becomes more exciting when the individual dancers imbue it with their own expressive manners. As with the singing, the emphasis is on dancing as a vehicle to allow num to boil. . . .
> If dancers are too intent on perfecting fancy steps or too concerned with how they appear to others, their dancing remains in the foreground and obstructs their ability to let their num boil. The male adolescents who typically dominate the beginning stages of a dance are examples. (Katz 1982:127–128)

Further evidence that the religious efficacy of the Ritual Healing Dance lies more in *num* than in music and dance is seen in the fact that the performing arts that they include are not themselves sacred. On the one hand, the Ritual Healing Dance provides an occasion not only for curing the sick but also for ribald joking and flirting; and, on the other hand, the music of the Ritual Healing Dance is commonly used in distinctly secular settings such as lullabies and the melodies people hum or sing spontaneously and for simple enjoyment.[10]

But if the sacredness of San music and dance are questionable, the aesthetics of San performing arts may have a deeper religious motivation in that these activities provide a means of unifying the San and their collective spirit. In Marshall's words, San dance "brings people into such unison that they become like an organic being" (Marshall 1965:271); and Katz observes that the Ritual Healing Dance "is, quite simply, an orienting and integrating event of unique importance" (Katz 1982:36).

These remarks, taken with other observations by Marshall and corroborated by various fieldworkers, indicate that ceremonial music and dance do constitute religious art for the San, directed not toward specific, tangible ends but intended as a means of enhancing the morale and spirit of the performers and their community.

To take stock of the picture of San aesthetics thus far: There is no ethnographic evidence that the San conceptualize their art in formal terms. Equally absent is a native theory that sets the aesthetic response apart from other affective states. Lastly, the role of art in San religion is limited in that it is not used for didactic purposes, nor is art believed to have supernatural efficacy in itself, improving San prospects for future well-being. Some body decorations occur in ritual contexts, although this has little more religious significance than, say, a Western bride's efforts to look her prettiest at her wedding. Some scarification is believed to bring good fortune, although the aesthetic qualities of the scars seem to be of little importance. Only music and dance appear to make a significant aesthetic contribution to religion by providing a feeling of community that is characteristic of San cooperative life.

But having factored out these considerations, we are left with a great amount of art activity, practiced primarily in the secular areas of body deco-

---

[10]No clear consensus exists regarding definitions to distinguish "sacred" from "secular" beliefs. Most however would emphasize not the content of the belief but rather the subjective stance of the believer. The realm of the supernatural, the sacred, or of religion and magic generally has a potential for provoking mystical, awe-inspiring feelings that are qualitatively unlike natural phenomena. But in some ethnographic settings, the distinction between the sacred and the secular is so blurred as to disappear.

ration, music, and dance, that is motivated *solely by the simple pleasure and gratification it brings.* The San—especially young adult San, and most of all young San women—are walking art objects, proud of their beauty and pleased by any satisfaction their beauty gives to others **(Figure 1-9)**. Music and dance, for their part, are intrinsic components of day-to-day life in a San encampment, providing a continual source of pleasure for performers and audience alike.

The fundamental aesthetic principle of the San is that art brings pleasure, whether by augmenting one's natural beauty or by providing enjoyable pastimes to make daily life happier. In religious contexts, San art enhances the sense of community among the living, mortal members of San encampments, but San art is justified primarily by the pleasure it gives. The satisfactions of art are, for the San, not extreme—no aesthetic ecstasies or flights of imaginative passion. But art is a continuous, reliable source of pleasure during every waking hour of San life. Just as the San make optimal use of the sparse resources of the Kalahari Desert, they seem also to get the greatest possible satisfaction from the aesthetic activities that their lifestyle permits.

FIGURE 1-9 San women with many types of jewelry, including ostrich eggshell beads in their hair. *(Photo courtesy John K. Marshall, Documentary Educational Resources, Watertown, Massachusetts.)*

Conclusion

Although at first glance one might think that the San have no art, closer scrutiny has produced several interesting findings. The San treasure beauty, and they go to great lengths to cultivate it—most certainly in body decoration and also in music and dance. They also appreciate the skills of individuals who are particularly capable in music-making. So if art entails beauty or skill, the San do indeed have art. Further, their ostrich eggshell beads, like Western "fine" arts, have a cultural and economic significance that far exceeds their overt contribution to physical well-being. So although the San are not well known for their art, they support the widely accepted notion that all societies have art.

It is particularly interesting to note what San art is *not*. First, San visual art is almost entirely confined to the medium of body decoration; about the only other things that receive any measure of adornment are utilitarian items such as their ostrich eggshell canteens and their pipes. Clearly this should not be ascribed to a lack of San creativity or imagination but represents an ingenious solution to the problems of living a nomadic life. Moving from one encampment to another and lacking beasts of burden, they obviously benefit by concentrating on music and dance (which weigh nothing in themselves and require only minimal instruments) and by decorating the things they must carry with them anyway—their tools, their clothes, and their own bodies. Earlier generations of San probably had one additional solution to the problem of art-making in a nomadic society—rock painting. Although they could not take these with them, they could leave the designs behind with the assurance that the decorations would be awaiting them the next time they visited the site.

Contemporary San visual art is not representational, nor does it carry a great weight of symbolism. Again, though, this should not be attributed to a lack of artistic ability. The highly sensitive rendering of people and animals found in the rock art of the past proves that the San's ancestors could make life-like drawings if they so desired. Instead, it is probably due to the media in which San art is created. Body ornamentation everywhere tends to call more attention to the decorated person, whereas the use of representational or symbolic techniques would direct attention to some other subject matter. Body decoration may be a means of displaying differentiated social status, but there is obviously little need for this in a small-scale, homogeneous society such as the San's.

As for music and dance, the San do have some program music in which melody and rhythm are used to convey specific emotions or subjects. (San songs are not narrative, and although traditional mood songs and the songs of Ritual Healing Dance have titles, they have few, if any, words.) Also, several San dances effectively mimic certain animals or activities. However, San art, like art elsewhere, does reflect the deeper cultural predispositions and values of the people. For example, Nicholas England, who carried out ethnomusicological fieldwork in the Nyae Nyae area, has observed that when a San man who is singing or playing a musical bow is joined by other men,

> they will also draw upon [the same] melodic phrases, choosing whichever they desire at the moment and perhaps adding their individual embellishments and variations to the basic phrase designs. . . . This interchanging of melodic phrases is a common method of music making in Bushmanland, and it is a principle that, to my mind, epitomizes the Bushman way in general: it clearly reflects the Bushman desire to remain independent (in this case, of the other voices) at the same time that he is contributing vitally to the community life (in this case, the musical complex).   (England 1967:60)

Lastly, it is noteworthy that although the San do have art, their aesthetic values are not set out as an explicit theory. This reflects, of course, the absence of full-time specialists in philosophy among the San. But this is only part of the story, because it is abundantly clear that the general absence of philosophical speculation in San culture is not due to their being so busy providing for the material necessities that they have no time left to philosophize. Systematic study by Lee (1979) shows that there is in fact an abundance of leisure time in San life.

This raises a second possibility. The San seem simply not to *need* an explicit theory of aesthetics, and this may be so for two reasons. First, San aesthetic values are not conceptually complex. In comparison to the systems of aesthetics found, say, among the Aztecs (Chapter 7), the precepts of San aesthetics are so self-evident that they can be summed up quite succinctly: To bring happiness and well-being to yourself and your people you should sing, dance, and adorn yourself and your possessions. An aesthetic system as straightforward as this can be handed down from generation to generation as part of the normal process of socialization. The San do not need special teachers of art appreciation or aesthetics.

But recalling again the cultural homogeneity of San society, we see another reason they do not need an explicit aesthetic system. In complex societies such as the West, art creators and art consumers are usually distinctly separate groups. In such a situation, one job for aestheticians and art critics is to mediate between these two groups, explaining the artist's works to patrons of the arts and commenting on the artist's role in the larger fabric of culture. Such mediation is not needed in a classless society such as the San's. Among the San, where no great gulf exists between maker and user, art is created not just for the patron's sake but for everybody's sake.

Having described the life-enhancing aesthetics of the San, we can return to the question that was raised at the beginning of this chapter—namely, to what degree do we, as products of the Western tradition, live in the same conceptual and emotional world as the San, whose material circumstances are as distant from our own as any people on earth?

With respect to feelings about art, at least, there is a remarkable similarity between us and them. Formal and affective considerations are admittedly important in Western fine art, but the role of art in contemporary Western *popular* culture is quite similar to that in San society. In religion we generally believe that art objects, though a traditional and desirable adjunct to religious ritual, do not by themselves have a supernatural efficacy, although art in general, and music in particular, may provide a sense of oneness among the faithful. But that aside, Western popular arts such as clothing, fashions, and home decoration are largely justified in the public mind by the sensuous pleasure they bring. Add to this the popularity of commercially recorded music so omnipresent at home and at work and the aesthetic parallels between San art and Western popular art become striking indeed.

And there is one further similarity. In both cases the arts spring not from explicit aesthetic theories but from a tacit consensus that the "natives" generally feel is too obvious to require elaboration—namely, that art makes life richer and more enjoyable.

This postulated parallel between popular culture in the West and traditional culture of the San should not, I feel, be written off as a finding that is too abstract to have any actual relevance for us. Admittedly there is a wide range of variation among members of Western society, with Western fine art finding no counterpart in San culture; and the amount of cross-cultural variation is greater still. So we cannot claim to have shown that *all* humans inhabit the same conceptual world and experience existence in the same way. But we *can* conclude that the San are kindred spirits to us. They are people who view art in terms similar to our own, a folk whose imaginative and psychic worlds are much in tune with ours. I, for one, find this a reassuring conclusion.

2

ESKIMO AESTHETICS
Art as Transformer
of Realities

"My Breath"
>This is what I call this song,
>for it is just as necessary to me to sing
>as it is to breathe.

I will sing a song,
A song that is strong.
>Unaya—unaya.

Sick I have lain since autumn,
Helpless I lay, as were I
My own child.

Sad, I would that my woman
Were away to another house,
To a husband
Who can be her refuge,
Safe and secure as winter ice.
>Unaya—unaya. . . .

Dost thou know thyself?
So little thou knowest of thyself.
Feeble I lie here on my bench
And only my memories are strong!
>Unaya—unaya. (From a song told to
>Knut Rasmussen (1931:321)
>by the Netsilik Eskimo, Orpingalik)

A life of moving nomadically from one location to another, accompanied by fewer than thirty relatives and friends, and providing for the material necessities of life with a technology not of iron and fossil fuels but primarily of wood, stone, and human muscle—such was the sole life way of humans for almost all our history. Only during the last 10,000 years has the primeval technique of hunting and gathering been supplanted in some locales by a sedentary existence; by clusters of population numbering hundreds, thousands, and even millions of people; and by a technology dramatically different from the flint knife and spear-thrower of the past.

Of course, compared to one person's life, 10,000 years is still a long time, so it is natural that these innovations (which were the basis for the "Neolithic Revolution") are often taken for granted and that we view as exotic cultural aberrations the few stone-age peoples that survived into the twentieth century. But we should constantly remind ourselves that such an assumption is as temptingly comfortable as it is dangerously wrong: In the true long-term picture of the human race, *we* are the aberrant ones, and nomadic hunter-gatherers are the norm.

This being the case, we are lucky that a handful of small-scale societies did survive into recent times and, wonder of wonders, that a few individuals had the foresight to study and record their cultures in detail. One such nomadic culture, well known in the ethnographic literature, is that of the Eskimos, or Inuit,[1] of the North American Arctic.

Admittedly, the Inuit of the late twentieth century differ markedly from most peoples of the pre-neolithic past. Fish and sea mammals have always been more prominent in arctic diets than in those of most hunter-gatherers, and vegetable foods have been relatively less important. Also, for many decades the effects of Western culture have been increasingly apparent, due both to the colonial policies of Western nations and to the Inuits' own appetite for Western technology.

But compared to other areas of the New World, most natives of the Arctic were still relatively unacculturated when Knut Rasmussen organized the Fifth Thule Expedition in the 1920s. Born in Greenland with Eskimo ancestry on his mother's side, Rasmussen spoke fluent Eskimo, and his and his colleagues' research led to the publication of extensive accounts of traditional Inuit "intellectual culture" (by which Rasmussen meant religion and mythology) and "material culture" (i.e., artifacts and technology). Taken together with

---

[1]People in some regions of the Arctic wish to be called "Inuit," their name for themselves in their own language, and others prefer "Eskimo." The issue is important, involving as it does the self-image of a sizable population. In the absence of a consensus among the people involved, I have chosen to use the two terms interchangeably.

the field reports of others, this literature gives us a good picture of traditional Eskimo life.[2]

Background: Origins and Art Production

The first Inuits probably migrated into North America from northeast Asia between 4,000 and 6,000 years ago (see map, p. 10). By 1000 B.C., they had dispersed across the entire Arctic region, living in hundreds of locations north of the treeline, from southwestern Alaska, across northern Canada, to the shores of eastern Greenland. And wherever they wandered, they took along characteristic cultural adaptations to the Arctic, many of which they shared with their near relatives in northern Siberia. (Eskimos differ genetically, linguistically, and culturally from the Native American Indians living south of the treeline, peoples whose ancestors had been in the Western hemisphere for thousands of years before the arrival of the first Inuit.)

Some eras of Eskimo prehistory have produced more art than others,[3] but art of one kind or another has been made in virtually all possible media. Western collectors and museums have long prized Inuit ivory carving (**Figure 2–1**), but Eskimo men also made durable figures in bone and wood (**Figure 2–2**), as well as ephemeral works in snow and ice. Most such pieces were smoothly molded human and animal forms, polished to a lustrous sheen, sometimes decorated with incised patterns of lines and dots. The exigencies of a nomadic life dictated that few, if any, such items served solely decorative purposes. Some served as tools for the shaman, others as toys for children. Many utilitarian items, such as bone tubes for storing women's needles, were carved in such a way as to suggest animal forms. Masks (**Figure 2–3**) were carved for various uses, and they ranged in size from two to twenty inches (5 to 50 centimeters).

If carving was a man's art, the leather, fur, and sinew used to make arctic clothing provided an avenue of artistic expression for Inuit women

---

[2]In addition to the rich literature, our appreciation of Inuit art and culture is aided by numerous excellent films. Of particular interest is a series made by Asen Balikci under the auspices of the National Film Board of Canada that documents the annual migratory cycle of the Netsilik of the Pelly Bay area.

[3]Robert McGhee (1976) has examined variations in the quantity of art produced in the Arctic from one time and place to another. Interestingly, he found that art production is not correlated with the availability of leisure time, nor was there a gradual increase in the amount of art with the passage of time. Variations were only weakly correlated with the duration and size of settlements, factors thought to be important in promoting art production elsewhere. In a more recent study, Taçon (1983) found that art production was particularly prolific during the Late Dorset period, 800–1500 A.D., and he speculated that this development may have been a result of stress due to adverse changes in the environment or the in-migration from Alaska of Eskimos bearing the new Thule culture.

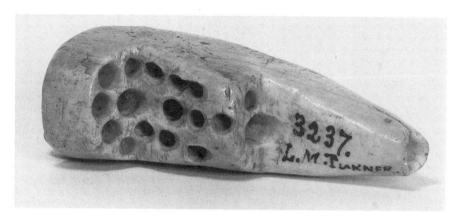

FIGURE 2-1   Eskimo carved ivory gaming device. *(Smithsonian Institution, Department of Anthropology, catalogue no. 90228.)*

(**Figures 2–4, 2–5, 2–6**). The design and the amount of decoration on cloth-ing varied from one locale to another, with especially elaborate parkas being worn for group festivities in both Alaska and Greenland. In some regions, specially decorated mittens and fans were made for use in dances. Most patterns were geometric and were created by the ingenious use of varying colors and textures of furs.

In some places, kayaks, mortuary boards, and dance drums bore painted and carved designs, but tattooing was the most widespread type of

FIGURE 2-2   Wooden box for storing harpoon blades used for whaling, carved at Port Clarence, Alaska. *(Courtesy, Field Museum of Natural History, Chicago, neg. no. 103530.)*

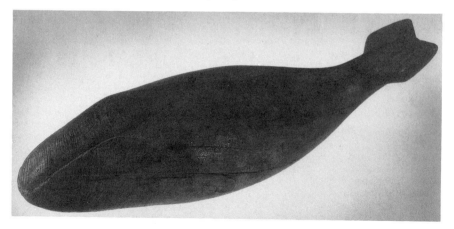

FIGURE 2-3 Asymmetrical Eskimo mask, ca. 1875. Alaska, Lower Yukon area. Wood, paint, feathers; 42 cm high. (The Saint Louis Art Museum, Friends Fund.)

FIGURE 2-4 Eskimo woman in decorated fur parka. (Photo courtesy National Museums of Canada, Canadian Museum of Civilization, neg. no. 51–571.)

FIGURE 2–5 Eskimo decorated parkas. *(Photo courtesy National Museums of Canada, Canadian Museum of Civilization, neg. no. 36–914.)*

FIGURE 2–6 Eskimo parka decorated with fringes and contrasting colors of fur. *(Smithsonian Institution, Department of Anthropology, catalogue no. 238533.)*

two-dimensional art **(Figure 2–7)**. Created mostly by women, tattoo patterns were made by either rubbing ashes into pin pricks, or else a needle and thread were covered with grease and ash and then passed under the skin (Birket-Smith 1959:119), a method that the Eskimos' counterparts in Siberia called *vyshiva,* Russian for embroidery. Cat's cradle string designs **(Figure 2–8)**, some of which were extremely elaborate, constituted the only other pan-Arctic three-dimensional art form. Alaskan Eskimos made basketry and pottery, but these media had limited importance for aesthetic expression.

By contrast, the performing arts of dance, music, and song were quite important throughout the Arctic, both in ceremonial and recreational settings **(Figure 2–9)**. In traditional times, at any given moment in an Inuit camp the singing of women could be heard (cf. Lutz 1978:43). Except for the songs that were sung to accompany juggling (and whose contents are not well understood), most songs' subject matter focused on hunting, on animals and birds, and on legendary beings of the mythic past. Eskimo dances ranged from highly formalized and rehearsed solos to freestyle, group performances; but even in the latter, dancers' movements came from a traditional repertoire of motions, and the best dancers were those who could combine subtlety with liveliness, not an easy feat. One field study

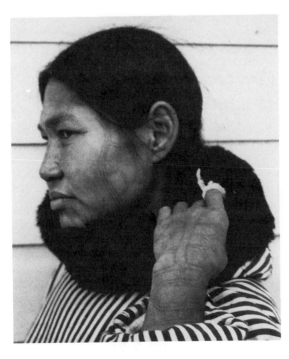

FIGURE 2-7 Daisey Okinello, of Gambell, Alaska, showing tattoos on wrist and face. *(Photo courtesy Denver Art Museum, Potosky Collection.)*

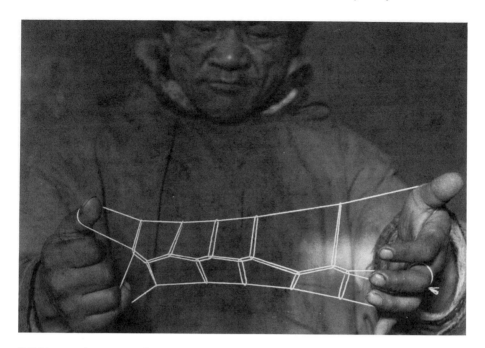

FIGURE 2-8 Eskimo cat's cradle figure. *(National Archives of Canada/PA11413/Photo by Richard Harrington.)*

reports that "it is remarkable to see a young dancer spring eagerly to the dance floor, spry, energetic, and enthusiastic, but give a disappointing and awkward performance, while an aging dancer who must be led to the dance floor blind and hobbling is transfigured at the first drumbeat to an angel of grace" (Luttmann and Luttmann 1985:58).

Whatever the medium, there is compelling evidence that the Inuit possessed exceptionally high degrees of manual and perceptual skills. Regarding the former, Carpenter (1973:17) remarks, "Aivilik men are first-class mechanics. . . . I have watched them repair instruments which American mechanics, flown into the Arctic for this purpose, have abandoned in despair." And as for visual perception and memory, several early explorers asked Eskimos to make maps of the land they frequently traversed. Although some drawings portrayed landforms that extended tens of thousands of square miles or more, they were accurate down to the most minute detail. Clearly, Inuit have no shortage of hand-eye coordination and visual imagery (cf. Rasmussen 1931:93–113; Nelson 1899:197; George Sutton, cited in Carpenter 1973:10–11).

FIGURE 2-9 Dance of natives of Dolphin and Union Strait given at a farewell celebration for members of the Fifth Thule Expedition. The dancer, accompanied by a drum, sings songs he composed and owns. *(Photograph by Leo Hansen, 1924; photo courtesy Nationalmuseet, Copenhagen.)*

How Much Can We Know about Eskimo Aesthetics?

Why did the Inuit, a people who lived in one of the earth's most demanding environments, expend great amounts of time and effort creating art? Surely they thought it to be an important human endeavor or else they would not have invested so much energy in making art. As we shall see, Eskimos *did* have good reasons for producing art, but before describing Inuit aesthetics we should take note of two possible problems.

First, we know that Eskimo bands were sparsely scattered over an enormous area of land—well over a million square miles, a territory that was probably larger than that of any traditional people in the world; and we also know that art media, quantity of art production, and skill of construction varied from one Arctic region to another. Is it, then, possible to speak of "Eskimo aesthetics" as a unitary entity? After all, the distance between the natives of western Alaska and those of eastern Greenland is greater than that from Scandinavia to West Africa, and no reasonable person would force the arts of these divergent and independent areas into a single aesthetic system.

But although variations exist, fieldworkers have found a remarkably uniform Inuit culture throughout the Arctic, especially in such conceptual and symbolic areas as language, religion, and myth. For example, Rasmussen was able to speak intelligibly with Eskimos across the Arctic using the language he knew from Greenland. Or, to give a more relevant example, Colby (1973) constructed a generative grammar to account for formal structures in North Alaskan folktales, and he found that stories from distant Eskimo groups in Canada and Greenland fit the same model with only slight modification. Such facts suggest that we can legitimately synthesize an integrated Inuit aesthetic system by using clues from wherever they are reported throughout the vast Arctic.

I say "clues" because that is really all we have to go on, and this is the second possible impediment to describing Eskimo aesthetics. Although much anthropological fieldwork has been carried out among Inuit peoples, and despite the existence of many books that lavishly illustrate Eskimo artifacts, no one ever thought to systematically question traditional Inuit themselves about the role of art in their lives.[4]

But if the ethnographic literature is examined for references to native ideas about art, clues for unveiling a coherent Eskimo aesthetic system are indeed found. Myths and creation stories situate art in a broad metaphysical context; native explanations about the day-to-day uses of art reveal the role of art in the affairs of Eskimo life; and ethnographic tidbits, such as the observation that two Inuit bands differ in their ideas about which fur makes a more beautiful parka—this is the primary data of aesthetic style and taste.

Validation of such a synthetic, catch-as-catch-can approach is always illusive. The best one can expect, I believe, is that when enough scattered and fragmentary observations are put together, a coherent and integrated aesthetic system will eventually emerge. Future research will undoubtedly sharpen our focus and give us a more detailed picture of Eskimo aesthetics, but the inductive approach I use below produces a first approximation of Inuit aesthetics. It reveals a system of thought in which art is believed to enhance a person's life today, improve one's prospects for tomorrow, and accomplish this through its unique capacity to transform reality.

Eskimo Aesthetics: The Enhancement of Present Life

In the minds of traditional Inuit, one important rationale of art's existence was that it made today's life more livable. This occurred in several ways, not the least of which was the enjoyment derived from artistic creation itself.

---

[4]Graburn (1974) has studied Inuit aesthetic values and critical standards regarding commercial soapstone carving, but that craft is young and is largely informed by considerations of the marketplace. As should be obvious, the account given here focuses on art made for traditional, indigenous purposes.

For example, one early explorer wrote, "In places where ivory is plentiful the men appeared to delight in occupying their leisure time in making carvings from that material or from bone, sometimes for use, but frequently merely for pastime, and many little images are made as toys for children" (Nelson 1899:196).

But Eskimos also realized that the pleasure engendered by art continues after the creative act is complete. That they savored beautiful things is proven in several ways. For one thing, although the Inuit language had no single word for art or aesthetics, there was a term, *takminaktuk*, meaning "it is good to look at or beautiful," that was applied to a wide range of referents (Graburn 1967:28). For example, the monolingual Pitseolak, who grew up in a traditional setting but who became a successful printmaker in her later years, once reminisced about her girlhood when she had "the most beautiful drinking water, the most beautiful water I have ever had" (Eber 1979, unpaginated). Significantly, many art objects were also said to be *takminaktuk*.

Myth, too, confirms the relish that Inuit feel for sensuous beauty. A major spirit being of the Central Eskimo is a handsome, and sometimes evil, young woman named Sedna, who in one story is courted by a fulmar, or large Arctic sea bird. "Come to me," says the fulmar; "come into the land of the birds, where there is never hunger, where my tent is made of the most beautiful skins." Sedna is won over by the bird's seductive promises but later is disappointed to discover that her new home "was not built of beautiful pelts, but was covered with wretched fishskins, full of holes, that gave free entrance to wind and snow. Instead of soft reindeer skins her bed was made of hard walrus hides" (Boas 1964/1888:175–176).

Inuit most commonly applied the concept of *beauty* to an individual's appearance, where one's natural features could be enhanced in various ways. Eskimos in southern Alaska could choose from lip, cheek, and ear plugs; nose pins; string of beads suspended from the lower lip; facial tattoos or paint—or they might decorate their black hair with white down. Ornaments were less profuse elsewhere, but Eskimos in most regions decorated themselves in one way or another, not for ceremony but for beauty's sake (cf. Hrdlicka 1975:43; Boas 1964/1888:151–153; Birket-Smith 1929:226, 229).

The themes of personal beauty and body decoration also appear in Inuit myth. The "Tale of the Red Bear," for example, tells of the time a group of women met Ta-kú-ka, a woman they had never seen before. They

admired [Ta-kú-ka's] face and its color, which was lighter than theirs, also several tattooed lines on her face, one up and down between her eyes and three that extended down across the chin from her lower lip; they were pleased also with the shape of her garments, which were very different from theirs. By and by one of the women said, "You are very handsome with the beautiful lines marked on your face; I would give much if you would teach me how to make my face like yours." "I shall not mind the pain," said the woman, "for I wish to be handsome, as you are, and am ready to bear it." (Nelson 1899:467–470)

As recounted by Nelson, the story ends with Ta-kú-ka tricking the vain woman by drowning her in a pot of hot oil, saying, "There, you will always be beautiful now!" (ibid.).

Like the woman in the myth, mortal Inuit women were willing to bear the discomforts and dangers of tattooing to appear aesthetically, perhaps even erotically, attractive. Among the Copper Eskimo, "tattooing on a woman had no religious significance; it was merely a time-honored method of adornment. . . . Just as there were no fixed rules regarding the exact time for the process [of tattooing], so there were no definite ceremonies surrounding it" (Jenness 1946:54; see also Carpenter 1973:160; Ray 1977:23; Hrdlicka 1975:45; Birket-Smith 1933:69).

Art enhanced Inuit life by giving pleasure to the creator and by adding sensuous beauty to the visual environment. But art also lightened the cares and tedium of mundane life through its role in recreation. Children's toys, for example, were often fashioned with aesthetic considerations in mind. Most Eskimo parents openly expressed love for their children, and they indulged their youngs' wishes when possible. In areas with particularly barren environments, natural objects such as small bones had to suffice as children's toys, but elsewhere men often went to great lengths to make ingenious and entertaining playthings. For example, some time in the late nineteenth century a father in St. Michael, western Alaska, constructed the object shown in **Figure 2–10** for his son. As Nelson describes the toy, it was

the image of a woodpecker made of wood fastened to a small wooden spatula by means of a stout quill in place of legs. The surface of the spatula is dotted over with red paint to represent food. By means of a string fastened to the point of the bird's beak and passing down through a hole in the spatula, the child is enabled to pull the bird's beak down. On releasing it, the elasticity of the quill throws it up again, thus giving a pecking motion and imitating the movements of feeding.   (Nelson 1899:341–342)

As in most societies, Inuit children's toys were adjuncts to the socialization process, serving as models that children could use to practice the skills of adult life. So Eskimo girls, who would one day become mothers, were given toy dolls; and boys, the future hunters and fishers, played with model animals (cf. Birket-Smith 1929:289; Nelson 1899:345; Ray 1977:10; Jenness 1946:146).

Adult Inuit had their toys, too. During the long Arctic winters when the small bands of summer coalesced into larger groups of fifty to a hundred individuals and when daylight lasted a few hours at most, Inuit stayed inside their igloos for extended periods of time. During this period, art, in the service of recreation, helped relieve the boredom of confinement. One game, called *ajegaung,* involved players taking turns with a small object that was perforated by several holes, such as the one shown in Figure 2–1. The

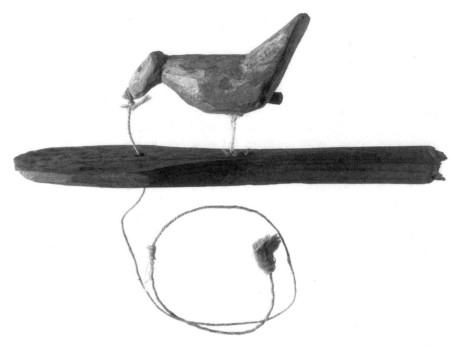

FIGURE 2-10   Eskimo child's toy, St. Michael, western Alaska.   *(Smithsonian Institution, Department of Anthropology, catalogue no. 33798.)*

idea was to toss it into the air and then, before it landed, deftly catch it in the proper hole with a slender stick. Sometimes a small animal skull was used, but usually the game was played with an ivory carving shaped like an animal.

A gambling game called *tingmiujang* was also popular. Players would sit around a piece of leather or a wooden board, and one after the other they would take several little figures, shake them, and toss them into the air. The winner was the one whose throw produced the correct number of figures standing upright, rather than lying on their sides or backs.

The performing arts were, if anything, even more important for relieving the tedium of the long winter months. Sometimes there were formal, planned get-togethers. Rasmussen's description captures the atmosphere of such activities over half a century ago:

> The great song festivals at which I have been present during the dark season are the most original and the prettiest kind of pastime I have ever witnessed. Every man and every woman, sometimes also the children, will have his or her own songs, with appropriate melodies, which are sung in the *qag·e*, the great snow hut which is set up in every village where life and good spirits abound.   (Rasmussen 1929:228)

A more recent observer noted that in such song "there is no literary, intellectual detachment; the Eskimo is emotionally immersed in immediate experience, including musical experience, for sound is fleeting" (Johnston 1976:6). Like music, there is good evidence that dance also gives great pleasure and enjoyment (Luttmann and Luttmann 1985:57).

Traditionally, impromptu opportunities for song were also common. Rasmussen again:

> Where all are well, and have meat enough, everyone is cheerful and always ready to sing, consequently there is nearly always singing in every hut of an evening, before the family retires to rest. . . . While one of the younger members takes the drum and beats time, all the rest then hum the melodies and try to fix the words in their minds. (Rasmussen 1929:228)

To complete the picture of the Inuit family whiling away a winter evening by singing together, we should remember that the mother's and father's hands are enjoyably busy making clothes and tools that are as practical as they are aesthetically pleasing.

Orpingalik once said to Rasmussen, "How many songs I have I cannot tell you. I keep no count of such things. There are so many occasions in one's life when a joy or a sorrow is felt in such a way that the desire comes to sing; and so I know that I have many songs. All my being is song" (Rasmussen 1931:16). The spontaneous satisfaction of artistic creation; the sensuous pleasure of experiencing beautiful things, actions, and people; and the enjoyment felt by child and adult alike when engaged in artistic play—in each of these ways, traditional Eskimo art enhanced life in an environment that gave few other pleasures.

Inuit Aesthetics: Insuring Future Well-Being

Eskimo art not only enhanced day-to-day life; in the traditional native view of things, art also improved the likelihood that future life would also be better—safer, healthier, and more prosperous. Art accomplished this through its role in religion.

Traditional Inuit religion had several dimensions. Many taboos prohibited specific activities. For example, if a Netsilik man killed a caribou with a bow and arrow, he was absolutely forbidden to eat its meat if he had eaten seal meat that day (Balikci 1970:219–220). A second component of Eskimo religion was shamanism. In most regions, shamans could cure illnesses and could also use their supernatural abilities to bring harm to enemies and to mitigate crises in the environment. Lastly, the world of the Eskimos was inhabited by numerous spirit beings, some dangerous and some benign, some subject to human control and some beyond the realm of human affairs.

Such spirits were not abstractions but were conceptualized in concrete terms. Rasmussen describes a revealing incident with one Iglulik shaman:

> One day I asked Anarqâq if he would try to draw for me some of his spirit visions. . . . He had of course never before drawn with a pencil on paper, but it must be said that he set about the new method of work with the true humility of an artist. There was no careless scratching or scribbling; he would sit for hours with closed eyes, solely intent upon getting the vision fixed in his mind, and only when this was done would he attempt to put it into form. Sometimes the recollection of the event affected him to such a degree that he trembled all over, and had to give up the attempt. (Rasmussen 1929:44)

Significantly, such spirits could be influenced by art: One of the major festivals among the Eskimos of Cumberland Sound included singing by shamans in an effort to marshall the legions of good spirits for protection against Sedna and other evil ones (Lutz 1978:103).

Such religious beliefs influenced Inuit aesthetics on several levels. First, some Eskimo art was made in service to religious belief. For example, although most women's tattoos were made for beauty's sake alone, some were prompted by a desire to supernaturally influence the future. Both Netsilik and Copper Eskimos believed that a woman's tattoos insured easier childbirth, and Eskimos in southern Alaska believed that tattoos on a woman's chest would increase the amount of milk she could provide her children (Birket-Smith 1933:69; see also Carpenter 1973:160; Rasmussen 1932:plate opposite p. 269).

Tattoos could also influence a person's fate after death. Birkett-Smith quotes one early explorer as quaintly reporting, "If the face be not thus embroidered [i.e., tattooed], the head, they say, becometh a grease tub which shall be placed under the lamp when they come to Heaven or the Land of the Soul" (Egede, quoted in Birket-Smith 1959:119; see also Birket-Smith 1924:215, Rasmussen 1929:148, 1931:313). Birkett-Smith notes, in an interesting reference to the importance of the differential distribution of skill, that one of the several underworlds to which a dead Inuit might go is the "Land of the Crestfallen." It is, he says, inhabited by "unskillful hunters and women whose tattooing has been badly done, [who] sit there, chin on breast, now and then snapping dully after the butterflies which are their only food" (Birket-Smith 1959:162).

If some ivory carvings were simply toys, others served a more serious purpose as amulets, or objects with the supernatural power to bring their owners either wished-for things (such as game for the hunter or else the strong shoulders and arms he would need to bring the game down), or desirable abilities (such as the shaman's skill of detecting evil spirits). The Netsilik were particularly amulet-oriented, with Rasmussen (1931:271) telling of a boy who wore a total of eighty amulets sewn inside his parka.

Some amulets were naturally occurring objects. For example, the Iglulik believed that if you place a bit of excrement from a newborn ermine inside your shoe so that it touches your foot, then you will be a good walker and will be protected against all types of foot problems. But usually amulets were products of the human hand. For example, "a small doll, made from the extreme hard point of bone in the penis of a walrus, skillfully carved with arms and legs, is sewn into a boy's inner jacket, and he will then, when out alone after caribou, never encounter the dangerous mountain spirits called ijErqät" (Rasmussen 1929:155).

Long ago Sir James Frazer coined the phrase "homeopathic" (or "sympathetic" or "imitative") magic for activities whose supernatural effectiveness derives from their resemblance to the desired end, and many Eskimo amulets fall in this category. An old East-Greenlander said, for example, that giving a child a doll carved from a straight willow trunk would make its owner grow up with a straight, strong back, "so that he can walk through life erect and fearless" (Meldgaard 1960:7).

Such items of homeopathic magic are effective, the Inuit thought, because their resemblance to the wished-for quality causes them to attract spirits of their own, spirits with the power to extend their distinctive characteristics into the lives of their mortal owners. But although Inuit had definite ideas about the appearance of spirits, they were not terribly literal-minded about amulets, which were rarely informed by photographic realism. The amulet needed to resemble the desired spirit only enough to convince the spirit to take up residence in it, so most amulets were conventionalized in style.

The Transcendent Dimension of Eskimo Art

If we were to end our account of Inuit aesthetics at this point, the result might seem to support the mistaken idea that people in small-scale societies are incapable of serious philosophical insight. Obviously, art's presence can make life more enjoyable, and the use of art in service of homeopathic magic may simply represent wishful thinking.

But Inuit myth, folklore, and art usage convey deeper ideas regarding art's role in the world. The Inuit world view implicitly distinguishes among three realms of existence—the supernatural world, with its out-of-the-ordinary and awe-inspiring qualities; the social world of day-to-day human interaction; and the natural world of animals, plants, and inanimate objects. Many peoples tacitly accept the existence of these three worlds but ignore the problem of how they are related to each other. How can cold, lifeless elements become warm, living human flesh; and how can the spirit that lives within the flesh transcend its mortal habitation and touch the divine? There is considerable evidence that Eskimos conceptualize art as a sort of cultural "philosopher's stone" that makes such transformations possible.

Consider, for example, a creation myth recorded in the late nine-teenth century in which First Man, having emerged spontaneously from a pea pod, encounters Raven. Seeing Man, Raven "raised one of its wings, pushed up its beak, like a mask, to the top of its head, and changed at once into a man" (Nelson 1899:451). The superhuman raven/man was astonished to see in First Man a living creature who looked so much like himself. Raven then set about creating the things of the world. For example,

> Raven made two animals of clay which he endowed with life . . . but as they were dry only in spots when they were given life, they remained brown and white, and so originated the tame reindeer with muttled coat. . . .
> [Finally, Raven] went to a spot some distance from where he had made the animals, and, looking now and then at Man, made an image very much like him. Then he fastened a lot of fine water grass on the back of the head for hair, and after the image had dried in his hand, he waved his wings over it as before and a beautiful young woman arose and stood beside Man. (Nelson 1899:454)

Aside from the fact that the myth has males coming spontaneously into existence whereas females are a product of male manufacture, the interest-ing point in this story is the way transitions occur between the natural, hu-man, and supernatural worlds. First, Raven, a creature with miraculous abilities, removes an art work—a mask—from his face and is thereby trans-formed into something resembling Man himself. Then, through another act of artistic creativity, the modeling of clay, Raven transforms inert earth into living animals and, ultimately, into Man's companion, Woman.

Another myth from the western Arctic reveals the same theme. Once in the ancient past, two men, one from the north and one from the south, fought over a woman, eventually pulling her apart at the waist. Each man returned home with only half a real woman but remedied the situation by carving a wooden model of the missing portion and attaching it to the part of the woman he brought home. Thus it happened that the upper half of the northern woman was made of flesh and bone, although her lower half was wood; and the southern woman was just the opposite. According to the story, soon the wooden portions became life-like too, so that the women were able to lead more or less normal lives. Thus in this story too, carving (that is, *art*) magically transforms an inanimate material, wood, into living flesh, thereby making each fragmented woman whole. Or at least nearly whole: Interestingly, the transformation is not perfect because the woman in the south was never able to excel at sewing inasmuch as her fingers had once been wood; and although the woman to the north was a fine seam-stress, the wooden origin of her legs made her a poor dancer. But these consequences are necessary parts of the myth because they explain why, down to the present day, women in the south have different talents than those in the north (Nelson 1899:479). Thus the progenitors of two contemporary tribes were created through artifice, and their art-making skills, sewing and dance, are reminders of their origins.[5]

In yet another tale, called the Origin of Winds (Nelson 1899:497–498), a childless couple carve and clothe a model doll which, in the middle of the night, turns into a child with extraordinary abilities.

Song, too, is associated with miraculous transformations in the context of myth: In 1970, Maija Lutz collected a traditional, but now highly enigmatic, song that went in part:

> Kayaks down there come on over
> You will be my husbands
> I am being stuck to this stone
> My legs are turning to stone. (Lutz 1978:54)

Later Lutz realized that the song referred to a legend that Rasmussen had collected nearly a half-century earlier in which a girl marries a stone—and as she sings this song she begins to turn into stone herself. Interestingly, Lutz (1978:104) also mentions a ritual in which a shaman, in a chant-induced trance, increases the effectiveness of hunters by bringing the soul of a seal into their minds or bodies.

Of course, all Inuit art made for purposes of sympathetic magic owes its efficacy to art's being able to cross the boundaries between the natural, human, and supernatural realms. For example, cat's cradle string figures, along with their accompanying songs, were believed to entangle the sun and prevent its disappearance. Consequently the figures were most common in the autumn when the sun's rays were waning (Johnston 1976:5).

Death, too, is a transition that, in the view of Eskimos, requires the soul to forsake its mortal abode for one of several possible realms of after-life; and art again aids the transitional process. Carvings of toy tools were often buried with the dead, and the souls of animals received similar treatment, so that in some places the killing of a bear necessitated placing a needle-case beside an adult female and a miniature bow and arrow beside a cub, "that they might not travel emptyhanded to the spirit-home of their kind" (Jenness 1928:169; see also Rasmussen 1929:199; Nelson 1899:307, 311).

As with the visual arts, the performing arts could also transcend the boundaries between the three planes of existence. In Igluklik thought,

> no one can become a poet who has not complete faith in the power of words. When I asked Ivaluardjuk about the power of words, he would smile shyly

---

[5]One might conjecture that the story also sheds light on Eskimo conceptions of "women's arts," distinguishing as it does between domestic skills, as quintessentially represented by sewing, versus the sensual and reproductive dimension that might be associated with dance.

and answer that it was something no one could explain; for the rest, he would refer me to the old magic song I had already learned, and which made difficult things easy. . . . His idea in citing this example was to show that the singer's faith in the power of words should be so enormous that he should be capable of *believing* that a piece of dry wood could bleed, could shed warm, red blood—wood, the driest thing there is. (Rasmussen 1929:241)

Other Uses of Art in Inuit Culture

Besides providing symbolic bridges between an Eskimo, the material world below, and the spiritual world above, art also helps define social relationships between one Eskimo and another. Compared to other societies, Eskimo culture is relatively homogeneous, with all families relying on the same subsistence techniques and living nomadic lives that prohibit the accumulation of many luxuries. Nevertheless, there are at least a few distinct social roles in Eskimo society: Men and women hold noticeably different positions in the culture, as do boys and girls from an early age; and art, in the form of body decoration and clothing, displays these statuses in a highly visible fashion (cf. Ray 1977:23).

In addition to these statuses, Eskimo shamans were also somewhat set apart, and this too was reflected in art, at least in some communities. When a young man attained the status of shaman in the central Canadian Arctic, he put on a special belt. His friends and relatives gave him small, carved figures of humans, fishes, and harpoons which he wore hanging from the belt. These figures insured his control over powerful spirits (Rasmussen 1929:114).

In a few Inuit groups, art also disseminated noteworthy information by recording the events of the past. The human and animal figures engraved on ivory tools in Alaska—especially on bow drills—related to hunts and other activities the carver had engaged in (cf. Ray 1961:22–23, 1977:25; Mason 1927:253, 279). Such subject matter was also recorded in song and thereby handed down from one generation to the next.

Conclusion

Given its sociological attributes and the harshness of the environment in which it exists, one might not expect Eskimo culture to be the site of significant art production and serious aesthetic thought. But traditional Eskimos produced items that have been held in high aesthetic esteem not only by Western art collectors but by Inuit themselves.

There is clear evidence that Eskimos recognized the difference between ordinary, run-of-the-mill productions versus things that stand out for their special artistic merit. Subtle ivory carvings are reported to have been "tests of the skill of the worker" (Martijn 1964:556); and Carpenter (1973:203), probably inspired by a remark by Leach (1961:29), has compared carving among Inuit to handwriting among members of literate societies. In both instances, most adults possess the skill in question, but a few individuals—called "sculptors" and "calligraphers," respectively—are recognized for their superior abilities.

Our perception of Eskimo ideas about aesthetic excellence is obscured somewhat by a native ethos that discourages competitiveness and that seldom overtly rewards an outstanding performance in any endeavor. But the consummate Inuit artist does sometimes get his or her due. Recall, for example, that a woman's well-made tattoos provide a pathway to a superior life after death whereas poorly made tattoos destined the wearer to a dreary eternity of subsisting on butterflies. Also, it has been pointed out that

> through dance an adolescent could demonstrate acquired knowledge and capabilities in the roles to be played in life, a significant outlet in a culture which censured any form of overt bragging or self-congratulation. . . . [Thus,] a young marriageable woman could demonstrate her desirability as a spouse by miming her talents in dance.   (Luttmann and Luttmann 1985:55)

Traditional dress, too, provided a domain for critical evaluation. The aging Pitseolak recalled, "I tried hard to learn how to sew because I envied the women who could sew nicely" (Eber 1979). And it has been said that in contemporary Northwest Alaska where almost all men make carvings, only a small fraction are considered to be experts, and every man knows his level of competence relative to all the other carvers (Ray 1961:133).[6]

Eskimos not only create art, but they make it for purposes that are important and profound. Again, the situation is obscured by a trait of Eskimo culture, namely the absence of a specific word for art: Some of the objects we have just discussed are simply said to be *sulijuk* (i.e., true or honest), but many others are indicated by the suffix, -*nguaq,* which connotes "diminutive-likeness-imitation-model-play" (Swinton 1978:81).

---

[6]Interestingly, those who are considered to be "experts" by other Eskimo carvers are also the ones judged to be "artists" by Western buyers (Ray 1961:132). But before we conclude that Inuit and Western notions of "expertness" are identical we should take into account the following anecdote recorded by Rasmussen:

> I shall never forget [the Iglulik poet] Ivaluardjuk's astonishment and confusion when I tried to explain to him that in our country, there were people who devoted themselves exclusively to the production of poems and melodies. His first attempt at an explanation of this inconceivable suggestion was that such persons must be great shamans who had perhaps attained to some intimate relationship with the spirits, these then inspiring them continually with utterances of spiritual force. But as soon as he was informed that our poets were not shamans, merely people who handled words, thoughts, and feelings according to the technique of a particular art, the problem appeared altogether beyond him.   (Rasmussen 1929:223–234)

But although the Eskimo vocabulary for discussing art may seem cumbersome, we must admit that the traditional Inuit philosophy of art was complex and subtle. In the first place, Eskimos appreciated the immediate pleasure that artistic production can give to artist and audience alike. The satisfactions of the creative process itself, the sensuous pleasure afforded by artistic beauty, and the enjoyment found in recreations that use artistic paraphernalia—all of these were recognized in traditional Eskimo culture. Moreover, Inuit were convinced that art has the power to influence the course of future events, bringing such desirable and important effects as health, food, and fertility.

The belief that art can do these things rests upon a fundamental conception of art that is as profound as any produced by the philosophers of the East and West. Eskimos recognize the frightening chasms that separate humans from, on the one hand, the cold, unresponsive material world that surrounds us, and, on the other hand, the transcendent realm of the supernatural and eternal that we conceive to be beyond us. Surely reflective people everywhere agonize over these alienating gulfs, instinctively feeling that something should bridge them—but what? The Inuit answer to the dilemma is that a link does indeed exist, and that it is art. (This notion is not altogether foreign to the Western student of art who firmly believes, say, that a masterpiece painting is far more than mere pigment and canvas.) Eskimos know that through art mortals can influence events in the otherwise indifferent realm of nature, and that art touches the spirits that stand above both humans and the natural world.

Phrased in these terms, it is easy to see the importance of art's role in Eskimo culture and little wonder that the Inuit, despite the simplicity of their material means and the hardships necessitated by their environment, produce art with such conviction.

3

ABORIGINAL AUSTRALIAN AESTHETICS
Sacramental Union
with the Eternal Dreamtime

[Australian Aboriginal art works] are tangible representations of the sacred mythological past in the present, the bridge that links man with his gods. (Berndt 1964:7)

The senses speak to us of one reality, a world whose palpable immediacy cannot be easily dismissed. But the mind, given an opportunity for reflection, often proclaims another, more significant realm, one that transcends the mundane plane of the senses. Most of us have had presentiments of such a world at one time or another, whether in experiencing the awesomeness of divinity, the ecstasy of love, or even, as in the words of a mathematician and philosopher, "the Pythagorean power by which number holds sway above the flux" (Russell 1967:13).

For most Westerners, such epiphanies are the exception rather than the rule, but for the aboriginal peoples of Australia the world beyond the empirical here–and–now is compellingly genuine and important. Spiritual concerns permeate Aboriginal life, and a careful examination of native Australian aesthetics reveals that, along with ritual, art is the primary means by which mortals may touch the world of mystery.

Australian Aborigines are among the few hunting and gathering cultures to survive into the twentieth century, and their being prolific producers of art makes them all the more important to us. Moreover, the spiritual quality of Australian aesthetics compels our attention, forcing us to probe into the dark corners of the heart to search out and examine the voice through which the soul of the mystic speaks to the transcendent spirit of nature. For aboriginal Australians, that voice is ritual art.

The Cultural Context of Aboriginal Art

The native peoples of Australia have never been numerous. In an island only slightly less vast than the continental United States, European explorers met about 300,000 people (fewer than one-third the current population of Rhode Island), and the colonial experience has reduced that small number by about 90 percent. Most of the approximately 500 traditional tribal groups were divided into seminomadic bands with less than a hundred members each. The demographic sparseness of the Aborigines is exemplified by Western Arnhem Land (see map, p. 10), a region located in northern Australia and the source of much of our information about traditional Australian art and aesthetics, and now inhabited by less than 1,000 people.

But these bands survived remarkably well in the inhospitable desert and grassland environment found in most of Australia, thanks largely to a technology that was simple but ingenious. Digging sticks and grinding stones allowed women to obtain and prepare food from the earth; and spears, spear throwers, and boomerangs helped men bring down game. (Not all groups had the boomerang; and among those that did, the non-returning type played a far more important role in hunting than did the returning type, which was used primarily for recreation.) The remaining inventory of utilitarian items was small: Aborigines made shields and clubs for fighting; string, bark, and wood containers; and houses of bark and grass. They cut and worked wood with stone axes, adzes, wedges, and chisels; and they lit fires using firedrills and firesaws.

Compared to the simplicity of their material culture, the intellectual life of Aborigines is quite complex. Australian kinship systems, for example, continue to tax the understanding of Western scholars. And though not as complex as kinship, Australian religion is also a subtle topic. Its most fundamental premise is that during some indeterminate period of the past that Aborigines call the "Eternal Dreamtime," mythical beings wandered through the countryside, their activities creating many notable features of today's landscape, such as waterholes. Also in their travels the Dreamtime spirits brought into existence a primordial abundance of plant and animal life, human beings, and many human institutions such as ritual, song, and the principles of descent. The spirits of the Eternal Dreamtime still exist today, and by recounting the stories of their travels (i.e., through myth—see **Figure 3–1**) and by reenacting their activities (i.e., through ritual—see **Figure 3–2**), the original harmonious and prosperous state of the world will be perpetuated. Ritual practices vary widely and are the responsibility of equally diverse totemic groups—that is, sets of individuals who share a symbolic identification with a particular species of animal, from which they trace their origin and with whom they retain a close association.

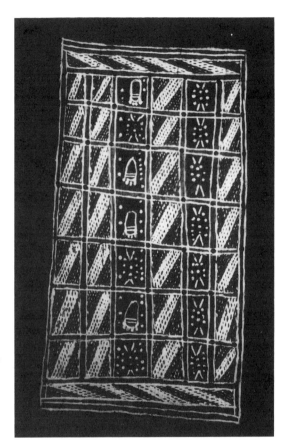

FIGURE 3-1 An Australian Aboriginal bark painting by Banakaka, a member of the Liyagalawumirri, northeast Arnhem Land. It depicts in a traditional style the characters and events that occur in the myth of the Wawilak Sisters, a story "owned" by the artist's clan. *(Courtesy Edward L. Ruhe.)*

Aboriginal Art

The traditional arts of Australia are profuse and varied; although native languages have no term equivalent to *art* in general, they do have words for specific art media, such as graphic art, carving, singing, storytelling, and ceremonial dance (Berndt and Berndt 1964:306).

Like other seminomadic peoples, Australian Aborigines capitalize on the most portable of all media, the human body itself.[1] They practice scarifi-

---

[1]The majority of Aboriginal art is sacred and its makers feel very strongly that it should be viewed only by initiated individuals. Therefore, most of the styles and media will not be illustrated by photographs. Some bark paintings may be seen by non-initiates, and three of them appear in Figures 3–4, 3–5, and 3–6. Although they do not exhaust the repertoire of Aboriginal techniques, they give the viewer a reasonable idea of the styles common in north-central Australia.

FIGURE 3-2 A bark painting by Manuwa, a member of the Djambarrpuyngu, northeast Arnhem Land. The painting shows the dancing post of the Banumbirr (Morning Star) ceremony. Sea gull feathers at the top of the post and at the ends of the strings represent stars. Also shown are several musicians—a dronepipe player, a man with clapsticks, and two songmen. The ceremony, "owned" by several clans, is performed to honor the dead of any of the allied clans. *(Courtesy Edward L. Ruhe.)*

cation, using both the common method of rubbing ashes or clay into fresh cuts and also the unusual technique of putting ants in the cuts to cause irritation (McCarthy 1957a). The resultant scars serve various purposes. Some are made as part of mourning or initiation rituals; others indicate the wearer's social status (male versus female, initiated adult versus uninitiated youth); and still others are created simply to make the wearer's body more attractive.

Many Aboriginal groups use paint to enhance a person's appearance. The people of northeastern Arnhem Land, for example, first grease the body and then apply ochres in complicated patterns. The painted designs are "owned" by individuals; and in addition to their ceremonial worth, the patterns have economic value in that they can be bartered or sold (Elkin, Berndt, and Berndt 1950:61–62).

Clothing is minimal or non-existent throughout aboriginal Australia. Some Aborigines wear a pubic tassel, but it is meant to decorate, rather than cover, the body. Others wear necklaces and head-, arm-, and waist-bands (see **Figure 3–3**). In some regions the body is painted, and textured designs are created on the body by sticking the fluff from kapok plants onto the body, using blood as an adhesive. Headdresses are perhaps the most elaborate additions to the body. The Arunta of central Australia, for example, pull their hair together atop their heads, surround the resulting bunch of hair with small twigs to form a helmet-like structure as much as two feet high, and sometimes decorate it further by adding several eagle-hawk feathers (Spencer and Gillan 1938:610–612).

But body decoration is not the only medium of Australian visual art. Some groups produce paintings on large, flat sheets of bark from the stringy bark tree **(Figure 3–4)**; and tens of thousands of paintings on rock walls have been documented throughout the continent. One style of rock art is characterized by "X-ray drawings," which depict not only animals' silhouettes but also their internal organs, painted in an anatomically accurate, polychromatic style **(Figure 3–5)**. Others, the so-called *mimi* drawings, monochromatically portray stick-figure humans; and stencil impressions of human hands constitute yet another variety of rock painting.

FIGURE 3-3 Australian Aboriginal pendant, with incised figures. *(Courtesy, Field Museum of Natural History, Chicago, neg. no. 97020.)*

FIGURE 3–4 A bark painting by Ngulmarmar, a member of the Ganalbingu. It depicts the Dingo Dreaming Place, a cave penetrated by the dingo of the sacred Dreamtime. The cave is inhabited by flying foxes, whose droppings on the floor of the cave are also seen. *(Courtesy Edward L. Ruhe.)*

Many bands of Aborigines produce three-dimensional art objects, the most important of which are *tjurungas*. These ritual objects are flat, oval, or circular slabs of wood or stone, from two inches to eighteen feet in length, often bearing complex painted and incised patterns (Berndt and Berndt 1964:367). Aborigines also make bullroarers by attaching oval pieces of wood to cords and whirling them in the air to produce an eerie, roaring sound. In some places, such as northeastern Arnhem Land, carvers make wooden heads or full figures of ancestral beings and animals. Elsewhere they cut large designs into live trees for use in initiation rites and as grave

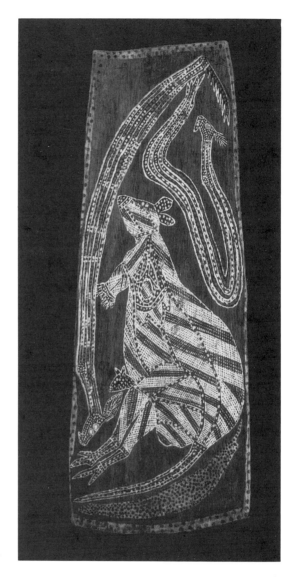

FIGURE 3-5 A bark painting by Mandarrg, of the Dangbon tribe, showing an X-ray kangaroo with the Rainbow Serpent, Borlung, rendered twice and costumed for a corroboree with a false beard and headdress. Note that the kangaroo's gullet, heart, lungs, diaphragm, liver, and spine are all visible, as is the baby in its pouch. A death adder appears below the kangaroo. *(Courtesy Edward L. Ruhe.)*

posts. Natives of Arnhem Land also use earth, sand, and logs to produce huge high-relief sculptures on the ground. Margaret Clunies Ross and L. R. Hiatt (1978) witnessed the construction of five such sand sculptures that eventually covered about 600 square meters. Some tribes make baskets, decorating them with pandanus fiber, red parakeet feathers, white down, human hair, and fur.

The appearance of Australian art varies somewhat, both regionally and from one medium to another, but it is always graceful and economical in style. Its makers use a "subjective vision," representing things not as they briefly appear to the eye but as the mind knows them eternally to be **(Figure 3–6)**. Artists also often conventionalize their work, allowing a few characteristic features to represent the whole subject. Kupka describes bark paintings in these terms:

> By stripping down, reorganizing, and recreating natural forms, the Aboriginal painter arrives at a sort of abstraction, as do many "modern" painters, however, abstraction is not at all his aim. On the contrary, every line and every dot in his painting has a real meaning that can be recognized by the initiated. The fact that outsiders cannot interpret them is often an advantage.   (Kupka 1965:96)

The performing arts are at least as important in Aboriginal culture as the graphic and plastic arts. Solo and ensemble singing are integral to both sacred and secular life; and the songs heard in many Aboriginal camps on almost any evening are usually accompanied by various gongs, rattles, and the *didjeridu*, a drone pipe made from a hollowed-out eucalyptus branch

FIGURE 3–6 A bark painting by Midinari of the Galpu, showing the place of the twelve sacred rocks. *(Courtesy Edward L. Ruhe.)*

which, when played, has an eerie and distinctive sound. Some song texts are organized into cycles of up to 300 individual songs, each with densely symbolic meanings (cf. Berndt 1976; Ellis 1985).

The Use of Art in Aboriginal Religion

Aboriginal religion, with its deep concern for the Eternal Dreamtime, is the wellspring from which all Australian art flows; and most Aboriginal religion, and its associated art, falls into two categories. It is either used for *increase magic* whose purpose is to insure the availability and growth of food supplies, or else it helps *initiate* young people into the status of adulthood.

The Aboriginal art that is a part of increase magic takes many forms. Success in hunting, for example, provides a motivation for much cave painting. As Elkin describes it, "A man sees a fine fish in the river; he paints it on the gallery, and then is sure he will see it again and spear it" (Elkin 1964:15). Some eastern Arnhem Land men believe that they can improve their hunting by wearing necklaces with congealed blood pendants (Berndt and Berndt 1964:275). And in the Kimberleys, these two agents—paint and blood—are united when men draw blood from their arms and smear it onto sacred paintings. Alternatively, some Aboriginal groups carve wooden poles and bullroarers shaped like animals to insure the fertility and increase of the species they are painted to represent.

A Fertility Mother, Kunapipi (or Gunabibi), is the focus of much increase magic, but the purpose of her ceremonies should not be misunderstood. Aborigines do not expect their rituals to compel Kunapipi to provide food directly to her devotees. More ambitiously, they hope she will be induced to perpetuate the natural order of all things as they were originally created during the Dreamtime, a condition that includes adequate rainfall, the consequent flourishing of flora, the resultant increase of fauna and, finally, the provision of food to humans (Elkin, Berndt, and Berndt 1950:28).

If increase rituals are meant to perpetuate the world of nature, then initiation ceremonies are performed to sustain the realm of the human spirit. Special ritual knowledge, possessed only by initiated adults, must be passed down from one generation to the next, and this is accomplished by psychologically compelling rituals in which young men (and, to a lesser extent, young women) undergo initiation into the mysteries of the Eternal Dreamtime.

The revelation of some secrets to the initiates is accomplished via song and dance; but the deepest meanings in initiation rituals reside in magically potent carved sticks, strings, wooden poles, ground sculptures, bullroarers, and the ubiquitous *tjurungas*, which are believed to actually embody the Dreamtime spirits and are the only items not destroyed after use in initiation ceremonies. The initiators typically alter the appearance of the initiates during these rituals by knocking out some of their teeth, pulling out their hair, or scarifying them. Most common, however, are various types of genital mutilation, including, for males, circumcision and subincision (i.e., slitting the urethra along the bottom of the penis) and, for females, ritual defloration.

Increase and initiation rituals are the most important parts of the Aboriginal religio-artistic complex, but they are not the only ones. For example, some bark paintings are made for initiation rituals but most serve as teaching devices to convey general information to children (and strangers) regarding the non-esoteric aspects of the Dreamtime.

Most Aboriginal Australian art is not only religious but, simultaneously, utilitarian in the sense that it is made in an effort to obtain desired, material results. It accomplishes this through supernatural means, since human well-being depends upon the continuing activities of the Dreamtime spirits. Berndt and Berndt believe that Aboriginal ritual painting and carving "are tangible representations of the sacred mythological past in the present, the bridge that links man with his gods" (Berndt and Berndt 1964:7).[2]

Aboriginal Aesthetics: Transubstantiation via Art

Art clearly plays an important role in Aboriginal religion, but the question remains, What is the basis of art's religious efficacy? In the Aboriginal view of the world, what makes art such a necessary adjunct of the Eternal Dreamtime?

A clue lies in the nature of the Dreamtime itself. The mythical beings that traveled through the primordial countryside never departed from this earth. Being eternal, they remain alive today. However, as supernaturals they can change their outer form; and today they usually have the appearance of natural phenomena such as particular rocks, mountains, and animal species. Despite their current guises, Dreamtime spirits still have close bonds with their human descendants. Indeed, members of a totemic group may not kill or eat their totemic animal because, for them, doing so would be homicide and cannibalism.

---

[2]An anecdote recounted by Catherine Ellis illustrates the great difference between Western and Aboriginal views regarding the importance of art in society. When she was in secondary school, Ellis participated in a debate in which she had to argue that she, as a musician, was at least as important in her (Western) society as a lawyer or a minister. She lost the debate, her friends telling her, "We wanted to vote for you but we couldn't. Why didn't you say you were a teacher, or a nurse, or a doctor? A musician is no use for anything." Years later Ellis learned that in Aboriginal culture "the most knowledgeable person in a tribal community was the person 'knowing many songs.' This individual encompassed within his knowledge of music, the wisdom of his people" (Ellis 1985:1).

The cooperation of the Dreamtime spirits is absolutely necessary for humans to survive. Elkin, Berndt, and Berndt remark,

> To trail the kangaroo is not enough; it is necessary also to influence it so that it will stand within range. To aim at the fish will not in itself insure accuracy. It must be drawn to the spear of the fisherman. For such purposes, charms, rites, paintings and sacred objects are . . . effective because [the hunter] and animals and plants and natural phenomena, both in the past and present, belong to one great moral or social order, each depending on the other— man's duty being ritual, nature's being food-producing. If man is remiss, nature will fail. (Elkin, Berndt, and Berndt 1950:2-3)

These observations bring us to the fundamental axiom of Aboriginal aesthetics: Art is a conduit that conveys the needs and wishes of mortals to the Dreamtime spirits. Every detail of an art work is said to represent

> events and situations in the career of the hero of the totemic group or lodge. As the artist engraves and paints he is 'impressing' that meaning into it— probably by chant. Later, it is handled reverently as the sacramental link between man and the hero or ancestor, and the creative condition to which the latter belongs. (Elkin, Berndt, and Berndt 1950:7)

To touch a *tjurunga* is to come into direct, physical contact with the realm of the supernatural, and such contact insures the perpetuation of both mortals and Dreamtime spirits.

Thus we see the underlying logic of Aboriginal aesthetics: Human welfare requires the blessings of the Dreamtime spirits; these supernaturals are influenced through ritual; and works of art—specifically song, dance, and decorated ceremonial objects—are the effective component of ritual. Since human existence ultimately depends upon art, it is not surprising that native Australians produce art in great quantities and of considerable conceptual sophistication.

Sometimes this central premise of Aboriginal aesthetics is taken one step further. Through art, mortals not only communicate with the Eternal Dreamtime; they may actually join the spirit world themselves.

For example, Elkin, Berndt, and Berndt (1950:3) say that a participant in a ritual "becomes the hero or ancestor. . . . By reenacting what the ancestor or great being did, he becomes a life-giver too, therefore, nature will be productive and food-species multiply." Similarly, the Walbiri believe that Dreamtime spirits are physically embodied (*balga*) in the dancers who impersonate them, decorated as the dancers are with sacred *gúruwari* designs (Munn 1973:198).[3] Some evidence even suggests that the identity of the

---

[3]Keali'inohomoku (personal communication) has pointed out that the transformation of mortals into spirits lasts only for the duration of the dance, but that the more often an individual is so transformed, the greater becomes his spiritual power—and the closer he comes (metaphorically) to joining the spirits himself.

dancer in this liminal state may be more genuine than his normal condition, since the Berndts report that the term *-jimeran,* which refers to men's activities on the sacred ground, may be translated as "making themselves"—that is, becoming their true, spiritual selves (Berndt and Berndt 1970:144).

Other components of traditional Australian culture support the idea that individuals are united with the world of the Dreamtime. For example, a common belief is that conception occurs when a woman happens to pass by an animal that is a disguised Dreamtime spirit. If it enters her body, she becomes pregnant and the child she later bears embodies a spirit corresponding to the species that was its supernatural father. Thus, a man may assert that he is himself a kangaroo; and he has a lifelong responsibility to join with other individuals who possess the kangaroo spirit to carry out the rituals appropriate to their totemic father (Berndt and Berndt 1970:200).

Aboriginal aesthetics rests on a religious and philosophical foundation, but it also has a very real psychological basis that imbues traditional Australians' personal lives with a potent spirituality. Formal instruction in Aboriginal religion occurs during initiation ceremonies for adolescents, but much earlier the formative minds of young people come under the sway of the Eternal Dreamtime. Joining in the singing or beating time to accompany the dancers in the great corroborees of song and dance that are not restricted to initiated men, even the youngest children must sense the power of the kindred ritual performances. And as the dancing continues into the night and the children drift asleep surrounded by song and dance, they enter their own, literal "dreamtime" under the influence of the visual and performing arts imbued with the Eternal Dreamtime (Elkin 1964:11). Thus the belief that within every individual is a "spirit child" is a credible portrayal of the Aboriginal psyche. Through the arts, an individual experiences a genuine identity with the spirit world.

Just as the individual's spiritual life begins before birth, it is believed to continue after death, a transition after which one continues to lead another life, much like the one before death. And again, art mediates the transition. The corpse is painted with the designs of his or her totemic group, and the hair may be woven into a string that is revered as sacred (Berndt and Berndt 1964:390, 409).

The concept of the body being a vessel of a Dreamtime spirit underlies many other traditional ritual practices. Because blood is as vital for spiritual life as for mortal life, many rituals require the drawing of blood from the celebrants' arms or penes so it may be sprinkled over ceremonial objects or people. (Red ochre is sometimes substituted for blood in such contexts.) And where circumcision is practiced, men's sacred baskets may be decorated with pendants of beeswax that encase the foreskins of the bags' owner or those of his close relatives (ibid.:381).

In their classic account of Aboriginal culture, Elkin, Berndt, and Berndt state,

> Ritual and life: without the former life would cease; and without the latter, the necessity, the urge, for ritual would not exist. But ritual implies art—at least for the Aborigines. Ritual is the ordered arrangement of symbols and symbolic actions, all of which expresses man's urge to conceive in outward forms the 'shades,' the inner life and meaning, the permanent element, in man and the world and his relations to it. (Elkin, Berndt, and Berndt 1950:4)

The role of ritual and art in Aboriginal thought is extremely powerful, coloring all aspects of native life. Any people that can survive the inhospitable semideserts of central Australia for tens of thousands of years by means of a stone-age technology obviously possess great practical ingenuity; Australians were, after all, the world's sole inventors of the returning boomerang. And they are confident of their position in the world and their reliance on time-tested subsistence techniques.[4] But in daily life the mystical and subjective dimension holds sway, with far greater importance attached to what they consider to be the spiritual foundation of life, the Eternal Dreamtime, than to the mundane, visible world.

Artistic Ramifications of Aboriginal Aesthetics

The Aboriginal aesthetic system that has just been described does not exist in isolation but has notable implications for art production and creativity, for art's role in male and female initiation ceremonies, for love magic and native standards of beauty, and for secular uses of art.

For example, since the mystical efficacy of art is present only in ritual settings, most sacred Aboriginal art has only a brief existence. After use it may be forgotten, left to disintegrate of its own accord, or deliberately destroyed. A few objects, such as *tjurungas,* which are believed to be the permanent residences of Dreamtime spirits, are exceptions to this rule, as are rock paintings and engravings; but bark paintings, ground sculptures, and, of course, most body decorations and the performing arts are ephemeral, despite the many hours of effort that go into their production.

The transubstantiating capacity of art also militates against innovation in Aboriginal art styles. Indeed, Australians say that the spirits of the Eter-

---

[4]"An Arnhem Land woman once said in effect, rather patronizingly, as she watched a Fijian missionary working on his mission garden, anxiously concerned because a few of the plants had died: 'You people go to all that trouble, working and planting seeds, but we don't have to do that. All these things are there for us, the Ancestral Beings left them for us. In the end, you depend on the sun and the rain just the same as we do, but the difference is that we just have to go and collect the food when it is ripe. We don't have all this other trouble'" (Berndt and Berndt 1964:93).

nal Dreamtime respond only to art that precisely replicates traditional patterns of graphic design or performance. Some groups believe that if the singers' memories momentarily lapse in the middle of a ritual performance and cause a minor error, the song should be stopped and started again from the beginning to insure its supernatural efficacy.[5]

Male initiation plays an important cultural role in Australian societies; and the blood that flows from the wounds of circumcision symbolizes the severing of a boy's close association with his mother and unites his soul with the spirits of older initiates. But on another level, the blood drawn from the penes and arms of the celebrants in these rites of passage establishes and validates a sacred bond with the spirits of the Dreamtime. The red blood, like the red ochre used on *tjurungas,* insures the well-being of the Dreamtime spirits, and this in turn promotes the fertility of humans and the natural species that provide human sustenance.

Although female initiations vary from region to region, most combine the themes of sexuality, fertility, and increase in the environment. Three long cycles of love songs collected by Ronald Berndt in Arnhem Land show this linkage clearly. The songs, which poetically reveal Aboriginal views on romance, are particularly illuminating regarding the relationship between spirituality and erotic beauty. For example, one song describes the attractiveness of the breasts of young women as they stand in the cold west wind, fluttering their eyes at men and swaying their buttocks (Berndt 1976:57). Significantly, the text describes the girls as *mareiin,* a term "usually translatable as 'sacred' [although] here it conveys an extra quality—of being extraordinarily attractive or beautiful" (ibid.). In another passage Berndt remarks,

> The girls, as they play among the cabbage plants, *are* sacred—, or, in an alternative meaning, they are out of the ordinary, which could also be a reference to their physical attractiveness. This usage of *mareiin* was quite deliberate on the part of the Aborigines concerned, and raises some interesting problems. In one sense, we may interpret it as having to do with sanctity, springing from the girls' direct association with basic elements of sacredness. In another sense, sacredness could well be said to imply ... aesthetic considerations of beauty, regularity, order and "natural" behaviours. (Berndt 1976:80)

The conjunction of sexuality, aesthetic concepts of beauty, and fertility appears in other contexts as well. For example, in songs from Goulburn Island, the spirit Yulunggul "symbolizes a penis, and rain [symbolizes] se-

---

[5]This does not necessarily mean that Aboriginal art is static and unchanging. Sometimes a group will adopt cultural elements from its neighbors; and there are recorded instances in which an individual introduced an entirely new song, dance, or visual design into a group. Among the Yirkalla, such innovations only come into existence through dreams, and once identified they obey the laws that constrain all other Aboriginal art works (cf. Waterman and Waterman 1970:107–108).

men; female attributes are blood and clouds. . . . Coitus, symbolic or actual, brings about the desired season of rain which, in turn, promotes fertility" (Berndt 1976:80).

Considerations of fertility and good health also provide the foundation for aboriginal concepts of personal beauty. Aborigines, who find deformities and handicaps ugly, place a high premium on a healthy body, clear skin, and even a good crop of hair; and they sometimes enhance their apparent healthiness by cosmetic efforts such as rubbing the hair and body with fats. But "the greatest stress is on youth. A girl who has just reached puberty is most desirable as a spouse—one with small, rounded breasts, not yet drooping after years of childbearing; so is a young man, newly initiated" (Berndt and Berndt 1964:162).

Love magic can be best understood as an effort to insure sexual conquests (and, at the same time, reproduction) by use of objects or actions whose powers depend upon their aesthetic component. Aborigines believe it is the poetic artistry of a love song that gives it the power to arouse the desired lover's sensuality and draw him or her inexorably into relations with the singer. Also, men sometimes make cave paintings that depict women with accentuated breasts or elongated vulvas; women dancing or making love with men as semen runs down their legs; or women whose bodies show clear signs of pregnancy. These are clearly instances of homeopathic, or imitative, magic, with the artists believing that their pictured fantasies will come true.

The Aboriginal aesthetic is pre-eminently sacred in nature, and most Australian art is produced for explicitly religious uses. But some traditional art does occur in non-ritual contexts. In northeastern Arnhem Land, for example, various groups make decoratively carved and painted spears, spear throwers, paddles, bobbins, and children's toys. Beautifully made baskets, mats, and nets are produced for everyday use; and some secular body decorations, such as necklaces and arm bands, are produced with great artistry.

Even though these items serve utilitarian purposes, their aesthetic value derives from the same belief system that prompts sacred art production. Regarding sacred designs on secular objects, Elkin notes,

> *The designs, which are really in themselves symbols of the mythical world—the world of spiritual power—together with the associated songs and changes, impart a 'virtue' to the weapon or other object which they adorn. A weapon so enriched is not only more pleasing, but more powerful.* It is endowed with a power which comes from the heroes of the creative past, a power which, through the medium of myth and ritual, is still available to men. (Elkin 1938:9; emphasis in original)

But although sacred associations inform secular art in traditional Australia, the two realms do differ, and the disparities emphasize the priority of the sacred. Secular art is less strictly tied to tradition than is sacred art in that the creators of sacred art must copy old designs precisely, whereas the makers of secular art can choose between realistic or symbolic techniques, and some innovation is permitted.

The sacred/secular distinction also influences the Aboriginal artist's status. In northeast Arnhem Land, to be able to paint sacred designs is considered a great gift, and only those few who are so blessed are elevated to a high status and are paid for their efforts. The maker of secular art, by contrast, gains neither status nor compensation (Elkin, Berndt, and Berndt 1950:110).

Sometimes the sacred associations of secular art emphasize the importance of the message communicated by the art. At Balgo in Western Australia, the Berndts saw men painting boards with maps of the surrounding countryside. Ostensibly, they were recording totemic information about specific locations, but as men traded the boards among themselves, they gained accurate information about the highly important matter of local terrain (Berndt and Berndt 1964:114). And the X-ray drawings provide similarly valuable anatomical maps, providing information that is useful to anyone wanting to butcher the animal portrayed. Finally, carved and decorated "message sticks" were common. A messenger to another camp would carry such a stick, not so much to convey information symbolically but as proof of the importance and accuracy of his verbal message (McCarthy 1957a:107).

Conclusion

Documenting the aesthetic systems of hunting and gathering societies proves that the artistic spirit is found even among those peoples who are most distant from the West in technology, population, and specialization. Australian Aborigines do make art, and although fieldworkers have consistently noted that traditional Australians do not create "art for art's sake," Aboriginal artists evince genuine pleasure in artistic production, a gratification that combines a sensuous satisfaction of the "pretty" with an intellectual appreciation of the spiritually and socially significant (Berndt and Berndt 1964:306, 350, 352; Mountford 1954:9–10, 1961:7–8; McCarthy 1957a:167; Elkin 1938:10; Elkin, Berndt, and Berndt 1950:10–11).

Fieldworkers also consistently report that Aborigines appreciate differences in levels of skill and that they reward exceptionally talented individuals. This is most true of Aboriginal song-men and didjeridu-players, who undergo elaborate and prolonged training and who sometimes become so well known that neighboring tribes ask them to come and teach their songs and music. But Aboriginal artists, although recognized, are not full-time specialists who can rely on commissions to provide their subsistence but are integrated into the social milieu, performing all the other activities appropriate to their sex (cf., e.g., T. Jones 1956/7:28; Elkin, Berndt, and Berndt 1950:110; Mountford 1961:7; McCarthy 1957b:13–14).

But the greatest significance of Aboriginal art is not the social integration of the artist but the cultural integration of the aesthetic system from which art derives. Aboriginal aesthetics not only fits into the broader conceptual system of the society, but it plays a pivotal role in unifying, explaining, and translating into concrete strategies one of the most fundamental components of Aboriginal philosophy, the belief that through art mortals can come into immediate, intimate, and genuine contact with the all-important spirits of the Eternal Dreamtime. One can hardly imagine art anywhere being devoid of a spiritual component, but rarely is this motive as important as among the native peoples of Australia. Clearly, if this dimension is taken to be the noblest part of art, then Australian Aborigines, for all the simplicity of their material culture, produce some of the world's most impressive art.

4

AESTHETICS OF THE SEPIK
Powerful Spirits and Phallic Aggression in New Guinea

> In its own culture, every work of art rouses emotions and appeals to ideas and associations which are not capable of being put into words. Let us never forget that we only know fragments of the culture which has brought forth those foreign works of art. It is impossible for us ever to undergo and enjoy the full effect of these works as they were intended to be—as they really are! (Carl A. Schmitz 1963:148)

Art is important in many societies of the Pacific islands, but nowhere in Oceania does art production reach such extravagant proportions as in the Sepik region of New Guinea. Consider, for example, the testimony of Anthony Forge, who lived with the Abelam of the Sepik for more than two years. Within a five-mile radius of his 1963 base village, he counted over a hundred ceremonial houses, each filled with carved and painted art work **(Figure 4–1)**; and Forge's Abelam neighbors built more than fifteen cult houses, complete with paintings and sculptures, during one six-month ceremonial season (Forge 1970:271). Such an enormous outpouring of art probably puts the Abelam ahead of the "art capitals" of the Western world in sheer quantity of art production.

And although the Sepik people live according to cultural premises that seem distant from our own—some societies practiced headhunting and cannibalism well into the twentieth century—their intellectual capacities are by no means inferior. Gregory Bateson has argued convincingly that in one Sepik

FIGURE 4–1 *Kwarambu,* a tambaran house in the Tagwatsapu hamlet of Kinbangwa village, northern Abelam. An initiation is in progress, and taboo areas beside the house are closed off with a fence of palm fronds. August 1962. *(Photo courtesy Anthony Forge.)*

tribe, the Iatmul, there is an appreciation of such intellectually subtle issues as the difference between emotional and cognitive truth and the potential monism, dualism, or pluralism of the natural and supernatural world (Bateson 1958:222, 235).[1] And the same Iatmul commonly accomplish feats of memory that we may well be envious of: An individual may have as many as thirty personal names, and Bateson once estimated that a learned Iatmul man knows between ten and twenty thousand such names for his associates.

---

[1]Like Einstein, the Iatmul view natural objects as being, in a sense, only patterns of waves. Therefore, those Iatmul who revere the East Wind as their clan totem believe that the waves are set in motion by the East Wind as she waves her fan at mosquitos. But members of other clans debate this belief, as shown by this anecdote recorded by Bateson:

> On one occasion I took some Iatmul natives down to the coast and found one of them sitting by himself gazing with rapt attention at the sea. It was a windless day, but a slow swell was breaking on the beach. Among the totemic ancestors of his clan he counted a personified slit gong who had floated down the river to the sea and who was believed to cause the waves. He was gazing at the waves which were heaving and breaking when no wind was blowing, demonstrating the truth of his clan myth. (Bateson 1958:231)

But despite this proven intellectual potential, most Sepik peoples seem to have little interest in creating elaborate and integrated philosophical systems to account for the nature of things. Phyllis Kaberry, for example, claims that among the Abelam, "there is no elaborate cosmology such as one finds among the Australian aborigines, and in reply to questions about the origin of the country, natives said matter-of-factly, 'marsalai [i.e., animistic spirits] made it'" (Kaberry 1941:359–360). Similarly, Margaret Mead says the Mountain Arapesh "have no cosmology and make no attempt to explain the origin of the earth and sky, the sun and the moon" (Mead 1970:239; see also Firth 1936:31).

The societies of the Sepik therefore present us immediately with a seeming paradox. They produce a spectacular profusion of art, but they have no explicit theory of aesthetics that justifies the existence of art, that places the goals of art in a wider philosophical context, or that provides broadly applicable principles of art criticism. However, in the absence of such theories, extensive research in New Guinea by several fieldworkers has revealed that Sepik art is indeed governed by implicit axioms, assumptions that play an important role in the fabric of Sepik society and culture. Uncovering these principles requires digging deeply into Sepik religion, personality, and, especially, Sepik conceptions of masculinity and femininity.

Peoples of the Sepik

The vast island of New Guinea (see map, p. 10), lying north of Australia and southeast of the Philippines, is divided into two political entities, the eastern half being the self-governing country of Papua New Guinea; the western half, the Indonesian province of Irian Jaya. The Sepik region lies in the northwest corner of Papua New Guinea, with a diverse terrain that includes offshore islands, swampy shoreline and riverine environments, and high plains that stretch up to the base of the towering Victor Emmanuel Range of mountains that form the spine of New Guinea's central highlands.

More than a quarter of a million people live in New Guinea's East Sepik Province and West Sepik Province, and they are organized into numerous tribes. These groups do not constitute an altogether uniform or homogeneous cultural area—for example, tribes that are adjacent to each other often speak mutually unintelligible languages. But despite such differences, several fundamental similarities may be found throughout the Sepik district. For thousands of years the residents of the Sepik have been village dwellers and have subsisted on farming, supplemented by hunting and gathering. Taro and sago plants, as well as pigs and dogs, are all long-established domesticates.

Another commonality through the area is that, at least at first glance, men dominate public and private life. Descent is reckoned through the male line, and men in most Sepik societies have highly competitive dispositions.

Men's secret societies, discussed below, constitute perhaps the most distinctive trait of the Sepik District tribes.

The inland reaches of New Guinea have had less contact with the complex societies of Asia, Europe, and America than almost any other area of the world. Colonizers have wrought some changes in recent decades, such as introducing steel axes and suppressing warfare and its attendant head-hunting and cannibalism. But until recently, traditional religions remained largely intact; the precedents of native social systems still held sway; and, most importantly for our purposes, traditional art was still being made well into the twentieth century, long enough for several careful fieldworkers to record the principles that influence native art production.

Art of the Sepik

Of the score of tribes and subtribes living in the Sepik region, anthropologists have studied the Abelam, Arapesh, Iatmul, Kwoma, and Wogeo in some depth. Others, such as Mundugumor and Chambri (formerly Tchambuli), have also been studied, although in less detail. This literature suggests that a fundamental similarity exists throughout the area regarding not only subsistence, kinship, and the high visibility of men's cult groups, but also in traditional attitudes toward art. (The following account of Sepik art and aesthetics will draw on information from all the well-studied Sepik cultures.)

Making art is a semispecialized activity in the Sepik. The more prolific art-producing groups recognize some individuals as "artists" and commission them to execute specific carvings and give them special food for their efforts. But even for these individuals, art is only a part-time occupation; and like everybody else, they and their wives must garden, gather, and hunt for most of their subsistence. The artist's profession does bring prestige, however. In Abelam society, for example, being an artist of repute is one means by which a man can attain an elevated social status, the other avenue to success being a reputation as either a good fighter or a successful yam farmer. In any case, the traditional tools of the visual artist's trade are, in Forge's phrase, "thoroughly neolithic" and include stone adzes; gravers; chisels; awls pointed with pig, dog, and flying fox teeth; lizard skins and rough-surfaced leaves for smoothing; and fire for hollowing large objects (Forge 1967:74).

Most Sepik art serves religious purposes—elaborate decorations of men's ceremonial houses, plus the masks, costumes, songs, and dances that constitute the core of men's cult activities **(Figures 4–2 and 4–3)**. But in addition to wood and wicker masks and the flat and low-relief paintings and carvings that decorate the ceremonial house, much secular and semisacred art is also made. A list of the utilitarian items that are decorated in one way or another is a virtual inventory of Sepik material culture: neck

FIGURE 4–2   Waupanal, a men's house in the Kwoma village of Bagwis. December 1973. *(Copyright Ross Bowden. Photo supplied by Dept. of Reprography, La Trobe University, Melbourne.)*

rests, shields, wooden hooks (used to suspend items from ceilings and walls), canoe prows, toys, clubs, taro pounders, mortars and pestles, and lime containers and spatulae. Portrait masks are made by modeling clay over human skulls (**Figure 4–4**), and a few groups produce other types of pottery as well. Crocheting and finger-weaving are variously practiced. Extraneous mate-

FIGURE 4–3 Inside Waupanal, with *yena* items on display *(Copyright Ross Bowden. Photo supplied by Dept. of Reprography, La Trobe University, Melbourne.)*

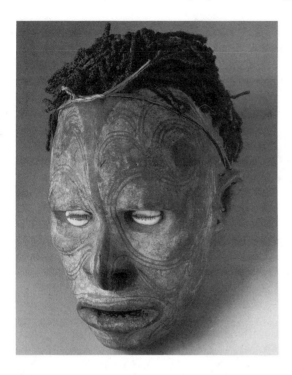

FIGURE 4-4 Iatmul trophy head, Middle Sepik. Human skull and hair, clay and shells, red and white paint. Maximum length, 32 cm *(Courtesy Saint Louis Art Museum, gift of Morton D. May.)*

rials such as shells, feathers, and animal teeth often adorn carvings, producing a dramatic, even theatrical, visual effect (Linton and Wingert 1971).

As in many small-scale societies, the human body serves as a major medium of aesthetic expression for the peoples of the Sepik. Hair may be decoratively cut, augmented with a wig, or adorned with feathers, shells, or sprigs of fern. Both men and women are scarified, although the scars usually last only a few years. Traditionally, clothing was minimal or non-existent, but the clothes that did exist were often decorated by adding fresh flowers or green leaves. Ornaments range from simple shell necklaces to woven arm- and leg-bands and include the use of bones, shells, dog teeth, feathers, and other items worn through holes pierced in earlobes or the septum of the nose. Body decoration is at its most spectacular in the Sepik during village dances and feasts, although it hardly matches that found among Mt. Hageners, who live 150 miles (240 kilometers) south of the Sepik delta (see Strathern and Strathern 1971; Kirk 1981).

The preceding references to slit-gongs (i.e., long, hollow, percussion instruments) and to flutes suggest the importance of music in New Guinea, and although there are no thorough accounts of music and dance for any of the Sepik River tribes, most descriptions of ceremonial activities include references to song and dance, and the music of flutes and slit-gongs is typically supplemented by drums, bullroarers, pan-pipes, and other instruments.

Despite the existence of several style provinces, some traits are common in all parts of the Sepik. Sculpture in the round and in high relief is usually painted, red being the most common color. Geometric designs generally tend to be curvilinear, with painted, limed, or engraved multiple outlines. Carved and painted figures often represent humans and anthropomorphized animals, usually with extremely long noses. Some seemingly abstract patterns may be stylized figures, as happens in other areas of New Guinea (cf. Salisbury 1959; Gerbrands 1967). Sepik artists integrate these design elements to produce an intense, sensual art **(Figure 4–5)** (cf. Linton and Wingert 1971:339).

The Social Functions of Sepik Art

The challenge of Sepik aesthetics is to understand why so much art is produced in the absence of an explicit philosophy of art. Answering this question requires some "aesthetic excavation" in that, like the archaeologist, we must start by digging into the most accessible stratum of Sepik culture—in

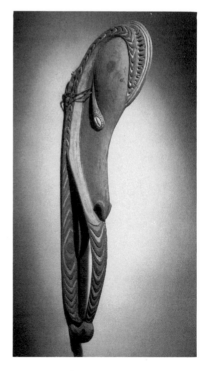

FIGURE 4–5 Mask from the Iatmul village of Kanganaman, Middle Sepik. Wood, shells, and cane; red, black, and white paint; 95 cm high. *(The Saint Louis Art Museum, gift of Morton D. May.)*

this case, the observable uses of art in day-to-day human affairs—and from there move to successively deeper and deeper levels of Sepik thought.

One obvious rationale for art's existence in the Sepik is as a means of displaying social identity. An individual's personal decorations are an infallible indication of his or her age because when a young man or woman is ritually initiated into adulthood, the climax of the ceremony is the giving of decorations befitting the initiate's newly attained status—handsome clothes, ornaments, and scars. The information conveyed by such body art is by no means trivial because in the Sepik, to know a person's age is to know his or her potential marriageability and also, for males, their status in the highly important initiated men's society, the tambaran[2] cult. Status *within* one's group may also be conveyed through personal decoration. In Wogeo society, for example, only clan leaders wear boar tusk ornaments. Lastly, body decorations display the unity of every village, with each group's characteristic style setting it apart from its rivals. As Marilyn Strathern says regarding Mt. Hageners' spectacular body art, "In using themselves to sig-nify their own achievements, people drape these qualities about their per-sons" (Strathern 1979:246; cf. also Mead 1963:90; Whiting 1941:63, 106; Hogbin 1934/35:318, 335; Kaberry 1941:360–363; Chenoweth 1979:8–23).

If art, as body decoration, serves to mark boundaries between groups, the trade of aesthetic items can also bring peaceful interaction between them. The intertribal trade of art takes several forms in the Sepik, including the tribes of the Wewak coast, who buy and sell entire dance complexes; the Mundugumor, who have little in the way of their own indigenous art style but who trade with their neighbors to get flutes that have fanciful, spirit faces; the Iatmul, who incorporate foreign artistic traits into their own well-integrated style; and the Abelam, Chambri, and Kwoma, who export art objects and whose styles, therefore, influence those of their trading partners (Mead 1963:170, 1970:20; Whiting 1941:119). (So much for the idea that art in small-scale societies is always thoroughly indigenous!)[3]

The Implicit Aesthetics of Sepik Art

If you ask a Sepik man why he produced a particular art work, he may well give a concrete reply: "This painting was needed for a cult ceremony";

---

[2]The words "tambaran" (i.e., male initiation and the cult houses used by initiated men) and "marsalai" (i.e., spirit beings) are not italicized here because they have been incorporated into both Neo-Melanesian, the *lingua franca* of the region, and the English-language ethno-graphic literature.

[3]The Mountain Arapesh have institutionalized art trade to the degree that every man inherits a path along which he can safely travel from one hamlet to another as he makes his rounds, acting as a middleman between the Beach Arapesh and the Plains Arapesh, each of which has incomplete repertoires of art production (Mead 1970:22).

"These ornaments must be worn by a man of my age"; or "We made these carvings to trade to our neighbors so we can get some of their valuable goods in return." But one may gain access to a deeper stratum of Sepik art by asking, "Why does it look as it does?" Although many men might answer, "Because that's the way such things have always looked," abstract ideas about beauty do sometimes appear.

Bateson, for example, quotes an Iatmul man as saying, "I am going to my beautiful dances, to my beautiful ceremonies" (Bateson 1958:141), and in a footnote he elaborates that "the native word for 'beautiful' is *yigun*, a common Iatmul word which is used to describe an admired face or spectacle" (ibid.). Other Sepik groups have taste preferences, too. For example, the Wogeo are avid body decorators, and on one occasion a Wogeo man asked Ian Hogbin for the loan of a mirror to see if it was true that

> his cockade of red cordyline leaves and white cockatoo feathers clashed with his hair, which he had smeared with a henna-coloured vegetable paste. The cockade being found to strike a jarring note, he removed it and pinned a large black and yellow butterfly in its place. Then, after rubbing the red paint from his cheeks, he took a packet of yellow ochre and a stick of charcoal from his handbag. "Black and yellow in the hair demand black and yellow on the face," he explained.   (Hogbin 1946:196)

Sepik peoples also evaluate the performing arts. Chenoweth found, for instance, that when the Usarufa dance, they quickly and bluntly criticize stragglers and inept dancers (Chenoweth 1979:86).[4]

Significantly, artists themselves are usually the most astute critics of art works, and Anthony Forge's remarks on the Abelam deserve to be quoted at length:

> [Abelam] artists, particularly when carving, discuss among themselves such things as the shape of a limb and its relation to other parts of the figures, but these things are not appreciated by the non-artist. I have heard carvers reproached for holding up the beginning of the painting [of a new sculpture] by fiddling about, taking a piece off here and there, when the figure already had all the attributes, legs, penis, navel, arms, and head. The artists, although they lack any specific terms, do talk about such things as form and proportion, and derive considerable pleasure from carving and painting things satisfying to their aesthetic sense. They carefully examine and discuss works by other artists and rate one another as more or less talented by criteria that are primarily aesthetic. Although not capable of, nor interested in, discussing art in the same terms, most non-artists asked to rate a group of figures or paintings

---

[4]Although the Usarufa can and do criticize individuals for poor performances, Chenoweth found that the songs themselves are not so judged. "Correct rendition is 'good' music.... The question was again put to them: 'Is there any bad music?' It was this time in expectation of a moral evaluation of music in regards to texts, connotations, or associated behavior. They both answered unequivocally: 'No, all songs are good'" (Chenoweth 1979:86).

in order of effectiveness, both in ritual power and secular prestige, rank them in the same order as do the artists and the ethnographer.   (Forge 1967:82)

The Religious Basis of Sepik Aesthetics

If the Sepik tribes are exceptional for the quantity of art they produce, they are also unusual in the importance of ceremony in the lives of Sepik men. Despite some intertribal variation, most Sepik supernatural belief and prac-tice fall into three categories that can be quickly sketched.

At about the time of puberty, Sepik males are ceremonially initiated into societies known as tambaran cults. Male initiation ceremonies among the Abelam show just how complex and aesthetically dense the tambaran cult can be. Rituals take place on four successive occasions, and each time, after much fanfare, cult members show initiates art objects that are said to be the tambaran spirits themselves. During subsequent installments they learn that the previous carvings were bogus but are shown different art works and *these* are said to be genuine spirits. In the fourth and final cere-mony, the initiates see the most sacred carvings of all. Each of the four parts of the Abelam initiation cycle occurs only once every few years, so going through the entire ritual requires well over a decade; and since a man who has just completed being initiated promptly becomes an initiator of the next generation, he may be actively involved in tambaran activities for as much as thirty years of his life.

The details of tambaran activities vary from tribe to tribe, but every-where women and uninitiated males are strictly proscribed from the cere-monies. So although Kwoma boys often clandestinely glimpse the "secret" objects, they must feign surprise when they finally see them legitimately during initiation. In earlier times, a Kwoma woman who accidentally saw initiation ceremonies is summarily killed, shot by an arrow from each initi-ated man in the village (Whiting 1941:54; Chenoweth 1979).

Long yam cults are the second focus of Sepik religion. These vary even more than tambaran practices (and are altogether absent from some groups), but the usual belief is that a village's welfare is magically related to the growing of a special variety of yams that commonly reach a length of eight feet (2.4 meters) and that, in a good season, are twelve feet long at maturity. Raising such yams is the responsibility of men in the yam cult. After harvest, they parade their longest yams through the village, the yams sometimes being decorated with painted designs and masks. Cult members believe that a good yam crop augers prosperity, and this provokes much boasting vis-à-vis other villages.

Marsalai are the third focus of Sepik religion. These are spirits through which the supernatural world interacts with mortals. They live in specific locations and have names, and their appearance is conceptualized in considerable detail. Although they are not thought of as ancestors, individual marsalai did create all the things of the world as it is now known, including the clans of living mortals.

Art as a Home for Sepik Spirits

Most religious activities in the Sepik have aesthetic components, including both the graphic and plastic arts (body decoration, masks, paintings, and architecture) and the performing arts (music, dance, and song).[5] The tambaran house itself illustrates the central position of art in Sepik cultures. For example, Abelam tambaran houses measure up to a hundred feet (30 meters) in length and have a triangular facade that soars as much as sixty feet (18 meters) into the air, visually dominating traditional villages and literally casting their shadows over the populous. These imposing structures hold the sacred *nggwalndu,* paintings and sculptures of the principle spirits of the village, and their preeminence in the village-scape accurately reflects the importance of the *nggwalndu* in the minds of Sepik men.

But although the relationship between Sepik art and religion is a powerful one, we have yet to specify its exact nature. Why are these two realms, which Westerners strictly distinguish, so closely linked in Sepik cultures? The answer lies in this logic: The effectiveness of Sepik ceremonials depends on the active co-participation of representatives of the spirit world; these, in turn, reside in the carvings, paintings, and masks used to depict the spirits during the festivities.[6]

Evidence that Sepik art actually embodies supernatural spirits is found in many tribes. For example, Kaberry learned that when Abelam men build a new tambaran house, they endow it with spirits by performing certain magical rites (Kaberry 1941:358); and Forge says explicitly that the paintings and carvings within the house are also thought to have in-dwelling spirits (Forge 1967:75; 1970:281).

A fieldworker among the Arapesh, Donald Tuzin, discusses the same issue at some length. He notes that although all of the paintings inside Arapesh ceremonial houses are "vitalized" by supernatural spirits, some are quite literally the residences of representatives of the spirit world, Nggwal. In the minds of cult members, these "are self-referential; they do not merely

---

[5]So important is the religious basis of Sepik art that most secular art reflects sacred themes. For example, Forge says of the Abelam, "Decorative art, of course, exists, but its *motifs* are drawn from the art of the tambaran cult; and it carries with it overtones of status from the cult" (Forge 1967:67).

[6]Sepik art styles have a strong tendency to resist innovation, since spirits will only dwell in ritual objects that exactly replicate the ones they have known in the past (cf. Forge 1967:80).

represent Nggwal, they *are* Nggwal, they partake directly of the same essence" (Tuzin 1980:190).

Mythology also suggests that spirits reside within Sepik art works. For example, Newton has reported creation myths from the upper Sepik in which the first flutes and slit-gongs magically played themselves because they were invested with spirit beings (Newton 1971:34, 52).

Thus, art production in the Sepik is motivated by a very powerful aesthetic principle: Art works provide residences for the members of the spirit world upon whom present and future life depends.

But a still deeper component of the Sepik philosophy of art may also be discerned. Some researchers have suggested that there is a sense in which Sepik art serves not only as a vessel for the powerful spirits of the supernatural realm but also for the souls of the men who make and use the art. The most detailed picture of the embodiment of mortal spirits in Sepik art comes from the Kwoma and a study by Bowden of *yena,* the first of three yam ceremonies held each year in traditional Kwoma villages. Of all Kwoma art, *yena* sculptures are believed to be the most powerful, and Bowden presents convincing evidence that "*yena* spirits *are* the men themselves" (Bowden 1983:99). His argument rests partly on the fact that, based on their comments about their own dreams, Kwoma men seem clearly to distinguish the physical body from the spirit that dwells within it. The former is mortal and is subject to the normal processes of the natural world. One's spirit, by contrast, is supernatural; and, as such, it is identified with *yena* spirits. (This spirit resides in one's head, thus leading to the enlargement and iconographic significance of heads in Kwoma art.)

The notion of equivalence between men's souls, *yena* spirits, and the art works made for *yena* ceremonies exists only as an unstated axiom of Kwoma metaphysics. If they were explicitly asked about it, Bowden says, the men would deny it. Nevertheless, Bowden cites indirect evidence that the axiom is unconsciously accepted. For example, when men carry out their *yena* ceremonies inside their ceremonial house, they tell the women that the singing and dancing is being done by the spirits. Moreover, Kwoma men clearly believe that *yena* spirits also reside in their yams, a predictable situation inasmuch as the *yena* spirits are first and foremost responsible for the fertility of the all-important yams. But the powerful equivalence between yam and *yena* spirit extends to the yam gardener himself. This is apparent in the Kwoma belief that if a man were to eat the meat of a cassowary bird or of certain types of spiny fish while his yams were growing in the ground, he would later harvest yams with tough, bristly rootlets, similar to the fish's spines or the cassowary's quills (Bowden 1983:110).

The triple identity among art work, supernatural spirit, and the soul of the maker appears elsewhere in the Sepik, too. For example, an Arapesh man told Tuzin a myth about how women learned to give birth to children.

Initially husbands delivered babies by cutting open their wives' stomachs, but this practice inevitably led to the women's death. Then on one occasion, a pregnant woman who had reached full term started having labor pains while her husband was out hunting. A spirit that resided in a carved post of the nearby tambaran house heard her cry out in pain so he came out of the post, found the woman, and taught her how to deliver the child through the birth canal. Later the woman was reluctant to tell her husband about the discovery, thinking he might become jealous of the spirit, but in fact he did not, the reason being that "it was actually the husband's own spirit in the house post, *'for he was the one who had carved it'*" (Tuzin 1980:169). Tuzin also reports that vitalized Arapesh paintings are hung inside ceremonial houses in such a way as to constitute a virtual kinship chart of the clan members who made the paintings (Tuzin 1980:177, 180). The same equation between man, art, and spirit has also been reported among the Iatmul (Bateson 1946).[7]

Thus whereas the peoples of the Sepik do not say so in as many words, their art *is* based on a coherent aesthetic system, and a very compelling one at that. The driving force behind Sepik art production is art's capacity to embody the all-powerful representatives of the spirit world; and more than that, the art is an incarnation of the souls of its makers. As such, its importance in Sepik intellectual culture can hardly be denied.

Phallic Aggression: Sex and Temperament in Sepik Art

Having unearthed this principle, we are now in the position to understand some of the characteristic features of Sepik art style. If Sepik art symbolizes men's souls, it must be understood that the souls in question are exclusively those of adult, initiated males. On this point, the men of the Sepik are both conscious and explicit: Art is men's work, and women are systematically isolated, forcibly if necessary, both from artistic production and from most of the religious matrix that prompts Sepik art.

---

[7]The foregoing account of Sepik art and aesthetics raises an interesting question. The spirit world's dominance of men's day-to-day lives, their belief that art embodies supernatural spirits and that mortals themselves in some sense enter the spirit world through art, an aversion to artistic innovation because the spirits will come only to art that replicates traditional forms—all of these beliefs of the Sepik are also, we have seen, present in the traditional culture of Australian Aborigines. Are these uncanny parallels the coincidental result of independent, parallel invention, or do both systems of thought go back to a common ancestor?

The continental island of New Guinea and about five hundred miles of ocean separate the Sepik tribes from Arnhem Land, and this would seem to put quite a barrier between the two culture areas. However, genetic and linguistic evidence indicates that although the two peoples are distinctly different from each other, some interaction between New Guinea and Australia has undoubtedly occurred.

Although several of the most prolific Sepik scholars have been women, neither they nor their male colleagues have described Sepik women's art and ritual as being more than, at most, a shadow of men's activities. Kaberry flatly asserts that Abelam yam ceremonialism "appears to have very little bearing on the life of the women except negatively, and in so far as it sets up a barrier against their direct participation" (Kaberry 1941:358). Mead's account of Mountain Arapesh women's situation is particularly illuminating:

> [Girls] learn not to speculate lest misfortune come upon them all. A habit of intellectual passivity falls upon them, a more pronounced lack of intellectual interest than that which characterizes their brothers' minds. . . . This prohibition cuts them off from speculative thought and likewise from art. . . . Women participating in art . . . would endanger the women themselves, [and] would endanger the order of the universe within which men and women and children live in safety. (Mead 1963:70)

The aesthetic disenfranchisement of women seems to spring from several factors. First, Sepik men view sexual relations with feelings ranging from marked ambivalence to high anxiety. Among the Kwoma, for example, the normal requirements of propriety lapse during the night-long dances that follow tambaran and yam cult ceremonies, and a generalized sexual license prevails between all men and women except for the young and between closely related individuals. But the male participants surely must have contradictory feelings about the affair since many of them have bled their penes and tongues during the preceding rituals (Whiting 1941).

Among the Wape, ambivalence turns into fear:

> A central assumption of any male version of Wape culture is that sexual desire is dangerous. The sexual act itself is no voluptuous and carefree dalliance under the tropical moon, but a furtive forest encounter, carefully rationed, with an aftermath of fear. . . . The sex act is a risky undertaking that drains the male and places both him and his partner in a position of demonic jeopardy. (Mitchell 1978:162)

Sexual anxiety such as this starts early, at least among the Kwoma. Whiting reports that although no clothing was traditionally worn, Kwoma men were not supposed to have erections in public, and "any female who observes a boy with an erect penis is expected to beat the member with a stick" (Whiting 1941:49).

Related to male sexual anxiety, either as cause or effect, is a second pervasive belief—women themselves are dangerous for adult men and inimical to their activities. In the origin myths recounted by Newton from the upper Sepik, women were the first owners of the enchanted flutes and slit-gongs. The myth notes parenthetically that "now, should women see [the flutes], their vulvas would close and they would grow testicles" (Newton 1971:34).[8]

As in myth, so in life: While an Abelam man's yam garden is growing, he is expected to refrain from sexual intercourse; and after a successful harvest he denigrates his rivals by saying that they do not "know how to plant yams; they only play with the women," thereby suggesting that the enemies lack the discipline to refrain from sexual intercourse (Kaberry 1941:355). Meanwhile, women must stay away from Abelam yam gardens and yam store houses, because, men say, "She has a vulva" (ibid.). Kwoma men use the same logic to prohibit women from watching the construction of *yena* sculptures that accompany yam ceremonies, arguing that being seen by women would cause the wooden figures to crack and hence be useless (Bowden 1983:102). Even the planting of yams has sexual connotations inasmuch as the Kwoma word for planting, *chuwa*, refers to any act "in which a long, roughly cylindrical object is thrust into something else, usually a hole" (Bowden 1983:120).

Lastly, Sepik men associate the hazards of sex with another threat—that posed by enemies. Like women, males' foes prompt feelings of vulnerability and fears of defeat, and Sepik males commonly respond to both types of adversaries with aggression and hostility. The Iatmul, for example, explicitly equate sex and headhunting, believing that both are dangerous ventures that do not necessarily end in successful conquest and that the shame of defeat in warfare is only slightly worse than that of being a passive object of sexual intercourse. In the thinking of Iatmul men, headhunting and sexuality are related in that the fathering of many children is believed to be a major reward for success in battle (Bateson 1958:140).

Phallic Aggression in Sepik Art

So men in New Guinea's Sepik River region share a distinctive constellation of assumptions about sex. The sex act itself is dangerous; female sexuality is hazardous and prompts male antagonism toward women; and the aggression against women is equivalent to that directed at enemies. In this set of ideas lies the fundamental rationale for Sepik aesthetics: *Through their art, Sepik men assert their masculinity and dominance over their adversaries, be the enemy their own women or men of hostile villages.* This belief permeates Sepik art, and men feel it so strongly that they make great quantities of art in a distinctively aggressive, masculine style **(Figure 4–6)**.

---

[8]Similar social and mythological situations appear elsewhere in the world. Murphy and Murphy (1974), for example, describe the adversarial relationship between men and women among the Amazonian Mundurucú. There too men believe that women were the first owners of three sacred flutes now jealously guarded by the men, a pattern that bears a surprising resemblance to the situation in the Sepik.

FIGURE 4–6   Carved wooden "Hook Figure," 19th century or earlier. Middle Sepik, upper Karawari Region, Arambak people. Wood and Shells, 225 cm high. *(The Saint Louis Art Museum, gift of Morton D. May.)*

Although the peoples of the Sepik are not generally inclined to speculate about the philosophical nature of things, they *do* acknowledge the messages of masculine identity and power conveyed by their art. Consider, for example, the explicit sexual imagery of yam cult art. The iconography of sculptures used in Kwoma *yena* dances, supported as it is by elaborate myths, is too rich to be described here in detail (see Bowden 1983:105–117); but briefly, the enlarged heads of *yena* sculptures symbolize masculine sexuality, fertility, and homicidal aggression. And if the head symbolizes manhood, the nose serves as its penis (and, sometimes, the eyes as its testicles). There is general agreement that the huge noses of Sepik figurative sculpture are overtly phallic, and in their downward extension they follow the Sepik convention whereby size, rather than upright position, indicates penile erection **(Figure 4–7)**.[9] (The association between noses and masculine aggression

---

[9]An anecdote recounted by Forge reveals the importance attached to the nose in the Sepik District:

> A group of Iatmul . . . had found a picture of Thoth, the ibis-headed [hence long-beaked] Egyptian god of wisdom—used as a trademark by an Australian book distributing firm— on the back of a mission school book. This, and the accompanying advertisement, they had copied out and showed to me as conclusive proof that the whites had also sprung from totemic ancestors. My translation of the text, which was irrelevant to the origin of man and the nature of the cosmos, convinced them that I, like the other whites, was determined to deceive them, to deny our common origins, and continue the pretense that whites were a different sort of being from blacks. (Forge 1971a:291)

FIGURE 4-7 Iatmul house figure, Middle Sepik. *(The Saint Louis Art Museum, gift of Morton D. May.)*

may be the basis of the Kwoma practice of wearing a boar tusk through the septum of one's nose, since the tusk is the principal weapon of the most dangerous animal in Kwoma territory.) When *yena* sculptures are displayed, they are adorned with shell and feather decorations fitting for a man who has successfully killed an enemy.

Most *yena* sculptures also have extended tongues, and this organ's associations with masculine aggression are also clear:

> During the weekly moots that the Kwoma hold in men's houses debates are frequently so intense that disputants commonly work themselves up into states in which they become literally speechless with rage.... [An enraged man] will adopt a conventional posture that expresses extreme anger and aggression. This involves holding the arms slightly apart from the body and bent inward, hopping slowly from one foot to the other, glaring at the opponent, and extending the tongue out as far as it will go. A man might hold this position for several minutes until he regains his composure or is restrained by clansmen.
>
> Informants interpret the extended tongues of *yena* sculptures in the same way; they indicate, as men say, that *yena* spirits are "hard" (*ow katawa*), i.e., that they are quick to anger and will strike a person down for the most trivial of reasons. (Bowden 1983:112)

The phallic association of tongues is also apparent in a Kwoma myth in which the protagonist, Sasap, lifts up two young girls to join him in a tree by extending his tongue down to them. His idea is for them to "stand one behind the other, and for each in turn to hook the end of his tongue into their vaginas" (Bowden 1983:114). The technique works, and the young women become Sasap's wives.

As another example of the pervasiveness of phallicism of Sepik art, consider the iconography found in Abelam paintings of their clan spirits, *nggwalndu*. Standing ten to fifteen feet (3 to 4.5 meters) high, they portray males with impressively oversized heads and large, downward-pointed penes, with a white drop of semen painted at the end. Some paintings show a pig or a bird (specifically, the clan's totemic bird) with its head nearly touching the tip of the penis. Cult members repeatedly told Forge that this picture of the nourishing of pigs or totemic birds was beneficial for their clan.

The symbolism of the Abelam tambaran cult house links sexual motifs with aggression toward enemies. The men refer to the structure as female, but male imagery permeates its construction. The ridgepole is erected (!) by men who have bled their penes; and like the men's genitals, the end of the pole is also pierced. Later, when the man responsible for decorating the ridgepole finishes his job, he shouts out his clan's war cry and throws a coconut to the ground, where waiting clansmen smash it with slit-gong beaters. Simultaneously another man drops a rattan decoration containing two skulls—formerly those of killed enemies, although wild pig skulls are now substituted. That these activities symbolize intervillage hostilities is shown by their similarity to a practice, now defunct, whereby one village would repay another for its aid in killing an enemy. In that ceremony, the killed man's testicles were given to the allies, who suspended them above the tambaran dance ground. Sticks would be thrown at them to knock them to the ground, where, Forge says, "they were pounded to pulp, again with slit-gong beaters" (Forge 1971a:304).

Although the artistically prolific societies of the Sepik have little in the way of an overt philosophy of art, they do have explicit and strongly held views about their own situation in life. They see themselves as being endangered on two fronts—by female sexuality and by hostile neighbors. Responding to such fears, they go to great lengths to assert their own superiority; and art is the primary medium for communicating that message. Sepik art, significantly, is a statement of the intended dominance of men over women and other adversaries. The urgency of this concern is indicated as much by the symbolism of phallic aggression that permeates the art style as by the frequency with which the statement is made. The Sepik stands, after all, as one of the richest regions for art production in the world, a testament to the potential power of male fear and insecurity.

Conclusion: Contradictions in Sepik Aesthetics

A central tenet of Freudian theory deals with men's problematic relationships with their mothers (whom they love but cannot marry) and with women other than their mothers (whom they must marry, whether they love them or not). Finding solutions to these problems, Freud said, are "tasks laid down for every man" (Freud 1956:346) and, he thought, failure in these tasks inevitably leads to serious psychological problems. (At one point in his writing, Freud hypothesized that artistic creativity could provide men with a productive outlet for the frustrations of unresolved relationships with women.)

But whatever its universality, surely the majority of men in most societies have less apparent sexual anxieties, and handle them with more grace, than do the men of the Sepik region. Men elsewhere have male adversaries too, but an ethos of phallic aggression permeates few societies as thoroughly as among many of the traditional tribes of New Guinea. Sepik men are obsessed with asserting their dominance over their "enemies," male or female—so obsessed, in fact, that they devote vast amounts of time and material to making art and performing rituals that display their power. The Mundugumor, for example, are not a particularly materialistic people, but the Mundugumor men's sacred flutes are an exception to this. Men lavish attention on their flutes, refer to them by kinship terms, offer them the choicest food, and decorate them with spectacular finery. Mead describes seeing "the sacred flutes with their tall, thin, shell-encrusted standards surmounted by manikin figures with a huge head, bearing a diadem of shell and hundreds of graceful and valuable decorations from the midst of which its mother-of-pearl eyes gleam—this is an experience of major importance" (Mead 1963:213).

What prompts such obsessions? Obviously, one can only speculate about answers to this question, but several factors may be involved. First, the sexual division of labor in the Sepik is strict and somewhat unusual. Despite their ceremonial preeminence, the contribution of Sepik men to the subsistence prerequisites of life is often limited. Although men in tribes such as the Iatmul are responsible for doing the occasional job that is physically taxing, including clearing land for gardens and building houses and canoes (Hauser-Schaublin, personal communication), many of the duties that are essential in day-to-day life are carried out by women. For example, among the Mountain Arapesh, women are responsible for tending the gardens, getting firewood and water, and cooking meals. Men do hunt and carry pigs and heavy logs, but much of their time is spent preparing ceremonial food and tending their special yam gardens; "the women," we are told, "do everything else" (Mead 1963:185). For the Iatmul, the division is even more clear: "Men are occupied with the spectacular, dramatic, and violent activities which have their center in the ceremonial house, while the women are occupied with the useful and necessary routines of food-getting, cooking, and rearing children" (Bateson 1958:123)—despite the fact that some Iatmul rituals include male transvestitism. The Wogeo simply say, "Men play flutes, women bear infants" (Hogbin 1970:104), and the pattern whereby women are more responsible than men for the practical necessities of life is found elsewhere through the region (cf. Mead 1970; Kaberry 1941:354–355; Forge 1970:104; Chenoweth 1979:69–61).

Sepik women, disenfranchised from expressive culture, often wield great authority in other, more practical spheres. For example, although the titular head of a Chambri household is the husband, who claims to "own" one or more wives, the real power lies in the hands of women, who fully realize that through their gardening and trade they hold the purse strings (Mead 1963:255). "Women's attitude towards the men," Mead relates, "is one of kindly tolerance and appreciation. They enjoy the games that the men play, [especially] the theatricals that the men put on for their benefit" (ibid.).[10]

And despite the heads, noses, and tongues that Kwoma men put on their *yena* sculptures, it is Kwoma women who usually take the initiative in sexual relations, both in premarital courting and also after marriage. If a Kwoma boy does want to attract a girl, his only options are either to use love magic or to dress in his finest clothes, decorate his face, and hope for a chance encounter with the girl of his fancy. And Kwoma women in general enjoy a status considerably higher than that implied by the ideology of Kwoma men (Bowden 1984:448).

Finally, Chenoweth discovered that Usarufa men feel that women are stronger than they themselves are, pointing out that women live longer, work more consistently, and have hair under their arms rather than their faces, body hair being a measure of strength (Chenoweth 1979:22).

Thus, Sepik men's fears of being vulnerable to women, so apparent in their arts, have some basis in fact. At home, women dominate many activities, leaving men only the symbolic dominance found in their "secret" cult activities, a subject that hardly interests women. It is illuminating, for example, to contrast the highly serious and self-conscious rituals of the men with women's rituals in those groups where they do occur. For example, the Abelam formally initiate into adulthood not only young men but also young women. Men are involved in the first stages of these rituals, but the men soon

> are frozen off their ceremonial ground, and the women perform their own secret ceremonial involving, among other things, transvestite women who magnificently imitate and mock the swaggering of their husbands and

---

[10]Forge states that in the Middle Sepik, "women are treated as inferior by men, who nevertheless believe them to be superior" (Forge 1971b:142, cited in Gewertz 1984:626). Gewertz observes,

> Sepik men do, however, actively seek in ritual to refute the culturally defined fact that men who are equal are produced through the power of inferior women. Indeed, their initiation of young men into patriclan membership involves scarification and bloodletting, each designed to free initiates from the deleterious effects of the mother's blood that they are bound to internalize before birth. (Gewertz 1984:626)

brothers. . . . I understand that pantomimes of sexual intercourse and advice on the conduct of love affairs are included, and there is certainly teasing and much riotous laughter. (Forge 1970:274)

Such goings on may confirm the worst fears of the already threatened Sepik men, prompting them to use every available avenue in an effort to legitimize their equivocal positions in Sepik cultures.[11]

And, of course, underlying all these details is the most fundamental fact of all: Whereas Sepik men ritually symbolize themselves as the guardians of fertility, the fact of social and biological life is that it is the women who actually provide the vital part of creation by giving birth to the young; and men, in their traditional roles as fighters and headhunters, are actually "life-takers."

Some evidence of the insecurity of Sepik men is actually apparent in their art. Sculptures of female figures occur in some ceremonial houses (Hauser-Schaublin, personal communication); and among some groups the houses themselves are thought of as being feminine. Bowden describes several ways in which the theme of feminine fertility occurs in Kwoma art production, such as the requirement that *yena* figures, as they are being painted, "must be placed on pillows made from rolled-up women's net bags *(kow)*, objects which in ordinary social life are not only directly associated with women, but are linguistically equated with wombs, the receptacles in which unborn children are carried" (Bowden 1984:456–457). Perhaps most strikingly, the men believe that women were the original inventors of all their rituals, as well as the associated arts.

Bowden observes that three theories might be suggested to explain the contradiction that is implicit in there being noteworthy themes of femininity within the quintessentially masculine art of the Sepik. It might, for one thing, reflect historical fact, representing a "survival" from a distant time in which women *did* occupy a position of leadership in society, a role now nominally held by men. A second possibility is that the men's art effectively conveys a message of total male dominance, not only in the traditional areas of male endeavor but even in those activities and objects (such as bearing children and using net bags) traditionally associated with women.

Somewhat hesitantly Bowden posits a third possibility, namely, that through their inclusion of themes of femininity in their preeminently male ideology, "men may be tacitly acknowledging what, at a conscious level at least, they are denying, namely that it is women, not men, who are the prime creators, for it is only women who can bring forth new human life" (Bowden 1984:457).

In the ideology of Sepik men, male and female principles are diametri-

---

[11]For an account of a similar situation in sub-Saharan Africa, see Keil 1979: 156–157.

cally opposed to each other, and although themes of male aggression dominate Sepik aesthetics, female themes are also clearly apparent. So instead of echoing Bowden's diffidence, I see this fact as evidence of art's inimitable capacity to embody and express ideas that, to the rational mind, are altogether contradictory. We will find instances of this phenomenon in some other societies as well, and we must postpone to Part Two a thorough examination of this feature of art. Suffice it here to say that the societies of the Sepik region of New Guinea make much highly compelling art. That it does so despite what seem to be significant contradictions within its theoretical rationale is as revealing of the nature of art as it is of the complex relations between men and women.

5

NAVAJO AESTHETICS
A Unity
of Art and Life

With beauty before me, I walk
With beauty behind me, I walk
With beauty above me, I walk
With beauty below me, I walk.
(Navajo prayer, Witherspoon 1977:153)

Many of us go through our lives believing that our view of the world is true and that other people share it; our grasp on reality usually seems valid enough for us to live from one day to the next. But occasionally this complacency is shaken, and one is confronted with a frightening possibility: What if the "reality" that I usually take for granted is not actually "out there" in the world that my senses seem to tell me about? What if it exists only in my mind and extends only to the limits of my own subjectivity? What if other people (assuming other people exist) live in different realities, traverse different worlds, and believe the universe around them (and within them) is fundamentally different from the world I inhabit?

Cultural anthropologists do not spend much time arguing about which world views are right and which are wrong, but we have taken on the job of documenting the world views found in other cultures. Because they reflect such fundamental assumptions about the nature of things, non-Western world views are often tacit and always abstract, making them more elusive to describe than, say, kinship systems. But we know one thing beyond a doubt: Other people do indeed live in different phenomenal realities. Nowhere is this more clearly the case than among the Navajos of the American Southwest.

Anthropologists have studied Navajo culture intensively for several reasons. The Navajos are geographically accessible—at least by comparison to New Guinea's Sepik District; their intellectual lives remain largely formed by indigenous culture, free of Western influences—at least as compared to most Native American peoples; and in contrast to their Pueblo neighbors, they are not adverse to allowing serious, sympathetic outsiders to study their life ways. These practical considerations have prompted four generations of scholars to spend much time among the Navajos. By one count (Witherspoon 1980:10), over 200 fieldworkers have studied the Navajos intensely, several devoting more than two decades of their lives to the endeavor—one result being an endless series of jokes about the typical Navajo family consisting of mother, father, unmarried children, numerous extended family members—and a cultural anthropologist.

But in addition to practical considerations, there is also a compelling theoretical reason for anthropologists' perennial interest in the Navajos, and it has to do with the nature of Navajo culture itself. Like individuals, some societies seem more prone to speculative thought than others. Every race produces its serious thinkers, but whereas some cultures give short shrift to their would-be philosophers, others nurture the reflective life and produce explicit and dense intellectual theories regarding the origin and abstract nature of material things, the role of humans in the larger universe, and so on. The Navajo are one such culture, disproving once and for all the ethnocentric notion that the west has a monopoly on the search for answers to life's important questions.[1]

The anthropologists who have focused particularly on the religious, philosophical, and intellectual dimensions of Navajo life—notably Father Berard Haile, Gladys Reichard, David McAllester, Gary Witherspoon, and John Farella—have revealed a people who view their world with a distinctively aesthetic sensibility. Whereas some societies relegate art and beauty to a narrowly circumscribed domain that is set apart from the rest of life, the Navajo view every word and thought as being imbued with a spirit that can only be called artistic. An examination of the Navajo aesthetic system provides us with an uncommon opportunity to see just how potent a force ideas about art can be. The Navajos' security in their ecological environment has always been tenuous; and the socio-political milieu of Anglo culture has often been hostile. Nonetheless, Navajos have sustained their way of life; and this may be partially a result of the general philosophy, including the philosophy of art, that underlies their culture.

---

[1]John Farella has observed, "The Navajos are not especially good at material culture, nor are they in the linguistic habit of describing their world concretely. Archaeologists and linguists who have studied them will tell you that. They are good at ideas, however" (Farella 1984:19).

Navajo Culture and Art

The Navajos, whom the literature sometimes refers to as Nava*h*os and who call themselves Dineh, "The People," are relative newcomers to the "Four Corners" region where Arizona, New Mexico, Utah, and Colorado meet (see map, p. 10). The ancestors of the modern Pueblo Indians had already been there at least 1,000 years when nomadic groups from the northern plains entered the region, probably before the thirteenth century. By the fifteenth century, two major migrant groups had settled in the area, the Navajos themselves and various Apache tribes.

The Navajos thrived in the Southwest and despite periodic depredations by Anglo culture, they have grown in population to become the largest single tribal group of Native Americans, numbering well over 200,000 and inhabiting 25,000 square miles of land. Sheep herding plays a central role in Navajo life, but they also rely heavily on horticulture, supplemented by some hunting and gathering. Unlike their Pueblo neighbors who have long lived in clusters of apartment-like buildings, Navajo families live in individual round houses called *hogans* that are widely distributed through their territory. Although men are formally the heads of Navajo families, in actual practice women have as much, if not more, importance in social life. Navajos reckon kinship through the female line; women are the owners of farm and range land, which they pass on to their daughters; and a husband usually comes to live in the locale of his wife's family.

Men do generally hold sway in the area of ceremonialism, an activity that looms large in Navajo life. The Navajos have an extensive and dense body of mythological stories, and the rehearsal of parts of this corpus in "Sings" by religious specialists and their assistants provides the basis for the most important ritual activities.

For Navajos, ceremony inevitably entails art. Sings are elaborate performances that last as long as nine days, featuring all-night singing, daytime prayers and chants, and ritual shampooing of the hair with yucca suds. In most (but not all—cf. Frisbie 1980:171) sings, much of the chanting reiterates the stories of creation and activities of the mythic Holy People. If a man falls ill, has misfortune, or is jeopardized by some condition beyond his control, his family will hire a singer, and the singer's assistants, to perform a Sing to restore the man's well-being. Other Sings are carried out in a prophylactic effort to maintain current health.

At certain junctures in a Sing, the ceremonialists make sandpaintings, illustrating in a richly iconographic style the story's events and personae **(Figure 5–1)**. First the sandpainters smooth an area of the hogan floor so they can work directly on it or else on a buckskin spread on the ground. Besides sand, they use pigments made from ground minerals, pulverized charcoal, corn pollen and corn meal, and other materials. The intricate

FIGURE 5–1   Navajo ceremonialists making a sandpainting of Blue Horned Toad as part of the Red Antway. *(Photo by Leland C. Wyman, courtesy of the Wheelwright Museum of the American Indian.)*

paintings are made freehand, with the leader and his assistants producing straight lines and uniformly colored areas by allowing an even stream of pigment to run out of the hand between the thumb and forefinger. Sandpaintings vary in size, from small ones measuring about three feet (1 meter) in width to ones that require a full day's work by the Singer and as many as forty assistants and that measure twenty-five feet (6 meters) across. When they have finished the sandpainting, the person for whom the Sing is being performed is seated in its center and pigments from certain parts of the painting are applied to his or her body, further insuring the efficacy of the ritual **(Figure 5–2)**. Then, having served its purpose, the sandpainting is ceremonially destroyed.

Navajo art is not confined to Sings, however. Navajos probably learned weaving (and, for that matter, sandpainting) from their Pueblo neighbors.[2] Whereas sandpaintings are made by men, women are the chief fiber artists, doing everything from carding and spinning the wool to executing a design on a vertical bar loom. Although the technology of Navajo weaving is rela-

---

[2]With regard to both sandpainting and weaving, there are so many differences between Navajo and Pueblo styles and manner of execution that some (e.g., Keali'inohomoku, personal communication) have questioned the consensus opinion that the Navajos simply adopted pre-existing Pueblo techniques.

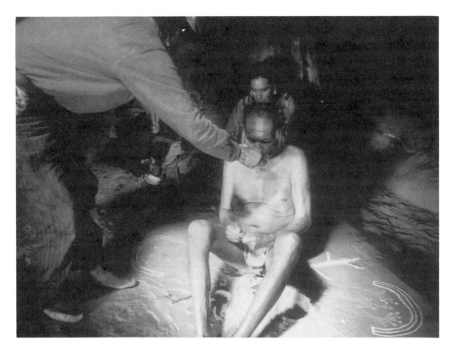

FIGURE 5-2   Traditional Navajo sandpainting, *Cactus People and Medicine Plants,* being used as part of the Windway ceremony.   *(Photo courtesy Natural Museum, Los Angeles County, catalog #A.5280-10.)*

tively simple, the resultant textiles are striking for their sophisticated use of design and color **(Figure 5–3)**. Weaving was initially a utilitarian art for the production of clothing and blankets, but trade goods now fill many of these needs, and today most weavings are sold off the reservation.

Silversmithing is the youngest Navajo art, learned in the late 1800s from Mexican smiths living in the Southwest. Navajo craftsmen began by decorating utilitarian items such as horse bridles, but since the turn of the century most smiths have produced jewelry, which is in great demand among both Anglos and the Navajos themselves (Adair 1944).

Hózhǫ: The Core of Navajo Philosophy

Shooting Way is an important Navajo Sing lasting nine days and composed of many songs, prayers, and sandpaintings. At its conclusion, the people sitting in the hogan pass around a small, leather pouch of pollen. Like the sun's path in the sky, the bag begins with the people sitting along the east side of the hogan, circles around the south, then up the west, and finally across the north. As each person takes a bit of pollen, touching some to the

FIGURE 5–3   A Navajo woman working at a vertical loom, weaving a blanket from home-spun, dyed wool. Photographed before 1934. *(Courtesy of the Southwest Museum, Los Angeles, ca. no. 30797.)*

tongue, some to the top of the head, and then scattering some to the world at large, he or she repeats the words,

> *Hózhǫ́ nahasdlį́į́*
> *Hózhǫ́ nahasdlį́į́*

That is, entire nine-day ceremonial has been successful, and in McAllester's translation [1980:211],

> Conditions of beauty have been restored,
> Conditions of beauty have been restored.

The seminal term, *hózhǫ́*, appears in many other ritual contexts, often in the phrase *sǫ'a naghái bik'e hózhǫ́*, as well as in frequent non-ceremonial settings in everyday Navajo life. If we can unlock the meaning of *hózhǫ́*, we will have gone a long way toward understanding the fundamental Navajo philosophy of art.

But explaining *hózhǫ́* is no easy matter. Washington Mathews carried out the first careful study of Navajo intellectual culture in the late nineteenth century, and he translated the first two words of *sǫ'a naghái bik'e hózhǫ́* as "in old age walking," the second two as "in his trail beautiful" (cited in Witherspoon 1977:24); and in a less literal translation, he equated the first phrase with long life, the second with health. Although thousands of pages have been published on Navajo religion and world view since Mathews's time, scholars continue to debate the precise meaning of *są'a naghái bik'e hózhǫ* in general and of *hózhǫ* in particular (cf. Farella 1984:153–188).

The best approach is to begin, as it were, at the beginning, with the Navajo account of creation. This is a daunting task in itself. Zolbrod (1983) recently used Mathews's original notes, along with other sources, to produce a complete translation of the story, and the result fills over 300 pages of text, plus another 76 pages of explanatory notes—clear evidence of the rich-ness of Navajo speculative thought.[3] But for our purposes, the most relevant part of the myth cycle is the passage that tells how First Man's medicine bundle, which is itself called *są'a naghái bik'e hózhǫ*, gave rise to First Boy and First Girl. First Boy is identified with thought and, according to the myth, is called *są'a naghái;* First Girl is associated with speech and called *bik'e hózhǫ*. A notable quality of First Boy and First Girl (i.e., of *są'a naghái* and of *bik'e hózhǫ*) is their radiant beauty, both having hair reaching down to their thighs (Witherspoon 1977:17). (Although they came from the same source and share some of the same traits, First Boy and First Girl are not brother and sister.)

The Navajo creation story says that First Boy and First Girl can no longer be seen, but their presence is still felt because they were the parents of Changing Woman, the benevolent Mother who is incarnate as the earth. Changing Woman is the source of all human life, and she controls nature's fertility; and, we must keep in mind that she is the offspring of First Boy and First Girl. So the fundamental proposition of the Navajo creation story is that the world and all living things are products of *są'a naghái* and *bik'e hózhǫ*

We have already learned several meanings of *są'a naghái* and *bik'e hózhǫ*. These phrases refer to First Man's medicine bundle, to two surpassingly beautiful supernaturals who came from that medicine bundle, and to the source of Changing Woman—the earth—and all her procreative power.[4]

---

[3]The complexity of Navajo philosophy taxes not only outsiders but Navajos themselves. Denet Tsosie told David McAllester regarding Shootingway, "Fifty-four years ago I began learn-ing some things about this, when I was twelve years old. But though I am always finding out more I will never know it all—and there is much that I have forgotten" (McAllester 1980:200).

[4]*Są'a naghái bik'e hózhǫ* even has a sexual component. After many discussions with John Farella about the meaning of *są'a naghái bik'e hózhǫ*, a thoughtful old Navajo man named Grey Mustache concluded his "lessons" by focusing on the reproductive dimension of *są'a naghái bik'e hózhǫ*. Grey Mustache claimed that First Man had produced First Boy and First Girl not from his medicine bundle but through intercourse with his wife, and his account is worth quoting at length. First Man, said Grey Mustache,

> was thinking about generations of growth, how animate beings would continually in-crease. And having thought about this he set to work on his wife, that is, he had inter-course with her. After he did that, she started out having children. He achieved what he had thought about, he had assured continuous birth in the future.

> It was by means of *są'a naghái bik'e hózhǫ* that this is assured. You see the semen of First Man is called *są'a naghái*, and the reproductive fluid of First Woman is *bik'e hózhǫ*. That's what *są'a naghái bik'e hózhǫ* is all about to this day. (Farella 1984:177)

But nearly a century ago, Washington Mathews translated the phrases as abstract qualities—long life and health—and it is these meanings that give them their greatest significance. Thus, the deepest meaning of *są'a nagháí bik'e hózhǫ́* is that *the world was created in a state of beauty, harmony, and happiness,* a condition that, by the nature of things, continues today and may persist into the future.

Before turning to *hózhǫ́'s* implications for art, one additional component of Navajo philosophy must be considered. Navajo world view is not filled solely with everlasting beauty and goodness. Individual Navajos evince a fear of the darker side of reality, as manifest in death, ghosts, witchcraft, and the like. Thus on the philosophical level, *hózhǫ́* has a counterpart in *hóchxǫ́,* the "evil, the disorderly, and the ugly" (Witherspoon 1977:34). Unlike the West, where evil is distinct from goodness, Navajos think of *hózhǫ́* and *hóchxǫ́* as "temporary, although cyclically reappearing, points in an ongoing process" (Farella 1984:36). They are not separate forces, locked in an eternal battle with each other. Their relationship is defined by the phrase, *alkéé naa' aashii,* meaning that all entities contain within them a vital opposition that insures continuous, dynamic change and that allows them to perpetuate themselves. Day and night exemplify the opposition of *alkéé naa' aashii,* as do the contrasts between "good" and "bad" deities, the changing of the seasons, birth and death, male and female, and so on.

Only those aspects of Navajo philosophy that are the most fundamental and relevant to Navajo aesthetics have been discussed here; the interested reader is referred to the primary sources, especially Witherspoon (1977) and Farella (1984), for additional information. But one thing should be clear: Navajo philosophy is thoroughly aesthetic in nature. It posits a world of manifest (albeit tentative) beauty and goodness, and of constant change and development.

Hòzhǫ̀ in Ceremony and Art

The concepts of *są'a nagháí bik'e hózhǫ́* and *alkéé naa' aashii* are not abstractions that Navajos discuss as an intellectual exercise. Instead, they have practical and far-reaching implications for Navajo ceremony, art, and daily life.

The non-Navajo can best understand the relationship between theory and practice by recalling that on one level, *są'a nagháí* means *thought.* People in the Western world usually assume that the mind's activities are largely determined by the world outside the mind. Navajos, by contrast, conceive thought to be an active and effective force that can influence the material and spiritual worlds. It was, after all, the union of thought and speech (i.e., *są'a nagháí* and *bik'e hózhǫ́,* or First Boy and First Girl) that brought the world (Changing Woman) into existence. In a parallel fashion, mortals can use thought and speech to effect change in the material world around them.[5] And, of course, that is exactly the intention of Navajo rituals, where traditional prayers, chants, and sandpaintings repeat the story of the initial creation of *hózhǫ́* and thereby create it once again. Whether a ceremony is performed to cure the sick or to bring rain during a period of dry weather, it is intended to restore the world to its natural condition of *hózhǫ́*.[6] So the central premise of Navajo aesthethics comes down to this: The world was created in beauty and harmony, albeit also with the potential for evil and chaos; mortals should sustain and restore the world's primal beauty; and this is effectively accomplished through the production of art—both in the controlled art of Sing chants and sandpainting, as well as in the artful living of day-to-day life.

It may sound too good to be true that a non-Western culture would equate art, life, and nature, perhaps more wishful thinking prompted by a "noble savage" sentiment than ethnographic fact. But Gary Witherspoon, with many years of first-hand experience in Navajo culture, provides ample evidence that the Navajo world view is indeed based on this concept. Navajos, we are told, "don't admonish one 'to be beautiful' or 'to see beauty' but to 'walk (live) in beauty' and to 'radiate beauty'" (Witherspoon 1977:32). A common Navajo prayer says,

> With beauty before me, I walk
> With beauty behind me, I walk
> With beauty above me, I walk
> With beauty below me, I walk.
> (Witherspoon 1977:153)

Navajos, we are told,

> Do not consider the generation or maintenance of beauty to be particularly elusive. Beauty is in the nature of things, as well as in people. It is the normal

---

[5]The Sapir-Whorf Hypothesis asserts that some aspects of language, to a greater or lesser extent, determine an individual's phenomenal world, rather than the external world determining the nature of language. Although empirical support for the Sapir-Whorf Hypothesis has proven to be elusive, Navajos go about their daily lives assuming that it is true—and presumably were doing so long before Edward Sapir and Benjamin Lee Whorf began to speculate about it. Witherspoon says explicitly, *"In the Navajo view of the world, language is not a mirror of reality; reality is a mirror of language"* (Witherspoon 1977:34, emphasis in original).

[6]Navajos realize that their attempts to use their inner force may miscarry. For example, Witherspoon witnessed ceremonies that were intended to produce rain on four different occasions. Each time, the previously clear sky became cloudy and rain fell within twelve hours, although significant rainfall occurred only once. After the unsuccessful efforts the singers "shrugged their shoulders with a slight sense of humor and not a little dismay and commented, 'How feeble-minded we have become'" (Witherspoon 1977:28).

Also, McAllester (1980:231–234) has questioned the concept of the "compulsive word," developed by Reichard (1944) and Witherspoon (1977), suggesting that Navajos do not, in fact, believe that the proper performance of ritual will necessarily lead to the desired results.

state of affairs. The Gods designed this world to be a beautiful, harmonious, happy, and healthy place. To be maintained, beauty needs to be expressed and renewed in ritual, song, art, speech, dress and in daily living. (Witherspoon 1981:32)

Finally,

The Navajo does not look for beauty; he generates it within himself and projects in onto the universe. The Navajo says *shil hózhǫ* 'with me there is beauty,' *shii'hózhǫ* 'in me there is beauty,' and *shaa hózhǫ* 'from me beauty radiates'. (Witherspoon 1977:151)

The Aesthetics of Navajo Music

David McAllester carried out one of the first empirical studies of non-Western aesthetics in 1950 among the Navajo, and although McAllester spent only four and a half months in the field, his findings set the stage for extensive later work both by McAllester himself and by others. He initially intended to analyze secular music but soon learned that all Navajo music has religious associations and that the Western distinction between sacred and secular music is not applicable in Navajo culture. Consequently he focused his study on the chant music used in Enemy Way, a Sing meant to protect Navajos from the ghosts of slain non-Navajos, and one that was widely known and commonly performed in the years following World War II as Navajo servicemen returned to the reservation.

McAllester also discovered that he was unjustified in assuming that Navajos would have ready answers to questions such as, "What is good tone?," and "What is your favorite instrument?" Eventually McAllester did discover some Navajo values regarding performance style: "Tonality should be consistent [and a song] should not change key while it is being sung" (McAllester 1954:73); and "A good voice is somewhat nasal, the vibrato is rather wide; the voice should be as high as possible, it should be capable of sharp emphases, and there should be an easy and powerful falsetto" (ibid.:74). But Navajos give no more attention to stylistic qualities such as these than to other traits that Westerners would not consider to be strictly aesthetic. A good singer, for example, ought to have a good memory and great endurance—a reasonable expectation inasmuch as the singing that begins at dusk should continue until dawn with minimal repetition and undiminished gusto.

Further discussion led McAllester to realize however that questions of performance are not very important to Navajos. Their principal concern about music is not, "How does it sound?" but "What is it for?" (McAllester 1954:71). When he asked, "What is it about a song that makes it sound

FIGURE 5–4   Sandpainting of Blue Corn People, part of a Red Antway ceremony that was performed in June, 1963. *(Photo by Charlotte Johnson Frisbie, courtesy of the Wheelwright Museum of the American Indian.)*

pretty?," the typical answer was, "It's songs like the Lightning Way and some of the songs in the Blessing Way that are most beautiful. It's good for the patient and makes him well. If it's worthwhile it's beautiful" (McAllester 1954:71). Although extracting aesthetic principles from the wider matrix of Navajo philosophy is contrary to their own thinking, this statement—"if it's worthwhile, it's beautiful"—can be taken as a central axiom of Navajo aesthetics. In 1950 Navajos even applied this idea to non-Navajo music: When McAllester asked a Navajo woman which Anglo music she preferred, she said, "I like Army songs because they saved the country" (McAllester 1954:71).

Subsequent fieldwork in Navajo culture and an improved understanding of the Navajo language have clarified these comments about music for outsiders. Navajos do not conceive music to be a trivial recreation, removed from the "important" aspects of "real life." Making music is serious business for Navajos, an activity that can make a sick patient well again or help a country win a war. In all cases, music restores the health, harmony, and goodness that the world is potentially heir to. McAllester found that although music may have varying stylistic qualities and be performed with differing degrees of expertise, first and foremost *it must work*, fostering the *hózhǫ́* that Navajos expect to come from all traditional activities.

Process Orientation versus Product Orientation

Navajo art is based on the premise that the beauty and goodness embodied in *hózhǫ́* are the natural conditions of existence and that every human endeavor manifests and helps perpetuate this state. But besides the harmonious principle derived from *hózhǫ́*, Navajo aesthetics also reflects the processual principle of *alkéé naa'aashii*. *Hózhǫ́*, remember, is not a static state, established at the beginning of the world and unchanged ever after. Instead, *hózhǫ́* is a dynamic process, always interacting with *hóchxǫ́*. To describe the situation accurately, the inherent beauty of the world should be spoken of in the present progressive, not the past tense: *Hózhǫ́* was not "created" but always "is being created." So another basic principle of Navajo aesthetics is that beauty is found in activities, not in products.

Again, Witherspoon's remarks cannot be improved upon:

> A Navajo experiences beauty most poignantly in creating it and in expressing it, not in observing it or preserving it. The experience of beauty is dynamic; it flows to one and from one; it is not in things, but in relationships among things. Beauty is not to be preserved but to be continually renewed in oneself and expressed in one's daily life and activities. To contribute to and be part of this universal *hózhǫ́* is both man's special blessing and his ultimate destiny. (Witherspoon 1977:178)

When this emphasis on process over product is combined with a Navajo belief in the general dominance of inner spirit over outer manifestation, the result is an approach to art that emphasizes the internal processes that produce beauty, rather than the external activities involving art media. For the Navajo, "beauty is not so much a perceptual experience as it is a conceptual one" (Witherspoon 1977:151).

These ideas have a profound influence on Navajo art. For one thing, the performing arts, which are all process and no product, are important components of Navajo culture, the many hours of chanting in Navajo Sings being an obvious example. (A family may spend several thousand dollars in staging a Sing, and over 1,000 people may participate in the event in one way or the other.) The value of ritual singing and prayer does not lie in the singer's emotional experience while chanting. Instead, most Sings are efficacious because the words recount the creation of a world of *hózhǫ́*, and as the singers tell the story, conditions of *hózhǫ́* are restored to the world.

Informal singing is also important in Navajo culture. Witherspoon says that daily activities are accompanied by "riding songs, walking songs, grinding songs, planting songs, growing songs and harvesting songs," and a Navajo often "counts his wealth in the songs he knows and especially in the songs he has created" (Witherspoon 1977:155).

But the Navajo emphasis on creativity extends beyond the performing arts. Besides chanting, Sings require the construction of sandpaintings.

Making even an average sized sandpainting requires several hours, careful work, and as many as forty men may work for ten hours to produce the most complex sandpaintings. But after all this effort, the singers use the finished sandpainting for only a few minutes, and then they sweep it up and ritually dispose of it. As with songs, the importance of sandpainting lies in the process of creation, and the finished product has no lasting worth.[7]

Aesthetics and Art Style

The aesthetics of *hózhǫ́* and *alkéé naa' aashii* provide not only a theoretical basis for Navajo art production, but they also inform the stylistic conventions found in the various Navajo art media. Navajos recognize a dichotomy between dynamism and activity on the one hand and stability and conservatism on the other, and they use it to symbolically account for the differences between Navajo women and men.

Navajo men are considered to be static, and this belief is reflected in the stylistic conservatism seen in the sandpaintings men make. For a sandpainting to be effective, it must replicate in almost every detail the designs that have been handed down from previous generations.[8] Also, sandpaintings display a strong impulse toward symmetry, both in total design and in details. But as we have come to expect of the Navajo world view, although static traits dominate their art, men are not innocent of the opposite characteristic of dynamism, so sandpainters avoid simple, mirror-image symmetry by using a rotational symmetry that is far more dynamic. In *Whirling Logs*[9] (**Figure 5–5**), for example, the figures on the right replicate those on the left, but rotated 180°. This type of symmetry also emphasizes the contrast between the static black cross in the center of the painting and the periph-

---

[7]The contrast between the process-oriented aesthetics of Navajos and the product-oriented attitude that has characterized most components of the Western aesthetic tradition is dramatically illustrated by the respective attitudes toward sandpaintings in the two cultures. In contrast to the Navajo practice of discarding sandpaintings soon after they are completed, Western collectors buy thousands of sandpaintings every year, as souvenirs, home decorations, and fine art. Commercial sandpaintings, which use either novel designs or modified traditional designs, are made on boards covered with glue, so they may hang, forever, on their proud Anglo owners' walls. Nancy Parezo (1982, 1983) has documented the transition of "religious act to commercial art."

On the other hand, not all contemporary Western artists are product-oriented. During his formative years, Jackson Pollock watched Navajo sandpainters at work. Some of his letters indicate that one inspiration for his technique of "action painting" was the Navajos' emphasis on process, rather than product, to say nothing of the procedural similarity found in Pollock's method of dripping paints, lacquers, and even sand onto a canvas lying on the floor (cf. Witherspoon 1977:174–178).

[8]For some sings, however, the singer composes the prayers that are used (cf. Frisbie 1980).

[9]The following stylistic analyses are based on Witherspoon (1977:163–168).

FIGURE 5–5   Navajo sandpainting, *Whirling Logs.* *(Photo courtesy K.C. Publications.)*

eral figures that move in a sunwise direction to produce a whirling visual effect—all held in check by the elongated figure that encircles most of the sandpainting.

The colors used in *Whirling Logs* also reflect the static/active opposition. Navajo color symbolism is complex, with any given color's connotations depending upon the other colors it appears with; but in this sandpainting, it is noteworthy that the black and white lines that cross at the center are considered to be static relative to the colors of the figures that spin around the outside. And of the two crosses, the black one is graphically more solid and steady in comparison to the white cross which, set on the diagonal, gives a feeling of energy that balances the black "X".

Navajo women are considered to have dynamic natures, at least as compared to Navajo men, and women's art reflects this belief. In contrast to the traditional designs that men faithfully copy in their sandpaintings, the dynamic minds of women always produce new patterns for their weavings, never replicating a pre-existing work. And in the same way that the energy of the mind can be used effectively only when it is controlled by ritual knowledge, the creativity of the weaver bears fruit only when she successfully controls the diverse elements of the weaving process, from spin-

ning the wool, through selecting the proper natural dyes to produce a desired color, to weaving weft threads through the warp to produce a
balanced, integrated design (Witherspoon 1981:30).

Other Aesthetic Factors

The philosophical concepts discussed above constitute the core of Navajo
aesthetics, but there are several additional cultural conventions that apply
to Navajo art, including both prescriptions and proscriptions. One early
field report, for example, claimed that in making a basket a woman should
only work on its concave side or else she would loose her mind; that she
should not allow a child to place sumac, from which baskets are woven, on
its head or its growth would be stunted; that she could not sleep with her
husband when she is working on a basket; and that any man who worked
on a basket risked impotence (Tschopik 1938). (Given such taboos, it is not
difficult to accept Tschopik's thesis that Navajo pottery and basket-making
became nearly extinct in the early twentieth century partly because of the
availability of trade goods but also because of the oppressiveness of these
restrictive regulations.)

Another generalized taboo concerns the avoidance of complete circles
in some design contexts. This has been noted for pottery, basketry (Newcomb 1940:37–38), and in the solid border that many women weave around
all four sides of a blanket. It is prompted by a fear of entrapping the weaver's spirit and energies in the rug (Hill 1938:178; Newcomb 1940:38; Bennett
1974:35).

Ramifications of Navajo Aesthetic Theory

From what has been said thus far about Navajo aesthetics, one might conclude that Navajos make art solely for practical ends such as healing the ill
and that, for example, when chants and sandpaintings are used in a Sing
to cure a sick person the participants in the ceremony experience feelings
comparable to those of the doctors and nurses in a Western hospital's operating room. This is not the case. When Navajos discuss art, they emphasize
its instrumental value, but sprinkled through the literature one finds comments that, taken together, give some clue to the Navajo affective response
to art. For example, based on her research in the 1930s, Gladys Reichard
wrote,

> The whole fabrication of prayersticks and [medicine] bundle paraphernalia
> is an aesthetic occupation, felt as such by the men who pursue it. The . . .
> materials . . . are handled not only with reverence by the men, but also with
> pleasure expressed verbally as they work. The same kind of satisfaction is

shown in the achievement represented by a sandpainting.   (Reichard 1977/ 1939:77)

On a less lofty level, Johnny Blanco told McAllester, "I like the [songs] that have a nice tune. When you hear a nice tune, that makes you happy" (McAllester 1954:83). Navajos' reactions to art rarely include the ecstatic, however. In fact, a person who experiences an odd or dizzy feeling upon hearing Enemy Way music is thought to need the ceremony performed over him or herself.

Pride in the quality of one's work and a feeling of awe at the master artist's consummate skill are also part of the traditional Navajo aesthetic response.[10] Given the underlying assumptions of their world view, all Navajos are, in a sense, artists; but some individuals are nevertheless singled out for their exceptional abilities. Kluckhohn and Leighton report,

> Experts are richly rewarded in prestige as well as money, and not without reason. Prodigious memory is demanded of the ceremonialist. The Singer who knows one nine-night chant must learn at least as much as a man who sets out to memorize the whole of a Wagnerian opera: orchestral score, every vocal part, all the details of the settings, stage business and each requirement of costume. Some singers know three or more longs chants, as well as various minor rites.   (Kluckhohn and Leighton 1946:163, quoted in McAllester 1954:79)

Although Navajo women are eager to find buyers for their weavings and to win prizes in exhibitions of Southwestern Indian arts and crafts, in the non-competitive atmosphere of traditional Navajo culture, prestige and money were not the primary motives for artistic activity, and even at the present time such considerations seem to be secondary. For example, most weavers today are lucky to receive a payment equivalent to the minimum wage for their long hours at distaff and loom. Given the limited economic resources of many Navajos, it would be sheer romanticism to assume that Navajo artists are indifferent to the income they derive from sales; but besides the profit motive, women also weave for the satisfaction they receive from successfully carrying out the creative synthesis that the craft represents in Navajo culture (Witherspoon 1981).

---

[10]Not surprisingly, emphasis was traditionally placed on conceptual skills rather than on perceptual and motor skills, and summoning the mental concentration needed to generate *hózhǫ́* was more important than having the manual or vocal skills necessary for flawless execution. Craftsmanship has, however, risen to paramount importance in arts and crafts made for sale to non-Navajos (cf. Adair 1944:96–101, 199; Leighton and Leighton 1944:51; Bartlett 1950:5–6; Reichard 1936:191–192).

Conclusion

Although most of us usually take our phenomenal world for granted, one sometimes must wonder what it would feel like to live inside another person's skin, to look out through their eyes, to think with their minds while walking through their world. Would the experience be the same as one's own perceptions, thoughts, and feelings, or would these all be different?

The accumulation of ethnographic studies makes us the first people ever to have systematic, empirical information relevant to these questions, and nowhere is that data more complete than in the case of the Navajos. Those who have studied Navajo culture in depth still disagree about some aspects of Navajo world view, but their clear consensus is that traditional Navajos do indeed look at the world in a way that is uniquely their own.

Navajos believe that the world was created in a state of beauty, balance, and harmony, held in dynamic balance with ugliness, chaos, and evil. These opposing forces persist today, and in the face of the hazards represented by dangerous spirit forces, Navajos seek to maintain and foster *hózhǫ́* by living lives of balanced harmony. By producing the arts that are the traditional components of ritual Sings, Navajos are confident that, as the conclusion of Shooting Way says, "Conditions of beauty have been restored." In a physical and sociopolitical environment that has often been hostile, Navajos have survived admirably, living their lives in the harmony, balance, and art embodied in *hózhǫ́*.

6

YORUBA AESTHETICS
Goodness and Beauty in West Africa

A man may be very, very handsome
Handsome as a fish within the water
But if he has no character
He is no more than a wooden doll.
(Yoruba verse, quoted in Thompson 1983:11)

European and American fascination with West African art goes back at least to the turn of the century, when Picasso, Vlaminck, and other Parisian artists became intrigued with the way in which African carvers treated the human figure and face. Since then our interest in West African art has spawned a vast literature that describes the colorful and varied arts of the Guinea Coast as a rich and sweeping panorama, meanwhile illuminating many specific topics in minute detail. For example, a doctoral dissertation by Henry Drewal records, among other things, the events that took place in the Yoruba (see map, p. 10) town of Aiyetoro, Nigeria, beginning on the afternoon of March 27, 1971, and continuing for the next twenty-four hours. Most of the present chapter describes Yoruba aesthetics in general and abstract terms, but to evoke the spirit and expressive feeling of Yoruba art, I will begin by recounting the events of that day, as seen through Drewal's eyes (cf. Drewal 1973; see also Drewal and Drewal 1983).

Anticipation of the activities has been growing in Aiyetoro for days. Various misfortunes had been plaguing the townspeople, and so several weeks ago the town fathers, following custom, consulted the *babalawo*, a priest in the cult of Ifa, the God of Divination **(Figure 6–1)** The *babalawo's* art was, as always, subtle and complex. From a special, elaborately carved wooden container, he

FIGURE 6-1 Yoruba *babalawo* (Ifa diviner) preparing to consult the spirit. Egado, Nigeria, 1978. *(Photo courtesy Henry John Drewal and Margaret Thompson Drewal.)*

took sixteen palm nuts, enough for a large handful. Again and again he attempted to pick them all up out of his left hand with one sweep of his right hand. After each try, one or two of the palm nuts remained behind, but this was as tradition dictated. After each attempt the *babalawo* made a mark in the wood dust that had been sprinkled on a carved wooden tray to indicate whether it had been one or two nuts that remained. Sixteen attempts yielded a column of sixteen marks in the dust; based on the resultant configuration, the diviner selected one verse from the thousand committed to his memory **(Figure 6–2)**, and this verse held a solution to the town's problem: It was imperative that the dual rituals of Ẹfẹ and Gẹlẹdẹ be performed.

Soon after the Ifa diviner called for the Ẹfẹ/Gẹlẹdẹ rituals, the men and women who belonged to the Ẹfẹ/Gẹlẹdẹ cult gathered in their meeting house and began preparing for the ceremonies, activities that would require an exceptional quantity of art, produced in many different media.

First, cult members examined masks used in past years, giving those in good condition a new coat of paint **(Figure 6–3)** and commissioning carvers

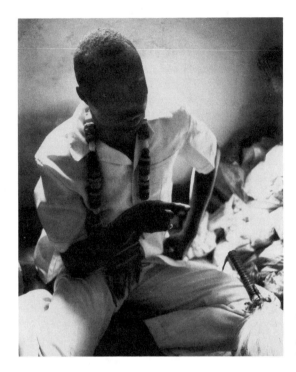

FIGURE 6-2   A babalawo consulting during a divination session. Ijebu, Nigeria, 1982. (Photo courtesy Henry John Drewal and Margaret Thompson Drewal.)

to make replacements for unusable ones. (**Figure 6–4**). Old or new, Ẹfẹ/Gẹlẹdẹ masks are elaborate creations, and often the carver uses intricate linear ele-ments to produce an elaborate sculpture in the round.

But masks makers are not the only residents of Aiyetoro who have been busy. Other members of the Ẹfẹ/Gẹlẹdẹ cult hierarchy have been making elab-orate costumes to be worn with the masks. Although the actual performers are men, they will portray both males and females, with masculinity conveyed by a bamboo hoop around the torso, over which flow layers of richly embroid-ered and appliqued cloth, giving the wearer a massive appearance. Femininity, by contrast, is indicated by a small waist and artificially enlarged breasts and buttocks.

Still other cult members have been busy composing the songs that will be a main attraction of the ceremonies. The Ẹfẹ performance lasts all night, and since new songs are composed each year, the Ẹfẹ/Gẹlẹdẹ song writers clearly faced a daunting task before the rituals can be performed.

But now, several weeks later, all such preparations in Aiyetoro have been completed. In the morning, cult leaders went to a sacred grove and offered the resident spirits various gifts of kolanut, whiskey, a white ram, and finally, cornmeal and waterleaf soup. These, along with prayers and songs, were given to insure good fortune not just for the Ẹfẹ/Gẹlẹdẹ ceremo-nies but for the entire coming year.

FIGURE 6-3 Elder in the Gẹlẹdẹ society painting a mask in preparation for a festival. Lagos, Nigeria, 1978. *(Photo courtesy Henry John Drewal and Margaret Thompson Drewal.)*

In the village itself, the air has become increasingly charged with antic-ipation, and as the excitement grows during the day, so do the crowds. Al-though Ẹfẹ/Gẹlẹdẹ cult members constitute only a small portion of Aiye-toro's total population, members of many other traditional cults have come to witness their ceremonies, as have local Christian and Muslim converts. Word has spread beyond the boundaries of the village itself, and some of the visitors have traveled as many as 150 miles to witness the events of the next twenty-four hours.

There are variations in Ẹfẹ/Gẹlẹdẹ performances from village to vil-lage, but if the ceremonies at Aiyetoro parallel those in traditional villages of Ketu and Idahin, then shortly after nightfall between 1,000 and 1,500 spectators will bring their lamps, food, mats, and chairs to the central mar-ket square in anticipation of the performance that will last till dawn. A spe-cial enclosure made of palm fronds stands at one side of the square, but the opposite side of the square gives the first unequivocal evidence that the ceremony is about to start. Five drummers begin the insistent beat that will continue throughout the night. Their playing provides more than just a

FIGURE 6-4   Yoruba Gẹlẹdẹ society mask, carved from cottonwood. *(Courtesy, Field Museum of Natural History, Chicago, neg. no. 109311.)*

rhythmic background to the festivities. The largest of the drums, the *iyalu* or "mother drums," are literally "talking." By mimicking the rhythmic and melodic patterns of the Yoruba language (which is tonal in nature), the mother drums sing out verbal messages, praising the Yoruba gods, remembering revered ancestors, and honoring illustrious elders—as well as giving voice to many well-known Yoruba proverbs. Against the mother drums, the beat of the smaller drums, tuned to various pitches, adds a complex polyrhythmic counterpart.

At last masked cult members begin to emerge from the enclosure and move into the center of the crowded square **(Figure 6–5)**. Some of their masks have moving parts that fascinate the youngest generation of spectators, who cheer and push to get a closer look. Other masks, more serious in nature, represent specific supernatural figures. One group of cult members forms a chorus that sings a hearty praise as each masked performer emerges from the palm frond enclosure, and they are soon joined by others from the crowd of onlookers. One is a figure known as Pa-ni-ina-njako, and when he rushes into the square with a pot of fire on his head, the people excitedly sing,

FIGURE 6–5 Masked Gẹlẹdẹ dancer. Lagos, Nigeria, 1978. *(Photo courtesy Henry John Drewal and Margaret Thompson Drewal.)*

> The burning of the bush comes without warning
> You farmers with fields near the bush
> You are warned to take precautions (Quoted in Drewal 1973:73)

Upon Pa·ni·ina·njako's entrance, all lamps are extinguished. The square remains dark, making later events all the more dramatic.

Sometimes the masked performer himself sings, and one, wearing a female mask named Tetede, heralds the arrival of the central figure of the Ẹfẹ night ceremony, Oro Ẹfẹ. After much fanfare from his attendants and tentativeness on his own part, the drummers fall silent and Oro Ẹfẹ finally emerges from the enclosure. He is literally larger than life, his girth being expanded first, by his costume's bamboo structure and, second, by the many layers of richly embroidered and appliqued cloth that cover him. Even the looming Ẹfẹ mask that sits above his head adds to his supernatural stature. Oro Ẹfẹ's iron ankle rattles, six on each leg, sound a slow, steady beat as he enters the square, swaying and stamping. He begins a series of chants honoring Yoruba gods, ancestors, and mothers, and his words are resoundingly seconded by onlookers who fire guns into the air and shout their approval.

After these preliminaries, Oro Ẹfẹ starts a routine that will continue for the rest of the night. He begins chanting a song, and soon members of

the Ẹfẹ/Gẹlẹdẹ chorus take up the words and move through the crowd teaching it to the onlookers until the thousand-plus voices of the entire group
are singing it in unison. After a while, Oro Ẹfẹ begins another song, and
eventually everyone is singing that one. Finally, as dawn approaches, a
masked performer on stilts enters the square. As he diverts the crowd's attention, Oro Ẹfẹ makes an unobtrusive exit, and the weary onlookers begin
to disperse. So goes Ẹfẹ Night.

The next day is devoted to the Gẹlẹdẹ Dance, staged by the same individuals who performed Ẹfẹ Night. Late in the afternoon, the crowd begins
to gather once more around the market square; and, again the cult's drummers take up their position opposite the palm frond enclosure. Their drumming brings still more onlookers until the expectant spectators are jostling
each other for good seats. (A Yoruba proverb says, in translation, "The eyes
that have seen Gẹlẹdẹ have seen the ultimate spectacle" [Drewal and Drewal
1987:243].)

Meanwhile, cult members are putting on their costumes, and again,
masks sit atop their heads and elaborate costumes cover their bodies. The
masked dancers are of all ages, and the youngest dancers go first. Boys as
young as five, individually or in groups of two or three, attempt to perform
the intricate steps of the Gẹlẹdẹ dance. Happy onlookers reward their efforts with enthusiastic praise—and sometimes with coins. Adolescent and
teenage dancers eventually replace the boys, and they in turn are followed
by young adult and adult dancers. Finally the most accomplished dancers
of all, the elders, appear. With each successive dancer, or group of dancers,
the crowd's enthusiasm grows, and cult members who have been assigned
the job of controlling the crowd are barely able to keep an open space
in the middle of the square for the whirling, stamping, explosively energetic
dancers. Meanwhile, other attendants vigorously fan those who have already
danced so they can redouble their choreographic virtuosity in another effort. After the most experienced dancers have performed to the shouts of
encouragement from the crowd—and sometimes accompanied by cult
members who cannot resist joining the dance—the Ẹfẹ/Gẹlẹdẹ ceremonies
end. The citizens of Aiyetoro return to their house compounds, happy and
confident that the joyous celebration will bring good fortune to the town
in the future.

The activities of Ẹfẹ Night and Gẹlẹdẹ Dance constitute a multimedia
artistic event, and as such they embody many of the principles that constitute the core of Yoruba aesthetics. Mask making and costumery, song and
dance—all are combined in Ẹfẹ/Gẹlẹdẹ to produce a powerful spectacle that
is distinctively Yoruba in nature. No witness to Ẹfẹ/Gẹlẹdẹ, whether native
or visitor, can fail to appreciate the richness of Yoruba art.

Drewal's account of Ẹfẹ/Gẹlẹdẹ gives us a vivid sense of a small component of the Yoruba art world. Other studies prove that Ẹfẹ/Gẹlẹdẹ is just
one of a vast number of equally striking artistic activities in Yoruba life.

And, as we shall see, Yoruba culture is not only rich in art; art plays an important role in the social and moral world of the Yoruba.

Yoruba Society

If all the world's societies could be placed in some approximate order, rang-ing from small-scale hunting and gathering groups to large-scale, complex civilizations, the traditional culture of the West African Yoruba would be closer to the complex end of the spectrum (cf. Thompson 1973:24–25). The Yoruba population, for example, numbers over ten million people, who live today in Nigeria and nearby regions of the People's Republic of Benin (for-merly Dahomey) and the Republic of Togo. (A great number of descendants of Yoruba who had been slaves now live in Sierra Leone, Cuba, Brazil, and the United States.) Cities have existed in this area of West Africa since the distant archaeological past; and modern Yorubaland has an index of urban-ization higher than that of Canada, France, or Greece (Bascom 1969:3), with half of the Yoruba population living in towns and cities, six of which have more than 100,000 residents. The largest, Ibadan, has evolved from an agri-cultural and trade center to become a thriving industrial metropolis and the largest inland city in sub-Saharan Africa. But like the much smaller Aiye-toro, whose Ẹfẹ/Gẹlẹdẹ celebration has been described, even Ibadan's popu-lation swells when major religious festivals are held (cf. Lloyd, Mabogunje, and Awe 1967).

The Yoruba homeland has seen the rise and fall of complex and pow-erful kingdoms for at least a thousand years, and although the details of the various strands of Nigerian pre-history remain unclear, the contemporary Yoruba are themselves divided into many kingdoms, each with an elaborate bureaucracy, impressive symbols of state such as beaded crowns and elabo-rately carved royal stools, and a political hierarchy whose pervasive influ-ence reaches down to the individual house compound **(Figure 6–6)**. Tradi-tional Yoruba culture lacked a formal means of writing, but formalized court singing and other genres of oral literature provide a wealth of histor-ical information.

Yoruba society has many other sorts of specialists besides those of state. On market days, traders (most of whom are women) sell everything from chickens and goats to ingredients for charms and medicines. Most Yoruba do at least some farming, but many people practice semiprofes-sional vocations. There are guilds of weavers, dyers, iron workers, brass casters, woodcarvers, and carvers of calabash gourds, leather workers, and potters, as well as drummers, diviners, and circumcisers, to name only a few Yoruba trades.

But for all its complexity, two features of Yoruba culture stand in marked contrast to the West: kinship and religion. Both play a more impor-

FIGURE 6-6 Yoruba king with beaded crown and staff of authority during annual rites of kingship. Ijebu, Nigeria, 1978. *(Photo courtesy Henry John Drewal and Margaret Thompson Drewal.)*

tant role in the day-to-day lives of traditional Yoruba than they do for most Westerners. The Yoruba reckon descent patrilineally, which is to say that every person belongs, for most practical purposes, only to his or her father's clan. The clan overshadows the nuclear family in importance, and every clan member lives under the authority of the clan's oldest male member, or *bale*.

Religion also plays an important role in the lives of most Yoruba; and although many Yoruba are Christians or Muslims, traditional religion is also a powerful force—as the Ẹfẹ/Gẹlẹdẹ ceremonies demonstrated. Yoruba religion centers around several types of supernatural beings. First is Olodumare (also called Olorun), a male supreme being who is the source of all life. Although he represents beauty *par excellence*, he never appears in Yoruba iconography, and unlike other Yoruba supernaturals he has no cult of devotees for his propitiation. However, his coeval, Onile, does play an active role in the affairs of mortals. As owner of the earth, she is attended by a special cult, Ogboni; and as the goddess of motherhood, she is also worshipped by all mothers.

Beneath Olodumare and Onile are the *orisha*, a large group of super-natural beings. Many are associated with specific natural phenomena (e.g., Shano, the god of thunder and lightning **[Figure 6–7]**) and human activities (e.g., Ogun, the *orisha* of ironworking). Other *orisha* are the spirits of deified ancestors. The *orisha* directly influence the lives of mortals, so to entice them to act favorably, every *orisha* is served by a cult of mortal worshippers. Cult members may feed the *orisha* by making sacrifices to it; they may wear distinctive clothes or ornaments to glorify it; or (and of particular interest to us) they may use sculpture, music, dance, and oratory to publicly praise the *orisha* and thereby win its favor. As we have seen, Ẹfẹ/Gẹlẹdẹ cult members in western Nigeria spend an entire night in public singing and another day in dancing. They do this in a concerted effort to please their *orisha*—in this case, another spirit of motherhood, who embodies powerful procreative, nurturant, and pacifying capabilities, and at the same time, cult members hope to nullify any harm that might come from women who are witches.

Yoruba Art Production

The Guinea Coast, a 200 mile-wide (320 kilometers) strip of land that begins in Sierra Leone in the west and runs 1,500 miles (2,400 kilometers) eastward

FIGURE 6–7 Interior view of cult house for Shango, Yoruba God of Thunder. Ibadan, Nigeria. *(Photo courtesy Field Museum of Natural History, Chicago, neg. no. 70014)*

to include the southern portions of the Ivory Coast, Ghana, Togo, Benin, and Nigeria, is extremely rich in art production. Why it has produced such enormous quantities of art is a matter for speculation (cf. Bascom 1973b:184–187); but whatever the reason, Guinea Coast art has had a magnetic appeal for Western sensibilities. The sensuousness, vitality, and visual inventiveness that Matisse, Picasso, Modigliani, and Brancusi found so striking in Guinea Coast art in the first decade of the twentieth century continue to excite Western museum goers and collectors today. For their part, scholars have been so fascinated by West African art that they have carried out more field studies and published more books and articles on West African art than they have on art from anywhere else in the world except the West, the Far East, and India. Moreover, Guinea Coast art continues to live and thrive today, with much art still being produced for traditional use.

The diversity of Yoruba art production is reflected in the training of Yoruba artists. Some families specialize in particular crafts, in which case a child's years of artistic training are an essential part of growing up. The child whose interests and talents do not coincide with the family profession may be apprenticed to a master artist in another medium.

In any case, the degree of specialization is remarkably high. For example, the guild of male weavers who use a horizontal loom to make narrow bands of material is separate from the guild of women weavers, who use a vertical loom to weave cotton fabric (Bascom 1973a:66).

As the Ẹfẹ/Gẹlẹdẹ activities showed, Yoruba visual arts often occur along with the performing arts—music, dance, drama, and oratory. If anything, these media play an even greater role in West African aesthetic sensibilities than do the visual arts (cf. Borgatti 1983:29).

The Yoruba distinguish between decorative and utilitarian arts, calling, for example, the carver of masks (**Figure 6–8**), *gbẹnẹgbẹna,* whereas the carver of mortars and other practical items is *gbẹgibe-gi* (Bascom 1973a:64). But even the carver of masks is not a full-time artist and must rely on garden farming to supplement the income he receives from commissions and from the occasional apprentice.

Although Yoruba art serves several purposes, religion is by far the most important. Hundreds of different cults exist in Yorubaland, each associated with a specific *orisha,* and most cults' duties require, in one way or another, the use of art. Recall the Ẹfẹ/Gẹlẹdẹ ceremonies. Not only did the dancers and singers use many masks, but also each wore an elaborate and striking costume that largely concealed the mask wearer as he appeared before the assembled audience. Furthermore, complex drumming, dancing, and singing were all integral to the performance, and each was distinctively the possession of Ẹfẹ/Gẹlẹdẹ cult members.

Or consider another cult, that of the *babalawo,* the diviner who asked his own deity, Ifa, whether the time had come for the Ẹfẹ/Gẹlẹdẹ ceremo-

FIGURE 6–8 Yoruba sculptor finishing the knifework on a headdress for an Egungun masquerade. Awori, Nigeria, 1981. *(Photo courtesy Henry John Drewal and Margaret Thompson Drewal.)*

nies. He probably stored the sixteen palmnuts needed for the divination ceremony in an elaborately carved container; he used a bell cast in brass to attract Ifa's attention; and **Figure 6–9** shows the handsome wooden tray upon which one *babalawo* scattered sawdust. Finally, the *babalawo* himself is distinguished by the decoration of his person: Bracelets of alternating green and tan beads (See Figure 6–2) are the emblem of the *babalawo*. The elaborate visual and performing arts associated with the cults of Ẹfẹ/Gẹlẹdẹ and Ifa are matched by many other Yoruba cults, so the quantity of Yoruba religious art is clearly enormous **(Figure 6–10)**.

Still more Yoruba art is produced for secular purposes, primarily as a means of indicating social status. Each ruler of a Yoruba kingdom has his own royal stool, beaded crown, umbrellas, fly whisks, scepters, gowns, slippers, and other regalia of state, and the finest carving graces each king's palace. Also, the reputation of a noble lineage is made visible to everyone by the impressive low-relief carvings on its compound door. But even this art is not wholly secular in nature. Yoruba religion and politics complement

FIGURE 6-9   Ifa divination tray.   *(Photograph courtesy Parkersburg [West Virginia] Art Center, from the Marietta College Permanent Collection, Marietta, Ohio.)*

and support each other; and, as we shall see below, the Yoruba strongly believe that excellent art, by embodying goodness and right, is a public confirmation of elevated political or religious status.

Yoruba Art Criticism

A thumbnail history of modern comparative aesthetics is contained in the following three quotations:

> It is for want of a conscious critical sense and the intellectual power of comparison and classification that the Negro has failed to create one of the great cultures of the world.   (Fry, quoted in Thompson 1968:44)

> It is important for us not to deceive ourselves into believing that we can understand the intention of an African sculptor simply by looking at his work. (Willett 1971:161)

> There exists in Sub-saharan Africa, locked in the minds of kings, priests, and commoners, a reservoir of artistic criticism. Wherever tapped, this source

FIGURE 6-10 Humorous Egungun *idan* (miracle) performers masquerading as Europeans. Awori, Nigeria, 1981. *(Photo courtesy Henry John Drewal and Margaret Thompson Drewal.)*

lends clarity to our understanding of the arts of tropical Africa. (Thompson 1973:19)

Taken together, these statements document a steady intellectual evolution, from Roger Fry's naive ethnocentrism of only sixty-odd years ago that tacitly assumed that "primitive peoples" were incapable of critical thought and subtle philosophical speculation; through a growing awareness of our ignorance of the aesthetic underpinnings of art from other cultures, as seen in the second quotation from Frank Willett; and finally the conclusions of Robert Farris Thompson, based upon sustained research aimed at learning native principles of aesthetics.

Many scholars have contributed to our knowledge of Yoruba aesthetics, the foremost of whom is Robert Farris Thompson. Thompson uniquely combines the art historian's visual sensitivity to style and form with the cultural anthropologist's rigorous fieldwork techniques. Since the 1960s, he has spent much time in West Africa interviewing Yoruba artists and critics; and although his early fieldwork was done through translators, Thompson was careful to recheck translations (using a native Yoruba speaker), both in the field and once more after returning to the United States. Thompson's writing in both lucid and deep, providing thorough descriptive material as well as thought-provoking analysis.[1]

Thompson has shown beyond a doubt that Yoruba culture does possess a living and sophisticated tradition of art criticism. He notes that although no Yoruba individuals make a full-time occupation of being art critics, criticism is a traditionally recognized activity. In fact, a Yoruba dictionary dating from 1858 has two entries that mean "knower of beauty" or "connoisseur" (Thompson 1973:26; 1983:5). A critic may be an artist or one who commissions art, male or female, king or commoner. Of the 200 art critics Thompson interviewed, twenty were farmers, "some of them of very humble economic means, who balanced the simplicity of their material possessions against the riches of their minds" (Thompson 1973:27). Despite this diversity, the critics all spoke with marked conviction and articulately evaluated Yoruba art works, using a highly developed vocabulary that is called upon only in the context of art criticism.

Yoruba art critics exercise their skills in several situations. They may be asked to evaluate the success of an art work when it is sold; and master carvers seldom hesitate to assess the merits of carvings made by apprentices and other sculptors. However, most critics are reluctant to comment publicly on their own work or work by a clansman, and they avoid discussing the carvings used in cult shrines.

Thompson describes his technique for collecting information thus:

> Artistic criticism was not requested in any village or town until data about carvers, dating of works, names of woods, and so forth had been collected. . . . The crowd was then asked, while pieces of sculpture brought out for study were still in the sunlight, was someone willing to rank the carvings for a minimal fee and explain why he liked one piece over another? . . . Almost without fail someone would step forward and immediately begin to criticize the sculpture. The rare delays did not stem from lack of verbal skill. Rather some informants were simply afraid that their efforts would not really be compensated. Others wished to study the works with care in the light, turning them around and testing their profile and mass.   (Thompson 1973:26)

Using these techniques, Thompson collected a rich body of information from which he has extracted the evaluative criteria used by Yoruba art

---

[1]A concise statement of Thompson's findings appeared in *Art News* (1968); his later book, *African Art in Motion* (1974) broadens his analysis to include Yoruba music and dance. Margaret Thompson Drewal and Henry John Drewal have also produced, and continue to publish, extremely rich studies of Yoruba art and aesthetics. See also Jean Borgatti's work (1979, 1982) on the neighboring Okpella.

critics. Granted, standards of art criticism exist on a different analytic level from the abstract assumptions that make up the Yoruba philosophy of art, which is our central concern here. However, the explicit principles of Yoruba art criticism do provide the best access into the implicit ideas of Yoruba aesthetics. The cannons of Yoruba statuary criticism are as follows:

1. A Yoruba figurative carving should be "not too real and not too abstract, but somewhere in between" (Thompson 1974:26). This value, which Yoruba call *jijora* and which Thompson terms "mimesis at the mid-point," requires that a carved human figure should look like a person but should possess none of the idiosyncratic flaws that set that individual apart from others.

2. A carved figure should possess *ifarahòn*, or clarity of form and line. Not only should the major sculptural masses be clearly demarcated, but also the fine lines representing clan scars should be clearly visible. One informant told Thompson, "If you want to marry a person you have to see the body completely" (Thompson 1973:36), and the elements of a carved figure should similarly be visible for all to see. The expert carver should (so the reasoning goes) have nothing to hide.

3. A carving should also possess a smooth surface, giving the piece a shining luminosity or *didón*. Creating such a high polish is one sign of the carver's art: "The adzemarks of the master, where the edges show, shine while the adzemarks of the apprentice lack formal separation and do not shine" (Thompson 1973:37).

4. Yoruba art critics are sensitive to several factors of composition. All parts of a figure should be properly positioned relative to each other, and their sizes should be correct—which is to say, neither too big nor too small. Indeed, as shall become clear later, Yoruba seek moderation in *all* facets of art and culture.

5. Surface details of carvings should be finely made, and delicacy is much appreciated.

6. Roundness—in buttocks, breasts, and other major body parts— is held in high esteem, but again, only in moderation. "Excessive curved swellings" and "sinister bulges" are appropriate only in the rare portrayal of the grotesque for purposes of satire, moral inquisition, and psychological warfare, situations that require carvers to violate the principles of beauty.

7. Proper Yoruba sculpture usually reveals a marked bilateral symmetry. The carver seeks to produce a noble, upright posture, giving figures an appearance of calm dignity.

8. Yoruba art connoisseurs recognize and appreciate the carver with exceptional skill. The master carver's talents are often alluded to in his *oríkì*, or attributive name. For example, an early twentieth-century carver named Taiwo was known far and wide as *Onípàsónòbe*, which means, "possessed of a knife like a whip. It is a miniature poem in praise of the carver's artistic cunning. Such was the skill of the late Taiwo that he summoned shapes, as with a whip, out of brute wood with his knife and made the shapes do as he bid them" (Thompson 1973:56).

9. A final Yoruba canon of beauty is ephebism (*òdó*), or "the depiction of mankind at the optimum of physicality between the extremes of infancy and old age" (Thompson 1971:378). The Yoruba have the highest regard for the sagacity of the elders, but when they are portrayed in wood carvings old people are flattered by being given the robust figures of a person at the physical prime of life that occurs in early adulthood. Ephebism is a fundamental principle of Yoruba art criticism: First, it is directly linked to underlying philosophical beliefs that determine the nature of Yoruba aesthetics, a fact that will be discussed below; and second, several of the preceding principles of Yoruba art criticism derive from ephebism. A statuette should not portray the slack, wrinkled skin of old age, but the *smooth* appearance of *lustrous* skin over firm muscle, with clan scars still clearly *visible* as in an individual's younger years. It should not show the stooped posture or hobbled gait of the elderly but the confidently *erect* and *symmetrical* stance of early maturity. Not the withered breasts and buttocks of a grandmother but the sensual *roundness* and swelling fullness characteristic of a woman just starting her reproductive years; and, most of all, not the ungainly frame of youth but the harmoniously *proportioned*, proudly *demarcated* elements of the mature body.

Yoruba arts constitute an integrated stylistic system, so it is not surprising that the criteria of dance and music criticism parallel those for carving. For example, the vitality implicit in ephebism is as important in dance as it is in carving. As elsewhere in West Africa, Yoruba dancers display both athletic energy and a sensitivity to rhythmic complexity that only years of practice can give. Thompson remarks, "Most dancers in Africa (elderly kings are sometimes an exception) step inside rhythms which are young and strong, and to this extent their bodies are generalized by a vital rhythmic impulse" (Thompson 1974:7). The use of syncopated, off-beat stresses produces this effect, as does playing one rhythm against another (**Figure 6–11**). A dancer's hands and feet may be following the four-four beat of one percussion instrument, the hips a three-four beat of another, and the back and shoulders a five-four beat of still another! But instead of executing this polyrhythmic wizardry with showy bravado, the audience expects the

FIGURE 6–11 Odudua devotees dancing during ceremony. Ijebu, Nigeria, 1982. *Photo courtesy Henry John Drewal and Margaret Thompson Drewal.)*

dancer to maintain a mature composure, as reflected in a "cool," unsmiling face (Thompson 1974:45).

The principles of Yoruba art criticism, then, are complex, elaborate, and sophisticated. Taken as a whole, they constitute a unique applied aesthetic, one significantly different from Western aesthetics.[2]

---

[2]"I would frankly doubt that curators, of whatever sensitivity, could, without careful study of the Yoruba aesthetic, make judgments which would unerringly coincide with those of the Yoruba connoisseurs. The canon of ephebism, for example, might intervene as an overlooked variable and it is not at all certain that eyes conditioned by a visual culture of abstract expressionism, Pop, and later modes are *ipso facto* in tune with the relative symmetries, straightness, and delicacy of the Yoruba round of art" (Thompson 1976: chaps. 3, 4).

The Moral and Ethical Bases of Yoruba Art Criticism

Although these principles of Yoruba art criticism are both broad and subtle, they are not particularly profound—they simply define Yoruba notions of beauty, particularly as applied to the human form. As such they seem arbitrary, perhaps only a rationale for sensuality. But if one looks more deeply into Yoruba philosophic assumptions, as manifest in Yoruba myth, religion, and secular belief, there emerges a sophisticated system of reasoning from which these standards of beauty are derived.

Roy Sieber has said that African sculpture is rarely art for art's sake; it is, rather, art for life's sake (Sieber 1962:8). This cardinal principle lies at the heart of Yoruba aesthetics. Most Yoruba art serves religious purposes, but the emphasis, we must be clear to say, is not upon attaining spiritual enlightenment for its own sake but upon using religious means to attain material well-being for the population at large. Yoruba theology is thoroughly pragmatic and it assumes that if the gods are praised, they will bring prosperity, fertility, and good health to those who honor them. (Sculptures of Yoruba *orisha* are not considered to be the gods themselves; they are vehicles that link mortals with the spirit world [Lawal 1974:244]).

In artistic contexts this means that if the *orisha* are praised through beautiful art, then they will be compelled to bestow their blessings upon the mortals who present the art. In essence, the Yoruba believe that human well-being depends on the disposition of the *orisha*; this, in turn, depends upon pleasing the *orisha* by making art in their honor. Of course, the entire argument rests upon the assumption that the art will be beautiful enough to please the *orisha* to which it is dedicated.[3]

This reasoning accounts for several of the formal principles of Yoruba art reported by Thompson. The criterion of "midpoint mimesis" requires that a representation of a person not show the unique traits, warts and all, that set the individual apart. Instead, the figure should be generalized to the degree that it represents the finest and best in the human form. (Thompson's informants often praised a sculpture with the phrase, *nitori o jo enia*— "the image is beautiful because it resembles mankind" [Thompson 1976:Chap.3/1].)

To please the members of the spirit world, a sculpture should possess exemplary beauty not only in physique but also in representing the highest ethical standards. This principle leads us to a still deeper level of Yoruba aesthetics, one which links standards of sensuous beauty with standards of ethical and moral worth.

---

[3]Other African societies have similar beliefs. For example, Vandenhoute found that among the Dan peoples, only *beautiful* masks are thought to bring favors to mortals from their revered ancestors (cf. Gerbrands 1957:91). And many individuals among the Baule own statuettes that are meant to please a spirit lover. If this spirit lover is happy, it will give both riches and children to the statuette's owner (Vogel 1979, 1980).

The belief that art should embody not only physical perfection but also ethical and moral ideals has implications for several of the stylistic conventions of Yoruba art. For example, the Yoruba carver focuses a disproportionately great amount of his attention on the subject's head, which is considered to be the seat of consciousness and moral capacity. The Yoruba, like other West Africans, see more in a face than Westerners commonly do. Not just the eyes, but the entire visage is, apparently, a "mirror of the soul" (cf. Abiodun 1987; Deregowski, Ellis, and Shepherd 1975; Borgatti 1982:34). Thus, heads are shown in oversized scale to the rest of the body, a "psychological realism" that conveys its own kind of truth.

The identification of sensuous beauty with sociocultural goodness is found again and again in Yoruba life. For one thing, the finest art is available only to those of elevated socioeconomic status among the Yoruba.[4] More importantly, scholars have learned that in many African languages, the same word means both "good" and "beautiful." For example, Daniel Crowley, whose extensive fieldwork in Central Africa focused on the arts of the Chokwe, has reported that although the Chokwe language has an extensive vocabulary for differentiating such things as degrees of kinship and types of musical instruments, it lacks a lexical distinction between "good" and "beautiful," both of which are termed *chimba* (Crowley 1971:322); and Harold Schneider found that in the language of the Turu of Tanzania, the word *majigha* means "beauty, a lovely thing," but "more precisely, it is a voluntary action which makes people happy" (Schneider 1966:158).[5]

It has been clear for some time that the (seeming) idiosyncrasies of a language provide useful clues for cross-cultural understanding, and the things that appear exotic in another tongue may provide the key to unlocking the speakers' philosophical system. The equation of goodness with beauty in sub-Saharan African languages may provide a valuable insight into the aesthetics of the Yoruba and other African peoples.

The equivalence between goodness and beauty prompts the question,

---

[4]The belief that the best art is that which represents the highest craftsmanship appears elsewhere in West Africa also. For example, the Dan peoples of the Ivory Coast admire careful finishing and good color in sculptures; and Warren and Andrews (1977) found that the Akan peoples they studied demand extreme smoothness in carvings. Often such criteria are linked to economic factors, so the "finest" of art is available only to the wealthiest of patrons because it can be made only by the most highly skilled of artists or else because it represents an exceptionally great investment of labor. The just-mentioned Akan appreciate and amply reward the consummate skill that ultra-smooth carvings represent, and they also place a high premium on closely woven, color-fast *kente* cloth, high-fired pottery, and well-forged and finished iron work, each of which embodies exceptional skill and effort.

[5]In a secondary review of the literature on this subject, Leiris and Delange note additional African languages in which "good" and "beautiful" are expressed by the same, or closely related, terms. In some cases, however, the situation appears to be more complex. For example, the Bulu, in Southern Cameroon, are said to "use the word *abeñ* (beauty) when speaking of a woman, a house or the weather, while other words are used indiscriminately to describe 'good' or 'fine' " (Leiris and Delange 1968:42).

In African thought, just what *is* goodness? The cultural context of language usage shows that the criteria of goodness-and-beauty are not thought to come from natural laws or from religious revelation; they are firmly grounded in social, humanistic reality. "Goodness" means ethical goodness, moral goodness; exemplary conduct is the foundation of all beauty. Consider, for example, these excerpts from John Miller Chernoff's work, based on his many years experience of learning the art of traditional drumming in Ghana:

> My education in African music was an education in my awareness of spiritual and ethical principles, the prerequisites of the clear mind and experienced judgement I would need to play really well. (Chernoff 1979:140)

> In music, random improvisation and imprecision spoil the delicate structure of the rhythms, and in society, random expressions spoil the delicate structure of communication. . . . In short, in Africa someone with bad character'is essentially someone who lacks respect, someone who has withdrawn from participation in society and whose intentions have become inaccessible. (Chernoff 1979:167)

And finally,

> One does not dance to go into a trance but to come out of a trance, to join a diversified assembly with a separate contribution, for dancing is a reminder that one is only part of the whole. (Chernoff 1979:150)

Returning to Yoruba we find that here too language is the best means of uncovering the relationship between goodness and beauty. The Nigerian art historian, Babatunde Lawal, himself a Yoruba, has reported that the word *ewá* refers to manifest beauty, but that it has two distinctly different levels of meaning. *Ewá ode*, or "facial beauty," refers to the outer beauty of a thing—the attractive appearance of an object or the sensuous good looks of a person. But *ewá inu*, "inner beauty," refers to the genuine, intrinsic worth of a thing. In an inanimate object, this utilitarian value is paramount, so that, for example, "a good-looking but fragile cutlass is useless and is dismissed as. . . . superficial beauty" (Lawal 1974).

In man or woman, the inner beauty of *ewá inu* is determined by his or her *iwà*, or character. This concept of *iwà* will lead us to a still deeper level of Yoruba aesthetic theory. Lawal says,

> *Iwá* is the very stuff which makes life a joy because not only does it please *Olorun* (the High-God), it also endears one to the hearts of all men. . . . The person who is outwardly beautiful but inwardly ugly or lacks character is called *awobowà* (literally skin covers character). . . . The physical beauty of such a person may be at first admired, but as soon as his inner ugliness surfaces he becomes repulsive. His beauty is immediately beclouded by the flames of

his character: for the Yoruba see character as manifesting itself like a flame. (Lawal 1974:240–241)

A Yoruba verse quoted by Thompson (1983:11) shows the importance attached to personal character:

A man may be very, very handsome
Handsome as a fish within the water
But if he has no character
He is no more than a wooden doll.

Iwà: Good Character

What are the traits of *iwà*? They are perhaps best summed up by the words *harmonious energy*—a phrase that stands at the very foundation of Yoruba aesthetic thought. We must, therefore, examine the implications of harmony and energy in the world of Yoruba society and art.

The person of good character maintains *harmony* in two "directions," as it were. From a diachronic perspective, he or she lives in harmony with the ancestors and the storehouse of Yoruba tradition that has been handed down from the past and that perpetuates the beliefs and institutions of the ancestors. All cultures are conservative, but the Yoruba make a cardinal virtue of this principle. However, from a different, synchronic perspective, Yoruba culture encourages harmony with one's immediate social environment. The Yoruba expect all adults to maintain a cooperative spirit in dealing with others and to be submissive to legitimate authority, be it the political authority of the king or the familial authority of the clan headman, the *bale*.

The striving for harmonious living has many implications for day-to-day Yoruba life. Emotions should always be kept in check, and one should maintain a tranquil countenance, whether engaging in political debate or participating in a vigorous dance. Lawal states, "*Iwà* fosters social harmony among men, thereby generating law and order in society" (Lawal 1974:247). Of course, the high value placed on harmonious living makes good sense in Yoruba culture, with its traditionally high level of urbanism and also with all the psychosocial implications of residence in house compounds in which many extended family members are in constant, face-to-face contact with each other. The Yoruba recognize the importance of social harmony, and as a consequence harmony stands as a pillar in the Yoruba value system.

Yoruba art and aesthetics reflect harmonious living in several notable ways, such as the pervasive concern with *moderation*. Recall, for example, that carved statuettes must be neither too realistic nor too idealized; body parts should be clearly delineated but not exaggerated; surfaces should be curved but "sinister bulges" must be avoided; and the sculpture should be compositionally balanced, with a nearly perfect left-right symmetry.[6]

The performing arts of the Yoruba also reflect their deep respect for social harmony. No matter how energetic the choreography, nor how demanding the polyrhythmic beat of the drums, a Yoruba dancer should not spin about the dance area with complete abandon but must always maintain control, staying "inside" the tempo, keeping a "cool" look on the face (cf. Thompson 1966). The content of Yoruba art reflects a similar concern with maintaining social equilibrium. For example, the songs composed for Ẹfẹ Night often ridicule individuals who have been notably antisocial during the preceding year (cf. Drewal 1973:92).

But the striving for harmony in Yoruba art and culture is not the whole story. A life of total harmony, devoid of creative novelty and social friction, is as stultifying in theory as it is impossible in practice, and the ideal of "harmonious *energy*" brings distinctly different values to the fore. Energy is conveyed by the Yoruba term *àṣẹ*, an important word that denotes "authority" and carries connotations of "spiritual command, the power-to-make-things-happen, God's own enabling light rendered accessible to men and women" (Thompson 1983:5). Power, growth, and individual uniqueness are basic character attributes, and little thought is needed to see that these too are not arbitrary values but spring from vital concerns of life. To insure protection from such plagues as drought, foreign invaders, and disease, one must be strong; and to provide for the welfare of one's family, one must lead a vigorous, active life. And although Yoruba culture is hierarchical and has distinctly conservative tendencies, Yoruba social life also includes a measure of competitiveness. In the political arena, for example, the self-made man can rise to a position of some power (Barbar 1981:724). All these needs and wishes require an outlay of *energy*.

A striving for energy, power, and prosperity is, if anything, even more apparent in Yoruba art than is the quest for harmony. The pre-eminent value of ephebism, of portraying individuals who are at the pinnacle of physical dynamism, springs from *àṣẹ* but so do such stylistic details as the flexed legs so often seen in carved figures. The feeling of equipoise conveyed by a carving's bilateral symmetry contrasts with its powerful legs that, from their flexed hip-joints and the tense bend at the knee, seem ready to send the subject leaping into the air.

---

[6]Lawal notes that this striving for harmonious moderation leads to an interesting dilemma in Yoruba notions of human beauty. For example, although very tall, good-looking, well-complexioned men are, in theory, the most handsome, "beauty is also seen in the *mean (iwontún wonsi)*, i.e., average height, complexion and looks. In fact most Yoruba would prefer the mean because while the extremely ugly is often despised, the extremely beautiful is often held suspect" (Lawal 1974:239).

To describe Yoruba sculptures by using the imagery of dance is not inappropriate. West African dance generally requires a quickness and energy of both body and mind if the dancer is to follow the music's complex beat with the appropriate, often highly athletic, movements. (Some Yoruba dancers jump and spin in the air while wearing helmet masks that weigh as much as sixty pounds, and dancers elsewhere in West Africa perform on fifteen-foot–high stilts while covered by masks and flowing costumes that conceal their bodies as well as their stilts!)

As with harmony, the Yoruba striving for energy has both synchronic and diachronic aspects. One should have power in the present, but one's influence and renown should also continue into the future. Since tomorrow is in the hands of the next generation, considerations of reproduction and sexuality play an important role in Yoruba moral and aesthetic thought. The Yoruba place a high premium on having many healthy children, and this too influences the plastic and performing arts. Women's breasts nourish suckling infants, so Yoruba art critics praise statuettes of women with breasts that show promise of feeding many children.[7]

Perhaps because there are few visible indications of an individual's fertility, the reproductive emphasis in Yoruba arts often extends to secondary sexual characteristics. In practical terms, men's muscular arms, legs, and torsos provide food and protection for their families, but when found in Yoruba dance and sculpture, these traits are beautiful in and of themselves. Similarly, smooth, lustrous skin, free of "sinister bulges" combines practical and sensual considerations. Such skin is an indication of good health and personal hygiene, but again it is considered to be intrinsically—and erotically—beautiful. Sizable buttocks may reflect the luxuries of the ample diet available to a prosperous family; and (as has been hypothesizd by Tobias [1961] concerning steatopygous San women) they may provide nutritional insurance for a nursing mother during periods of food shortage. But these practical factors merge with (and ultimately serve as a basis for) an erotic and aesthetic appeal. They reflect present wealth and prosperity and at the same time they contribute to the well-being of the next generation.

The core value of *àṣẹ*, or dynamic power and growth, informs Yoruba art on several different levels. In sculpture *àṣẹ* justifies sensuous ephebism and vitality; it provides a rationale for the pulsing energy of music and dance; and it inspires a creative force in the arts as a whole. Drewal and Drewal (1983) believe that the wide diversity they found in Gẹlẹdẹ dance is a direct consequence of the inventiveness and spirit of growth that permeates Yoruba culture and art.

---

[7]Interestingly, the Anang, the Yoruba's not-too-distant neighbors to the southeast, prefer carvings of women with pendulous breasts, evidence that they have *already* fed many children.

Beauty, Goodness, and Civilization

The power of Yoruba art is obvious to the untutored eye, but viewed in the context of traditional West African culture, it has an even more sweeping effect on human life and sensibility. As we have seen, art is absolutely necessary for Yoruba religion, and it effectively communicates Yoruba social status. Both of these uses, however, derive from the equation of beauty with goodness. In Yoruba thought, anything that is beautful is necessarily *good*, not just aesthetically but also spiritually, ethically, and politically (**Figure 6–12**).

But the Yoruba philosophy of art is more than an after-the-fact justification for the superiority of the political and religious elite. At its foundation, art makes a crucial contribution to Yoruba culture by conveying the fundamental theme of *harmonious energy*.

This concept is important because it embodies a basic existential contradiction. On the one hand, when Yoruba art, through its subject matter and stylistic conventions, admonishes people to lead lives of *harmony*, it is

FIGURE 6–12   Araba, the head Ifa priest of the community, dancing during Ifa festival. Lagos, Nigeria, 1977.   *(Photo courtesy Henry John Drewal and Margaret Thompson Drewal.)*

calling for acquiescence to authority, obedience to custom, and ultimately a reliance on the security of hearth and home. *Energy*, by contrast, requires a person to expand his or her own income and autonomy, usually at the expense of others, or else to abandon traditional life ways in order to forge new means of success. At the very least, the energetic life requires one to leave the safe haven of home in search of a spouse with whom to raise a family and to prosper. Thus, the demands of harmony and energy inevitably pull in opposite directions, and the wonder of Yoruba art lies in its combining these contradictory motives.

Think again of the dancers of the Ẹfẹ/Gẹlẹdẹ cult who opened this chapter. Their choreographic style, which simultaneously captures the divergent impulses of stability and dynamism, is purely intentional. Like other Yoruba artists, their dignified but vital masks, movements, and costumes say, "Live well with others, but develop your own potentialities too." The merits of such a message are clear. In his *Flash of the Spirit*, a study of the aesthetic influences of Black Africa on the arts and cultures of Black Americans, Robert Farris Thompson has argued that "a civilization like that of the Yoruba, and the Yoruba-Americans, pulsing with ceaseless creativity rightly stabilized by precision and control, will safeguard the passage of its people through the storms of time" (Thompson 1983:97).

Phrased in these terms, Yoruba art addresses a universal human problem, a dilemma faced by every person in all societies—namely, the precarious balance between social cohesion and individual autonomy. Everyone ultimately must ask, How can I conform to the demands of society and still be true to myself? Yoruba art does not dispel or resolve the dilemma, but by simultaneously embodying principles of both harmony and energy, it says unequivocally that neither goal should be pursued to the extreme, that each must always be balanced and held in check by the other.

Conclusion: The Metaphysical Basis of Yoruba Art

The literature on Yoruba art is quite rich, but until recently attention has been focused primarily on its most prominent aspect—namely, its capacity to convey important, indeed profound, social and ethical messages. But now evidence is coming to light of a deeper, more abstract level of Yoruba aesthetics. In fact, the existence of such a metaphysical foundation for Yoruba art should have been expected. After all, how could a culture invest art with such vital information unless it attributes to art a communicative efficacy of considerable power?

Margaret and Henry Drewal recently suggested one source of art's power in Yoruba thought. Based on extensive fieldwork, they have reexamined the Yoruba concept of àṣẹ, "energy" or "authority." As noted earlier, àṣẹ applies to personal behavior, as exemplified by the vitality of a good drummer or the stamina of an excellent dancer; but the Drewals have learned that *àṣẹ* also has a more generalized meaning as a "sheer activating [or] generative force" (Drewal and Drewal 1987:225). *Àṣẹ* exists in all substances, but it is concentrated in some things. Blood, for example, is rich in *àṣẹ*, making it a suitable food for the *orisha*—hence the sacrifice of the white ram at the beginning of the *Ẹfẹ* ritual described at the start of this chapter.

In Yoruba intellectual thought, *àṣẹ* is conceptualized as wind; and inasmuch as speech is impelled by wind from the speaker's lungs, words are believed to have a power all their own. Words that are uttered in ritual contexts (in the form of proverbs, songs, and incantations) can actually make things happen; and when many voices speak as one, as in the songs sung by the hundreds of participants and observers in *Ẹfẹ* ceremonies, the words have an irresistible force (Drewal and Drewal 1987:226).

The Drewals claim that the very structure of Yoruba arts (and, for that matter, of Yoruba society) rests ultimately upon *àṣẹ*, but it is the work of another Yoruba scholar, Rowland Abiodun, that reveals how this is so by examining the source of *àṣẹ* itself. Abiodun states that the power of *àṣẹ* is dependent upon another Yoruba concept, *Ọ̀rọ̀*; and although *Ọ̀rọ̀* is a complicated idea, the light it ultimately sheds upon Yoruba aesthetics justifies a close examination of its nature.

As in other cultures, a part of the Yoruba creation story provides a vital clue regarding *Ọ̀rọ̀* and the metaphysical foundation of art. According to the oral literature associated with Ifa divination, at some time in the mythic past the high god, Olodumare, "realized that he needed an intermediary force, since he was too charged with energy to come into contact with any living thing and have it survive" (Abiodun 1987:254). Therefore he produced the three seminal elements of creation: *ogbón* (wisdom), *ìmọ̀* (knowledge), and *òye* (understanding), which are known collectively as *Ọ̀rọ̀* (or *Họ̀ọ̀*). Holding them in the palm of his hand, Olodumare told Wisdom, Knowledge, and Understanding to fly away and look for a proper place to live. None was successful in this search, however, and one by one they flew back to him, humming like bees, and Olodumare swallowed them.

This situation prevailed for a long, long time, but eventually Olodumare lost patience with the incessant humming of Wisdom, Knowledge, and Understanding. In an effort to get some peace for himself, he expelled them from his stomach and ordered them to descend to earth, an event that Abiodun describes in dramatic terms: "Since they were heavily charged lifeforces from heaven, their descent was accompanied by lightning and thunder. All solid matter melted and became jell-like. For a while, *Ọ̀rọ̀* was suspended in mid-air like an egg and did not melt, but then it dropped to earth and split" (Abiodun 1987:255).

On earth, *Ọ̀rọ̀* is associated with several things: On a literal level it is identified with the deity of Ifa divination, and in particular with the proverbs (Òwe) that are the core of Ifa divination; but of central interest to us is the fact that by extension Òwe "can metaphorically apply to the communicative properties of sculpture, . . . dance, drama, song, chant, poetry, [and] incantations" (Abiodun 1987:255). Thus, when all is said and done, the Yoruba conceptualize the verbal and visual ritual arts as earthly incarnations of divine wisdom, knowledge, and understanding.

There is another way to portray this situation: In Yoruba thought there are two kinds of beings, the "people here on earth" (Ará Ayé) and the "beings in heaven" (Ará Òrun) (Abiodun 1987:256), and each category has a profound need for the other. For their part, divine Wisdom, Knowledge, and Understanding (Òrò) are too energetic and restless to remain in heaven, and they require earth as their dwelling; and at the same time, mortals must have the help of the deities on high in solving their own mundane problems. Significantly, art provides both parties with a means to meet their needs: On the one hand, Òrò descends to earth via proverbs, the oral literature of Ifa divination; and on the other hand, the performing and visual arts of Yoruba ritual provide a channel of communication between Orí-Inú, the Inner Head (or destiny) of the individual and Orí-isese, the primal Head in heaven.

These are by no means simple ideas, and much detail has been omitted.[8] Further, the situation is likely to become more complex as scholars pursue additional research along these lines. But already it is clear that the visual and performative sophistication of Yoruba art is matched by an equally complex body of abstract, philosophical thought that attributes to art a central role in both Yoruba society and Yoruba intellectual culture. The Yoruba view art as a well-defined conduit whereby heaven and earth gain necessary access to each other.

---

[8]The Drewal's show convincingly how the conception of àṣẹ as a vitalizing force unique to every being, leads to a stylistic feature of Yoruba art that they call seriate composition; and Abiodun discusses at length how the idea that art provides a means of communication between mortal and divine heads underlies the emphasis upon the head that is so apparent in Yoruba art.

7

AZTEC AESTHETICS
Flower and Song

Jade Shatters,
the quetzal feather tears apart.
Oh God, you mock us.
Perhaps we really do not exist.
(León-Portilla 1971:448)

The aesthetics of the pre-Colombian Aztecs deserve our attention for several reasons. For one thing, the Aztecs, along with the Olmecs, Mayas, and other Mesoamerican societies, made a prodigious quantity of art work, most of it reflecting exquisite standards of craftsmanship. Also, these states, like the handful of other complex civilizations that emerged during the course of human history, possessed a high level of economic specialization, with some people farming, some trading, some producing art works—and some focusing their attention on the creation of intricate aesthetic systems that were discussed extensively and, at times, hotly debated.

But the most compelling reason to examine Aztec aesthetics is because the New World civilizations developed independently of Old World traditions. Therefore, if parallels exist between New and Old World aesthetics, they are unlikely to have resulted from diffusion but probably represent independent, convergent development. And this in turn has an important bearing on our basic question—namely, to what extent do aesthetic systems reflect fundamental, pan-human predispositions toward art?

The Aztecs in Mesoamerican Culture History

When the Spanish Conquistadors arrived in the early sixteenth century, they found a land dominated, from the Gulf Coast to the Pacific, and from the deserts of north-central Mexico to the mountain forests of Guatemala, by the mighty military state of the Aztecs. A few small groups such as the Mixtecs

FIGURE 7-1　Map of Tenochtitlán and a scale model showing what the ceremonial center of the city might have looked like. *(Photo courtesy Garcia Valades Editores, S. A.)*

existed as autonomous enclaves, but the Aztecs, ruling from their capital of Tenochtitlán,[1] were the lords of the land.

Tenochtitlán itself was a wonder to the Spaniards. Built on an island in Lake Texcoco (which has since been drained and is the site of modern Mexico City), Tenochtitlán had a population of perhaps 200,000—far greater than that of London of the same period (see **Figure 7-1**). Its massive stone architecture, including impressively decorated temples, had few European parallels; and the fine arts flourished there in a way envied by many Europeans of the day. For example, Albrecht Dürer, after viewing some of the spoils of conquest, wrote, "All the days of my life I have seen nothing that rejoiced my heart such as these things, for I saw amongst them wonderful works of art and I marveled at the subtle ingenuity of men in foreign lands" (quoted in Fraser 1971:25).

The impressive Aztec state of 1520 represented the culmination of sev-

---

[1]Regarding the pronunciation of Aztec words, all letters have the same sound as in Spanish except that *h*'s are aspirated as in the English *hot; x* is pronounced as in the English *sh;* and the sound indicated by *tl* is pronounced as a single consonant, not as two distinct consonants, the same being true for *tz.* Stress is usually on the next to the last syllable, with exceptions, such as Tenochtitlán, indicated by an accent mark.

eral thousands of years of economic, political, and cultural change in Meso-america. Before about 10,000 years ago, two distinct cultures lived in the area, the Big Game Hunters and the Seed Gatherers, and the names given them by modern archaeologists accurately reflect a significant difference in specialization. A decline in the availability of large game animals, such as mammoth, llama, and bison, gradually tipped the balance in favor of the better-adapted Seed Gatherers. Around 9,000 years ago, these peoples, for one reason or another, took a step that was unprecedented in the New World and that eventually had enormous consequences: They started encouraging some plants to grow when and where they met human needs, rather than tailoring human needs to the plants' natural life cycles. In doing this, they started down the path that led to agriculture. Eventually maize (corn), beans, squash, and many other plants were domesticated; and by 4,000 years ago, some groups in central and southern Mesoamerica had become full-time farmers.

As in the other areas of the world that witnessed the "Neolithic Revolution" (if a 4,000-year-long process may be termed a revolution), Mesoamerican farmers eventually developed the whole constellation of traits that we have come to associate with civilization. As farming became more intensive, the formerly nomadic hunter-gatherers found they could support not only permanent villages but also ceremonial centers inhabited by priests and graced with monumental architecture; the division of labor became far more complex; and calendar and record-keeping systems came into use. Development was not an even, gradual process, but instead there was a succession of different peoples and places at the forefront of change. Olmec culture, near the coast of southern Mexico, flourished from about 800 B.C. to 400 B.C. During the later so-called "Classic" Period from 300 A.D. to 900 A.D., the distinctive Mayan civilization emerged in what is now northern Guatemala and neighboring regions; at about the same time, Zapotec culture developed in Oaxaca; and in central Mexico the city of Teotihuacan was the center of a third vigorous culture.

Between 500 and 900 A.D., all three of these kingdoms fell into disarray, due at least in part to invading Chichimec ("barbarian") groups from the north. Arriving with the simpler hunter-gatherer technology associated with the ancient Seed Gatherers, these nomads quickly adopted the sedentary, horticultural lifestyle of the people they displaced. One such group was the Toltecs, who were to build a spectacular city at Tulla, not far from the fallen Teotihuacan, and who established their own political hegemony in the Valley of Mexico until, in the twelfth century, they too fell to later waves of invaders. The Toltecs are particularly significant because they spoke a Nahuatl language and were eventually "adopted" as the spiritual forbearers of another Nahuatl-speaking group of hunter-gatherer-fighters that arrived from the north in the thirteenth century, the Aztecs.

The Aztecs' legendary histories claimed that they had begun their travels at Aztlán (hence their name, Aztec); that along the way they found their own principal deity, Huitzilopochtli ("Hummingbird-on-the-left"), a god of sun and war; that Huitzilopochtli told them they were destined to rule the world and that they should change their name to "Mexica," after the place he told them to go, the Valley of Mexico. Spurned there by the descendants of the Toltecs, the Aztecs eventually settled on an inhospitable island in Lake Texcoco, founding their city of Tenochtitlán there in 1337. Within a hundred years, they had secured their island and were rapidly expanding their influence by warfare and alliance to become the most powerful single state in Mexico. By 1502, their empire included nearly all of Mesoamerica, and it was this Aztec kingdom that Hernán Cortéz encountered upon his arrival in the New World in 1519.

The Aztec hegemony lasted only from about 1480 to 1520. By 1521, the Spanish had conquered Tenochtitlán and the Aztec empire was in ruins. Several factors led to the rapid defeat of the Aztecs, not the least of which was the willingness of many of the peoples whom the Aztecs had conquered to side with the Spanish against the Aztecs.

From 1521 onward, all the native peoples of Mesoamerica suffered the ravages of colonialism. Probably more than 80 percent of the native population died between 1519 and 1650 as a result of warfare, starvation, and the introduction of European diseases. Those who survived found themselves at the bottom of economic, political, and social hierarchies dominated by an aristocracy that was Spanish-speaking and Western-thinking. Nahuatl-speaking descendants of the once-mighty Aztecs continue to exist today, but little of pre-conquest Aztec culture remains in the isolated Nahuatl communities (cf. Madsen 1960).

Our Knowledge of Aztec Thought

The broad outlines of the history of Mesoamerica are unearthed by the archaeologist's shovel and trowel; and the sites of the Mexican high civilizations, with their promise of sensational finds, attracted classical archaeologists long before anthropological archaeologists began their more extensive (if less lucrative) study of pre-historic peoples. Excavations in Mesoamerica began in 1839, and since that time a wealth of artifacts and information has been uncovered.

Archaeologists usually face the task of reconstructing a past society armed solely with the mute stones and bones of a forgotten era, but evidence of the late Mesoamerican civilizations exists in another valuable form—the written word. Since the 1950s, there has been a steady growth in the field known as ethnohistory, a discipline that studies no-longer extant societies by examining written documents dating from the era when the society existed. For Aztec society, such resources are comparatively rich. Like the other areas of the world where the Neolithic Revolution ran its course, Mesoamerica developed a notation system for record-keeping—at first for dates, payments of taxes, and other mundane data, but by later pre-Columbian times the partially phonetic system of writing was adequate for recording more complex information. The Spanish conquerors found native Aztec libraries of codices (singular, codex) dealing with history, astronomy, and astrology (see **Figure 7–2**).

Although the Spanish destroyed some (but not all) of this native literature, they themselves created an extensive body of what amounts to Aztec ethnography. Eight years after the collapse of the Empire, a twenty-nine-year-old Franciscan missionary, Fra Bernadino de Sahagun, arrived in "New Spain" and began two decades of systematically recording the beliefs and customs of the Aztecs. Sahagun and his Aztec "research assistants"—young men of the nobility who would have become priests had the Spanish not arrived—collected information on a wide range of subjects. Between the deductions from the archaeological record and the commentary in such ethnohistorical sources as these, we have a surprisingly complete picture of life in a complex, thoroughly non-Western culture as it existed nearly 500 years ago.

FIGURE 7–2 A page from the Codex Borgiano, probably of Aztec origin. *(Courtesy, Field Museum of Natural History, Chicago, neg. no. 2561.)*

Aztec Culture

The Aztec Empire was far too complex a social system to be analyzed here in detail, but a few of its basic features do require brief mention. The Aztec economy had two bases. Remarkably fertile floating gardens (*chinampas*) in Lake Texcoco produced as many as seven harvests per year, in addition to which conquered territories sent enormous amounts of food to Tenochtitlán each year as tribute. Aztec documents record Tenochtitlán annually receiving tens of millions of pounds of corn and beans, as well as vast numbers of cotton cloaks, shields, feathers, precious stones, and other items.

Aztec society was composed of twenty ranked clans, each with many lineages which were also ranked, ranging from the highest aristocratic families from which members of the priesthood were drawn, to the majority of clans of land-holding farmers. Such a structure provided kinship bonds among the Aztec people and embodied a hierarchical spirit that permeated Aztec society. Above the twenty clans was the family of the king and below them was a large population of non-Aztec laborers (including guilds of artists and craftsmen), largely drawn from conquered tribes and chiefdoms. Although they were bound for life to their trade or to the Aztec families they worked for, these individuals were not quite slaves since they could own property, maintain families, and see their children grow up to become free men and women. The *pochteca,* or traders, made up another growing class in the last years of the Empire. All Aztec men, including priests, periodically bore arms for the state, and an atmosphere of militarism colored all aspects of Aztec life and thought.

Aztec religious practice lay primarily in the hands of a priesthood that was both influential and numerous—Tenochtitlán alone probably had 5,000 priests. Their chief responsibility was a complex series of ritual ceremonies that recurred annually and was organized into an elaborate fifty-two–year cycle. A central tenant of Aztec thought was the belief that the world would be created and destroyed five times and that four destructions had already occurred. The final, violent destruction of the present world by earthquake was expected to occur at crucial junctures of the ritual cycle and was most likely to occur at the end of the fifty-two–year period. Only if Huitzilopochtli, Tlaloc, and the other deities were propitiated might this apocalypse be forestalled.

Aztec Art

Aztec artists worked in many media, probably the most dramatic of which was architecture. Houses and secular public buildings were modest in design, but temples were grandiose stone structures that included huge, stepped pyramids on whose truncated tops stood small wooden structures.

Large stone figures surrounded the pyramid's base (see **Figure 7–3**) and painted mural frescoes decorated the pyramid itself. Small items, both religious and decorative in purpose, were also carved in stone. (Wood carving was practiced, but little of it remains today.) Painting merged with calligraphy to produce the illustrations of the Aztec codices. A black-on-orange decorated pottery was made in a style that had its origins many centuries earlier in Teotihuacan culture. Fiber artists wove fine textiles, including velvets and brocades, and these were further embroidered, tie-dyed, or served as the ground for feather mosaic. Mosaics were also made of shells, turquoise, and other semiprecious stones. When the Spanish arrived in Tenochtitlán, they found great quantities of gold and silver which Aztec craftsmen had worked using lost wax casting and other complicated techniques.

Religion provided the subject matter for most Aztec art. Gods were portrayed, religious paraphernalia was made to order, and the underlying thrust of it all was the embodiment and glorification of religious belief—although it should be said that the goals of Aztec religion and politics were indistinguishable, and both were focused on forestalling the apocalypse and realizing the Aztecs' promised destiny as rulers of the world.

Covarrubias (1957:321–326), himself an artist and art historian, be-

FIGURE 7–3   The Aztec Sun Stone, a olivine basalt monolith, 3.57 meters in diameter and weighing 24.5 tons. Originally part of the High Temple, it is now on display in the National Museum of Anthropology, Mexico City. *(Courtesy, Field Museum of Natural History, Chicago, neg. no. 90742.)*

lieves that Aztec artistic style had three components—a generalized geometric propensity that is indigenously Aztec; many architectural conventions copied directly from the pyramids of the Toltecs; and a graphic, pictorial style borrowed from the Mixteca-Puebla tradition. Like the European art patrons of the Renaissance who glorified classical Greek and Roman culture, the Aztecs looked back upon the Toltec and early Mixtec civilizations as their cultural and intellectual forbearers, and as the Aztecs expanded their empire they brought master Toltec and Mixtec artisans to Tenochtitlán to produce the art they desired.

Aztec style was an amalgam of both naturalism and conventionalized representation. Mortal humans and animals were rendered with extreme subtlety, but the Aztecs visualized their gods as fierce, anthropomorphic beings with faces resembling native Mesoamericans but clothed and decorated with all the elaborate regalia appropriate to deities. The iconographic traits that identified a given god included the color of his face (Huitzilopochtli's was blue with a horizontal yellow stripe) and the shape and color of his nose and ear ornaments, headdresses, items worn in his hair or on the back of his head and neck, plus objects—frequently shields—held in his hands (cf. Nicholson 1976).

Dance was another important component of the Aztec arts. From the codex texts we know that both sacred and secular dances were performed, and from their illustrations and from Aztec ceramic figurines, we even have some idea of the patterns of movement that characterize Aztec dance (cf. Marti and Kurath 1964), although the theoretical basis of dance has yet to be worked out.

In sum, Aztec society produced a tremendous quantity of art with a high degree of craftsmanship and technical sophistication, reflecting its being produced by full-time specialists. Domestic items were also made with care, but by far the most intensive effort went into the creation of art used in the politico-religious system upon which Aztec society was based.

Aztec Aesthetics

Evidence bearing on the nature of Aztec aesthetics was long thought to have disappeared. Vaillant, in his classic *The Aztecs of Mexico,* stated flatly, "We have no way, except by analogy with living groups, to ascertain the Aztec attitude toward their . . . art" (Vaillant 1944:156); and Westheim, surveying Aztec art and aesthetics in the thorough-going tradition of German art history, states, "There does not seem to have been a Mesoamerican Aristotle. At least, no maxims [about aesthetics] such as his have been preserved. . . . We must derive the esthetics expressed in that art from the works of art that have been saved" (Westheim 1965/1950:54–55).

Despite these statements, both common sense and ethnographic analogy lead us to assume that Aztec art was indeed linked to a canon of aesthetic theory, and a few remarks by the early Spanish invaders support this assumption. For example, Díaz, in a description of a battle that occurred just before the fall of Tenochtitlán, said that many Spanish soldiers drowned because they overloaded their boats with loot of gold and silver, whereas he himself survived because he took only jade beads, jade being more valuable to the Aztecs than either silver or gold (cited in Covarrubias 1957:319).

Since the mid-1950s, however, ethnohistorians such as Angel Ma. Garibay K. and Miguel León-Portilla have begun to reveal the major themes of Aztec philosophy. Contrary to Westheim's remark, Mesoamerica *did* have its Aristotles—men called *tlamatinime* (singular, *tlamatini*), or knowers-of-things, who were respected for their wisdom, whose chief interest lay in speculative thought, and who, like many Western philosophers, sought to illuminate the major metaphysical questions of life by examining traditional beliefs, correcting and extending them when possible. One codex described the *tlamatinime* in the following terms:

> He is the way, the true guide of others. . . .
> He teaches the truth. . . .
> He holds a mirror before others,
> he makes them mindful and judicious. . . .
>
> He shines his light on the world
> he inquires into the region of the gods above,
> and into the region of the dead below. . . .
> (*Códice Matritense* fol. 118rx, cited in León-Portilla 1971:448)

As noted previously, Aztec religious thought turned on the belief that a fifth and final destruction of the world by the wrathful gods was imminent. The *tlamatinime* translated this popular fear of an impending apocalypse into questions of a more philosophical nature, the foremost of which concerned the tentativeness of the material world and human mortality in particular. For example, a late Aztec philosopher wrote the following lines of lament about the fifteenth-century king, Itzcóatl, who had glorified the Aztecs as the People of the Sun:

> You were celebrated, Oh Itzcóatl
> exquisite were the words you spoke
> but you are dead. . . .   (fol. 29v, cited
> in León-Portilla 1971:448)

Carrying this line of thought one step further, the Aztec wise men realized that *all* earthly things are transient and by their nature doomed for destruction:

> Hence, I weep,
> for you are weary,
> oh God.

Jade shatters,
the quetzal feather tears apart.
Oh God, you mock us.
Perhaps we really do not exist.
Perchance we are nothing to you?
(*Cantares Mexicanos,* fol. 12v, cited in León-Portilla
1971:448)

The logical consequence of the *tlamatinime's* concern about the impermanence of all things is summed up in the penultimate line of the preceding excerpt: *Perhaps we really do not exist;* perhaps life

   ... is just a dream ...
   And here no one speaks the truth....
   (*Cantares Mexicanos,* fol. 13r, cited in León-Portilla
   1971:450)

If life is transitory, or only a dream, the *tlamatinime* asked, how should
one live out one's days? One proffered answer was to live life to the fullest
during the brief time that remains:

   Here man lives on earth!
   Here there are lords, there is power,
   there is nobility....
   There is ardor, there is life, there is struggle,
   the search for a woman, the search for a man.
   (*Códice Florentine* bk. 6, fol. 44r, cited in León-Portilla
   1971:449)

But this doctrine of *carpe diem* appears to have been only a minority
opinion. Other *tlamatinime* held different views about *neltiliztli,* or truth that
is solidly established and "rooted" in the fundamental nature of things.
Most interesting is a theory that had a wide currency but that found its most
complete elaboration in the works of one Tecayehuatzin and his associates.
According to this school of thought, the only things in life that are real, the
only things that are "rooted," are "flower and song."
   The phrase "flower and song" appears often in the writings of the
tlamatinime; it is an example of Aztec *difrasismo,* whereby two words are con-
joined to convey one important idea.[2] The concept conveyed by "flower
and song" is art, in the broadest sense of the word, including poetry, symbol,
metaphor, and all that has meaningful beauty (see **Figure 7–4**). Using

---

[2]In a similar way, English speakers sometimes use the phrase "bread and butter" to refer
to subsistence generally. Apparently flowers had more than just a metaphorical significance
for the Aztecs. Covarrubias (1957:321) relates that at the time of conquest, "The Spaniards
were much impressed with the haughty manner of the Aztec nobility toward them, and wrote
with candor of the nobles' extreme cleanliness: They bathed often and held bouquets of flowers
to their noses whenever they had to approach a Spaniard."

FIGURE 7-4   Stone sculpture of Xochipilli, Aztec god of song, poetry, theater, love, dance, vegetation, and springtime. Some of the decorations on his throne represent flowers. Height, including throne, 1.15 meters. *(Photo courtesy Garcia Valades Editores, S. A.)*

"flower and song," the *tlamatini* Nezahuqlocóyotl explained one way out of the dilemma of transience and death:

> Finally, my heart understands it: I hear a song,
> I see a flower,
> Behold, they will not wither!
> (Ms. *Romances de los señores do la Nueve Espana,* fol. 19v,
> cited in León-Portilla 1966:35)

Elsewhere he continues,

> They will not end, my flowers,
> they will not cease, my songs. . . .
> Even when the flowers wither and grow yellow,
> they will be carried thither,
> to the interior of the house
> of the bird with the golden plumes.   *(Cantares Mexicanos,*
> fol. 13v, cited in León-Portilla 1966:36–37)

That is, art is everlasting; and even if the tangible embodiment of art should fade, its essence will, like the Gods to whom it is dedicated, last forever.[3]

---

[3]Jane H. Hill (1987) has demonstrated the pervasiveness of the metaphoric association between "flower" and poetry throughout the Uto-Aztecan language family, extending well north of the Rio Grande.

Discovering the origin and true nature of "flower and song" was so important an issue that the Nahuatl manuscript *Cantares Mexicanos* describes a meeting convened by Tecayehuatzin and attended by various *tlamatinime* at which the efficacy of "flower and song" was debated at length. The host of the gathering began asking whether "flower and song" are perhaps the only things that are genuinely real and lasting—that, in language of the *tlamatinime*, are "rooted." Ayocuin Cuitzpaltzin, Lord of Tecmachalco, answered first, claiming that art is simply the gift of the gods through which we humans, in our clumsy way, may find immortality:

> From the interior of heaven come
> the beautiful flowers, the beautiful songs.
> Our desire deforms them,
> our inventiveness mars them. . . .
> Must I depart like the flowers that perish?
> Will nothing of my fame remain here on the earth?
> At least my flowers, at least my songs. (*Cantares Mexicanos,*
> fol. 10r, cited in León-Portilla 1966:51–52)

The poet's reasoning here may be that inasmuch as genuine art comes from the gods, it will (like the gods) last forever. Even after the inevitable disintegration of the material art work with the passage of time, the *concept* that it once embodied is true and eternal. This, at least, seems to have been in the mind of a second speaker, Azuiauhtzin, who suggested that flower and song "are the form of invoking the supreme giver of life. The giver of life may perhaps become present by way of the world of symbol" (León-Portilla 1966:52). Just as one might take a gift of flowers when visiting a friend, the gift of sacred art may warm the gods' reception of mortals and thus give the makers of the art some prospect of immortality.[4]

Then another participant, Cuauhtencoztli, questioned whether "flower and song" have any worth at all, to which the host, Tecayehuatzin, replied that at least they have value in that they can alleviate sorrow and bring joy to one's life. (After all, the person who is genuinely engaged by art is oblivious both to the passage of time and to the troubles of the mundane world, a condition not unlike immortality itself.)

But a final speaker, Xayacámach, says that this line of reasoning is shallow, questioning whether "flower and song" are merely

> like hallucinating drugs, the best means of intoxicating the heart and making oneself forgetful of sadness here. When in the sacred gatherings the drugs are consumed, one sees marvelous visions, evanescent forms of different colors, all more real then reality itself. However, afterward this fantastic world van-

---

[4]The practice of giving art objects to the gods in return for favors had parallels in the earthly realm of Aztec society: Archaeological and ethnohistoric evidence reveals that it was fairly common for Aztecs to give craft items to those whom they asked for favors. (See Brumfiel 1987.)

ishes like a dream, leaves the man weary, and no longer exists.[5]   (León-Portilla 1966:53)

The meeting eventually closes on an ambiguous note. The host admits that the matter has not been resolved and that "his heart continues to be open to doubt," but all present will agree that, "if nothing else, 'flower and song' at least make possible our friendship" (León-Portilla 1966:53), presumably by providing a topic for stimulating discussions such as the one in which they have just participated.

Two themes may be discerned in this thoughtful debate on flower and song. First, and more superficially, some of art's secular functions are noted. Art can serve as a source of pleasure and provide a basis for friendship. But the second and far more serious use of art relates to the human soul. Art invokes the gods and insures the maker's immortality, no small accomplishment in a world whose imminent destruction was taken for granted both in Aztec popular thought and in the more rarified philosophies of the *tlamatinime*.[6]

The extensive analysis of all aspects of "flower and song" suggests just how important this idea was in the minds of the *tlamatinime*. Again and again they affirm the divine origin of flower and song:

> The Flowers sprout, they are fresh, they grow;
>   they open their blossoms, and from within emerge the
>   flowers of songs; among men
> You scatter them,
> You send them.
> You are the singer!   (*Cantares Mexicanos*, 35v, cited in León-Portilla 1963:77)

But the gods do not scatter their flowers among humans indiscriminately; instead, art's spiritual blessings come only to the enlightened few. Only people who learn to "converse with their own hearts" have any hope of bringing genuine "flower and song" into the world.

In essence, then, Aztec aesthetics is founded on a belief that true art comes from the gods and is manifest in the artist's mystical revelation of sacred truth. Through such revelation the artist transcends mortality and the transient world of the senses and partakes of the eternal. The Aztec sages believed that art is the only thing that is actually real, and as such

---

[5]This note of skepticism may reflect the speaker's belief that the philosophy of "flower and song" is less compelling than a competing ideal that saw military victory and blood sacrifice as the only means of propitiating the gods (cf. León-Portilla 1983).

[6]There is some irony in the fact that the Aztec's world *was* soon destroyed—not by an earthquake sent by the gods, but by the conquering Spanish; and this irony is heightened when one realizes that the essence of Aztec culture *did* survive this experience largely through art works such as architecture, the illustrated codices, stone sculpture, and so on.

it can protect humans from the inevitable destruction of our fragile and temporary world.

The application of this theory to actual Aztec art production is interesting. The *tlamatinime* presumably considered themselves to be on the road to spiritual enlightenment, and they believed that their poems embodied "flower and song." But as previously noted, the visual arts were created not by Aztec nobles, or even by Aztec commoners. Instead, most visual arts were created by craftsmen brought to Tenochtitlán from subjugated peoples. A few were Mixtecs, but most were Toltecs. Indeed, the Nahuatl word *toltécatl* meant "artist," and the highest form of artistry was isomorphic with Toltec production.[7]

This seeming paradox—that although art was viewed as the gods' blessing upon the Aztecs, in practice most visual art was produced by non-Aztecs—is resolved by recalling the high regard in which the Aztecs held Toltec culture. A memory of the elegance and sophistication of the long-fallen Toltec kingdom haunted the parvenu Aztecs. Therefore, they were willing to accept art being made by the illustrious Toltecs—especially since the Aztecs saw themselves as the spiritual heirs of the Toltec civilization and were, in any case, the undisputed masters of Toltec artists.

These views became even more credible in light of Aztec notions about artistic talent, which was thought to depend upon two factors. First, one must have been born on a propitious date (the day One Flower was good); and, second, one must possess the proper temperament to seek, through meditation, the spiritual enlightenment of a "deified heart." One codex described at length the characteristic qualities of artists:

The artist: discipline, abundant, multiple, restless.
The true artist, capable, practicing, skillful,
maintains dialogue with his heart, meets things with his
    mind.

The true artist draws out all from his heart;
works with delight; makes things with calm, with sagacity;
works like a true Toltec; composes his objects; works
    dexterously; invents;
arranges materials; adorns them; makes them adjust.

The carrion artist works at random; sneers at the people;
makes things opaque; brushes across the surface of the face
    of things;
works without care; defrauds people; is a thief. (*Códice Matritense
de la Real Academia* Vii, fols. 115v and 116r, cited in León-Portilla 1963:168)

---

[7]In some passages from the codices "flower and song" refers only to the art of poetry, which *was* composed by the *tlamatinime,* but in others they assert that visual arts such as painting, pottery, and metalsmithing also come from a "deified heart." See León-Portilla 1963:79, 103, 171–175.

The same manuscript goes on to specify the traits of the practitioners of various crafts. For example,

> The good painter is a toltec, an artist;
> he creates with red and black ink, with black water. . . .

> The good painter is wise,
> God is in his heart.
> He puts divinity into things;
> he converses with his own heart.

> He knows the colors, he applies them and shades them;
> he draws feet and faces,
> he puts in the shadows, he achieves perfection.
> He paints the colors of all the flowers,
> as if he were a Toltec.   (*Códice Matritense de la Real Academia,*
> fol. 117v, cited in León-Portilla 1963:172–173)

Thus the Aztecs maintained what León-Portilla calls an "aesthetic conception of the universe and life [for] 'art made things divine,' and only the divine was true" (León-Portilla 1963:182).

Conclusion

The elegance and coherence of Aztec aesthetics should not be seen in an ethnographic vacuum, and the nobility of their philosophical system requires as a postscript some mention of a component of Aztec culture that has not yet been discussed. In practice, Aztec society was one of the most brutal known to history. Not only was their empire created by bloody wars and political maneuvering, but after its boundaries were extended to the limit, the Aztecs continued their policy of extreme militarism, fired by a belief system that sought to stave off the final destruction of the earth by constantly asserting their dominance as The People of the Sun. The Aztecs glorified war *per se:*

> There is nothing like death in war,
> nothing like the flowery death
> so precious to Him who gives life:
> far off I see it: my heart yearns for it.
> (Cited in Coe 1962:168)

As this passage reveals, the term "flower" referred symbolically not only to art but also to warriors (Zantwijk 1957:168).

The "flowery wars" of the late Aztec Empire provided another means by which the Aztecs hoped to propitiate their deities and postpone the final destruction of the earth, namely through providing captives for human sacrifice. Earlier Mesoamerican societies had practiced ritual execution, but not to the degree, nor apparently with such fervor, as did the Aztecs (cf. León-Portilla 1983:10–23). Cortéz's chronicler, Díaz, reported what he saw in one city: "I remember that in the plaza . . . there were piles of human skulls so regularly arranged that one could count them, and I estimated them at more than a hundred thousand. I repeat again that there were more than a hundred thousand of them" (quoted in Farb 1978:190). The total number of humans ceremonially killed each year by the Aztecs was once believed to be about 20,000, but the current consensus is that the figure was probably larger, the highest estimate being a quarter of a million victims per year. In any case, there can be no doubt that Aztec society, for all its high-minded metaphysics and elegant aesthetic theories, also had a dark side which prompted the Aztecs to carry out, consistently and on an enormous scale, some of the most bloodthirsty policies ever devised by the human mind (see **Figure 7–5**).

The Aztec aesthetic tradition apparently did not survive the Spanish Conquest, although Zantwijk (1957:108–114) claims that traces of the Aztec

FIGURE 7–5 Stone sculpture of Coatlicue, Aztec goddess of the earth and death. She wears a necklace of human hearts and hands, and her skirt is made of serpents. 2.57 meters high. *(Photo courtesy Garcia Valades Editores, S. A.)*

world view still linger in some contemporary Nahuatl poetry. Records from 1569 indicate that native Mesoamericans were engaged in a wide range of crafts of mostly Spanish origin such as glove-making, saddle-making, and glass working (Gibson 1964:397–398). The most skilled artisans were still often Toltecs, and, perhaps due both to their comparatively good wages and also to their history of making goods in accord with their masters' wishes, they were adept at learning the new trades.

In the early 1960s, Peggy Golde (cf. Golde 1963; Golde and Kraemer 1973) carried out an interesting study of aesthetic values in an isolated village of contemporary descendants of the Aztecs. She found that although the aesthetic preferences of the 114 people she interviewed varied somewhat, two-thirds shared several aesthetic norms. When shown photographs of pottery, most preferred pieces that (in descending order of importance) reflected intensive work by the potter; whose surface had "clarity" (as judged by the fineness of surface, care of decoration, and meaningfulness of subject matter); and which depicted people of robust good health and endurance.

But 500 years ago, the Aztec *tlamatinime* believed that art was divine in origin, that it was the only lasting true reality; and that art (along with the blood of human sacrifice) provided the only means of saving an otherwise doomed world. The Aztecs placed art on a high pedestal indeed.

8

AESTHETICS
IN EARLY INDIA
Rasa and the Theory
of Transcendental Enjoyment

Two birds, deepest of friends,
live on the same tree.
One eats the sweet fruit.
The other, without eating, watches.
(Abhinavagupta, 10th century A.D.)

The Indus River valley occupies a special place in Western thought. In the first place, it was one of the few locations where our distant human ancestors, who had spent millions of years living in small bands as nomadic foragers, discovered agriculture. This innovation eventually had sweeping consequences: People exchanged their earlier transient existence for village life based on farming; populations grew dramatically in size; and, one thing leading to another, the Indus River valley eventually saw the rise of a civilization whose size and complexity were unprecedented in the Indian subcontinent. By 2000 B.C., the cities of Harappa and Mohenjo-Daro had such luxuries as wide, well-drained streets lined with spacious, two-storied houses. Elsewhere the emperors of the Indus Valley Civilization ruled an extensive and sophisticated state from grand palaces.

But there is a second reason for the perennial Western fascination with Indian civilization: India probably had trade links with the civilizations that had also sprung up in Mesopotamia, and as such it may be thought of as a "first cousin" to Western culture: Not only are the populations of India and Europe closely related genetically, but several important languages of the Indian subcontinent such as Sanskrit and Hindi are members of the far-flung Indo-European language family, which also includes most European languages.

But for all their kinship, India and the West remain alien to each other in many respects. The Westerner may be astounded at the aesthetic sophistication of Indian sculpture, such as the bronze Shiva shown in **Figure 8–1**, a masterpiece of craftsmanship and elegant grace. But although the beauty of such metalwork dazzles the Western eye, traditional India did not consider

FIGURE 8–1   Shiva Nataraja, the Dancing Lord. Bronze sculpture, 34 1/4″ high, made in Tamilnadu, South India, in the thirteenth century.   *(The Nelson-Atkins Museum of Art, Kansas City, Missouri [Nelson Fund].)*

sculpture (or, for that matter, painting) to be a major "art." Dramatic poetry and music—those were the finest of arts in the minds of Indian theorists.

Or, to note another seeming incongruity, the Westerner quickly learns that almost all Indian art uses religious subject matter—only to be confronted by Indian sculpture and literature that are blatantly erotic (see Figure 14–4).

How can these apparent anomalies be explained? Certainly not by relegating them to the status of "errors" and assuming that Indian artists were unaware of what they were doing. To the contrary, few of the world's artistic traditions have been as carefully scrutinized by native aestheticians as those of India. When Indian art surprises us, it is because of our ignorance of the aesthetic system that has informed Indian art for nearly 2,000 years.

The belief that sculpture and painting are, at best, secondary in importance, far outranked by drama and music, makes sense when one accepts the Indian belief that art should have a dimension of time. A painting or sculpture freezes the action of its subject in a single instant whereas drama unfolds an elaborate narrative; and Indian aestheticians believe that this time dimension makes drama intrinsically superior to painting and sculpture.

An explanation of the presence of erotic subjects in otherwise sacred art works is more complicated. To understand its rationale, we must recreate the historic, artistic, and philosophical context that produced the theory of *rasa,* a concept that distinguishes Indian aesthetic theory from all other philosophies of art.

Background: Indian History, Art, and Aesthetic Writing

The empires of the early Indus Valley Civilization fell into disarray by about 1500 B.C., and although successive events in Indian history are complicated, they generally follow a pulsating pattern whereby periods of unification alternated with periods of political breakdown, often coinciding with invasions from the west or north. Our own primary interest lies in the classical and medieval periods of Indian history, spanning the third to thirteenth centuries A.D., which saw the maturation of a distinctively Indian aesthetic system, with the most exciting developments taking place in the short span of the ninth through the eleventh centuries.

The dominant religion of India during the period in question was Hinduism, although Buddhism and several other religious traditions also had some influence on the aesthetic thought of the time. The charter for Hinduism is found in the four Vedas, or collections of ancient Sanskrit sacred writing that record hymns, prayers, and descriptions of Hindu ritual. The last section, called the Upanishads, contains the mystical and speculative core of Hinduism. The Upanishads claim that ultimate reality takes the form of Brahman, which is sometimes personified as a god but which more accurately is the Absolute—pure consciousness and pure bliss, permanent and immutable.

The world of the senses, being neither perfect nor immutable, is deemed to be unreal, and the proper goal of Hindu life is transcendence of the material world. This may be accomplished through ritual, self-control, and meditation. It is a striving that began in each person's past life and that will continue in future incarnations until an ultimate merging with Brahman occurs.

Speculative thought in India was the domain of a small caste of priests, called brahmins (see **Figure 8–2**). Similarly, art production was confined to sub-castes of professional artists, whose high level of technical expertise reflects their having received artistic training from an early age. Religion provided the subject matter for most Indian art, much of which was narrative in nature. If Indian intellectuals relegated painting and sculpture to positions of minimal importance, they held dramatic poetry, along with architecture and music, in high regard.

FIGURE 8–2 Brahmin at worship, Madras, India. *(Courtesy, Field Museum of Natural History, Chicago, neg. no. 86507.)*

During the classical and medieval periods, numerous intellectuals of the brahmin caste focused their attention explicitly on art. They asked, Is art a part of the Absolute (or Brahman) or is it a component of the mundane, illusory world of the senses? And in either case, What are the varieties of art, and how can art have such a strong affect on human consciousness? The brahmins often wrote down their speculations, and although we have lost most of the original documents and others remain in only fragmentary form, scholars have reconstructed many early theories, sometimes by using the commentaries of later brahmin writers.

Of the dozen or so sources of Indian aesthetics, two writers deserve particular mention. The oldest document in the Indian aesthetic tradition is the *Nāṭyaśāstra,* which dates from about the third century A.D. and is ascribed to "Bharata," a name that, like the ancient Greek "Homer," probably stands for several anonymous authors. Bharata was chiefly concerned with practical problems of drama, such as instructing writers, stage managers, and actors on the proper constituents of plays and of dramatic presentation generally. But Bharata also addressed some theoretical points. In one important passage, he says, "Without *rasa* no dramatic device is of any importance," (quoted in Masson and Patwardhan 1970:1), and this remark opened a line of inquiry that was the primary concern of Indian aestheticians for a thousand years.

If Bharata represents the beginning of Indian aesthetic writing, the tenth century work of Abhinavagupta (often simply called Abhinava) was the high point of the tradition. Like many later Indian aestheticians, he was born in Kashmir and was influenced by Tantricism (see below). Although Abhinavagupta absorbed and synthesized earlier aesthetic writings, he gave more attention to the philosophical and religious dimension of art than did any other Indian writer. His two surviving works are *Abhinava bhāratī,* a commentary on the ideas found in Bharata's classic text and *Dhvanyālokalocana* (or simply, the *Locana*), a commentary on a work by Ānandavardhana (which is itself another commentary on Bharata's writings). Both works are extremely difficult, so complex in reasoning, so elliptical in style, and so fragmentary in their current state of preservation that competent Sanskrit scholars often disagree significantly on the meaning of crucial passages.[1]

There were few additions to the Indian philosophy of art after Abhinavagupta's time, but the ancient writings are still studied in India. This may be a testament to the richness of the writers' speculations, for there is no doubt that Bharata, Abhinavagupta, and others produced an aesthetic theory as profound and complex as can be found in any human culture.

---

[1]Compare, for example, Masson and Patwardhan (1969:62–77) versus Gnoli (1968). Masson and Patwardhan (1969:1n) provide an excellent bibliography of general and specialized works on Indian aesthetics. A more recent work, Dhayagude 1981, although intended to systematically compare Western and Indian aesthetics, also provides a good overview of the major primary Sanskrit sources.

Art as the "Fifth Veda"

Early in the ancient *Nāṭyaśāstra,* Bharata recounts the story of the origin of art. In this tale, Brahman is the anthropomorphic leader of many lesser gods who come asking him for something to amuse themselves with besides the purely religious writings found in the four Vedas. Brahman says,

> Since these [original] Vedas cannot be heard by women, by Śudras and other classes, I will create a fifth Veda, different from these, that will be for *all* people. I will create a fifth Veda called "drama" out of past stories, that will lead to righteousness, to material gain, to fame, with good advice and full of wise sayings. It will display the deeds of all people in the world to come. (Masson and Patwardhan 1970, vol. 1:18–19)

Thus at the dawn of the classical period, Bharata identified two distinct reasons for art's existence: Art gives pleasure to mortals, and at the same time it shows them how to better themselves. In saying this, Bharata apparently gave voice to a deeply held and enduring belief within Hindu Indian thought because the aesthetic principles of pleasure and edification were still accepted by brahmin writers who lived a thousand years after Bharata's day. Although most believed that the more important of the two is art's capacity to engage a person's emotions, it is easier to explain Indian aesthetics by starting with the other rationale for art—namely, that it provides an excellent means of instruction.

Art as Instruction

As noted previously, the Vedas portray humans as existing in greater or lesser states of imperfection. We mortals are inherently ignorant and often waste our lives on sensuality and lust. The arts, however, provide one means of liberating us from this sorry condition and of putting our passions to good use. Just as the Vedas instruct devotees regarding the path to unification with the Absolute, the arts also lead to the moral betterment of those who experience them, and this is the first axiom of classical Indian aesthetics. But here we must be clear about what the Vedas consider to be "moral betterment." That phrase may suggest a purely spiritual development to most Westerners, but from a Hindu perspective, moral betterment implies the successful pursuit of the *puruṣārthas,* or the four proper goals of life, which include not only righteousness and spiritual emancipation but also the acquisition of material prosperity and the enjoyment of refined, worldly pleasures. So when Indian writers say that art exists to help a person progress along the path to Brahman, they are thinking of individual improvement in what Westerners would consider to be both the sacred *and* the secular dimensions of life.

Many centuries after Bharata told the story of Brahman creating the arts for (among other things) the edification of lesser gods and mortals, Abhinavagupta was still convinced that an important value of art lies in its capacity to instruct "in the ways of the world and in the means leading to the [four] goals of life" (quoted in Masson and Patwardhan 1969:55). But again, "instruction" must be understood in its Vedic context. Abhinavagupta did not condone didactic art that preached an obvious sermon or told a narrowly cautionary tale. Immediately after his claim that art should teach people how to attain the four goals of life, Abhinavagupta asks, "Question: does the drama instruct the way a teacher (or an elderly person) does? (Answer:). No. Rather it causes one's wisdom to grow" (ibid.).[2]

A later writer, Mammaṭ, elaborates on art's ability to teach. Art instructs, he says, "in the delicate, subtle manner of a beloved wife, not in the high hortatory tone of a master nor in the indifferent 'take it or leave it' manner of an acquaintance" (paraphrased in Dhayagude 1981:167). And not only is instruction via art more subtle than other forms of learning, but also the recipient of instruction is no ordinary student. Abhinavagupta says, "Even a stupid man can learn [philosophy] from the teachings of his professor. But poetry is only given to the person who has the imaginative genius. . . . and that only once in a while" (Masson and Patwardhan 1969:19).

Art's special instructional efficacy becomes more understandable when we recall Vedic metaphysics. If Brahman is the only genuine reality, then the individual self, still striving to attain Brahman, obviously is less than real. But, on the other hand, the creators of Hindu philosophy realized that it is counterintuitive to believe that the phenomenal world and human consciousness are totally unreal. One does, after all, experience the world and one's self. The solution lies in the concept of *māyā,* which asserts that the world of the senses is neither real nor unreal, but that it *is* empirically true.[3]

For the more theoretical Indian writers, art is also *māyā.* The world portrayed in art does not have the same reality as the subject matter it portrays; but even the most empirically oriented observer must admit that it does have some sort of reality because art can prompt a powerful emotional

---

[2]It is common practice for modern translators of Sanskrit to add words, enclosed in parentheses, that they believe to be likely substitutes for those now missing from the original documents. I have followed the same convention in this chapter, although I have omitted the Sanskrit words that are left in texts (in parenthesis) by some translators. I have used brackets in the usual way, to add a clarifying word or two in direct quotations that otherwise would not make sense outside their original context.

[3]To explain the apparent contradiction between the sensible world seeming to be simultaneously real and unreal, "Sankara, the great teacher of Advaita Vedānta, uses the analogy of a rope which appears to be a snake because of darkness or defective sight. Here the snake is pure illusion since it has no correspondence with the reality of the rope. Still the apprehension of the snake is real enough for it produces fear which is an undeniable empirical fact" (Dhayagude 1981:11).

response in the percipient. Because of this, art can instruct in a way that is different from, and superior to, the education that one might receive through formal channels. As Masson and Patwardhan (1969:5) put it, "Preachers inform us; only poets invite us to experience."

The Transcendental Pleasure of Art

Abhinavagupta's writings stand at the pinnacle of Indian aesthetic thought. The breadth of his learning and the depth of his analysis conjure up a man who possessed the combined talents of Plato and Aristotle. But before we form an image of him as a hardworking academic thinker, engrossed in purely cerebral activities, we should consider the following description of Abhinavagupta. It is the only extant account of him, but it apparently was written by a person who actually saw Abhinava at work.

> He sits in the middle of a garden of grapes, inside a pavilion made of crystal and filled with beautiful paintings. The room smells wonderful because of flower garlands, incense-sticks and (oil-) lamps. Its walls are smeared with sandal-paste and other such things. The room is constantly resounding with musical instruments, with songs and with dancing. There are crowds of women Yogins and realized beings with magic powers. It is equipped with a golden seat from which pearls are hanging. It has a soft awning stretched over it (as a canopy). Abhinava is attended by all his numerous students, with Kṣemarāja at their head, who are writing down everything he says. To his side stand two women, partners in Tantric rites, who hold in one hand a jug of wine and a box full of betel rolls, and in the other hand a lotus and a citron. Abhinava has his eyes trembling in ecstasy.   (Masson and Patwardhan 1969:38–39)

The account goes on to describe a mark of ashes on Abhinavagupta's forehead, a bead dangling from one ear, and flower garlands hanging about his neck. Lastly, "One hand is held on his knee holding a rosary with his fingers clearly making the sign that signifies his knowledge of the highest Śiva. He plays on his resonating lute with the tips of the quivering fingers of his lotus-like left hand" (Masson and Patwardhan 1969:39).

So much for the picture of Abhinavagupta as a dusty old pedant who thought art should be used principally for instruction. It has been said that if one side of Hinduism is ascetic and world-denying, its other side is sensual and resolutely life-affirming (cf. Organ 1975). The latter impulse is especially evident in the sect known as Tantricism, which was present in both Hindu and Buddhist India. Tantricism emphasized identification with the deity through meditation and also through rituals which included the religiously sanctioned eating of (otherwise forbidden) meat, the drinking of wine, and engaging in ritualized sexual intercourse. The above description portrays Abhinavagupta as a central participant in Tantric ritual.

FIGURE 8-3   The Mother Goddess as a Yogini. Carved in Greenstone, about 900 A.D.; 52 1/2" high. *(The Nelson-Atkins Museum of Art, Kansas City, Missouri [Nelson Fund].)*

Although the major Indian writers recognized that art can teach a person how to attain the four goals of life, they consistently placed greater stress upon art giving pleasure that verges upon transcendental ecstasy, and this belief is the second axiom of Indian aesthetics.

Rasa Theory

The Sanskrit word for the emotional satisfaction that one experiences via art is *rasa,* and the history of Indian aesthetics is largely a chronicle of speculation about the nature of *rasa.* From the beginning of Indian aesthetics (recall Bharata's claim that "without *rasa* no dramatic device is of any importance") through Abhinavagupta (whose *Locana* says, "*rasa* alone is the soul of poetry" [see Masson and Patwardhan 1969:81]), Indian aestheticians were unanimous in placing *rasa* at the center of their theories.

Rasa has more than one meaning. Most superficially, the word may be translated as "taste," "flavor," or "relish." Bharata used an extended analogy with food to convey his conception of *rasa.* In part he said,

Relish is produced from the combination of various spices, herbs and other materials. . . . Just as people enjoy relish while partaking of food made relishable by various ingredients, and experience happiness, etc., even so enlightened spectators relish the permanent feelings made relishable by the operation of the various elements accompanied with verbal, physical and emotional gesticulation, and experience happiness. (Dhayagude 1981:179)

Indian writers select their metaphors with care, and Bharata's likening of *rasa* to the delight that spicy food can produce is no exception. A distinctly piquant flavor is definitive of the spice that in English is called "curry powder"; and this taste is the *essence* of the spice and of the dish the spice is used in. The phenomenal experience of the curry powder is qualitatively different from the cumin, turmeric, ginger, and so on, that blend together to produce curry powder. Although curry is a substance, its significance, indeed its essence, lies in its distinctive taste.

The situation with art is similar.[4] Art does have an existence in the world of the senses—living actors on actual stages make audible utterances. But these are only a secondary feature of art. Art's fundamental and essential existence is found not on this empirical level but in the distinctive aesthetic reaction that the play prompts within the properly attuned audience member. So a deeper and more important meaning of *rasa* refers to the state a person is in when totally engaged by a work of art.

The analogy of *rasa* with food has additional dimensions. Just as curry powder is a compound of several individual spices, the total emotional response of a person who perceives art may be—indeed, should be—a combination of several elemental emotions. *Rasa* theorists specified that of the eight (or, for some writers, nine) recognized emotions (see p. 168), a successful poem should usually be dominated by only one, the others being relegated to secondary roles that complement the pervading mood of the poem.

Finally, like a food's flavor, *rasa* is characterized by a feeling of indivisible immediacy, an instantaneous experience of oneness between the audience and the art work, free of all distractions. The engrossed audience member cannot draw a boundary between where the self ends and where the aesthetic response begins any more than the eater can distinguish between the tongue and the taste upon it.

Thus, *rasa* means not only *taste* but also the sensuous pleasure that the aesthetically attuned individual may experience as a result of art—the thrill of excitement or, at the least, the soothing of grief, that can come about when a person is immersed in an art work.

But the deepest of the Indian theorists go beyond the sensuous level of *rasa*, reminding us that art may be gratifying not just to the senses but to

---

[4]The sense of wonder or surprise evoked by art is called *camatkāra*, a word coined, perhaps, for its onomatopoeic resemblance to the sound a person's tongue makes when something spicy is eaten (cf. Gnoli 1968:xlv).

the spirit as well; and this line of reasoning returns us to the previously mentioned belief that art may serve as a means of instruction and spiritual liberation. To quote Abhinavagupta, "delight (can be said to be) the cause of moral instruction. Imaginative experience consists in delight; delight is (the essential part of) drama, and drama is the only Veda" (Masson and Patwardhan 1970, vol. 2:22). Thus, he concludes, "delight is the final and major result [of art]" (Masson and Patwardhan 1969:55).

   The Indian view is that anything that is morally uplifting or leads to a more prosperous life must necessarily give pleasure; and conversely, nothing could be enjoyable if it despoils one's character. Goodness and happiness are inseparably linked in Vedic thought. Moral betterment is not just a means to a higher plane of consciousness in some future incarnation. Since moral improvement brings one closer to the pure bliss of Brahman, the experience itself is deeply satisfying. In another passage Abhinava says, "What we call bliss is nothing but a full illumination of one's own being, accompanied by a form of cogitation which pervades all one's own nature, one's own Self" (Gnoli 1968:xlii). Although art is not the only path to enlightenment (meditation and ritual are alternative means), it plays an extremely important role in Indian thought because it brings one closer to Brahman, the Great Enjoyer, and his *Ras Lila,* the Play of the Universe (cf. Raffé 1952:105fn).

The Source of Art's Power

How does art accomplish this feat? *Rasa* theorists debated this question for centuries. All concur that *conscious* use of art to obtain pleasure and moral betterment should not be necessary; poetry should be intuitively enjoyed, not laboriously studied (Masson and Patwardhan 1970, vol. 1:20). Nor should art explicitly exhort audience members to elevate their minds or spirits.[5]

   One contribution to art's efficacy comes from its subject matter. Classical and medieval Indian drama was concerned with the play of heroic supernaturals, and one theory of *rasa* held that in watching divine characters perform their roles, the sympathetic viewer would identify with the enlightened actions of the gods and would be raised to a higher level of spiritual

---

[5]Dhayagude observes that although there might seem to be a contradiction between art's affective function, as manifest in the doctrine of *rasa* and art's anagogic, or instructional, function, the contradiction "disappears if we bear in mind that the instruction which poetry gives is inseparable from the delightful experience which it occasions. If there is no *rasa* there is no poetry; if there is *rasa* but no instruction, one need not complain; if there is *rasa* and instruction, one need not quarrel. But in poetry instruction must not be superadded; it must accrue as part of aesthetic experience; it must be inseparable from the enjoyment of *rasa*" (Dhayagude 1981:169).

development. Again, however, the relationship between art and its moral lesson should not be explicit; one should not come away from a dramatic performance with a resolution to emulate the holiness of the characters in the play. Instead, *rasa* should arise "from the apprehension of the Absolute . . . , characterized by complete identity between the subject [i.e., the viewer] and the [*rasa*-inspiring] object. In it the mind contemplates itself in its freedom and as such is infinite and attaining the stage of the Absolute" (Pandy 1952:485). Moved by art, the sympathetic audience member forgets the personal, idiosyncratic self and merges with the cosmic Self that is Brahman.[6]

Other Indian writers attributed art's power to its stylistic conventions rather than its subject matter. Poetry, they said, was defined by its hyper-eloquent language, dramatic figures of speech, and various other embellishments. Certainly, they argued, art does not gain power through its imperfect imitation of specific individuals and actions. Instead, the truths found in art are generalized and relevant to all times and places. Poetry, by its nature, does not portray its subject matter in particularities; instead, its stylistic conventions allow it to convey universal principles. The superficial details of the dramatic action should not distract the "percipient" (the person who perceives the art work). Not *this* actor with *these* mortal idiosyncrasies, but rather the eternal, omnipresent god that the actor represents.

As with many other issues, Abhinavagupta went further than anyone else in analyzing the source of *rasa's* power. Because every mortal has lived a multitude of previous lives since Brahman first set the universe in motion, and since we have experienced all possible emotions during our past existences, Abhinava argued that we all come into our present lives with an instinctive capacity to feel all eight of the possible emotions—happiness, pride, zest (or laughter), sorrow, anger, disgust, fear and wonder (cf. Dhayagude 1981:182). So when a person clears the mind of all distractions and becomes totally immersed in an art work, these eight inborn emotions are transformed into the higher affective responses that we associate with art, some examples of this being that one's innate capacity to feel delight is the basis of erotic art, laughter is elevated by art to become comedy, sorrow is transmuted into pathos, and anger is the basis of furious art.

There is a pervasive tendency in Indian philosophy to typologize, enumerate, and systematize. Writers long before Abhinava's time had equated the eight emotions with eight *rasas,* but Abhinava added a ninth, *śānta,* the artistic manifestation of tranquility. Furthermore, although all nine types

---

[6]Indian aestheticians believed that the audience member's being engrossed in an art work is qualitatively equivalent to the total immersion of the artist in his or her work. The *Brahmā Sutra* says, "The arrow-maker perceives nothing beyond his work when he is buried in it; but he has nevertheless consciousness and control over his body" (cited in Coomaraswamy 1924:21).

FIGURE 8-4   Shiva Vishapaharana. Bronze with green patina, dating from the ninth or tenth century; 19 1/4" high.   *(The Nelson-Atkins Museum of Art, Kansas City, Missouri [Nelson Fund].)*

of *rasa* are highly desirable, he considered some to be more elevated, de-individualized, and universal than others. For example, *kama,* the *rasa* of the erotic, has somewhat less value than *śānta*—not because of prudishness but because the transcendence that occurs via sensuality is still highly dependent upon the senses, whereas the meditative experience of tranquility found in *śānta* has no such ties to the material world and can bring one directly to Brahman (cf. Munro 1965:76).

Whether art's power is thought to come from its portrayal of divine subject matter, from its ability to use stylistic devices to transcend the particular and transient and to express the universal and everlasting, or from its capacity to transform the emotional history of past lives into the higher spiritual responses that may pave the way to the pure bliss of the Absolute, the aesthetic writers of classical and medieval India clearly respected art's significance in human life. Like the other four Vedas, the "fifth Veda" of art provides a means of escaping the limitations of our mortality and ascending to a higher plane of existence.

Implications of *Rasa* Theory

Having examined the core of the theory, we can complete our discussion of *rasa* by looking at it in the broader context of medieval Indian thought and art.

First, although being in a state of *rasa* has a close kinship with the experience of religious meditation, Indian aestheticians distinguished clearly between the two. The rare mortal who attains complete spiritual emancipation is completely removed from the phenomenal world (Dhayagude 1981:23). By contrast, although *rasa* can free the *rasika* (susceptible person) from the passions and petty distractions that life usually holds, the art work itself continues to link the *rasika* to the world of the senses; even *śānta* must be prompted by some sensible work of art. As Pandy puts it, *rasa* "is different from the mystic experience of the brahmin because it is a limited experience, though without the consciousness of limitation at the time it takes place" (Pandy 1952:478). (By contrast, the bliss of the lover differs from the bliss of the *rasika* in that its fulfillment requires reciprocal feelings from the loved one.)

On a less ethereal level, we do not know how much the theory of *rasa* influenced the individuals who actually produced Indian art (cf. Vatsyayan 1968:103; Organ 1975:12; Saraswati 1969:89). *Rasa*-theorists agreed, however, that artists—especially poets—have great potential power. After all, their creations can alter the course of a person's practical and spiritual life. In the *Dhvanyāloka,* another major record of Indian aesthetics, Ānandavardhana says, "In the shoreless world of poetry, the poet is the unique creator. Everything becomes transformed into the way he envisions it" (trans. in Masson and Patwardhan 1969:12).

However, it is not a personal, subjective vision that makes the artist a serious force in the world; nor is the percipient's private and distinctive reaction to art particularly important. An art work's power comes from its objectively manifesting one of the eight (or nine) *rasas,* and Indian aestheticians relegate an individual's idiosyncratic, subjective response to art to a position of minimal importance. Artist and audience member alike tap the powerful energy of art only insofar as they engage the emotions that are systematized in the theory of *rasa.*

The arts of the poet and dramatist provide most of the examples used by *rasa*-theorists, although some writers occasionally refer to other media, including the other Indian "fine" arts, music and architecture. In Pandy's words, for example, "Music idealizes the sensible. It represents in tone, not the material extension, but only the movement and quivering of the inner parts of the material body. . . . Music is beautiful because in it the Absolute shines through the pleasant sound" (Pandy 1952:484–485). Likewise, architecture "represents heaven on earth and therefore arouses wonder . . . and leads to the aesthetic experience" (ibid.:486). Music and architecture, like drama, provide an avenue whereby one's self is transcended; and, in medieval Indian thought, such transcendence is the definitive and invaluable purpose of art.

Conclusion

We cannot hope to totally reconstruct an aesthetic system whose development ended nearly a thousand years ago, so several interesting questions remain unanswered. Written records and oral traditions combine to reveal an extensive aesthetic of drama and, to a lesser extent, music and architecture; but what assumptions, explicit or covert, provided a foundation for such arts as painting and sculpture, body decoration, and folk dancing? And although we must be grateful for our knowledge of the aesthetic speculations of brahmin intellectuals, one wonders to what extent the populous at large knew about—much less, agreed with—these rarified ideas.

But despite such gaps in our knowledge, the aesthetic system that does remain from classical and medieval India is remarkable for its internal consistency, complexity, and depth. *Rasa* theory begins with an important empirical fact, one that all of us have probably experienced at some time: Art can sweep us away, transporting our spirits from the tedious cares and anxieties that besiege our daily lives. Momentarily unconcerned about our petty, unfulfilled desires, we cease wondering who we are, what we want,

FIGURE 8-5   Shiva and Parvati on the Bull Nandi, attended by musicians and dancers. Buff sandstone, 18″ high; 973 A.D.   *(The Nelson-Atkins Museum of Art, Kansas City, Missouri [Nelson Fund].)*

and how we can get it. And in this moment of suspended self, we experience a focused intensity, a merging with not just the art work but the harmony of all creation. The Indian writers knew that although the art experience begins with the senses, it provides a means whereby we can transcend the sensory world around us and escape to a state of superior pleasure, practical betterment, and, ultimately, spiritual bliss.

9

JAPANESE AESTHETICS
An Exultation
of Beauty and Bliss

Art is an inspiration; life a fact. (Masaharu Anesaki 1933)

Contemporary Japan may bring to the Western mind a country of urban bustle and industrial growth, but a moment's reflection reminds one of another Japan, a land where beauty is cultivated and art thrives. This seeming contradiction cannot be attributed to historical succession, with the delicate aesthetic sensibilities of the past being bowled over and replaced by a twentieth-century ethos of commercialism. As the following poem shows, a thousand years ago Fujiwara no Kintō juxtaposed a crass vessel of trade, a sailing ship, with the natural beauty of morning mist in a scenic bay to convey a poignant feeling of melancholic loss.

> Dimly, dimly
> The day breaks at Akashi Bay;
> And in the morning mist
> My heart follows a vanishing ship
> As it goes behind an island.
> (Fujiwara no Kintō (966–1041))

As the poem suggests, Japan has a long history of simultaneously cultivating art and commerce. Indeed, few societies have been as successful as Japan at maintaining a fundamentally aesthetic sensibility throughout a long history of political, social, and religious upheaval and change. Fortunately for us, Japan also has an enduring tradition of literacy, scholarship, and aesthetic self-awareness. This allows us to uncover the primary philosophical and religious principles that have produced a society so pervaded by art that in the considered opinion of one Western scholar, aesthetics constitutes "the very essence of Japanese life".[1]

Background: Japanese History and Art

The wealth of available information about Japanese aesthetics and the technical sophistication of Japanese art make Japan a particularly interesting subject of study. But this same richness can also overwhelm the non-specialist. In the following paragraphs, I give only enough information about Japanese history and art to provide a context for our main concern, Japanese aesthetics.

For thousands of years, the residents of the Japanese archipelago lived as nomadic hunter-gatherers. A tribal stage followed, during which the Japanese acquired from the Asian mainland the skills of wet rice cultivation, pottery, metallurgy, and, in the sixth century A.D., writing. Finally there emerged a society dominated by a few large clans and small kingdoms, each led by a powerful priest-chief. Political unity was established in the seventh century, and the stability of the Imperial Era lasted until nearly the thirteenth century. This was followed by a chaotic Medieval Period of nearly four hundred years (1192–1568), during which provincial lords and their *samurai* retainers engaged in constant civil war. The strict rulers of the Tokugawa Period (1568–1867) reestablished law and order, but in 1867, the repressive and xenophobic policies of the Tokugawa shoguns gave way to the influence of Western powers and the era of modern Japan began.

The following account focuses on the art and aesthetics of the Imperial, Medieval, and Tokugawa periods. Except for the oral tradition of Shintoism, scholars know little of Japanese culture before 600, and the primary aesthetic developments since 1867 have resulted largely from Western-style industrialism and trade.[2]

Japanese visual artists have worked in painting, watercolor, printmaking, sculpture, pottery, textiles, and architecture—in fact, they have exploited all the media used by Western artists. But the Japanese have also used other visual media, such as calligraphy and flower arrangement, that have been only little developed in the West. Still other activities in Japan, such as sword-making and the tea ceremony, have a distinctly aesthetic dimension that has no counterpart in the West.

---

[1]"So important is the aesthetic in Japanese culture that it has been accepted by many students of Japan as the outstanding positive characteristic of Japanese culture as a whole. . . . In comparison with other cultures, the aesthetic has been considered to be the essentially unique expression of spirituality in Japan, as is ethics in China, religion in India, and, possibly, reason in the West" (Moore 1967:196).

[2]Ueda (1967:viii) remarks, for example, that "the history of traditional Japanese aesthetics ends in the mid-nineteenth century."

As in the visual arts, the history of Japanese literature reveals a complex interplay between mainland and indigenous forces, a process that ultimately produced art forms of a distinctively Japanese character. For example, although writing came initially from China, by the tenth century the calligraphic characters used in Japanese writing had evolved into forms that were distinctly different from those found in China. Chinese remained the language for state documents during the Imperial Era, so courtly Japanese women, deemed to be inferior by traditional Confucian dogma, were not taught Chinese, although they did commonly learn to write Japanese. It was predictable, therefore, that when some women began writing stories of their own imaginative creation, they set them down in Japanese; and, free of the strict conventions that applied to writing in Chinese, they invented a unique tradition of Japanese fiction writing. Indeed, because of these writers' concern with their characters' private lives and psychological states, books such as *The Tale of Genji* and *The Pillow Book* may reasonably be regarded as the world's first true novels. Similarly, Japanese poetry and drama, though influenced by mainland cultures, exhibit characteristically Japanese qualities.

Japanese Speculative Thought

All cultures have their speculative thinkers and possess subtle systems of abstract philosophy. Some Westerners facilely assume that religion is the primary vehicle of such thought in small-scale societies, whereas secular philosophy largely supplants religion in complex societies. Japan, however, does not follow this pattern. As the following pages prove, although Japan is rich in religious thought,[3] formal philosophy has never been well developed in Japan, as Japanese writers themselves have recognized.[4] Thus Japanese speculative thought, like Japanese art, often substitutes insinuation and suggestion for explicit, concrete propositions. But this inexplicitness

---

[3]Religion remains a potent force. A survey of religious affiliation in Japan in 1970 (Hori et al. 1972) revealed the presence of 165 different Shinto sects and subsects (with about 70 million adherents), 162 Buddhist sects (81 million adherents), and about three-quarters of a million Christians. That the total number of "adherents" is more than 50 percent higher than the population of Japan does not reflect a methodological error but rather reveals that many individuals actively subscribe to more than one doctrine. Furthermore, these figures fail to note that many Japanese also accept the ethical and political principles of Confucianism.

[4]For example, Ienaga (1979:90) says, "there is no denying the poverty of Japanese output in the field of theoretical speculation as compared with the excellence of Japanese achievements in the fields of literature and art." Similarly, Hajime Nakamura has observed that although the Japanese language has always had "a rich vocabulary of words denoting aesthetic and emotional states of mind, words denoting intellectual, inferential processes of active thought are notably lacking. . . . It is extremely difficult to express abstract concepts solely in words of the original Japanese" (1967:182; see also Izutsu and Izutsu 1981).

should not be confused with indifference. As we shall see, Japanese religions contain profound concepts that are applicable to many domains of culture—including art.

Shintoism's Seminal Influences on Japan

Shintoism, Buddhism, and Confucianism form the triumvirate of belief systems in traditional Japan, but only Shintoism is indigenously Japanese, the other two having been imported from the Asian mainland in the sixth century. Unfortunately, we have an incomplete understanding of early Shintoism because Japan had no system of writing before the sixth century, and written accounts of Shintoism after the sixth century may reflect Buddhist and Confucianist influence. But by combining early historic writings with the oral traditions passed down to contemporary Shinto priests, scholars have constructed a detailed picture of traditional Shinto belief.[5]

Shintoism is concerned primarily with Kami, or spirits, that are "invisible to the human eye in our normal state of consciousness [but that are] capable of exerting an influence on our visible universe, and to which worship should be offered" (Herbert 1967:25). The Kami can have good, bad, or ambiguous natures; and although some Kami are more powerful than others, none are omnipotent or omniscient. Shintoists recognize many Kami, with new ones occasionally being added to the pantheon as others fade into obscurity. Shintoism has little to say about human ethics, nor does it make many pronouncements about one's morality or fate after death. Instead, it focuses on the rites at shrines where the more important Kami reside.

Although such a religion might seem just a fabric of what Ienaga (1979:18) calls "magical ceremonies," devoid of philosophical insight, Herbert's (1967) interviews with members of the upper echelons of the Shinto priesthood revealed that a Shinto metaphysics does indeed exist. Shintoism provides much of the philosophical foundation for Japanese aesthetics, including many ideas about art's origin, nature, and purpose. (In a sense, Buddhism seems merely to have built on this foundation.) *Change* and *purity* are fundamental concepts in Shintoism, and to understand Shintoism's contributions to aesthetics, we must examine each of these in detail.

For Shintoists, *musubi* expresses the abstract idea of change. Shinto priests told Herbert that this is the single most enlightening word in their religion. The term, Herbert says, may be translated as "the spirit of birth

---

[5]The account of Shintoism by Jean Herbert (1967) is particularly valuable for its methodological rigor and objectivity.

and becoming, also birth, accomplishment, combination; the creating and harmonizing powers. It embraces everything, including the Deities. Even Magatsuhi, the cause of every evil, is understood as a deviation of *musubi"* (Herbert 1967:67).

Musubi—change—is personified by the rising sun, which is a symbol of both Japanese identity and the pre-eminent Shinto goddess, Amaterasu-ô-mi-kami. Moreover, *musubi's* "intangible meaning is a dynamic power uniting a pair of correlative opposites such as man and woman, day and night, and subject and object" (Herbert 1967:67). Such opposition generates change that is neither unilineal nor predictable. Instead, change is spontaneous and triune, with the potentialities of expansion, contraction, and evolution all aptly symbolized by Shinto's emblem, three comma-shaped figures whirling together to form a circle.

The Shinto belief that dynamic, ever-changing spirits reside in nature, led to an aesthetic principle that is cross-culturally uncommon. According to Shintoism, some natural phenomena, such as mountains and streams, are the residences of animistic spirits that differ from human spirits only in being far stronger than any mortal. If art is to portray the truly significant, then it must be a faithful representation of nature (cf. Ueda 1967:214). This principle partially explains Japanese visual art's uncommon interest in landscapes, still life, and animals (see **Figure 9–1**)—a preoccupation whose uniqueness can be appreciated when one considers that humans (or deities that are either anthropomorphic or else combinations of human and animal traits) provide almost all the subject matter for representational art in most of the rest of the world. Admittedly, not all Japanese paintings of nature are meant to represent Shinto Kami. Zen Buddhism, for example, has for its own purposes inspired a tradition of landscape painting. But the naturalistic bent of Japanese art surely reflects to some degree "the most characteristic feature of Shinto [which] is a basic conviction that Gods (Kami), men and the whole of Nature were actually born of the same parents" (Herbert 1967:21).

Like change, the Shinto concept of ritual purity has deep roots in Japan, going back to a prehistoric period when people may have feared coming in contact with any contaminating substance such as blood (Herbert 1967:26). An aversion to impurity remains prominent in Japanese thought, especially in Shintoism. Not only do Shinto devotees maintain high levels of bodily cleanliness, but paths to Shinto shrines are typically located close to a small fountain or body of water where one is expected to rinse the mouth and otherwise purify the body (see **Figure 9–2**). At some shrines, the same end is accomplished by routing the path to the shrine over a small natural stream.

The Shintoist equation of beauty with cleanliness and goodness has informed Japanese thought throughout history. Kōsaka (1967:257) observes, "morality in ancient times was aesthetic"; and a distinguished, contempo-

FIGURE 9-1   *Sakyamuni Triad with Sixteen Rakans.* First half of the fifteenth century; ink and color with gold pigment on silk, 69" high.   *(The Nelson-Atkins Museum of Art, Kansas City, Missouri [acquired through the Edith Ehrman Memorial Fund].)*

rary Shintoist told Herbert (1967:90), "anything that impairs the aesthetic order is thereby 'impure.'" The association of beauty with purity has implications for Japanese artistic style, a subject that will be dealt with near the end of this chapter (pp. 191–196).

The Shinto creation myth sheds much light on Japanese aesthetics. The long and complex story cycle centers around the Sun Goddess, Amaterasu-ô-mi-kami, and the creation of all material things. In a pivotal episode, Amaterasu-ô-mi-kami's brother has frightened the goddess into the Rock

FIGURE 9-2 Photo of a Shinto Shrine at Futami ga ura, Japan. *(Courtesy, Field Museum of Natural History, Chicago, neg. no. 50240.)*

Cave of Heaven. Since she is the source of all sunlight, and hence necessary for the growth and nourishment of all living things, the other Kami desperately need to lure her out of the cave. To this end, they create many things that later mortals value highly, including all plant and animal life. But, still frightened, she continues to cower behind the cave's heavy door, seemingly unmoved by such workaday things as the plants and animals that now provide for mortal subsistence.

Then, according to the story, a Kami named Ane-no-uzume approaches the door of the cave and begins to play music and dance. And as she dances, Ane-no-uzume exposes her pudenda and nipples, simultaneously suggesting sensuality and revealing the parts of the body most directly related to child-bearing and nursing. In so doing she reminds the Sun Goddess of her responsibility of bearing and nurturing the entire line of Japanese Emperors.

Ane-no-uzume's dance piques the timid Sun Goddess's curiosity, and she opens the door just enough to look out of the cave. Having gotten her attention, the Kami hand Amaterasu-ô-mi-kami a perfect mirror; and this, finally, induces the goddess to emerge from the cave, restoring her sunlight to the world.

Japanese art and aesthetics reflect several components of the Shinto creation story even to the present day. For example, Ane-no-uzume's music came from a bamboo flute and a zither-like instrument, the koto; and the flute and koto are still commonly used in Shinto temples as well as in secular settings. But more important are the clues the story gives regarding an underlying Shinto philosophy of art. What is it about the arts that made them so appealing to the Sun Goddess? An archaic version of the story says that what caught the Sun Goddess's attention was the general merriment taking place outside the Rock Cave, and in one rendition the praise expressed by Ane-no-uzume's song was also an important enticement for the Sun Goddess, who said, "Though of late many prayers have been addressed to me, of none has the language been so beautiful as this" (quoted in Herbert 1967:308). These interpretations of the seductive music and dance of the Kamis provide a rationale for the music and dance, as well as the games and sports, at modern Shinto shrines, whose explicit purpose is to "pacify, console and give pleasure" to the Kami (Herbert 1967:175).

Thus, in the most general of terms, the Shinto creation story implies that making art pleases the all-important spirit world, thereby significantly enhancing human existence. This principle alone goes a long way toward accounting for the sweeping importance of art in Japanese culture. Mason has observed, "Practicality and beauty are commonly associated in Japan, for the Shinto conception of creative action sees an increase of value when the aesthetic and the practical are united.... Art and utilitarianism are more naturally co-ordinated in Japan than in any other country" (Mason 1935:195).[6]

A second important aesthetic principle underlies the Shinto creation story. Music and dance may have persuaded Amaterasu-ô-mi-kami to peep out of the Rock Cave of Heaven, but it was the perfect mirror that finally brought the sun's light back into the world. One consequence is that many Shinto shrines still preserve mirrors as sacred relics. But beyond that, the mirror of the myth may be thought to symbolically convey an important feature of Japanese visual art. Like a mirror, art should depict a palpable reality; it should portray an objective subject matter as it truly is, not the fancies or fantasies of the artist. This is true no matter how spare or abstract the art may seem. Some works, such as Zen ink paintings, use a cryptic iconography to convey obscure subjects, but its intent is realism nevertheless.

Thus the Shinto story of Amaterasu-ô-mi-kami and the Rock Cave of

---

[6]This merging of the functional with the aesthetically pleasing also appears in many non-Shinto contexts. For example, when a home-owner builds a tea house, he constructs it at a place on his land some distance from his home. By removing the tea house from the bustle of the household itself, he ensures the tranquility necessary for the tea ceremony, but this arrangement also yields a measure of privacy, something often lacking in traditional Japanese residences, with their paper partition walls.

Heaven conveys a message of great aesthetic importance: Life as we know it, including the regenerative powers of the rising and setting sun, was made possible by art, as symbolized by Ane-no-uzume's music and dance and by the perfect mirror itself.

Shintoism is the wellspring of Japanese aesthetics, and a powerful one at that. Over 100,000 Shinto shrines, each with one or more simple but elegant architectural structures, dot the countryside of contemporary Japan; and there are many more shrines that have little or no material accouterments. Religion always reflects society's values, and the Shinto creation myth leaves little doubt that art has played a central role in Japanese Culture. Quite literally, Shintoists have the arts to thank for the very rising and setting of the sun each day.

Esoteric Buddhism and Japanese Aesthetics

Buddhism began in northern India, but it spread rapidly to the east. By the sixth century A.D., it entered Japan, championed by the then-dominant Soga clan. In contrast to the polytheistic beliefs of Shintoism, Buddha's teachings emphasized a unified reality underlying the individual gods and promised salvation to those who became one with that reality. Buddhists eschew the rituals of Shintoism, attempting instead to gain enlightenment through the powers of the mind. Attachment to personal possessions inevitably causes suffering, so enlightenment comes only to those who disengage themselves from material things, which in any case are so changeable that they can only deceive the unwary.

Hundreds of years passed before Buddhism became popular with the common people of Japan, and even among the courtly aristocrats, early Buddhism complemented, rather than competed with, Shintoism. Furthermore, early Japanese Buddhism was not so much a means of enlightenment as it was a symbol of the elevated status of the elite, prompting the construction of spectacular Buddhist monasteries and temples.

This situation began to change in 794 when the Japanese capital was moved from Nara to Kyoto, where it was to stay during the 400-year Heian period of relative peace and prosperity. Contacts with the Asian mainland continued to bring new concepts to the imperial court, and of particular importance were the preachings of two Buddhist monks who had studied in China, Kūkai (also known as Kōbō Daishi, see **Figure 9–3**) and Saichō. Kūkai established a sect known as Shingon Buddhism, and Saichō founded Tendai Buddhism; and both groups began a sweeping reformation of Japanese Buddhism. In contrast to the prior tendency to simply say prayers and perform appropriate rituals in hopes of insuring the safety of the Japanese state, Kūkai and Saichō both emphasized the principles of personal faith and spiritual development.

FIGURE 9-3 Fifteenth-century painting of Kōbō Daishi (founder of Shingon) as a child. Hanging scroll in ink, colors and gold on silk, 54" high. *(The Nelson-Atkins Museum of Art, Kansas City, Missouri [Gift of Mrs. George H. Bunting, Jr.])*

Kūkai's teaching was more influential than Saichō's during the ninth century because he convinced the emperor that his was the best form of Buddhism that the powerful T'ang court of China had to offer. His teaching, he said, came from the greatest of Chinese Buddhist monks, who passed on to him a doctrine that had come down orally and in a direct line of succession from the Buddha himself, offering "the easiest and quickest means of obtaining Buddhahood" (Ryusaku, deBary, and Keene 1958:146).

The definitive trait of Kūkai's teaching is contained in his assertion that the essence of Buddhism "is called the esoteric treasury; the words are secret and of absolute truth" (quoted in Ryusaku, deBary, and Keene 1958:148). It is not unusual for a religion to claim a monopoly on absolute truth, but whereas most religions hold out the promise of salvation to all people, Kūkai asserted that only those few who learned his secrets had any hope of achieving total enlightenment.

Kūkai's contemporary, Saichō, claimed that although his doctrines were quite similar to those of Kūkai, *he* was the one who had received the true, secret word of Buddha; and although Saichō's sect of Tendai Buddhism remained distinct from Kūkai's Shingon, the two faiths are often referred to collectively as "Esoteric Buddhism," to distinguish them from the "exoteric" Buddhist doctrines, which were general knowledge. Kūkai said, "By these [exoteric] teachings the dust and stains of the world are cleansed away, revealing the splendor and solemnity of the [esoteric] *world of the Mandalas*" (quoted in Ryusaku, deBary, and Keene 1958:153, emphasis added). The world of the Mandalas—this phrase provides the vital link between Esoteric Buddhism on the one hand and Japanese art and aesthetics on the other. In describing his extensive training in China, Kūkai wrote,

The abbot informed me that the esoteric scriptures are so abstruce that *their meaning cannot be conveyed except through art*. For this reason he ordered the court artist Li Chen and about a dozen other painters to execute ten scrolls of the Womb and Diamond Mandalas, and assembled more than twenty scribes to make copies of the Diamond and other important Esoteric scriptures. He also ordered the bronzesmith Chao We to cast fifteen ritual implements. (Quoted in Ryusaku, deBary, and Keene 1958:145, emphasis added)

Mandalas, here as well as in other Buddhist sects, are square or round paintings, decorated with either geometric designs or an orderly array of figures.[7] The Womb and Diamond Mandalas that played such important roles in Shingon were both of the latter type, depicting various Buddhas, lesser deities, saints, and other supernaturals. They are said to symbolize "the two aspects of cosmic life, its being and vitality, in the ideal or potential entity and in the dynamic manifestations. The point emphasized was the harmony between unity and diversity" (Anesaki 1963:126).

Esoteric Buddhists use mandalas as didactic devices, not only to instruct newcomers but also to remind the initiated of the many forms of absolute truth that are manifest in the Buddha and that are potentially present in every devotee. Esoteric Buddhism promulgated a powerful aesthetic system, one that justified art's existence in the most convincing of ways: Only through art can one find salvation. And, practicing what he preached, Kūkai himself became a painter and effectively used the visual arts, music, and dance to aid his proselytizing for Shingon Buddhism.

Granted, Shingon art was highly formalized (a wrongly colored lotus petal could subvert an entire mandala). But the 400 years of the Heian period saw an impressive quantity of art production, with courtly life filled with ceremonial music, dance, and a general and refined appreciation of the visual arts. The art-nurturing atmosphere of Esoteric Buddhism prompted the production of secular arts as well. Scroll painting flourished, and books such as the *Tale of Genji* testify to the richness of the period's

---

[7]A Tibetan mandala is shown in Figure 13–3.

literature. Also, the first recorded discussions of a distinctive Japanese artistic style date from the Heian period.

Even after the tumultuous Medieval Period supplanted the Imperial era, the principles espoused by the founders of Esoteric Buddhism remained alive in Japanese religion and art. A thirteenth-century monk named Nichiren called for a renewed commitment to spiritual purity and, like Saichō long before him, Nichiren found in a Buddhist text, the Lotus Sutra, the only true means to this end. Still later, Hon-ami, the leader of the influential Kano school of painting, perpetuated the influence of Esoteric Buddhism in Japanese art.

The Aesthetics of Amida Buddhism

Although Esoteric Buddhism continued to exist, the chaos and confusion of medieval Japan spawned additional religious movements. An important tenth-century reaction to the practices of the aristocracy's Tendai and Shingon Buddhism appeared in the guise of Amida, or Pure Land, Buddhism. The Amida sect exchanged arid intellectualism for personal fervor; and by the twelfth century, Amida Buddhism had become a genuine mass movement.

Whereas Esoteric Buddhists sought enlightenment through knowledge of many Buddhas, Bodhisattvas (Buddhas-to-be), and so on, the new doctrine looked solely to Amida, the Buddha of Boundless Light. Devotees cited passages in the sutras where Buddha made an "Original Vow" promising that anyone who called out his name in perfect trust would spend an eternity of bliss in the "Pure Land" that Amida had prepared in the west (see **Figure 9-4**).

The appeal of such a doctrine is obvious. Whereas Esoteric Buddhism had given followers only dispassionate enlightenment, Amida Buddhism offered a life of bliss—a reward that must have seemed especially attractive during the turbulent Medieval Period. Further, whereas success in Esoteric Buddhism demanded extensive secret knowledge, passed down orally from teacher to a select group of initiates, the new sect promised salvation to anyone who would call out the name of Amida.

Amida Buddhism had sweeping consequences for Japanese art and society. Many monks, giving up their scholastic endeavors, moved out of monasteries and either adopted secular lives or traveled through the land seeking converts to the new faith. (Ippen, a thirteenth-century evangelist, reputedly had over two million names on his roster of converts!) The popularity of the movement was matched by its members' strength of conviction. A monk named Yōkan is said to have repeated the name of Amida 10,000 times a day in his youth and 60,000 times a day during the prime of his life (Hori 1968:119–120).

FIGURE 9-4 *The Paradise of Amida Buddha,* second half of the fourteenth century. 47 3/4" high. *(The Nelson-Atkins Museum of Art, Kansas City, Missouri [Nelson Fund].)*

What was the role of art in Amida Buddhist belief? The contrasts between Esoterism and Amidism are illuminating. Whereas the mysteries of Esoterism were so profound that they could only be conveyed through the highly formalized art of the mandalas, the goals and methods of Amida Buddhism were so easily accessible that proselytizers used popular art to spread the doctrine of Amidism throughout the land. Consider, for example, the techniques of an early advocate of Amida Buddhism named Kūya (903–972): Dancing through the city streets with a tinkling bell hanging from around his neck, Kūya called out the the name of Amida and sang simple ditties of his own composition such as,

Hito tabi mo	He never fails
Namu Amida bu to	To reach the Lotus Land of
Yū hito no	Bliss who calls,
Hasu utena ni	If only once,
Noboranu wa nashi. . . .	The name of Amida. . . .

In the market places, all kinds of people joined him in his dance and sang out the invocation to Amida, "Namu Amida Butsu" (Ryusaku, deBary, and Keene 1958:193).

In contrast to Kūya, the "saint of the streets," was Genshin (942–1017), who never left his monastery at Mt. Hiei, but whose careful study of the sutras convinced him of the spiritual efficacy of Amida and of the need to spread the message to as many people as possible. To do this, Genshin wrote a book that described the horrors of Hell and the delights of the Western Paradise with such literary power that it became a virtual best-seller in tenth-century Japan.

But because custom dictated that Genshin write his masterpiece in a modified form of Chinese that many could not read, the writer/poet also used painting and sculpture in an effort to make his message even more widely heard. The result was a dramatically new style of religious art. Forsaking the stiff, formal iconography of Esoterism, Genshin made paintings of Hell and Paradise whose realism was so affecting that they were said to cause nightmares among the ladies-in-waiting at the palace court (Ryusaku, deBary, and Keene 1958:196).[8]

Although Genshin modified the *style* of Japanese religious art, the basic assumptions of Amida Buddhism are true to the Shinto roots of Japanese aesthetics. Art's primary purpose was still to affect an identification between mortals and the forces of the supernatural world, and this goal was to be attained by realistically portraying the places where the spirits reside. The only difference was that whereas Shinto art deals with Kami who live in mountains and streams, Amida Buddhist art depicts the paradisal home of the fortunate and the hellish land of the damned.

Zen Aesthetics

The twelfth century saw a final major development in Japanese Buddhism, the importation from China of Zen beliefs and practices. Esoteric Buddhists

---

[8]Anesaki, who rarely indulges in overstatement, asserts regarding Genshin, that "as a writer on the vices and miseries of life, on the varieties of existence and on the states of perdition or spiritual beatitude, he may be compared to Dante; while as a painter of paradise and saints he may be called the Fra Angelico of Japanese Buddhism" (Anesaki 1963:151).

had placed their faith in a body of secret and exclusive learning as a means of gaining spiritual enlightenment, and adherents of Amida Buddhism sought a paradise of bliss for anyone who faithfully repeated the name of Amida. In a sense, Zenists combined elements of both these sects. Like Esoteric Buddhists, their goal was enlightenment rather than ecstasy; but, like Amida Buddhists, they proposed to gain this end through a technique that was, at least in theory, available to all, namely silent meditation.

Buddha himself set the precedent for Zen Buddhism. To pass the core of his belief on to his foremost disciple, Mahā-kāśyapa, Buddha simply held up a flower; and the student, in silence, smiled. The significance of the event lies in its being a face-to-face encounter between master and student, and also in the student's response being intuitive, immediate, and personal, rather than resulting from rational thought and the didactic learning of explicit doctrines. Anesaki says, "Every Zenist should receive his spiritual illumination through the medium of his own soul, directly from the vast sources of the cosmos. All instruction is but as a finger pointing to the moon; and he whose gaze is fixed on the pointer will never see beyond" (Anesaki 1915:49).

Early Zen leaders were divided on many issues—on whether written teachings had any value, on the validity of the Esoteric teachings, on the worth of *koans* (seemingly insoluble riddles given by the master to the student as a topic of meditation), and on whether meditation was a means or an end in itself. But all Zen sects believed, first, that the material world should be understood for what it is—namely, a place where disorder and flux are inevitable; and, second, that a person can transcend such a world only by replacing the soul's tumultuous passions and consciousness with an intuitive and unconscious acceptance of the oneness of the universe.

Zen Buddhism never gained the wide popularity of Amida Buddhism, but it did find many converts in influential sectors of Japanese society. Besides intellectuals, Zen appealed to Samurai warriors because its doctrines accepted and transcended the rough world in which they lived; and bureaucrats and traders were interested for the same reason—and they also sought the advice of Zen monks on questions of foreign affairs because the holy men had recent and firsthand knowledge of China.

But for our purposes, Zen Buddhism is interesting because of its pervasive effect on Japanese aesthetics. The twin foundations of Zen aesthetics are _transcendental naturalism_ and _spontaneous intuition_ (cf. Anesaki 1915:53), each of which warrants our attention.

The transcendentalism of Zen lies in its assertion that all boundaries, as between subject and object or between observer and observed, are illusory. Enlightenment cannot be found in consciously and rationally identifying with nature, but in *experiencing* a unification with the Oneness that is reality. ("The real flower is enjoyed only when the poet-artist lives with it, in it; and when even a sense of identity is no longer here," says Suzuki

[1983:184].) Since transcendental reality is a manifestation of perfect beauty, as symbolized by the flower that Buddha held up before Mahā-kāśyapa, the religious endeavor becomes, in a sense, an aesthetic endeavor.

Unlike Esoteric and Amida Buddhism, Zen did not use art to explicitly convey its message or to gain converts. After all, Mahā-kāśyapa grasped the core of Buddha's meaning in a flash of insight, not as a result of laborious, scholarly study. But the *technique* of much Japanese art since the thirteenth century, in whatever medium, reflects Zen beliefs. Japanese artists have long believed that "only when the artist's mind is as calm as the surface of a mirror can the real nature of the outside object be grasped" (Kishimoto 1967:117). In this remark, the art-as-mirror metaphor, an image that reaches back to pre-historic, Shintoist Japan, appears once again. And although it takes for granted that art reflects nature, Zen emphasizes the *transparency* of the artist's sensibility. Far from "interpreting" nature, the Zen artist, in bold and unstudied brush strokes, extends nature itself into his art.

Carried to its extreme, the Zen approach to art led to ink paintings in which the viewer's own intuitions supply color to an otherwise monochrome drawing (see **Figure 9–5**). Such emotional reserve and economy of style produced an art that differed strikingly from the busy mandalas of Esoteric Buddhism and the dramatic depictions of heaven and hell of Amida Buddhism.

Although Zen influenced the style and technique of Japanese art more than its content, its impact is apparent in almost all media. In literature, the sparseness and suggestiveness of Zen aesthetics influenced Nō drama, with its inexpressive masks and minimal plot, as well as the poetic forms known as *tanka* and *haiku*, composed of thirty-one and seventeen syllables respectively. The idea of intuitively merging oneself with nature encouraged the arts of flower arrangement (see **Figure 9–6**) and landscaping. And the acceptance of Zen Buddhism by members of the Samurai class led to such "martial" arts as sword-making, horsemanship, swimming, and archery. In the latter, for example, the archer's goal is not simply hitting a target. An ingenious machine could probably shoot arrows more accurately than the best archer. From the perspective of Zen, the challenge of the sport is more spiritual than mechanical: The bowman attempts to maintain his limbs in a relationship of harmony, to calm his soul, and to concentrate his mind. If he successfully accomplishes this, his arrow will inevitably be unified with the target (cf. Anesaki 1933:121–122).

Finally, of all the factors that inform the Japanese tea ceremony (p. 195–196), none are more important than those derived from Zen Buddhism. Indeed, the cult of tea cannot be understood without reference to the assumptions and sensibilities that derive from Zen thought. But as the tea ceremony embodies several aspects of Japanese aesthetic style, a fuller account of it will be left for a later point in the discussion.

FIGURE 9–5 *Priest Sewing Under Morning Sun,* painted by Shokado Shojo, 1584–1639, inscribed by Ryutan Shuken. Ink on paper, 43 1/2" high. *(Courtesy Denver Art Museum.)*

FIGURE 9-6   *Young Man Arranging Flowers.   (Courtesy, Field Museum of Natural History, Chicago, neg. no. 49367.)*

Zen was the last major innovation in Japanese Buddhism, and it may not be coincidental that Japanese art also changed little after the fifteenth century. But during Buddhism's first thousand years in Japan, developments in art were as rich as those in religion. New art styles and media accompanied the earliest phase of Buddhism when it was still the private domain of a small, status-conscious aristocracy. With Esoteric Buddhism came the belief that only the art of the mandala could convey the profound teachings that pointed the path to enlightenment. Then Amida Buddhists used popular music and dance to attract converts; and paintings of heaven and hell brought renewed conviction to believers. Finally, Zen beliefs provided a metaphysical theory of art production: Total focusing of concentration, nurturance of inspired insight, and a rigorous mental discipline that could demolish the apparent boundaries between self and a universe of perfect beauty—these led to a unification of art with reality.

Japanese Confucianism

Confucianism also had an effect on traditional Japanese art, albeit in a more subtle way than did Shintoism and Buddhism. Like Buddhism, Confucian doctrine entered Japan from the Asian mainland in the sixth century; but whereas Buddhism strongly influenced Japanese religious and philosophical thought, Confucianism was applied largely to secular matters—individual ethics and questions of government. It emphasized such abstract and general human qualities as virtue, magnanimity, and humanheartedness, and such social values as loyalty, courage, and politeness. Whereas Buddhism encouraged its adherents to turn away from the material world because of its changeability, Confucianism attempted to negate change by encouraging cultural stability. By codifying both the leader's responsibilities as well as the follower's duties, Confucianism generally appealed to those who held (and hoped to maintain) privileged positions.

Confucian ethics forbids movement from one social class to another, and for a long time the only effect of Confucianism on Japanese art was to increase the tendency for individual families to specialize in certain crafts, generation after generation.

But the ideology of Confucianism became more influential after the Tokugawa shogunate restored political unity to Japan after the long period of medieval discord. In the arts, Confucianism primarily meant constructing elaborate temples; and in the Shogun's court, it encouraged such conservative and "edifying" arts as studying the classics of literature and painting, composing poems in the Chinese style, and writing official histories of Japan's past glories (cf. Hall 1959:285).

The motive for these activities was as much political as aesthetic. Whether it was a spectacular neo-Confucianist temple or an account of Japanese history written out in artistic calligraphy and illustrated by refined paintings, Confucian art depicted the high points of the Japanese state at the same time that it displayed and validated the pre-eminence of its current rulers.

Japanese Aesthetic Preferences

Aesthetics is made up of abstract ideas about art's fundamental nature and reason for being. *Art,* by contrast, refers to paintings, poems, and dances—or the mental and physical activity that goes into producing such things. The richness of information about Japanese culture allows us the rare chance to pursue an interesting question—namely, how are aesthetic theories linked to actual art production? Obviously, aesthetic assumptions tend to influence the subject matter of art. Esoteric Buddhism, for example, conceives art to be the sole means to spiritual enlightenment, so that it is not surprising that the subject matter of Esoteric Buddhism is largely made up of depictions of Buddhas, Bodhisattvas, and so on.

But besides subject matter, there may be a more covert link between aesthetic abstraction and material art work—namely, the possible influence of aesthetics on artistic *style*. Donald Keene has convincingly argued (1971) that four stylistic traits—suggestion, perishability, irregularity, and simplicity—characterize most Japanese art. Are these qualities completely autonomous or have they grown out of the Shinto, Buddhist, and, to a lesser extent, Confucian foundations of Japanese art? An examination of them, one by one, reveals that they *are* related to Japanese aesthetic values, but that their relationships to those values are complex, sometimes inverted, and always subtle.

For Westerners, perhaps the most alien feature of Japanese art is its avoidance of the straightforward and the explicit and its preference for the implied and the *suggested*. Consider again the poem on page 173, near the beginning of this chapter.

> Dimly, dimly
> The day breaks at Akashi Bay;
> And in the morning mist
> My heart follows a vanishing ship
> As it goes behind an island.

Fujiwara no Kintō wrote this tanka about a thousand years ago to illustrate standards of excellence in poetry. Whatever its appeal to the contemporary reader, the writer himself believed that its chief value was its suggestiveness. The poem is vague about the scene's temporal setting: It is after daybreak, but the "morning mist," far from conveying a specific hour, reminds us of a hazy morning when, lacking an unequivocal sunrise, we feel suspended in a phenomenally timeless state.

The poem is also suggestive in being about a virtual non-event. A sailing ship is involved, but all we know is that it has just disappeared! Its size, appearance, and destination are all left to the reader's imagination. (Similarly, the title of the Zen painting in Figure 9–5 is *Priest Sewing under Morning Sun*, but we view the priest from behind and can only guess at the work that presumably lies on his lap.)

The poem's emotional nexus lies in the statement that the author's "heart follows" the ship, but again we are left to speculate on the reasons for his feelings. Did he have a loved one on the boat? Was he longing to travel with the boat to another land? Fujiwara no Kintō believed that his tanka benefited by suggesting many possibilities rather than explicitly stating a set of factual events.

A similar taste for suggestiveness pervades most Japanese literature and art—the haiku, with its spare seventeen syllables, the cursory treatment of a subject in a Zen ink painting, or the Nō theater.[9]

Japanese artists are well aware of their use of suggestiveness, and they have discussed at length the concept of *yūgen*, an idea closely related to suggestiveness. In the fifteenth century, Shōtetsu Monogatari said that *yūgen* is "suggested by the sight of a thin cloud veiling the moon or by autumn mist swathing the scarlet leaves on a mountainside. If one is asked where in these sights lies the *yūgen*, one cannot say" (quoted in Ryusaku, deBary, and Keene 1958:285). The theory of *yūgen* focuses on an individual's emotional reaction to an aesthetic situation. (*Yūgen* is "just as when we look at the sky of an autumn dusk. It has no sound or color, and yet, though we do not understand why, we somehow find ourselves moved to tears," wrote Mumyō Hisho [quoted in Ryusaku, deBary, and Keene 1958:285].)

The most obvious place to seek the philosophical roots of *yūgen* is in Zen Buddhism. Zenists, after all, forsake the conscious study of explicit dogmas and seek instead the spontaneous insights of intuitive, private meditation. The parallels between this technique and the artistic sensibility associated with suggestion lie in their shared emphasis on the personal, unconscious response, attained by the use of a suggestive stimulus—the Zenist's *koan* or the artist's art work.

But since *yūgen* theory existed in Japan several centuries before the arrival of Zen Buddhism, the former obviously did not spring from the latter. At most, Zen nurtured a stylistic preference that already existed. However, Buddhists had long displayed a preoccupation with the obscure and with the belief that the palpable, sensory world is only a reflection (or suggestion!) of the invisible world of true Buddhahood. After all, the sutras did record the tale of Mahā-kāśyapa's spontaneous, inspired smile when Buddha held up a rose. So perhaps the Buddhist outlook does contribute to the Japanese artist's penchant for suggestion.

Zeami Motokiyo (1363–1443), the pre-eminent theorist of Nō drama, suggested another possible source of suggestiveness of Japanese art. He believed that *yūgen* should not be sought as an end in itself, but as a means of gaining deeper truths: "*Yūgen*, then, is the beauty not merely of appearance but of the spirit; it is inner beauty manifesting itself outwards" (quoted in Ueda 1967:61). This typically Shintoist concern for things' inner spirits prompted the sixteenth-century aesthetician Tosa Mitsuoki to remark, "All good works of art are lifelike, not so much in the sense that they copy all the outward details of real life, as in the sense that they observe all the

---

[9]Keene says of Nō: "The undecorated stage, the absence of props other than bare outlines, the disregard for all considerations of time and space in the drama, the use of language that is usually obscure and of abstract gestures that are scarcely related to the words, all make it evident that this theater . . . was meant to be the outward, beautiful form suggestive of remoter truths or experiences, the nature of which will differ from person to person" (Keene 1971:16).

inward laws of nature" (cited in Ueda 1967:131). Shintoism, like Buddhism, encouraged artists in Japan to focus on the inner spirit of an art work and to recognize that the work's tangible manifestation could never be more than a "suggestion" of this essence.

Perishability is another stylistic trait found in much Japanese art. Keene says,

> Whatever the subject matter of the old poems, the underlying meaning was often an expression of grief over the fragility of beauty and love. Yet the Japanese were keenly aware that without this mortality there could be no beauty. Kenkō wrote, "If man were never to fade away like the dews of Adashino, never to vanish like the smoke over Toribeyama, but lingered on forever in the world, how things would lose their power to move us! The most precious thing in life is its uncertainty."[10]   (Keene 1971:24)

An infatuation with perishability probably explains the Japanese near-obsession with cherry blossoms. Although their appearance and scent are not intrinsically more charming than plum blossoms, cherry blossoms are short-lived and, like the ideal *samurai* warrior, they fall at the peak of their beauty (Keene 1971:12–13).

Both common sense and contemporary psychology support the Japanese belief that the gratitude we feel for something increases when we understand its impermanence. But artists in most cultures, especially those in complex societies, often strive for permanence anyway. Where does the Japanese preference for perishability come from?

If a Japanese love of suggestion derives from the concept of *yūgen*, artistic perishability is related to *aware* (or *mono no aware*). When it first appeared in Japanese writing, *aware* meant "an exclamation of surprise and delight," or one's reaction to "the 'ahness' of things" (Ryusaku, deBary, and Keene 1958:176). The concept evolved with the passage of time, however, so that by the eleventh century, it meant "pity and sympathy" (Anesaki 1963:156) and often appeared in romantic accounts of unrequited love.

Like *yūgen, aware* has a curious relationship to Buddhism. Granted, an awareness of the inevitable transience of the material world is important in Buddhist thought; and the ephemerality of the sensory world is, for Buddhists, the strongest evidence of its being inferior to the realm of the spirit, or true Buddhahood. But this line of reasoning leads most Buddhists to renounce the material world rather than to glory in its supposedly greatest flaw, its impermanence. So perhaps the high value that has been placed on perishability came about, in part, as a reaction against the world-denying aspect of Buddhism—and, for that matter, also a reaction against the re-

---

[10]Adashino was a graveyard, and Toribeyama the site of a crematorium.

stricting and unemotional code of conduct prescribed by Confucianism (cf. Anesaki 1963:159).

Motoori Norinaga, a contributor to the Shinto revival of eighteenth-century Japan, gives a clue to a possible Shintoist origin of *aware*. Norinaga was highly critical of rationalism and placed his faith in the prescient, creative, and seemingly irrational Shinto deities (Ueda 1967:196). The alternative to unproductive rationalism, Norinaga said, was *mono no aware—* through *feelings* one touches true meaning. Literature, for example, should not be used for didactic ends but should serve a higher purpose. "Through literature man can return to his innermost self—the self that is energetic and creative as bestowed by the God of Creation. . . . Literature helps one approach Shinto gods, who are more truly human than modern men" (Ueda 1967:212).

Admittedly, Norinaga was writing long after *aware* had become an influential concept in Japanese art style, and he does not explicitly emphasize the implications of *aware* for the Japanese concern with perishability. But he does point the way to a possible link between *aware* and perishability. The Shinto deities, as spirits of nature, are unmoved by human reason. But, as we are reminded by the dance of Ane-no-uzume that enticed the Sun Goddess to peep out of the Rock Cave of Heaven, the Kami do respond to more elemental forces such as delight, fear, and simple aesthetic pleasure. Herbert, speaking not of artists but of Shintoists, says that "one of their key-phrases is *mono-no-aware*, sympathy with all creatures" (Herbert 1967:21).

So the philosophical basis of the Japanese fascination with perishability in art may be this: Buddhism and Shintoism both emphasize the sad fact that all material things have only a brief existence. Humans, too, are not long for this world. In the transience of art works, one sees one's own fate, a vision that prompts the strongest of emotional reactions.

Keene (1971:18–23) cites many examples to illustrate the Japanese penchant for stylistic *irregularity* and *simplicity.* Prime numbers, for example, play an important role in the poetic form of the tanka, whose thirty-one syllables are broken into five lines of five, seven, five, seven, and seven syllables each. Also, although Japanese Buddhist monasteries were originally patterned after Chinese monasteries that had symmetrical floorplans, Japanese architects soon began using asymmetric plans for their own buildings. Finally, Japanese ceramic works are often irregular, both in shape and in glaze; and the famous rock gardens of Japan stand in striking contrast to the obsessively geometrical layout of formal gardens in the West.

But the traditional Japanese tea ceremony is the best example of these qualities. An early form of tea had inspired a small tea cult as long ago as the eighth century, but green tea did not appear in Japan until it was brought from China by Eisai (1141–1215), the Buddhist monk who also introduced Zen Buddhism. Initially, monks used tea to avoid falling asleep when they meditated, and tea soon became popular beyond the walls of the monastery (Hayashiya, Nakamura, and Hayashiya 1974).

The traditional tea ceremony takes place in a small structure that is notable for its simplicity. Only muted colors and a minimum of adornments are found within; and this, complemented by the faint scent of astringent incense, creates a pervasive effect of tranquility. The tea itself is prepared and served by the use of implements that, though costly, are unostentatious. When the tea is ready, "it is placed before the visitor, who must lift the cup in both hands, feeling its texture and warmth. He drinks the tea, not in one gulp but three sips, savoring the liquid as refreshing as some precious elixir though made of a most common, ordinary leaf" (Ryusaku, deBary, and Keene 1958:266).

The tea ceremony's symbolism, which is too elaborate to describe here in detail, reflects Zen beliefs. For example, although the privy that typically stands outside the tea house may seem anomalous to the Westerner, it suggests to tea ceremonialists "the incessant changes through which the human body passes" (Ryusaku, deBary, and Keene 1958:264). Also, just as Zen meditation should lead to spiritual enlightenment, the tranquil setting of the teahouse should promote *furyu*—a combination of elegant refinement and simple amusement (Hayashiya, Nakamura, and Hayashiya 1974). Similarly the irregularity and asymmetry found in the tea house's design, its decorations, and the ceremony itself reflect, as does much Japanese art, an appreciation of the uniqueness of every art work and the idiosyncratic aesthetic response of every individual, a principle in keeping with Zen beliefs.

Again, however, the facts of history confound the analysis because the Japanese taste for irregularity and asymmetry pre-date Zen Buddhism. They might reflect the perennial Buddhist belief that the material world's diversity and imperfection conceal an underlying unity of the cosmos. And, too, Shintoism may be involved—in two ways. First, it seems logical that the Shinto obsession with purity would lead to a preference for the clean and simple over the fussy and ornate. Second, Shintoism's emphasis on nature may have contributed to the Japanese avoidance of symmetry. As Anesaki has pointed out, nature itself is rarely symmetrical (Anesaki 1933:18–19).

As in most of this analysis of the relationship between Japanese style and aesthetics, this argument seems strained, and we must conclude that although theory usually influences practice, aesthetic philosophy and artistic production are, at most, only loosely linked to one another.

Conclusion

The richness of the literature on Japanese art, religion, and culture allows us to understand Japanese aesthetics in greater depth than is possible in almost any other society. But this same richness also has a humbling effect, making one aware of the incompleteness of even our best efforts. A central assumption of Buddhism is that reality is fundamentally enigmatic; similarly, as Ueda has remarked, "Japanese aesthetic writings tend to be metaphorical rather than analytical, and impressionistic rather than rationalistic" (Ueda 1967:225).

If the essence of Japanese thought is elusive, some of its more superficial aspects also resist our understanding. For instance, this account has said little about the psychological functions of art. What emotional reaction should art prompt in the audience member? A review of literary theorists has led one scholar to claim that the aesthetic response should be cathartic, that it should liberate one from life's inevitable pettiness and boredom, and that it should evoke the joy of learning (Ueda 1967:23–35), but this important subject has not been sufficiently explored in other art media.

Equally unclear is the way in which Confucianism has influenced Japanese art and aesthetics. The early poet, Ki no Tsurayuki (868–946?) claimed that poetry "strengthens men's moral sense and helps create order in this world. Rulers educate their people by means of poetry, and people advise their rulers by means of poetry" (quoted in Ueda 1967:23); and 500 years later, another poet, Yoshimoto, asserted that the Confucian axiom, "That which makes all men follow is good" (Ueda 1967:39), applies to literature. These remarks only whet one's curiosity regarding the general influence of Confucianisms on Japanese aesthetics.

But for all these shortcomings, the study of Japanese aesthetics does pay genuine rewards. Japan has been called an "aesthetic culture," and an examination of Japanese history and society indicates this to be true on several levels.

First, art plays a crucial role in several influential religious traditions. Shintoism accords art a special place in its creation myth; and a striving for harmony and a concern with creativity are at the core of Shinto thinking. Buddhism also stresses unity and intuitive development, and several Buddhist sects proclaim art's efficacy for spiritual development. Specifically, the message of Esoteric Buddhism is believed to be so obscure as to be communicable only via the art of the mandala; Amida Buddhism uses song, dance, and other popular art forms to gain converts and to insure their loyalty through graphic depiction of the horrors of hell and the bliss of heaven; and the meditation required of Zen Buddhists promotes an intuitive sensibility and focused concentration that is as appropriate to art as it is to religion.

A second reason for considering Japan to be an aesthetic society is the extent to which artistic factors influence many day-to-day activities. Keene notes that the visitor to modern-day, industrialized Japan is inevitably impressed by "the flowers gracefully bending down from a wall-bracket over the toilet; or the artistically brushed signboard in the railway station which proves to mean 'Left Luggage Room'" (Keene 1971:11).

Lastly, the rich literature on Japanese art and thought allows us to get a rare insight into the relationship between, on the one hand, the abstract principles of aesthetics and, on the other, the stylistic traits that give Japan's art its distinctive qualities. The four values that Keene discusses—suggestion, perishability, irregularity, and simplicity—are highly consistent among themselves, but their relationship to Japanese aesthetics seems tenuous at best. Certainly there are resonances between the two systems, but it is equally certain that each possesses a fair degree of autonomy from the other.

10

WESTERN AESTHETICS
A Quartet of Traditions

"Aesthetics is for the artists as ornithology is for the birds."
(Barnett Newman, quoted in Wolfe 1975:79)

What might we gain by studying how others live their lives? One obvious answer is that by documenting the vast range of possible options that have been
explored by people in different times and distant places, we chart the remarkable range of human potentiality. This seems to be an intrinsically interesting
and worthwhile activity.

But there is a second good reason for learning about different life ways,
one that often remains unspoken. By looking at others, we gain new perspectives on ourselves—on the society that bore us and on the psychological terrain that constitutes our own minds. If we seek to understand ourselves, perhaps trying to bring to conscious formulation a vague and unconscious feeling
of dissatisfaction, the study of anthropology becomes a reflexive endeavor, an
effort to find secure moorings for our own social or personal cosmos. In short,
the study of the Other can foster a deeper and more critical understanding
of Self.

So, armed with some grasp of aesthetics in nine other societies, we now
look into the mirror and scrutinize Western thinking about art, subjecting it
to the same questions that were productive in learning about philosophies of
art elsewhere.

We often assume that the hallmark of the West is its science and technology, or else the amazing productivity of our business economy. After all, these
were the features that led to the West's partial or total domination of many
of the societies whose philosophies of art we have already discussed. In such
a view, the aesthetic dimension of Western culture is definitely of secondary
importance.

But if we are to avoid applying a double standard, we must approach
Western art in the same way as we did art in non-Western societies. Elsewhere
we took "art" to include not just those things and activities that were created

by full-time specialists to fulfill "aesthetic" (in the narrowest sense of the word) needs; but we were also interested in such things as body decoration, recreational music, oral literature, artifacts of religious significance, and so on.

Applying a similarly broad definition of art to Western culture, we see just how artistically fertile Euro-American civilization has been and continues to be. For example, consider your own surroundings at this very moment. You are reading a book that was printed using a *style* of type that was created by an individual with years of training and experience in designing type faces that are both *expressive* and *pleasing to the eye*; the book's cover and overall *design* received similar attention by others. *Architects* designed the room and building in which you sit, again prompted by considerations of function, cost, and *appearance*; and you (or, depending upon the room you are in, interior designers) gave similar thoughts to the room's *decorations*. Your clothes reflect not only your *tastes* but also the *fashions* of our era. If not just now, then probably sometime today you will hear *music* of one *genre* or another; and this evening, the *dramas* or *light comedies* of television will be conveniently at hand for relaxation unless you choose to end your day by seeking more active recreations such as *live music, theater, film*, or *dance*. Then again, you might indulge your taste for *literature* by settling down with a good—or, at least, engrossing—book.

Many of the activities that fill our day-to-day lives cannot be considered to be "art," much less "great art"; but when one considers the pervasive concern with objects and activities that are "expressive" and "pleasing to the eye," that reflect "taste," "fashion," and "style," or that are popular manifestations of traditional art media—music, drama, dance, and so on—then one realizes just how much art and quasi-art surround us at every moment. The affluence of Western society is proverbial, and it allows us not only to meet the primary needs of food, shelter, and reproduction, but also to consistently decorate and sensuously enhance virtually everything we make and do, to say nothing of creating art for its own sake. An evaluation of the relative merits of fine art versus popular and folk art is not the issue here (cf. Gans 1974). What is relevant is the simple conclusion that the West has produced, and continues to produce, vast quantities of things that can reasonably be considered to be art.

Likewise, the West has a considerable storehouse of speculative thought related to the art it has produced. We are all "natives," and although we often disagree about the "grey" areas between what is and is not art, between good and mediocre art, and between valid and spurious reasons for art's existence, few of us would be unable to give examples that fall unequivocally in "black" and "white" areas on each of these questions. Thus, DaVinci's *Mona Lisa* is an instance of fine art, a police "mug shot" is not; the Rolling Stone's "Satisfaction" is an example of popular art, and the "rat-tat-tat" from a jack-hammer outside the window is not.[1]

---

[1]Of course, it is possible that either of these—a "mug shot" or a jack-hammer's sound—might be transformed (through selection and method of presentation) into art by a conceptual artist.

Overview: A "Quartet" of Aesthetic Systems

During the long course of Western history, countless views have been aired concerning many of the same questions that have challenged thinkers in the nine societies discussed in the preceding chapters. Although many writers claim that theirs is the sole embodiment of truth, in fact distinct patterns of aesthetic thought are evident; and close inspection reveals that virtually *all* Western philosophies of art fit fairly neatly into one of four traditional categories. Indeed, although the historians of philosophy who have attempted to systematize Western aesthetic theories have sometimes used different labels in their taxonomies, there is a surprising amount of agreement that there has been a "quartet" of aesthetic traditions in the West, with each voice in the ensemble representing a tradition that can be traced back to ancient Greece and that remains viable today (cf., e.g., Abrams 1953, Stolnitz 1960; Pepper 1945).[2]

Examinations of the four major theories of Western aesthetics will form the main part of the present chapter, but before launching into the first of these, a very brief overview of the four theories is in order to provide a comparative perspective for each theory.

Mimetic theories focus on the relationship between the work of art and some material object in the sensible world which the art work "imitates," either literally or else by capturing it in an idealized form that transcends the mundane world.

Pragmatic theories emphasize the functional (or "instrumental") capacity of art, requiring that art make some sort of positive contribution to the well-being of individuals or society. Religious art, with its goal of enhancing the spiritual condition of the art audience, constitutes the most common type of pragmatic art, but political art also has a pragmatic goal.

Emotionalist theories focus neither on the material nor the social world but rather on the psychological realm of inner experience and the feelings of the individual. Again, the specific locus of interest varies.

---

[2]Three qualifications should be made explicit at this point. First, although specific Western aesthetic *theories* tend to fall into one of four categories, actual *people* and *art works* cannot be so straightforwardly classified. A person inevitably uses different aesthetic criteria to evaluate varied art works; and a particular work may be responded to from more than one aesthetic perspective.

Second, although the four traditions are usually distinct from each other, at times they overlap or are complementary in their concerns.

Third, Western theories of art *criticism* may be more numerous and varied than Western art *philosophies*, which deal with the ultimate nature or purpose of art. For example, Guerin, Labor, Morgan, and Willingham (1979) describe five major critical approaches plus eleven additional approaches to literature, almost all of which are uniquely different from the others. Some of them grow out of the four major Western aesthetic traditions, but many come from the application to literature of other conceptual schemes, such as analyzing fiction in light of Freud's or Jung's theories of the unconscious.

Emphasis may be on the artist's expression of emotion, on cathartic purging of audience members' emotions, or on the creative act itself. *Formalist theories* do not deal with the material, social, or psychological worlds, but rather with the stylistic world manifest in the art work itself. Art is thought to be a unique manifestation of "significant form," a manipulation of an artistic medium that is capable of producing a unique and definitively arresting response in the aesthetically attuned audience member.

The following pages discuss each of these four theories in depth. The remarks will be organized, first, in roughly chronological order. At any given point in time, one of the theories has generally prevailed over the others, so we shall begin with mimetic tradition, which dominated aesthetics in the classical civilizations of ancient Greece and Rome, then move on through pragmatic and emotionalist theories, and conclude with formalism.[3]

Besides chronology, the following remarks will also be given structure by the distinction between "fine" and "popular" arts. The four major traditions have focused on the stylistically sophisticated fine arts that thrived in the West under the perennial patronage of a political and economic elite. But the West has a long and fertile tradition of producing popular art as well, and I believe these arts also rest on the four aesthetic traditions described below. So in each of the four sections that follow, an aesthetic theory will be described in its historical context in relation to the fine arts, and then examined for its applicability to the popular arts. The final picture that emerges is of a culture that not only created prodigious quantities of fine and popular art but that also has produced a rich and complex body of speculative thought concerning art's meaning and its role in human affairs.

Mimetic Theories   DaVinci

If the four Western aesthetic theories are thought of as constituting a vocal quartet, with one part carrying the lead while the others sing in harmony, then mimetic theories were the first to have the melody. A Greek-derived term related to such English words as "imitate" and "mime," the term *mimesis* is now used with reference to art that is made with the conscious intention of representing and conveying to the percipient some concrete, specific, extra-artistic subject matter. Praxiteles's sculpture portraying the quintessentially athletic *Discus Thrower* (or the Roman *Male Torso* seen in **Figure 10–1**); Leonardo's portrait of a burgher's smiling young wife, *Mona Lisa;* and the battle for Leningrad during the Russian Revolution, as de-

---

[3]For the most part, the post-modernist theories that have followed on the heels of formalism will not be discussed here inasmuch as a state of controversy, rather than of consensus, seems to prevail in this area at the present time.

FIGURE 10-1   *Male Torso,* second century B.C., Greek. Marble, 36 1/2" high. *(The Nelson-Atkins Museum of Art, Kansas City, Missouri [Nelson Fund].)*

picted in Sergei Eisenstein's film, *Potemkin*—each is an example of a classic work of art that was created in an effort to portray some unequivocal subject matter. Undoubtedly, most Westerners recognize the consummate skill with which such artists have used art media to bring their subjects to life in the viewer's imagination.

No matter what divergent courses Western art theorists have followed, Western artists themselves have continually attached great importance to art's capacity to imitate the world around them—thus giving support to the quip attributed to the American artist and critic, Barnett Newman, "Aesthetics is for the artists as ornithology is for the birds" (quoted in Wolfe 1975:79).

For example, in his *Treatise on Painting*, Leonardo asserted that among various paintings, "That painting is most praiseworthy which conforms most to the object portrayed" (translated by McMahon 1956, frag. 433). Certainly many developments in the visual arts, from the Renaissance down to the present day, have been prompted by artists' efforts at simple, mimetic art, be it fourteenth-century Italian painters' discovery of ways to depict geometric perspective or nineteenth-century French impressionists' efforts to render the dazzling play of light on natural subjects. And, equally obviously, an impulse toward realism remains a very important force in contemporary popular art forms, such as television drama and sidewalk charcoal portraits.

But straightforward, literal imitation has found only limited support among Western speculative thinkers on art. Of the major philosophers, only Plato conceived art to be no more than an effort at imitating sensible reality; and for this reason he belittled art's value. After all, if ultimate reality resides in abstract Platonic Ideas, and material objects are mere shadows of such Ideas, then an art work that portrays objects would necessarily be no more than "shadows of shadows," twice removed from reality! And artists, too, often admit that there is indeed more to art than simple imitation. For example, even the most realistic of artists (such as the nineteenth-century artist, William Harnett, who was arrested by Treasury Department agents for his *trompe l'oeil* paintings of American currency) cannot resist the temptation to heighten the color and texture of their subjects (Stolnitz 1960:115–116).

But Plato's student, Aristotle, sounded a note that has been repeatedly heard in the mimetic tradition. In *The Poetics,* he argued that art can accomplish far more than literal imitation; it can convey the *essence* of the subject matter at hand. Aristotle asked, for example, What makes poetry different from other kinds of serious writing, such as history? He believed that the answer lay in the fact that whereas history merely replicates nature, poetry "is a more philosophical and a higher thing than history: for poetry tends to express the universal, history the particular" (*Poetics,* 1451a 36).

This assertion provided a charter for a different sort of mimetic aesthetic. Art was still conceived as being an imitation of some specific subject matter, but this subject was not just palpable, material reality. Rather, although the artist must begin with a specific, concrete subject, the art work ultimately transcends this literal subject to convey abstract, ideal concepts. Aristotle himself argued that the definitive trait of tragedy lies in its portrayal of characters who embody pan-human weaknesses and struggles. Following the same line of reasoning, the visual arts should depict ideal and perfect beauty (see **Figure 10–2**), not the unique imperfections and idiosyncrasies that distinguish one model from another. (Thus an often-repeated story that was first told by Pliny recounts that the Roman painter Zeuxis, in an attempt to sculpt the preternatural beauty of Juno, "had the young maidens of the place stripped for examination, and selected five of them, in order to adapt in his picture the most commendable points in the form of each" [cited in Abrams 1953:37].)

Medieval writers continued to assume that art was basically mimetic, but they emphasized the religious functions of mimesis, a theme that will be later discussed along with other pragmatic theories. But the Renaissance

FIGURE 10–2   Lucas Cranach the Elder, *The Three Graces*. Oil on panel, 1535; 19 7/8″ high.   *(The Nelson-Atkins Museum of Art, Kansas City, Missouri [Nelson Fund].)*

brought a renewed interest in mimesis for its own sake, and the result was the triumph of geometric perspective and the sophisticated figurative painting techniques that typify the era (**Figure 10-3**).

With the neo-classical period, 1550–1750, the mimetic impulse merged with idealism, leading the visual and literary arts to depict not only classic beauty but also ideal principles of ethical and moral perfection. The old Aristotelian approach of portraying the transcendent and pan-human, rather than the particular and idiosyncratic, regained popularity. Speaking for his time, Joshua Reynolds criticized Rembrandt's paintings because they sometimes showed mere commoners in mundane settings, using well-observed details to convey the uniqueness of each subject. Such art, the neo-classicists believed, could never serve art's highest purpose, which was to produce an uplifting effect on the audience.

Mimetic theories have not been prevalent in serious aesthetic writings since the romantic rebellion against neo-classicism 200 years ago. But even if mimetic theorizing and criticism is passé in the fine arts, it remains a powerful force in popular thinking about the arts in the West. Consider, for example, the fate of *Star Thief,* a large painting by the contemporary American, James Rosenquist. It portrays the vast reaches of outer space by

FIGURE 10-3 Frans Hals (1581–1666), *Portrait of a Burgher.* Oil on canvas, 42″ high. *(The Nelson-Atkins Museum of Art, Kansas City, Missouri [Nelson Fund].)*

setting against a black, starry background the images of modern machinery and architecture juxtaposed against a fragmented woman's face and floating slices of bacon. In 1981, a Florida arts committee proposed purchasing the work (for more than a quarter of a million dollars) to hang in the Eastern Airlines concourse in the Dade County Airport. The plan was vetoed, however, by the president of Eastern Airlines, Frank Borman. As a former astronaut, Borman had seen outer space firsthand, and he knew perfectly well that it did not look anything like Rosenquist's painting! The painting was, in Mr. Borman's opinion, poor because there was "no correlation . . . between the artist's depiction and the real thing" (quoted in Park 1986:22), a judgment that reflects a staunchly mimetic philosophy.

Or, to cite another illuminating case, in the 1920s, U.S. customs officials seized a semiabstract sculpture named "Bird in Space" by Constantin Brancusi on grounds that it was not art and should therefore not enter the United States duty-free. At the trial, the government lawyer argued, "Mr. Brancusi claims that this object represents a bird. If you met such a bird out shooting, would you fire?" (quoted in Stolnitz 1960:135)—a view that again is based on mimetic assumptions about art. (Ultimately, the court decided that the work was indeed art, a ruling that reflected the ascendancy of formalism in the twentieth century.)

At the same time that mimetic thinking underlies much popular criticism of contemporary fine arts, it also provides much support for popular art. The photograph on the bedroom dresser is treasured because it reminds its owners of the idyllic vacation trip to the mountains many years ago; a popular song about young romance becomes a favorite because it encapsulates an experience sought for and shared by many people; or a movie about a World War II submarine crew has a forceful impact on the audience because of its portrayal of a heroic will to survive a tragic, impersonal war. Each of these cases derives from an understanding that art can have significant value because of its capacity to represent, either literally or ideally, some subject in our actual lives.

The mimetic tradition has been pervasive and enduring in the West, providing a major philosophical basis for art during several historical periods. Even the largely religious art of the Middle Ages tacitly assumed that art's spiritual efficacy comes from its ability to effectively depict religious belief; and the emotionalist aesthetics of, for example, romanticism assume that art's special capacity to provoke high feelings is due to its representing subject matter that is affecting. Moreover, mimetic notions about art underlie much popular thinking about art.

But although one could force most Western aesthetic thought into the mimetic mold, to do so would be misleading. For one thing, no matter how we try we cannot convincingly explain some sorts of art in mimetic terms. Many art forms, including much instrumental music, most dance, all non-representational art and architecture, and many popular arts such as haute couture, do not depict a material subject outside the art work itself. Their styles undoubtedly reflect certain cultural tendencies and convey certain sorts of ideas, but they are not mimetic in the way that, say, a figurative painting is.

An even more compelling argument for a pluralistic model of Western aesthetics is that some aestheticians and artists have defined art in terms that are distinctly different from the mimetic ones discussed thus far. For a complete picture, then, we must, look at additional theories.

Pragmatic Theories

Pragmatic (or "instrumental") theories of aesthetics are based on the assumption that art should do something worthwhile for the members of the community that produces the art. Specifically, art should pave the way to a world that is socially, politically, or (most frequently) spiritually better.

Many varieties of art find their justification in pragmatic aesthetic theories. For example, art used for purposes of political propaganda is made to convince people to support a different, and arguably better, political regime; and the recently developed technique of "art therapy" attempts to use artistic media to improve the mental health of individuals who suffer from psychological problems. But by far the most common type of pragmatic art is made for religious purposes.[4]

The roots of aesthetic pragmatism can be traced back to the Old Testament of the *Bible*. In contrast to the Greeks, who saw art's value as lying primarily in its intrinsic, formal qualities, the Hebrew tradition usually emphasized the effect art had on the percipient: "Let me see thy countenance, and let me hear thy voice, for sweet is thy voice, and thy countenance is comely," says the *Song of Songs* (cf. Tatarkiewicz 1970b:8).

But it was not until the Middle Ages that the anagogic potential of art was fully realized (see **Figure 10–4**). During that period the artist was expected to create beauty, but this was largely thought of as an aesthetic means to a moral end: Beautiful objects that symbolize heaven and the laws of the universe were thought to be the most effective teachers of God's ways (cf. Tatarkiewicz 1970b:291). Thus Suger, the twelfth-century Abbot of St. Denis, wrote of his church, "I delighted in the beauty of the house of God; and the diverse colour and shapeliness of the gems detached me from my outward cares and, bearing me from the material to the non-material sphere, inclined me to reflect on the diversity of holy virtues" (trans. in Panofsky 1955:60–64).

---

[4]Religious art is sometimes said to be *anagogic*, in that it is thought to possess the mystical capacity to lead the audience member to a higher spiritual plane.

FIGURE 10–4   *The Flagellation of Christ,* from Troyes Cathedral, France. Stained glass, lead, thirteenth century; 53.3 cm in diameter. *(Courtesy Denver Art Museum, Dora Porter Mason Collection.)*

Such a philosophy influenced all aspects of art. The subject matter was overtly Christian, and an elaborate symbol system enlisted colors, flowers, items of dress, and so forth to convey additional messages (cf., e.g., Ferguson 1954). During the Middle Ages, the observance of time-honored methods and rules was far more important than creativity, and the identity of the artist was overshadowed by the religious ends that art served.

Religious art is still produced in the modern era, of course. Some is in the form of popular art with, for example, gospel music enjoying a large audience.[5] And a few fine artists, such as Georges Rouault and Edward Elgar, have produced profoundly religious art. Nevertheless, Western art since the Renaissance has clearly tended toward secular themes and has rarely been genuinely anagogical in motivation.

But the notion that art should serve a higher purpose did not die with

---

[5]Popular, contemporary religious art often combines the anagogic motive of pragmatic aesthetics with the emotional assumptions that gained ascendancy with the romantic rebellion. Thus much gospel music emphasizes "feeling the spirit" rather than didactically extolling moral virtues.

the Middle Ages. As noted previously, neo-classicism represented a merging of mimetic means with pragmatic ends. The resultant aesthetic is apparent in Sir Philip Sidney's *The Apologie for Poetry,* which, dating from the 1580s, is perhaps the first work of art criticism to be written in the English language. Sidney observes that poetry "is an arte of imitation, for so Aristotle termeth it in the word *Mimesis,* that is to say, a representing, counterfeitting, or figuring foorth—to speak metaphorically, a speaking picture: with this end, to teach and delight" (quoted in Abrams 1953:14). Similarly, Dr. Johnson praised Shakespeare's portrayal of reality because, Johnson believed, "the end of writing is to instruct; the end of poetry is to instruct by pleasing" (Abrams 1953:19.[6]

Echos of pragmatic aesthetic thinking have come down to us in the twentieth century in several forms. As noted, political art serves such a function, as does utopian literature, which is intended to direct people toward a better way of life. Equally pragmatic are authors who hope their writing will bring about social reform, a tradition that can be traced from Charles Dickens through Upton Sinclair to James Baldwin, all of whom *reveal* in order to *instruct.* Realism in photography (e.g., Riis's photographs of turn-of-the-century New York slums) and in cinema (e.g., Costa-Grava's films about political oppression in various countries) fit the same pattern.

But pragmatic aesthetic theories remain largely out of fashion in most contemporary writing on the fine arts; and in the opinion of most critics, political art succeeds despite its message, rather than because of it. It is a rarity when a theorist, such as Suzi Gablik, argues that the visual arts should have a moral or ethical dimension, or when John Gardner calls for a literature that "establishes models of human actions, casts nets toward the future, carefully judges our right and wrong directions" (J. Gardner 1978).

Perhaps representative of common contemporary beliefs about what art should "do" is a list, found in Monroe Beardsley's widely read *Aesthetics,* which attributes the following functions to art: Art, says Beardsley "relieves tensions and quiets destructive impulses," "resolves conflicts within the self," "refines perception and discrimination," "develops the imagination," and is "an aid to mental health." Only at the end of the list does one find functions of art that are as socially significant as those that concerned medieval and neo-classical thinkers: Art "fosters mutual sympathy and understanding" and it "offers an ideal for human life" (Beardsley 1981/1958:574–575). The gulf is vast indeed between this list of art's contributions to human well-being and the older, pragmatic belief that was expressed perhaps most

---

[6]The notions that art is representational and that it should be a model for ideal behavior are ironically supported by cross-cultural research that indicates that art generally *does* reflect a culture's fundamental themes, although the message is structural and implicit rather than didactic and explicit (cf. Fischer 1971; Anderson 1979:46–48).

succinctly in Dostoevsky's remark, "beauty will save the world" (Zenkovsky 1962:136).

Emotionalist Theories *Aristotle*

In the mid-eighteenth century, dominance in the quartet of Western aesthetic traditions began to shift from the pragmatism that spawned neoclassical art to the emotionalist beliefs that fueled the fires of the romantic rebellion. It might be said that if the reality of mimetic art lies in the material and social world, and the truth of pragmatic art lies in the moral, ethical, and spiritual realms, then emotionalist theories take as their universe the inner landscape of the individual's emotions and feelings.

But the roots of the emotionalist tradition antedate romanticism. As noted above, the ancient Hebrews were less interested in an art object's external characteristics than they were in its effects on the subjective experience of the percipient. Aristotle developed a similar concept in his theory of catharsis. Tragic poetry was valuable, he believed, because by engendering pity and fear it purged the reader's (or listener's) spirit of the pent-up emotions that could otherwise be harmful. (Aristotle also noted that in the art of rhetoric, persuasion is accomplished by, among other things, stirring the emotions of the speaker's audience.) The later Roman writer, Lucretius, also contributed to the emotionalist tradition by asserting that emotions are of fundamental human importance because they stem from a primordial past in which men were supposedly "endowed only with instinct, passions, and mere potentiality of reason" (Abrams 1953:83).

The voice of emotionalist aesthetics can even be heard during the Middle Ages, as a counterpoint to the prevailing anagogic thinking of the time. For example, some genres of oral literature, such as Goliardic verses and the fabliaux, were created principally for entertainment, and there was a widely held belief that a regular dose of "literary pleasure" helped sustain one's mental, and even physical, well-being (cf. Olson 1982).

But it was in the late eighteenth century that a coherent and pervasive theory appeared in the form of the romantic movement which viewed art as an embodiment and expression of emotion. Romantic artists focused on the internal world of the human spirit, rather than on some aspect of the external world. The creative process itself became a major focus of interest; and art's "subject matter," if it may still be called that, became the artist's personal thoughts, perceptions, and feelings. Thus it became popular to speak of artistic "expression," a term suggesting that something is "forced out by a pressure from within" (Abrams 1953:138); indeed, fine art was increasingly thought to be produced by individuals who, because of their exceptional sensitivity, possess an abnormally great measure of emotion and feeling, psychological states that well forth in the form of art.

Because of its great popularity, and also because of the easy availability of the written word, the tenets of emotionalist theory can be found in the words of modern artists themselves. For example, the mid-nineteenth-century French painter Corot called explicitly for emotionalism, individuality, and sincerity in painters: "Be guided by feeling alone . . . [follow] your own convictions. It is better to be nothing than an echo of other painters. . . . If you have really been touched, you will convey to others the sincerity of your emotions" (quoted in Stolnitz 1960:158). Wordsworth, for his part, defined poetry very simply as "the spontaneous overflow of powerful feelings" (quoted in Abrams 1953:21).

Such emotionalist thinking had interesting and important ramifications for art. Nature scenes and common people, both of which were portrayed so as to emphasize their honest emotions and passions, provided common subject matter (see **Figures 10–5** and **10–6**). Also, criticism in the visual arts shifted away from either a concern with the artist's skillfulness in representation (as mimetic aesthetics had dictated), or the social and moral message of the subject matter (as prescribed by aesthetic pragmatism). Instead, the first requisite of an art work was its uniqueness: Since every person's feelings are individual and inborn, no art work could be a copy of another.

FIGURE 10–5   J. M. W. Turner, *Fish Market at Hastings Beach.* Oil on canvas, 35 3/4" high; 1810. *(The Nelson-Atkins Museum of Art, Kansas City, Missouri [Nelson Fund].)*

FIGURE 10-6 Jean Auguste Dominique Ingres, *Portrait of the Sculptor, Paul Lemoyne.* Oil on canvas, 1808–1820; 18 3/4" high. *(The Nelson-Atkins Museum of Art, Kansas City, Missouri [Nelson Fund].)*

Formalism has supplanted romanticism in most serious, contemporary writing on the arts, but emotionalist aesthetic values remain alive and well today, providing a foundation for much Western popular art. However, whereas artists themselves are still commonly thought to possess heightened sensibilities, the greater emphasis today tends to be upon art's effects on the audience member's emotions.

Thus, emotionalist aesthetics provides a clear fiat for most popular art forms. Rock concerts; recorded background music in shops, restaurants, and offices; and the interminable broadcast of music to home and car radios—all are intended to bring pleasure, diversion, and some degree of enjoyment to those who hear it. And the same motives prompt Westerners to spend millions of dollars each year to go dancing and to the movies; and still more millions are spent by advertisers in order to sell their products through association with the comic and/or dramatic offerings of television.[7]

The important role of emotions and feelings in the aesthetics of Western popular art is revealed by research conducted by Mihaly Csikszentmiha-

---

[7]Fear of the supposedly harmful effects caused by art "only" making one happy can be traced back to the *Old Testament,* although the few empirically based studies of the question have produced contradictory results.

Iyi and Eugene Rochberg-Halton, reported in *The Meanings of Things: Domestic Symbols and the Self* (1981). The researchers interviewed 315 individuals from 82 families living in the Chicago metropolitan area. The sample represented diverse socioeconomic classes, races, and generations.

After background information had been collected, each person in the survey was asked, "What are the things in your home which are special to you?" Then the interviewer went on to ask why the objects mentioned were "special," what life would be like in their absence, and so on. The responses were tape recorded, verbatim transcripts were made, and from these data the researchers extracted a fascinating picture of "the meaning of things."

The 1,694 objects that people mentioned as being "special" fit comfortably into 41 categories, and about half of them fall into just ten types of objects, as shown in Table 10–1.

These ten categories alone provide an interesting picture of contemporary American culture inasmuch as all of them are either directly connected with art (e.g., "visual art," "stereo") or else are objects that are typically associated with aesthetic gratification (e.g., "plants" and "plates," both of the decorative variety). (Many of the other, less frequently mentioned items, such as jewelry, clothes, quilts, and silverware, have similar aesthetic associations.) Only very rarely did people have feelings of specialness for non-aesthetic objects such as "sports equipment," "telephones," or "refrigerators."

But the actual meanings attached to these objects are even more interesting, providing substantial evidence of the importance of emotionalist factors in people's feelings about their most "special" possessions. The 7,875 reasons people gave for these objects' specialness fell into eleven general

TABLE 10–1   Categories of Items Most Frequently Said to Be "Special" by 315 Individuals in the Chicago Metropolitan Area.

OBJECT CATEGORY	PERCENTAGE OF PEOPLE MENTIONING AT LEAST ONE SPECIAL OBJECT IN CATEGORY
Furniture	36
Visual Art	26
Photographs	23
Books	22
Stereo	22
Musical Instruments	22
TV	21
Sculpture	19
Plants	15
Plates	15

(Csikszentmihalyi and Rochberg-Halton 1981:58)

"meaning classes," and many of these are aesthetic in nature. For example, many objects were considered special because of their "style." The reasons people gave for the specialness of objects in the categor- ies of "visual art" and "sculpture" are the most interesting of all. Although one might have thought that art objects would be valued because of their aesthetic qualities, this was the case in only 16 percent of the cases (Csiks- zentmihalyi and Rochberg-Halton 1981:65).

Nevertheless, the art objects that people held to be special did prompt very strong feelings in people, a finding that parallels the ancient Hebrew aesthetic belief that emphasized an art work's impact on the audience member's spirit. Csikszentmihalyi and Rochberg-Halton learned that one of the most common reasons for valuing such objects was their association with other family members. One woman remarked, "I am going to keep this thing [a bust] forever. I wasn't even in school and me and my mother went to the store and I told her this looked like her, so she bought it. I'm going to keep this for life. It reminds me of my mother" (ibid.:77).

The special way in which art objects can evoke feelings and emotions, not only among connoisseurs of the fine arts but also in people with no special training in the art, is vividly revealed in the case of another of Csiks- zentmihalyi and Rochberg-Halton's respondents, an old Black man who had done domestic work most of his life. At the beginning of the interview he insisted that nothing he owned was particularly "special" to him.

> Toward the end of the interview, however, a look of recognition passed over his face; he walked to the mantle shelf and pointed at two black porcelain figures representing crouching panthers. These, he said, were special to him in a way that the other things were not. He told a long story about how he had always admired panthers and that his nephew, who was aware of this predilection, during a trip to the South found these two statues in a pawnshop window in Nashville and called him up, asking if he should buy them? The old man said yes and the nephew bought the panthers, which have been crouching above the fireplace ever since. (ibid.:77–78)

But besides reminding him of his nephew's thoughtfulness, the figurines were also important to the man because of the qualities he associated with panthers: "They are so smooth, so powerful, yet they don't scarcely show it" (ibid.:78)[8] This man clearly had strong feelings about his porcelain figurines, reminding him as they did of valued character traits and his neph- ew's thoughtfulness.

---

[8]Although the owner of the porcelain panthers had not previously associated them with the Black Panther political party, his attraction to this particular species of animal may reflect his Black heritage. Robert Farris Thompson's article, "The Aesthetic of the Cool" (1966) dis- cusses the ways in which values such as those attributed to the porcelain figurines parallel the philosophies of West Africa, which place a high value on both personal vitality and the re- strained, or "cool," display of emotion. See also the preceding chapter on Yoruba aesthetics.

Many of the people whom Csikszentmihalyi and Rochberg-Halton interviewed provided equally heartfelt explanations for their deep attachment to "special" objects. And even in the occasional mention of aesthetic qualities, personal associations were often involved. For example, one individual said, "It's a picture of a ship, under water. There's a certain light effect, and color effect. There are rays of light coming down on the sunken ship. It's the first time we ever bought any art and I really enjoyed that, looking at it" (ibid.:66), a rationale that suggests not only aesthetic appeal but also sensuous satisfaction—and a desire to be seen as something of a connoisseur.

The study by Csikszentmihalyi and Rochberg-Halton shows unequivocally that the art that is important in most people's day-to-day lives is not valued merely because of art's unique ability to portray subject matter in compliance with mimetic theory, nor for the pragmatic reason that it improves people religiously or politically. Rather, art works are important because of the feelings they evoke in their owners. The feelings themselves may not reflect the high romanticism of Corot or Wordsworth, but they are very potent nonetheless. Art plays a significant role in the contemporary Western world, verifying and embodying those principles that are most important in people's lives, namely their concepts of themselves and their feelings about others.

Formalist Theories

Just as in the early nineteenth century, when emotionalist aesthetics under the banner of the romantic rebellion supplanted the mimetic and pragmatic concerns of neo-classicism in the fine arts, in the early twentieth century romanticism itself was largely replaced in serious writing on art by the aesthetic of formalism. This school of thought asserts that art is valuable and important because of its "formal" qualities—the painter's use of color and composition; the composer's mastery of counterpoint or the sonata form; or the poet's choice of words to fit a rhyme scheme, effective use of assonance, or establishment of an ironic tone.

Like the other three aesthetic traditions of the West, the roots of formalism can be traced back to classical sources. Pythagoras (or one of his followers) said, "order and proportion are beautiful and useful, while disorder and lack of proportion are ugly and useless" (quoted in Tatarkiewicz 1970a:86); and several generations later Aristotle asserted in *The Metaphysics* (ibid:31) that "the main species of beauty are order, symmetry, and definiteness." This outlook, which was subtly injected into Christian writings by Greek translators, led classical artists and aestheticians to seek harmony, proportion, and measure in art works—goals that were as natural to medieval and renaissance thinkers as they were antithetical to baroque and romantic artists. By the late nineteenth century, however, signs of change became apparent. For example, the painting popularly known as *Whistler's Mother* was actually named *Arrangement in Gray and Black* by its creator, because, he said, "That's what it is. To me it is interesting as a picture of my mother; but what can or ought the public to care about the identity of the portrait?" (quoted in Canaday 1981:214)

In the early twentieth century these ideas were forged into an influential school of criticism known as formalism. Roger Fry, Clive Bell, and others found perfection not in God's design but in the "significant form" of the finest of art, a quality that is identified by its capacity to provoke in the sensitive audience member a powerful and distinctive "aesthetic response." Bell asks,

> What quality is shared by all objects that provoke our aesthetic emotions? What quality is common to Santa Sophia and the windows at Chartres, Mexican sculpture, a Persian bowl, Chinese carpets, Giotto's frescoes at Padua, and the masterpieces of Poussin, Piero della Francesca, and Cezanne? Only one answer seems possible—significant form. In each, lines and colours combined in a particular way, certain forms and relations of forms, stir our aesthetic emotions. (Bell 1958:28)

Formalism's uniqueness becomes more apparent when it is contrasted with the three preceding aesthetic traditions. Unlike mimetic theories, formalism does not emphasize art's ability to communicate semblances of extra-artistic subject matter. Indeed, formalism can be seen as a natural consequence of twentieth-century artists' shift away from representationalism and toward abstract art **(Figure 10–7)**, a trend that was to ultimately provoke the dictum, "The meaning of painting is paint!"

Formalism is equally distant from pragmatic theories. In fact, the "preachiness" of much representational art is considered by formalists to be a liability rather than an asset, so that art may be important *despite* its subject matter rather than because of it. Thus Bell says, "Let no one imagine that representation is bad in itself; a realistic form may be as significant, in its place as part of the design, as an abstract. But if a representative form has value, it is as form, not as representation" (Bell 1958:42).

Finally, although formalism resembles emotionalist theories in its definition of art as that which evokes a response in the percipient, it differs from other emotionalist approaches in two ways. First, formalism claims that the emotions spawned by art are unique: The experience of viewing a masterful abstract painting, for example, is totally distinctive. According to formalist thinking, such an art work is in a completely different class from, say, an illustration of a tow-headed boy digging a grave for his beloved but recently deceased dog, Rover. The latter picture may bring a tear to the sentimental viewer's eye, but the formalists asserted that such a maudlin response has no more to do with true art than the tear shed by a loyal

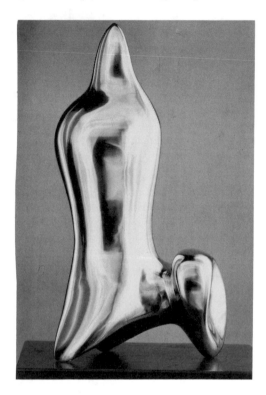

FIGURE 10-7   Hans Arp, *Vue et Entendue.*
Guilded bronze, 13 1/4" high; 1942.   *(The
Nelson-Atkins Museum of Art, Kansas City,
Missouri [Gift of the Friends of Art].)*

sports fan whose team has just lost a pivotal game of its otherwise promising season.

Formalism also differs from other emotionalist theories in focusing primarily on the quality of the art work, rather than on the quality of emotional response prompted by the art work—hence the phrase, "art for art's sake."

Formalism has had particularly interesting implications for literary criticism, since the written word inevitably conveys some subject matter. Formalist critics, from the earlier era of *new criticism* to the current school known as *deconstruction,* have attempted to look at literature as an artifact that exists above and beyond its overt meaning. Formal analysis concentrates on such qualities as the work's conformance to its genre or its style of word use. The assumption behind such approaches is that the critic's proper goal is "to explore the concept of the poem as a heterocosm, a world of its own, independent of the world into which we are born, whose end is not to instruct or please but simply to exist" (Abrams 1953:27).

Almost all formalist writing, from Aristotle to the twentieth century, has used examples from the fine arts to make its case. However, insofar as formalism is concerned with the artist's consummate mastery of his or her medium, it is identical to a concern that the public at large typically has regarding all the arts, whether fine or popular: Artists possess levels of skill that far exceed those of non-artists, so that in many people's minds the mere ability to perform a piano concerto, to dance *sur les pointes,* or to realistically render a likeness in oil paints insures that the maker is popularly recognized as an "artist." And although the skills required for most of the popular arts may not require a lifetime of study, these practitioners too are respected for their talents and training. Furthermore, the common tendency to define art as being non-utilitarian, to believe that art does not *do* anything (except bring some grace into one's life!)—this too resembles the formalist perspective on art.[9]

Formalism has been criticized by some because of its inherent circularity: Art is defined as that which, because of its significant form, engenders a distinctive reaction in the sympathetic percipient; but at the same time, such a reaction is recognized only by being prompted by the significant form that characterizes genuine art (cf. Stolnitz 1960:145–146). Nevertheless, formalism, both as narrowly applied to the fine arts and in its influential and enduring application to the popular arts, has played a significant role among Western aesthetic traditions. As native members of Western culture, many of us must admit that the basic premise of the formalist argument does strike a resonant note in our thinking about art. There *is* something very special about those things we consider to be art, a quality that somehow transcends art's mimetic, pragmatic, and emotionalist potentialities.

Conclusion

The West has produced vast quantities of art, and nearly as great an effort has been directed toward speculation about art's underlying purpose and nature. The long sweep of Western history has seen many permutations of religious and ideological belief, so that despite the general coherence of aesthetic thinking, each age has emphasized now one, now another line of artistic thought. Western aesthetics has been steadfastly pluralistic, a "quartet" of traditions made of four related but distinctive voices.

The four traditions of Western aesthetics have not been mere academic exercises but have had a significant impact on the evaluation of actual art works. For example, George Boas's clever paper, "The Mona Lisa in the History of Taste" (1963/1940) traces the vicissitudes of critical thought regarding Leonardo da Vinci's portrait of a burgher's young wife. During

---

[9]The study by Csikszentmihalyi and Rochberg-Halton of things that Americans consider to be "special" found that although emotional factors (e.g., "it reminds me of my mother") were given most commonly to explain people's attachment to their special things, formal qualities ("style" and "aesthetic considerations") were also mentioned for more than one-quarter of the items of visual art. Even the concern that, say, a painting "goes with the drapes" is in a sense formalistic.

the painter's lifetime, the work was apparently not considered to be particularly outstanding; but by the mid-sixteenth century, Vasari voiced the dominant mimetic standards of the Renaissance by praising Leonardo's uncanny
accuracy in portraying his subject. With the passage of time, this view gradually changed, and comments on the painting increasingly emphasized the
way in which it captured its quintessentially feminine subject, a view whose
mimetic underpinnings were being influenced by neo-classical idealism.

Critics of the romantic period continued to praise the *Mona Lisa* for
its subject matter, but the face that had been seen as a paragon of sweetness
and light became, by 1800, that of a *femme fatale,* about whom critics could
embroider emotionalist fantasies of intuition, feeling, and all things unlike
the stereotypical male rationality.[10] Thus did the popular evaluation of the
Mona Lisa weather the major sea change as the mimetic and pragmatic values of the neo-classical period were replaced by the emotionalist assumptions of romanticism.

Clearly the artistic and aesthetic pluralism of the West reflects the
complex currents and counter-currents that have characterized Western
economic and political systems. For example, Karen Field (1982) has described art education in three distinctly different situations—an art college,
an art department in a large university, and an amateur art club. In the
course of a year's fieldwork, she collected information on, among other
things, the criteria used by instructors and artists in evaluating art works.
The critical criteria most often mentioned in these settings can be arrayed
along a continuum, from attitudes within the artist (expression, confidence,
honesty) to object-centered qualities (e.g., beauty, economy, and rhythm).
Field found that critics in the art college tended to emphasize artist-
centered qualities reflecting the spirit in which the work was created,
whereas art club teachers were more concerned with the objective features
of the art work itself. (Instructors in university art departments tended to
fall between these two extremes.) Thus even today and in the fine arts alone,
Western aesthetics is adamantly pluralistic in nature.

Although the outlines of the four Western aesthetic traditions are now
known, issues such as those that we have just touched upon are inadequately
understood. What factors in the broader sociocultural environment lead to
the ascendancy of one "voice" in the "quartet" and the lessening of importance of others? How does this pluralistic situation impinge on art education and on the actual production of a specific art work? These and other
important questions remain to be studied.

---

[10]Boas observes that three hundred years before the romantic rebellion, women in the
West were stereotyped by most men as being "cruel, coquettish, vain, deceitful, gentle, fickle,
tender, weak, but they had rarely been enigmatic. On the contrary, men knew them only too
well" (Boas 1963/1940:584) It was the new "woman-as-enigma" idea that prompted the romantic
critics to praise the *Mona Lisa's* ambiguous smile.

PART TWO
11

INTRODUCTION
TO PART TWO

Aesthetic theory has often been pretentious. . . . Each theory has to
do with a *possibility* of art, but not, as they have often claimed, to
do with "Art." This is especially evident when the arts of non-
western cultures are included in the art world, (a not unreasonable
request). (Deutsch 1975:x–xi)

The chapters of Part One have examined many "possibilities" of art; but the
question remains, what conclusions can be drawn about "Art"? That is, what
do the preceding accounts of aesthetics in ten societies tell us about the general phenomenon of art cross-culturally? Each culture we have looked at has
had a unique reigning spirit of art, its own characteristic Calliope. But how
significant is the distinctiveness of each of the muses we have met? Is every
one truly a unique entity, fundamentally unlike all others; or are the culture-
specific idiosyncracies of Calliope's sisters relatively superficial, masking a single genius of art?

Part One attempted to bring each society's aesthetic system alive by calling attention to its coherence, its credibility—and ultimately its nobility. But
for purposes of comparison, we must now reduce these individualized accounts to their fundamental principles and state them in terms that are abstract enough to allow cross-cultural similarities and differences to become
apparent. As with any reduction, much is lost in the process. For the moment
we must ignore both the native rationales that justify each society's aesthetic
principles as well as the distinctive tone of feeling and style that characterizes
each culture's philosophy of art.

But just as we must necessarily neglect much ethnographic detail, we
must also be certain that the retained information is correct. The principles
must be formulated accurately, avoiding the temptation to modify concepts
slightly—for example, saying "fertility" when the operant native concept is a
generalized desire for human well-being. (Appendix One presents a précis of
each of the aesthetic systems discussed in Part One.)

The quest for aesthetic universals has engaged many Western thinkers since at least the fifth century B.C. Their efforts have often failed because they began with untestable axioms about art and proceeded to conclusions via deductive logic. I am adopting the opposite approach: Instead of beginning with premises assumed to be true *a priori,* I start with the hard-earned discoveries of the many fieldworkers who have studied the arts of other peoples in depth and at first hand. From this information, we can only *hope* that a logically consistent picture can be discerned, but the existence of such a pattern is not taken for granted. However, as the following chapters reveal, I believe that the available data do clearly reveal a single Calliope and go a long way toward disclosing her fundamental nature.

The chapters of Part Two use the data from Part One for several specific purposes. First, Chapter 12 looks for systematic patterns of cross-cultural variation. That is, insofar as philosophies of art do vary from one place to another, to what extent are these variations linked to concomitant variation in other sociocultural factors? Then Chapters 13 and 14 discuss features of aesthetics that occur in all ten of Part One's societies and that may well be universal. Finally, as an epilogue, Chapter 15 compares Western aesthetics to the philosophies of art found in other cultures.

12

COMPARATIVE AESTHETICS
The Many Faces
of the Muse

"Different strokes for different folks!"

When someone walks through a museum's non-Western art collection, his or her strongest reaction is that it *looks so different*, at least in comparison to the art that most Western artists make. This person might accept the experience, dismissing the differences as being no greater than those between, say, a Renaissance painting by Rembrandt and a modern sculpture by Louise Nevelson. It's all striking, creative, and a pleasure to look at, so it must be "art." (After all, it *is* in a museum, isn't it?[1]) This view may evaporate, however, as our hypothetical museum-goer reads the labels that accompany the non-Western art works: "Cult figures" stand next to "initiation masks," "lip ornaments," and a "chief's royal stool." Surely such uses set these art works apart from each other—and even farther apart from the pieces by Rembrandt and Nevelson.

In Chapters 13 and 14, I hope to show that a common unity *is* shared by art throughout the world, with artists everywhere using their special skills to imbue sensuous media with potent meaning. In so doing, art seems to fill a need that is universal throughout the human race. This realization, though abstract, should convince our hypothetical museum-goer of the legitimacy of housing the diverse objects of non-Western art under the same roof as Renaissance painting and contemporary sculpture.

But it would be disingenuous to ignore the museum-goer's reaction to the apparent diversity of art. It does, after all, reflect a second characteristic of our species—namely, our restless creativity, as manifest in a wide compass of cross-cultural diversity. Although a particular society may be uniform and

---

[1]Clifford Geertz (1983:119) has remarked, "Most people, I am convinced, see African sculpture as bush Picasso and hear Javanese music as noisy Dubussy." It is also worth noting that "museum" derives from the Latin, "temple of the muses."

enduring, there appear to be dramatic differences *among* societies. The resident of Manhattan cannot ignore considerations of subsistence any more than can the Eskimo, but hunting seals through the winter sea ice is quite unlike working on the New York Stock Exchange, and we should not overlook the differences between the two subsistence techniques. If the first goal of science is to uncover the fundamental unities that underlie our universe, the second is surely to discover the principles whereby these unities interact to produce a world of considerable diversity. Therefore, this chapter focuses on what may be properly called *comparative aesthetics*—that is, cross-cultural differences between conceptions of art, and the extra-aesthetic, sociocultural factors that may cause these differences.

Small-scale Versus Complex Societies: Contemporary Comparisons

Some of the more embarrassing skeletons in cultural anthropology's closet are the evolutionary theories that were constructed by the discipline's first generation of scholars in the late nineteenth century. At their worst, those writers assumed that the institutions found in the complex, industrial civilizations of their day were perched atop an evolutionary ladder and that the practices found in other societies could legitimately be assigned to lower rungs, representing stages through which the more "advanced" institutions had passed.

The notion that the institutions of the West are always more advanced (in the sense of being better) than those found elsewhere is now rejected as an ethnocentrism with racist ramifications; and the labors of several generations of careful fieldworkers have forced us to appreciate the subtle complexity and functional suitability of alien customs.

We shall turn later to the question of aesthetic evolution, but we should first explore a territory that is considerably safer. In addition to the differences between cultures past and present, there are also important differences among contemporary societies—not in their worth or their legitimacy but rather in such unarguable areas as their size, the complexity of their technology, and the degree to which the division of labor and other differentiating factors (such as social class or ethnic identity) create a relatively high degree of internal diversity. Indeed, these three factors—population, technology, and heterogeneity—generally vary with one another, and taken together they define a dimension that differentiates relatively small-scale from relatively complex societies.[2] If the reigning question of this chapter concerns the systematic differences that are found among various societies' aesthetic systems, then one

---

[2]Elsewhere (Anderson 1979:2–8) I have discussed the hazards of using the word "primitive" to refer to those societies that are here designated "small-scale" (see also p. 4, footnote).

interesting issue to explore is the possibility of systematic differences between the aesthetics of small-scale versus complex societies. If the ten cultures described in Part One are representative, then this sociological dimension does indeed include distinctive differences in ideas about art. (And it should be remembered that one factor in selecting this sample of ten societies was that they represent all parts of the continuum that ranges from small-scale to complex societies.)

Because of their relatively simple technology and low level of social heterogeneity, the three non-agricultural societies discussed in Part One—the San, the Eskimos, and the Aboriginal groups of north-central Australia—show certain similarities in their art production. Their nomadic lifestyle and their lack of draft animals prompt one obvious commonality in their art: It is *portable*. Song, dance, and oral literature are the ultimately transportable art forms, and as a consequence they are very important among nomadic groups.

Body decoration is important for the same reason. Distinctive haircuts, tattoos, decorative scars, and body paint constitute negligible baggage for nomads. Jewelry and distinctive clothing weigh only little more, and they also have the advantage of leaving the hands free for carrying objects, tending children, or food-collecting while on the move.

The decorations on necessary utilitarian items—the San's ostrich egg-shell canteens, Inuit harpoons and needle-cases, and Australian boomerangs—exemplify another solution to the nomad's problem. Among these necessities are artistic objects used for religious purposes—Eskimo amulets, Australian tjurungas, and San oracle disks. But the dearth of secular, three-dimensional art suggests that aesthetic considerations are secondary to religious ones in objects such as these. That is, hunters and gatherers probably carry "religious art" with them because it is religious rather than because it is art.[3]

Small-scale societies are not unique in producing easily portable art. Complex societies also practice the performing arts, lavish attention on the appearance of the individual body, and decorate some of their tools, so it is the *absence* of bulky art (e.g., the "permanent collections" that are stored in stately museums) that sets nomadic groups apart—that, and the absolute importance of the transportable art that is produced. Recall the picture of a San encampment. At any given time, one or more people are making music, stories are being told, and the bodies of young and old alike are

---

[3]As noted in the chapters on San and Australian Aboriginal aesthetics, nomadic peoples sometimes paint on caves and on other permanent stone faces. Such groups rarely wander randomly; instead, they typically visit the same sites, one after the other, with the passing of the seasons. Thus the labor-intensive art is left temporarily, to be seen and used on subsequent visits to the same site.

adorned with tattoos, beads, and other decorations. Restricting art to easily portable media obviously does not necessitate relegating art to insignificance.

The foregoing remarks concern the production of art rather than the philosophy that underlies it. Regarding aesthetics, the most obvious difference between small- and large-scale societies is the explicitness with which aesthetic ideas are articulated, a fact that has important consequences. If the predominantly mobile nature of art in hunting-gathering-fishing groups is a consequence of the nomadic lifestyle of those societies, then the explicitness with which art is discussed in complex societies results from another characteristic difference between the smallest and largest of societies— namely, the more elaborate division of labor that is inevitably found in the latter cultures, such as those of the Aztecs, early India, Japan, and the West.

All societies, even the smallest in scale, have their native philosophers; but in small-scale societies, such intellectuals must perforce engage in subsistence activities along with the other adult members of their sex. But agriculture, especially as it becomes more intensified, typically brings with it a class of part- or full-time specialists who, freed of manual labor, have time to devote to the skills of the mind. Historically, most members of this class were probably no more than priests, bureaucrats, and tyrants, but the speculative thinkers among them did produce such things as a cosmology to accompany recently refined calendrical systems, ideologies to justify increased political centralization, and, significantly, aesthetic theories to explain the new art and craft techniques that had appeared.

Despite the lack of such specialists, hunter-gatherer-fishers have definite ideas about the meaning and value of art, just as their belief systems include many cosmological and ideological propositions. But in small-scale societies, such concepts are either implicit and couched in the matrix of folklore, myth, and world view, or else are only narrow statements about why one thing or act is preferred over another. But this picture changes dramatically as the division of labor increases and intellectuals become part-time and then full-time specialists in speculative thought. For example, the Aztec *tlamatinime* defined themselves as men whose mission was to "shine their light on the world, to inquire into the region of the gods above and into the region of the dead below" (León-Portilla 1971:448). Similarly, classical India had its Hindu *rasikas*, whose exceptional sensitivity and enlightenment allowed them to experience the complex emotions associated with *rasa*. In the complex Japanese tradition, we repeatedly read of individuals, primarily priests, who made pronouncements about the role of art in the various sects of Buddhism. And Western intellectuals going back to at least Plato have consciously analyzed art, either in conjunction with broader philosophical arguments or else as an intellectual challenge in itself.

If aesthetic ideas are generally implicit in small-scale, hunter-gatherer societies and explicit in complex societies, then agricultural societies fall between these two extremes. For example, the Yoruba language contains words—*amewa* and *mewa*—that refer to individuals who are known for their ability to judge beauty; but an *amewa* is not a full-time aesthetician or critic but a farmer, a village chief, or a practicing artist who is especially skilled at judging and discussing art. Further, the expertise of these connoisseurs is in verbalizing the stylistic strengths and weaknesses of specific art works, and more fundamental and general aesthetic beliefs are, for the most part, implicit.

The explicit/implicit contrast cannot be taken too far, of course. Not *all* of the aesthetic ideas in complex societies are explicitly formulated by professional theoreticians. To the contrary, such societies have their share of aesthetic notions that are never more than implied within the general fabric of the culture. For example, the popular arts in the West have seldom caught the attention of aestheticians; and in Japan the aesthetics implicit in Shintoism, despite its importance for the Japanese aesthetic tradition generally, never seems to have been overtly articulated. (This is not surprising since Shintoism goes back to the animistic beliefs of pre-Neolithic Japan, and its aesthetic ideas were well accepted before the arrival of the Buddhist tradition and its acceptance by the aristocracy.)

If much aesthetic thought in complex societies is available via the explicitly written and spoken word, aesthetic principles in small-scale societies may be equally accessible, but in a different way. They are straightforward enough that all members of the society find it easy to understand them. In small-scale societies, normal processes of socialization suffice for transmitting ideas about art from one generation to the next. Courses in "art appreciation" are unnecessary; no arcane and specialized vocabulary is needed; and complex metaphysical argument is absent.

The self-conscious nature of aesthetics in complex societies leads them to cover the same general territory as those in small-scale societies, but to do so in more detail. For example, all societies have ideas about beauty, but in small-scale societies, such ideas are fairly general and are applied primarily to the appearance of humans and their close associates, such as the pastoralist's cattle. By contrast, complex societies typically have an intricate canon of beauty or, more generally, of formal appropriateness. For example, the West and India both developed complicated mathematical formulae for the proportions proper to not only the ideal human body but also to architecture, music, and calligraphy. The Inuit doubtless distinguish between the smoothly curving arc of a well-made igloo and the ungainly shape of an ill-made one, but their standards of architectural beauty are far less elaborate than, for example, the calculations Michelangelo used in designing a dome for St. Peter's Basilica, where he was challenged to design an edifice that was not only structurally sound but would also comply with the complex, classical norms of correct proportion.

As aesthetics is relegated to the province of an intellectual (and, generally, socioeconomic) elite, it also becomes more intricate and densely textured in its ideas about the emotional response that art can provoke. Again, the development is not so much a matter of exploring new aesthetic territory but is rather a movement toward mapping known territory in ever greater detail. Presumably Greeks before Aristotle and Indians before Abhinavagupta experienced the whole gamut of aesthetic feelings, but it remained for these two seminal thinkers, writing in their respective traditions, to set down typologies of emotions. Thereafter artist and audience alike could approach art with a conscious awareness of the potentialities of the aesthetic response, aided by the intricate vocabularies that Aristotle and Abhinava formalized.

But "intricate" is not the same as "profound," and we would be mistaken to assume that aesthetics in small-scale societies is on the whole less intellectually sophisticated than that in complex societies. Recall for example, the Inuit, with their realization that art has the capacity to transmute things among the realms of the natural, the human, and the supernatural. Surely the insight of this theory equals that of, say, the four traditions that Western aestheticians have developed.

Nor do large and small societies differ in the pragmatism of their aesthetic ideas. In all societies, it is common to view art as a means to an end, usually a supernatural end at that. Australian Aboriginal concern with the Dreamtime and Navajo ideas about nature's harmony and beauty, as embodied in *hózhǫ* are not qualitatively different from religious aesthetic thought in Aztec, Indian, Japanese, and Western culture.

The theories of the elite class in complex societies are not only explicit; they are also often self-serving, extolling the virtue and refinement of the aristocracy. In *rasa* theory, only those brahmins who had attained a high enough level of spiritual consciousness could relish genuine aesthetic delight. And for their part, Aztec wise men reasoned that only the enlightened ones, those with "deified hearts," would have their flowers and songs accepted by the gods.

Matters are more complex in Japan and the West because their aesthetic pluralism is accompanied by cultural pluralism, and the shifting tides of political ascendancy have caused periodic changes in the make-up of the elite. However, in Japan both Esoteric Buddhism and Zen Buddhism claimed that salvation and enlightenment would come only to the select few—specifically those who could grasp the ineluctable core of art's message. Amida Buddhism, a far more popular religious movement, had a correspondingly more egalitarian aesthetic; however, the Confucian influence on Japanese aesthetics emphasized stability of the state and the use of the arts to perpetuate the status quo.

Intellectual (and sometimes sociopolitical) elitism is a recurrent feature in the West also. The classical and neo-classical tendency to equate beauty with ideal form, "ideal" being known with certainty only by the privileged arbiters of taste and convention; the claims by religious thinkers that the anagogic glories of art are available solely to the elect; the arguments by Romantic theorists that only those with heightened emotional sensitivity could truly appreciate art; and the formalist modification of this last tenet that substitutes formal for emotional sensitivity—all are ways of saying that only the *cognoscenti* recognize or appreciate "true" art.

The elitism common to aesthetics in complex societies is predictable when one looks beyond the abstract components of philosophies of art to consider the actual methods of art production. The technical subtleties of a "fine" art style may well be lost on individuals who have limited experience with the medium; they can be appreciated only by the artists themselves (hence the "artist's artist") or by individuals who have had the luxury of free time to study the medium, acquiring a refinement of taste that the less privileged never know (hence the "critical success but popular failure"). Also, complex societies include not only the social strata of class but also gradients of ethnic and regional diversity, with each sector practicing its own art forms. Thus, when the Aztec philosophers praised the art of the "true Toltecs," they were elevating their fellow Nahua-speakers above the many other ethnic groups they had welded into their vast empire.

The distance between the aesthetic elite and the majority of common people in complex societies is often accompanied by a gap between aestheticians and artists. The discontinuity between theory and practice is sometimes the basis for assuming that artistic talent is inborn, rather than acquired; it may provide a rationale for artists being confined to distinct castes or guilds; and it leads to the requirement that artists perform certain purifying rituals before undertaking their work. That such a breach is not inevitably present in complex societies is evidenced by the occasional aristocrat-theoretician who is also an artist, as in the writing, painting, and sculpture of the Amida Buddhist priest, Genshin,[4] the poetry of several Aztec priests, and the occasional Westerner, such as Susan Sontag or John Berger, who not only theorizes about art but also produces it.

The art and aesthetics of small-scale societies may differ from those in complex societies in terms of *structural* attributes such as explicitness and intricacy, but what about the *content* of their aesthetic systems? One may well ask, Is the art of hunter-gatherers more oriented toward the supernatural than art in complex societies? As the next chapter, 13, shows at length, a comparative study of contemporary societies reveals only that art in *all* societies embodies culturally significant meaning; and small-scale societies seem

---

[4]The relatively broad appeal of Amida Buddhism may be relevant in accounting for this anomaly.

to have at least as great an interest in the secular significance of art as do complex societies.[5]

Nor does symbolism appear to differ systematically between small- and large-scale societies. In both, some art is iconographic while other art is genuinely symbolic in that its relationship to its referent is wholly conventional and not based on any apparent resemblance. Perhaps the iconographic repertoire increases in size as societies become more complex— more gods, spirits, ancestors, mortals, and natural objects provide the artist with a superabundance of subject matter. The emergence of a class of religious specialists may also permit the development of a larger pantheon, although one should not underestimate the complexity of oral traditions of myth.

Evolutionary Aesthetics?

The foregoing comparison of aesthetics in small-scale versus complex societies has focused on contemporary and relatively recent cultures, but this question necessarily suggests a companion query, one concerning cultural evolution. After all, each civilization is the culmination of a long historical development; given sufficient archaeological effort, every high culture's roots can be traced back thousands of years to pre-Neolithic bands of nomadic hunter-gatherers that, with the passage of time, gradually evolved into the formidable empires of history.

How have philosophies of art changed during this evolutionary process? There are serious obstacles to using evidence from contemporary or recent societies to construct evolutionary theories of change, not the least of which is that modern-day, small-scale societies cannot be equated with the societies of the distant past. At most, they are only suggestive, providing clues about what people did and thought during distant times.

Some of these clues can never lead to anything more than untestable speculations, but others do lend themselves to empirical study and eventu-

---

[5]Unless the vicissitudes of ethnographic reporting are misleading, my reading of the available data is that secular and sensuous uses of art outweigh sacred uses among the San; for Eskimos, the two potentialities of art seem to be of about equal importance; and Australian Aboriginal art's greatest emphasis is on the sacred dimension.

This is, however, such an important issue that the glaring lacunae in the data are particularly troubling. The visual arts among the San are indeed predominantly secular; but the situation is less clear regarding San performing arts: The Ritual Healing Dance of the San is highly important in San culture, but in this ceremony dance is only one of several requirements for success, sweat and fire being others. Moreover, San secular music and dance (which occur more frequently than do religious music and dance), are sometimes derived from the Ritual Healing Dance. Given such a situation, the relative importance of secular and sacred elements in San performing arts is difficult to ascertain. (See Anderson 1979:49 for other societies in which the arts appear to be largely or entirely secular.)

ally receive sufficient archaeological support to become accepted as fact. For example, we are quite certain that the literate societies of the historic era evolved from prior, non-literate societies; and it is equally well established that the large, stratified states found in a few locations in the modern world evolved out of small, relatively leaderless societies that existed previously.

If philosophies of art are considered in light of these two well-established evolutionary patterns, then it is altogether plausible that the patterns we have seen in contrasting aesthetics in small-scale contemporary societies and those of complex societies parallel an evolutionary change in aesthetics that has occurred in those parts of the world where the Neolithic Revolution has run its course. Thus, I would postulate the existence of what might be called "meso-evolutionary"[6] aesthetic change: Until 10,000 years ago or so, all human societies possessed aesthetic systems that, though they may well have been quite profound, were implicit, relatively non-intricate, and pervasive throughout their respective cultures. Then in those locations where the domestication of plants and animals brought about increasing specialization in the division of labor and social stratification, aesthetics tended to evolve into relatively explicit and intricate systems of thought that were largely the concern of small, specialized groups of people.[7]

It remains to be seen what the full implications of aesthetic meso-

---

[6]"*Meso*-evolution," because the process emerges due to processes within the culture itself. Later in this chapter, I will define aesthetic "peri-evolution" as the patterns of change that occur when traditional cultures are confronted and overwhelmed by larger, colonizing states.

[7]Thomas Munro's (1963) monumental *Evolution in the Arts* puts forward a similar thesis, but instead of focusing on aesthetic theory, it examines art styles, media, and methods of production. After making many qualifications (e.g., that evolution is not necessarily the *only* process by which art changes), Munro argues in favor of Herbert Spencer's nineteenth century theory that the passage of time brings about greater diversity in the "technics, materials, cultural settings, modes of transmission, spatio-temporal and causal organization, psychological components, and modes of composition (utilitarian, representational, decorative, etc.)" (Munro 1963:250) of art in the Western tradition.

There is mixed cross-cultural evidence in support of Munro's thesis. For example, Carneiro (1970) found that as societies increase in overall complexity, they are likely to adopt the following institutions—in this order:

Craft specialization
Craft production for exchange
Full-time craft specialists
Monumental stone architecture
Full-time painters or sculptors
Full-time architects

But these craft institutions are not as closely correlated to overall complexity as are such things as technology and population size. And although an extensive study by Lomax (1968) seemed to reveal a correlation between sociocultural complexity and certain musical variables, a restudy by Erickson (1976) found that several of the relevent traits were determined more by geographic location than by complexity. Even studies of the *quantity* of art production (e.g., Wolfe 1969, Houlihan 1972) have found little influence by any factors other than the amount of social segmentation.

evolution are for art, artists, and audiences. (For example, the invention of writing and the cultural pluralism that appeared during the process of state-formation would seem to have led to fertile cross-pollination between aesthetic thinkers of different times and places.) But the picture of aesthetics in the ten societies that were presented in Part One leaves little doubt that there *are* systematic differences between aesthetics in modern small-scale societies versus complex societies; and these seem directly related to the increased specialization and stratification that is known to have occurred during the long course of evolution that led some small-scale societies to gradually evolve into complex cultures.

Whatever the evolutionary pattern may have been, there clearly are some notable differences between recent small- and large-scale societies' aesthetic systems: Complex societies, being sedentary, are not restricted to producing art that is mobile; and one consequence of their characteristically complex division of labor is the presence of aesthetic specialists—individuals who develop explicit, intricate theories regarding the fundamental nature and role of art.

These differences, however, are relatively small by comparison to the universal features discussed in the next two chapters; and they seem far less significant than other kinds of sociocultural variation. If one considers our urban mode of living, the industrialized economies our subsistence is based upon, or our capacity to destroy the world through nuclear holocaust, the gulf between ourselves and people in small-scale societies seems enormous; but in matters of art, the distance is small indeed.

Aesthetic Milieu

When the Enlightenment philosopher and critic Hippolyte Taine tried his hand at explaining art, he attributed much to what he called "milieu." Many have dismissed Taine's work, thinking that his use of that term implied *physical* environment, when in fact his prime concern was with *cultural* environment. For the most part, I will follow Taine's lead by focusing on situations in which the aesthetic system of a small-scale, traditional society reacts to the impact of the colonial experience. But it is interesting to first ask if the natural environment does indeed have any influence on the way people conceptualize art.

The aesthetic systems described in Part One suggest one intriguing line of inquiry. In one way or another, several of them contain the premise that human well-being depends upon artistic activity. Western concern with the anagogic capacity of art during the Middle Ages; Indian *rasa* theory; Aztec fears that the world would suffer its final destruction unless the gods were supplicated with flower and song; Navajo efforts to maintain *hózhǫ́* via the creation of art; and Australian Aboriginal uses of art to sustain the fer-tile and harmonious conditions of the Eternal Dreamtime: Each represents an effort by the society to survive by means of art production. And interestingly enough, in each of these cases, the society in ques-tion was indeed existing in a state of duress. Each lived under prolonged attack by outsiders or, as in the case of the Navajo, moved into an ecologic-ally marginal environment. Only the Aztecs were successful in overcoming the inhospitable setting of the barren and rocky island in Lake Texcoco upon which they first lived, but this hazard was replaced by hostile neigh-bors over whom the Aztecs were never able to establish more than tenuous control.

It is easy to speculate that people redouble their involvement with art when times are hard and nothing else seems to work; but proof of such a theory is elusive. One might hypothesize, for instance, that the emphasis on health and fertility found in Yoruba aesthetics came as a response to a need to stimulate birth rates in an area of the world where the introduction of slash and burn horticulture some centuries ago caused a rise in malaria. But the scarceness of the archaeological record in West Africa makes testing such a thesis difficult.

Limited support for this model can be found in some places, however. For example, Dorset culture prevailed across the North American arctic for about 2,000 years, but art production in the region did not remain constant. Taçon (1983) has shown that Late Dorset peoples faced two growing threats—changing climatic conditions and Thule invaders from the west; and significantly, these challenges coincided with a dramatic increase in the production of Dorset art.[8]

Powerful and acquisitive neighbors and poor luck with climatic and environmental conditions are threats that societies rarely have effective de-fenses against. In such difficult circumstances, it seems reasonable that people would turn to symbolic means of trying to protect themselves. Such a strategy could take any of several forms; but in the cultures mentioned above, art seems to have been called upon, perhaps as a last resort, in an effort to survive difficult circumstances.

Intercultural Influences

The effect of the human environment on art is somewhat easier to docu-ment than that of the ecological environment. The very presence of art re-

---

[8]Mimbres culture, discussed in a later context, may be another instance of people react-ing to an environmental crisis by expanding their artistic efforts. J. J. Brody (1977:210) has suggested that a crisis in food production stimulated not only the novel pottery style of the Mimbres people but also a variety of innovative rituals.

gions, in which the art and aesthetics of adjacent groups share wide-ranging similarities, is proof of how important borrowing can be.

Often the influence of neighbors is motivated by factors far removed from art. For example, when Chagnon first visited the Yanomamo village of Momaribowei-teri in Venezuela, the residents told him that long ago they had forgotten how to make pots, that the local clay was unsatisfactory for pottery, and that in any case their allies in the village of Mowaraoba-teri made enough pots for everyone. Later, when this alliance became strained, the same villagers "remembered" how to manufacture clay pots, and Chagnon realized that their earlier statements had only been a rationalization for their desire to trade and socialize with the other village (Chagnon 1983:150). And the Yanomamo case is by no means unique. Intergroup exchange of art works often "lubricates" the exchange of goods and ideas between neighboring peoples. The ostrich eggshell beads made by the San and the decorative feathers and shells of the New Guinea Tsembaga, both mentioned in Part One, follow this same pattern.

These cases have involved art works, rather than art ideas; and in any case such situations result from the chance interaction of random neighbors, and I see no systematic pattern in aesthetic diffusion. There is, however, one very important and pervasive instance of patterned culture contact, namely, the interaction that occurs when traditional, small-scale societies are confronted by powerful, colonizing outsiders, usually (in modern times) representing Western nations. Based on the available information, it appears that a common response is for the victims of the colonial process to eventually discard the sophisticated systems of aesthetic thought they once possessed and adopt more commercially pragmatic, materially utilitarian, and aesthetically superficial values.

Recall, for example, the contemporary Aztec village where Peggy Golde (1963; Golde and Kraemer 1973) found that only technical mastery, not spiritual significance, differentiated good from mediocre pots. Whereas the artist in pre-contact times had to have a "deified heart," his modern descendant needs only a steady hand. In another Mesoamerican setting, Kearney found that among the Zapotec villagers of Ixtepeji, "aesthetic criteria are based on functional utility and materialized worth rather than on some abstract notion of beauty. . . . In Ixtepeji things are 'beautiful' because they are well-made and wear well" (Kearney 1972:68). At the very least, art produced for home use comes to incorporate subject matter from the dominant culture. Barbara Tedlock's study of Zuni Kachina Dance songs revealed allusions to such foreign subjects as the bombing of Pearl Harbor and American astronauts' landing on the moon (Tedlock 1980), which the Zuni composers intentionally included to puzzle and challenge the listener.

Often such colonized societies turn their talents to producing art works for sale in the world economy that they have become party to, in which case market value becomes the dominant aesthetic standard. Betty

LeFree's (1975) study of modern Pueblo pottery, especially at Santa Clara, revealed that a pot's quality is determined primarily by the makers' craftsmanship as reflected in smooth surfaces and evenly spaced designs. Such standards are obviously well-suited for intercultural appreciation: One need not understand the subtleties of Pueblo religious thought or philosophy to recognize a well-crafted pot. And since relative degrees of manual skill are easily distinguished, buyers and sellers of such pots have an unequivocal basis for differentiating the pottery of the "best" artists from lesser work. Thus, considerations of the market place have displaced any older, deeper beliefs about the role of art in human life.

In addition to market value and skill of execution, a third aesthetic consideration often appears in the culture contact situation: Producers and consumers alike may view the art work as symbolizing the ethnic identity of the culture of origin. Thus, even though Canadian carvers only started working in soapstone in the late 1940s and have adopted many conventions that pre-contact Inuit sculpture lacked, both they and those who buy Canadian soapstone carvings see the works as an effective channel whereby the ethnic identity and nobility of traditional Eskimo culture can be communicated to non-Eskimos—people who, in fact, have a determining influence over contemporary Eskimo lives and welfare. Or, to cite a different example, Joann Keali'inohomoku (1985) has examined pre-contact Hawaiian and Hopi cultures with regard to their response to the arrival of European culture. Both societies once had viable visual and performing art traditions, but in Hawaii music and dance have evolved into commercial successes while the visual arts became virtually extinct, whereas Hopi pottery and silversmithing have thrived as crafts of trade while Hopi music and dance continue to be used only for traditional purposes.

The culture contact situation is as volatile as it is varied, but for all its complexity a distinct pattern may be discerned with regard to aesthetics. It might be labeled aesthetic "peri-evolution," and it occurs in the course of culture contact when traditional, indigenous aesthetic systems, which inevitably view art as conveying significant cultural meaning, fall into decline or disappear, to be replaced by values that emphasize the maker's technical skill, the trade value of the art work in the context of a larger, state economy, and considerations of ethnic identity or subcultural pride.[9] (The case in

---

[9]I have elsewhere argued (Anderson 1979, 1989), and I continue to believe, that the art that emerges from the culture-contact situation is legitimate and that we must not ignore its importance for both art and culture. In documenting peri-evolutionary changes in aesthetics, I do not mean to belittle the aesthetics of the culture-contact situation. In our own culture, there is a long history of concern with both craftsmanship and the commercial value of art works, so it is hypocritical to scorn these factors when they appear in cultures that we have impinged upon. And to my mind, the embodiment of ethnic identity in art is altogether justifiable on political, if not aesthetic, grounds. The world-wide trend toward a reduction of artistic and aesthetic diversity is tragic, but it is only a part of a larger tragedy—namely, the loss of cultural diversity in all spheres of life within the human species.

which a society's art and aesthetics are influenced by its interaction with a neighboring society of comparable scale falls into neither meso-evolution nor peri-evolution. No patterns are apparent in such interactions, and I doubt that any general rule could describe them.)

As with aesthetic meso-evolution, more case studies and analyses are necessary to uncover the details of aesthetic peri-evolution: Although the last two decades have seen a welcome growth in studies of art in contact situations, virtually none of them has made as its primary focus the abstract, philosophical principles that underlie the art. Nevertheless, the broad outlines of the phenomenon seem clear. Traditional cultures inevitably possess philosophies of art that are subtle, compelling, and diverse. When such cultures fall under the sway of colonizing world powers, the outcome is art production that reflects the economic and political aspects of the culture contact situation.

Conclusion

Like the adage about a coffee cup being either half full or half empty depending on a person's point of view, Part One's descriptions of aesthetics in ten societies could lead either to conclusions that emphasize fundamental similarities in aesthetics, perhaps reflecting universal traits of art; or else one could stress the cross-cultural diversity found in philosophies of art, dwelling on the features that distinguish one art from another.

Obviously, differences between philosophies of art can easily be found, but the question remains, how fundamental are they? On close examination, many dissimilarities turn out to be fairly superficial. In several societies, for example, it is thought that art has the capacity to perpetuate the conditions that are necessary for life itself, but this axiom takes different guises in those cultures in which it occurs.

But other differences are deeper. The most important of them become apparent when societies are arrayed along a continuum that ranges from small-scale to complex. Philosophies of art in complex societies are explicit, intricate, and the domain of a small cadre of specialists; such philosophies in small-scale societies tend to be relatively less so. These differences have more to do with the structure of aesthetic systems than their content; and they probably parallel historical patterns whereby complex, class-structured societies have evolved out of small-scale, relatively homogeneous bands, a process I have called aesthetic meso-evolution.

The one change that has involved the subject matter of aesthetics may be seen when one looks at the culture-contact situation. There, aesthetic peri-evolution occurs when the cross-culturally diverse and individually profound aesthetic systems of traditional societies disappear, replaced by a situation in which art is made and esteemed for its trade value, its display of craftsmanship, and its ability to symbolize ethnic identity and pride.

Having duly noted these patterns of variation, the focus now turns to the features of art that occur in all of the societies surveyed in Part One. That is, the quest for the elusive Calliope must resume.

13

ART AS CULTURALLY
SIGNIFICANT MEANING

All art is quite useless. (Oscar Wilde)

Art . . . is necessary only in that without it life would be
unbearable. (Richard Selzer 1979:196)

Many philosophers have given up the search for an absolute and eternal definition of art. In a particularly influential article, Morris Weitz (1967/1957)
has argued that although there may be agreement on art's definition at any
particular place and time, even a cursory look at the history of intellectual
thought reveals that people have held quite different views at other periods
and in different places. Perhaps, said Weitz, the only constant lies in art's
always being creative, always evolving in style, in purpose, and, significantly,
in definition. This being the case, art can only have an "open" definition
that specifies several traits that are *usually* present in those things commonly
designated as art, even though no single trait is definitively present in *all* art.
Using a line of reasoning developed by Wittgenstein, Weitz claimed that art
is like a large family, the members of which share a genuine resemblance with
one another even though no single trait is found in every individual.

Having surveyed aesthetic systems in ten largely independent and highly
diverse societies, we can now ask whether or not any open definition can
subsume art cross-culturally. The answer, I believe, is yes; and I propose the
following open, cross-culturally applicable definition of art: *Art is culturally
significant meaning, skillfully encoded in an affecting, sensuous medium.* Although this
definition reads syntactically as a sentence, it is in fact a list of qualities—
"culturally significant meaning," "skill," "code," and "affecting, sensuous medium"—and I believe it can be shown that each one of the diverse congeries
of "arts" that were described in the chapters of Part One have most or all of

these qualities. Furthermore, these traits are notably present in those things that we commonly consider to be art from other times and places.[1] Granted, art traditions and individual art works vary in the relative emphasis placed upon each of these qualities. Australian Aborigines, for example, think of their *tjurungas* as embodying the deepest of spiritual meanings, whereas the manual skill of the *tjurunga*-maker may be no greater than those of most other men in his tribe. Or to cite another case, the sensuousness of most types of San and Inuit body decorations is paramount in native thought, whereas the cultural significance of the decorations is limited to notions about social status and personal beauty, values that may be somewhat superficial to the cores of the cultures involved. But despite such variations (which, after all, are inevitably present in an open definition), most or all of these qualities seem inevitably to be present in those things that we consider to be art.

Moreover, those things not commonly considered to be art rarely have all of the qualities listed above. (That is to say, the traits specified in the definition are not only *necessarily* present in art, but their absence is *sufficient* to set non-art apart from art.) Thus although Western religion embodies cultural meaning of great significance and the execution of religious ritual typically requires the skills of a specialist, only those things that are executed in such a way as to capitalize on the affecting qualities of a sensuous medium are considered to be religious "art." For example, a passage from the Bible is not generally considered to be art unless its aural delivery is enhanced by setting it to music or its literary qualities are heightened by poetic techniques, such as those found in the *Psalms* or the *Song of Songs*.

Although the majority of things can unequivocally be classed as either "art" or "non-art" by the definition proposed above, some things fall in an indeterminate area between the two categories. The traits that make up the definition obviously do not lend themselves to quantification; and we will probably never be able to specify precisely *how much* of the traits qualify something as being art. Such a situation is inelegant and aesthetically unpleasing, but it reflects disagreements in the real world, where consensus

---

[1]Weitz's tentative definition is that art implies "there being present some sort of artifact, made by human skill, ingenuity, and imagination, which embodies in its sensuous, public medium . . . certain distinguishable elements and relations" (1967:9). If my proposed definition bears a "family resemblance" itself to that of Weitz, this may, of course, be because I read Weitz's definition some time before I began the present study. However, it was *after* I had formulated the above definition that I found one that Clifford Geertz proposed: "If there is a commonality in art it lies in the fact that certain activities everywhere seem specifically designed to demonstrate that ideas are visible, audible, and—one needs to make up a word here—tactible, that they can be cast in form where the senses, and through the senses the emotions, can reflectively address them" (Geertz 1983:120). Osborne (1974) and Cohen (1983/1962) have discussed similar issues.

sometimes gives way to heated debate about whether a particular thing is "really" art or not.

Each of the qualities that constitute the open definition of art requires extended discussion. The first—culturally significant meaning—is the most complex and will be the sole concern of the remainder of the present chapter. The other issues—code, skill, and medium—will be dealt with in the next chapter.

When this survey is completed, we will, in effect, have revealed Calliope. In keeping with the nature of an open definition, we must be prepared to see Calliope take on differing guises in varied cultural contexts; and there is every likelihood that she, like art works themselves, will evolve creatively with the passage of time. But for the first time, we will have a cross-cultural definition of art that derives not from *a priori* assumptions about art but rather from a systematic examination of the empirical world of the makers and users of art.

Meaning in Art

Human existence is predicated on the well-developed human capacity to manipulate meaning—to comprehend meaning, to communicate meaning, and, in our most distinctively human capacity, to create meaning. Within the genus *homo,* we are the species designated *sapiens:* Our highly developed ability to be sapient—to think, to understand—distinguishes us from our hominid ancestors and relatives.[2]

Sometimes nature dictates meaning ("that fruit's redness means it is ripe enough to eat"), and the possibility of a fundamental, manifest meaning in the cosmos cannot be ruled out. However, much of our environment is surely devoid of intrinsic meaning and indifferent to human concern. Nevertheless, humans do *create* meaning, postulating that the fruit's redness is "beautiful," and that, perhaps, a man from the "red" clan may not marry a woman from the same "red" kin group. The result, of course, is a "logico-meaningful system of symbolic relationships" (Fernandez 1973:194)—that is, the vast and remarkable artifact we call human culture. In our eternal drive to create meaning, we have generated social structure, systems of myth and religion—and art. And, by all accounts, culture is a human imperative. To paraphrase the previously quoted remark (p. 34) by the Netsilik Eskimo, Orpingalik, culture is as necessary for us as our breath.

All the societies examined in Part One invest art with significant cul-

---

[2]Several of the themes discussed below are also dealt with, albeit from quite a different perspective, by Robert Plant Armstrong (1971, 1975, 1981).

tural meaning. That is, in addition to an art work's being "about" its own stylistic conventions and the emotional response that its use of a sensuous medium can evoke, it is also "about" some subject in the sociocultural matrix of which it is a part.[3]

Spiritual Meaning in Art

This is especially apparent in the cases where art is charged with supernatural significance and embodies the essence of human life and thought. Thus for Navajos, art denotes the world's most fundamental qualities—goodness, harmony, and beauty. Likewise, art in New Guinea's Sepik River region conveys messages of spiritual power. And for their part, Aztec philosophers believed that art alone was true, eternal—and meaningful.

Art's spiritual meaning is crucial even in societies where it does not serve as the nexus of supernatural belief. Thus, Japanese art provided the only means of conveying the profound truths of Esoteric Buddhism, aided the proselytizing efforts of Amida Buddhism, and embodied such fundamental Zen concerns as focusing one's concentration and aiding the devotee in experiencing spontaneous, intuitive insight. Although most San visual art serves secular purposes, the performing arts are absolute prerequisites for the Ritual Healing Dance, where heat and focused attention combine with chanting and repetitive movements to bring some dancers' spiritual energy, or *num*, to the boiling point. Finally, in the Western tradition of pragmatic aesthetics, art's efficacy rests upon its capacity to convey to the percipient a message that is religious, ideal, or essential in nature. Thus in over half of the societies examined in Part One, we see art performing an important service for society by carrying a meaning that transcends the mundane and commonplace and that embodies, or at least touches, the plane of the supernatural.

In other societies, art's meaning is more secular; however, it is not necessarily less important for being so. For example, one important dimension of Yoruba art is its capacity to simultaneously communicate principles of both goodness and energy through its sensuous embodiment of beauty. And in Sepik aesthetics, art is a manifestation of phallic aggression, expressing the quintessence of masculinity by conveying messages of male fierceness and pride, to friends as well as to enemies.

Lastly, art may carry a sacred or idealized message by mere affiliation

---

[3]One might simply say that art everywhere tends to be "symbolic," but I intend here to suggest a more polysemous, or multivocal, quality in art. Art may be narrowly symbolic (by referring to something outside itself that it does not resemble), iconically representational, or even reflexive (by making statements about itself or the stylistic conventions it uses). For that reason, I shall speak of art being "meaningful," rather than "symbolic."

with religious affairs. In Australian Aboriginal thought, the value of secular decorations comes from their association with sacred contexts. They carry a "spiritual connotation" as it were. Or, to take a superficially different example that amounts to much the same thing, Japanese stylistic preferences for simplicity, symmetry, and so on, highly valued in and of themselves, all seem to derive from religious, principally Shintoist, beliefs in purity, cleanliness, and the indwelling spirits of nature.

Means as Meaning

Art's cultural significance may also lie in its capacity to bring about some desired end—that is, the conventional meaning of art is as a *means* to some end. In the same way that the most salient meaning of "hammer" is "means of driving a nail," the meaning of an art work may be the means it provides to attain an extra-artistic end.

Again, religious meanings are often involved. For example, an item of sacred Australian Aboriginal art, such as a painted bullroarer, is not so much an embodiment of sacred meaning in itself but a means of influencing the sacred realm—insuring the natural, eternal order of things, especially fertility, the perpetuation of human life and culture, and so on. Eskimo art is also made for utilitarian, though sacred, purposes—namely, assuring future, personal well-being in this life and the next. Similarly, art *cognoscenti* among the Yoruba, Navajo, Aztec, and Japanese Shintoist thinkers believe that art induces supernatural spirits to act to the benefit of mortals. Art in classical India and medieval Europe was equally purposeful, yielding desirable spiritual results by bringing the mortals into closer accord with the supernatural realm.

Means-as-meaning is widespread, but it varies in the form it takes. Sometimes the end is thoroughly concrete and definable. Certain tattoos on Eskimo women are intended to ease their labor pains during future pregnancies; and a perfect mirror was used to lure the fearful Shinto Sun goddess, Amaterasu-ô-mi-kami, out of the Rock Cave of Heaven. Or the end may be abstract in nature. Navajo sandpainting, for example, insures a continuation of the world's natural state of goodness and harmony. Art's ends may be sacred, as in the preceding cases, or wholly secular, as with the sensuous pleasure and aesthetic delight that San and Inuit art inspire in their percipients. Moreover, the sacred and the sensuous are not necessarily mutually exclusive, and in actual practice the two qualities often complement each other.

There is ample evidence that art conveys significant cultural meaning not only in the societies discussed in Part One but in other groups as well. Bohannan, for example, observes that the West African Tiv "are more interested in the ideas conveyed by a piece of art than they are by its manufacture" (Bohannan 1971:175). And Graburn (1978) found that California museum-goers preferred Eskimo carvings to objects made by Naskapi-Cree, probably because they misunderstood the works' meanings: The viewers erroneously assumed that Cree Craft objects represented a greater degree of commercialism than did the Inuit carvings, and since this motivation was antithetical to the meaning of "art" for them, they placed a lower value on the Cree works.

Sacramental Meanings in Art

Not only does art typically convey culturally significant meaning, but it often communicates several such meanings simultaneously. When the messages reinforce each other, the effect is particularly powerful, transcending normal modes of discourse.[4] Gregory Bateson has called such communication "sacramental," as in this hypothetical dialogue between a father and his precocious daughter about the ways in which the ballet *Swan Lake* has a meaning beyond the merely quantitative and rational:

> FATHER: The swan figure is not a real swan but a pretend swan. It is also a pretend-not human being. It is also "really" a young lady wearing a white dress. And a real swan would resemble a young lady in certain ways.
> DAUGHTER: But which of these is sacramental?
> FATHER: Oh Lord, here we go again. I can only say this: that it is not one of these statements but their combination which constitutes a sacrament. The "pretend" and the "pretend-not" and the "really" somehow get fused together in a single meaning. (Bateson 1972:37)

Or we can recall a remark attributed to Isadora Duncan, who was instrumental in developing modern dance in the early twentieth century. When asked what her choreography meant, she replied, "If I could tell you the meaning, I wouldn't have to dance it!"[5] Not all art is sacramental, but a distinctive property of art is its capacity to ineffably convey meanings in a way that transcends the rational, the explicit, the unambiguous.

The phallic meaning of Sepik art is a good example of the sacramental dimension of art. The wood, fiber, paint, and shells that make a mask, shrine object, or tambaran house decoration are recognized as such, but at the

---

[4]Mihali Csikszentmihalyi sums up a widely held opinion in suggesting that "a different mode of knowledge is necessary to cope with the dimensions of reality reason is incapable of handling. . . . In this context, we are interested in art as a complementary alternative to rational cognition" (1978:17).

[5]Similarly, Stravinsky is claimed to have said, "I haven't understood a bar of music in my life, but I have felt it."

same time they are ardently believed to be embodiments of spirit beings. As with the Catholic sacraments of communion, where bread and wine *are* the body and blood of Christ, the Sepik art objects convey a potent message. Surely this must result from both the synergistic effect of unifying sensuous medium with spiritual meaning, as well as the nature of the abstract message itself. The Sepik spirits *are* powerful, but they rarely, if ever, exist in a tangible form. In art, they become palpable, dynamic beings.

Some meanings are overt and unambiguous, and language serves well for communicating them. And too, art often conveys explicit messages. But other meanings that are no less important cannot be expressed so easily and in many such cases art serves as a medium for their transmission. Before considering why art lends itself to such communication, we should examine some of the specific powerful meanings commonly found in art.

Art and Beauty

Often art's meaning lies in its being a tangible embodiment of abstract norms of beauty and social goodness. For example, the search for the root of Yoruba aesthetics began with examining standards of sensuous beauty as they apply to art objects, but these were clearly derived from criteria of human beauty. Searching for the source of these standards, we came to the generalized principles of harmony and energy, two social values that hold sway in Yoruba culture at large. In Yoruba, the words for "beauty" and "goodness" are synonymous, and the same is true in many other African languages. Similarly, Navajos use *hózhǫ́* to mean not only "beauty" but also "goodness" and other positive things. So although Westerners often equate art with one's idiosyncratic emotional response, elsewhere art usually conveys meanings that transcend the individual psyche and that are collective, public, and traditional.

Since art is often related to beauty, we would do well to ask about the source of native standards of beauty. Beauty criteria vary from one society to another, of course, but they generally do so within certain restricted limits set by sociocultural norms; these, in turn are often rooted in practical considerations. "Beautiful" skin is usually healthy skin, free of the blemishes of disease and the wrinkles of age; and it is surely no coincidence that sound, white teeth are both attractive and practical. Where women nurse their children, the female breast is often a focus of interest, the ideal being either young, firm breasts that show the promise of nurturing many children (as in Yoruba and north-central Australian cultures) or else pendulous breasts that have already done so (as among the Mountain Arapesh and Anang). And the standards of male beauty found in many societies are often at least as rigorous as those for women and derive from considerations of health, strength, and vigor (cf. van Offelen 1983).[6]

Beauty standards may be unrelated to subsistence and procreation but still serve a practical purpose. Shintoists, for example, see beauty in cleanliness and purity—perhaps because these qualities enhance healthiness. Even in the Western aesthetic tradition, Dostoyevsky writes, "Beauty inheres in everything healthy. . . . It is harmony, and it contains a guarantee of tranquility" (quoted in Zenkovsky 1962:141).

The East African Pakot show how other peoples may find beauty in places not expected by Westerners. Pakot women are gardeners, and they find beauty in "a healthy, green field of eleusine plants" (Schneider 1956:105). Interestingly, Pakot men, who are cattle herders and who have little to do with gardening, see no beauty in eleusine plants. They do, however, often wax rhapsodic about the beauty of certain types of steers, a passion beyond the ken not only of most Westerners but of Pakot women as well.

Evidence of an appreciation of the practical value of beauty comes from many places. The Yanomamo of South America, for example, believe that their welfare requires the blessings of supernatural spirits called *hekura,* to whom the men chant while under the influence of a powerful hallucinogen called *ebene,* exhorting the spirits to enter the men's own bodies. On one occasion during his extensive fieldwork with the Yanomamo, Napoleon Chagnon participated in the chanting:

> We walked silently over to Kaobawa's house for that is where the daily activities were to begin. "Let me decorate you, my dear brother!" said Rerebawa softly, and I knelt on the ground while all my friends generously made their special feathers and decorations available to me so that I might become more beautiful and therefore more worthy to the *hekura.* (Chagnon 1983:208)

For the Yanomamo, members of the spirit world are not only beautiful in themselves; they are summoned by beautifully decorated mortals. And, in fact, the decorations were efficacious for Chagnon. After inhaling powdered *ebene,* he did see the *hekura.* Thus, at least some standards of beauty are based on practical considerations; and, in the opposite way, beauty itself

---

[6]Freud wrote, "The love of beauty is a perfect example of a sentiment whose aim is inhibited. It is remarkable that the genitalia themselves, the sight of which is always sexually exciting, are hardly ever regarded as beautiful; beauty seems to accrue rather to certain secondary sexual characteristics" (quoted in Comfort 1962:100). Inhibition or no, it appears that most societies do attach more importance to the appearance of secondary sexual traits than to genitals; however, these secondary traits—men's legs and torsos, women's buttocks and breasts, and so forth—are also of practical importance. And where genital preferences are stated, as among the Anang (Messenger 1981), they are often emblems of gender rather than marks of beauty.

can be conceived as an instrumentality for bringing about desirable, practical ends.

Art and Social Values

If art often embodies messages about beauty, it also frequently suggests ideas of social goodness, although the connection between beauty and goodness may seem arbitrary. Aesthetic values may involve individual personality traits. Since ancient Greece, for example, Westerners have equated certain "attractive" facial features with desirable qualities of character, while others are "ugly" and found only in unsavory individuals, as in Aristotle's claim that straight eyebrows indicate an undesirable "softness of disposition" (cf. Liggett 1974:181–215).

The most pervasive pattern linking beauty and goodness focuses not on qualities intrinsic to the individual but rather on those that have a *social* dimension. Terence S. Turner has observed that among the central Brazilian Kayapo, to be dirty is to be actively antisocial because personal dirtiness contravenes a primary value of social life. Beauty is thought by the Kayapo to be a quintessential expression of society itself (Turner 1980:115, 135).

Or, to take a different example, consider the traditional conception of the artist in Chinese culture: He is a man "who is at peace with nature. . . . Above all, his breast must brood no ill passions, for a good artist, we strongly believe, must be a good man" (Lin Yutang 1935:288). Harold K. Osborne observes, "While the Western artist typically aimed to produce a replica of reality, actual, imagined, or ideal, the Chinese artist—although he might in fact do this—made his first aim to bring his own personality into keeping with the cosmic principle so that the Tao would be expressed through him" (Osborne 1968:107). The Chinese artist can only create beauty if he himself is a paragon of goodness, a model for everyone to emulate and revere.

Art and Truth

Two common value-meaning associations of art have already been noted—namely, art's link with human health and physical well-being and its involvement with social goodness. But art's value dimension has a third component. Art may also be conceived as a manifestation of *truth*. One is reminded of John Keats's dictum,

'Beauty is truth, truth beauty,'—that is all
Ye know on earth, and all ye need to know

which expresses the popular belief that the greatest verities serve as a foundation not only for society but for art as well. Similarly for the Central African Lega, the vocabulary of aesthetic values is isomorphic with Lega sociocultural values. Only those Lega individuals who have attained the state of *bugosa* are admitted to the highest levels of society. This term refers not only to beauty but also to goodness; and *bugosa* is goodness of a complicated sort, implying, among other things, *izu*, or "deep insight and wisdom, as opposed to *kizio*, simple knowledge" (Biebuyck 1973:129).

Or consider a different Black art form, the idiom of blues music:

> The main aesthetic standard . . . for early folk blues was truth. But it was a truth based in universal human experience or at least a kind of experience that was known to the singer and audience. Unlike other major forms of black folklore, the blues did not deal with the imaginary animal world of Br'er Rabbit or the deeds of legendary heroes like John Genry or Stacker Lee. . . . Along with this went traditional melodies and instrumental patterns and techniques. These too had to be delivered by the performers with conviction and "truth." Julius Lester states this point well when he says, "The roots of the blues . . . [are] social. The rural blues men were intent on telling their listeners what the listener already knew, but could not articulate. . . . Even the most personal blues of the rural blues singers never said, 'Look at me!' Invariably, it said, 'Look at you!' " (Evans 1982:52f)

So blues music, like the sculpture of the Lega, is a public and tangible embodiment of important truths.

The maxim of Navajo aesthetics, reported by David McAllester, has nearly universal applicability: "If it's worthwhile, it's beautiful" (McAllester 1954:71). The relationship between art and value is reciprocal in that an important message necessitates important art. But one can also ask (as we later shall), what features of art make it so affecting a human contrivance that it is often pressed into service as a medium for conveying value? Far from belittling Calliope's status as a handmaiden to extra-aesthetic domains, we should appreciate the venerable personages she serves, namely truth, goodness, and human well-being. But before we can properly examine the source of art's great communicative power, we must look at its relation to religion, a domain through which art often embodies goodness, beauty, and other high principles.

Art and Religion: Transformation and Communion

Although the metaphysical messages of art are sometimes implicit, the meanings of religious art are explicit and concrete. The cult usages of Yoruba sculpture, costumery, dance, and song; the music and dance of the San Ritual Healing dance; Australian Aboriginal dance, song, and drawings of the Eternal Dreamtime; Sepik art made for the Tambaran cult and other ceremonial uses; the amulets and some of the tattoos made by Eskimos; Navajo sandpaintings intended to maintain or reestablish a state of *hózhǫ́;* Aztec art given to please the gods and thereby forestall the final destruction of our earth and all who live here; Indian art's embodiment of *rasa,* with its capacity to elevate one to a higher spiritual plane; and Japanese art, with its close ties to Shinto spirits and the various sects of Buddhism—each is an example of art conveying a specifically religious meaning.

The combined issues of religion, morality, and ethics have been dominant themes even in the supposedly secular West. In addition to the obviously religious art of the Middle Ages, mimetic works have also usually had as an ulterior motive the moral and spiritual betterment of the viewer. Also, the tenets of romanticism and formalism have often been advocated with a religious fervor (Beethoven once remarked, "Music is a moral force"); and they generally present art as a means whereby the sensitive individual can be transported to the high realms of aesthetic bliss.[7]

As with beauty, the religious functions of art fall into a limited number of possible categories. For one thing, art may bring about miraculous, qualitative transformations. Eskimo art metamorphoses things between the natural world, the human world, and the world of the supernatural. Similarly, Australian Aborigines believe that art transmutes mortals and mundane objects such as painted pieces of wood into the spiritual realm of the Eternal Dreamtime. Yoruba dancers, when they don mask and costume, *become* the *orisha* in whose praise they are dancing; and in the Sepik, the *tambaran* and long yam spirits reside in the objects that are painted and decorated in their honor.

Where art is not an actual manifestation of the supernatural, it may provide the prime means whereby mortals can come into intimate contact with the sacred. Navajo sandpaintings embody *hózhǫ́;* and Aztec art, made as a gift to the gods, came from the gods in the first place. Indian *rasa* is the primary tangible means whereby mortals apprehend higher spiritual principles of religious belief, and the same could be said of the anagogic art of the Middle Ages in the West. Finally, regarding Japanese aesthetics, one is reminded of the Shinto creation myth in which it was the arts— music, dance, and the perfect mirror—that lured the Sun goddess out of the Rock Cave of Heaven. Thus, at least some of the art produced in each of the cultures discussed in Part One is an embodiment of the spirit world

---

[7]One should not, of course, assume that *all* art is religiously oriented. As Part One revealed, societies at all levels of complexity make art for distinctly secular purposes. San and Inuit body decorations make one look beautiful not in the eyes of spirits but in those of mortals. Navajo weaving and silversmithing are apparently void of religious meaning. And even the Aztec thinkers, despite their singular preoccupation with religious matters, recognized that art and poetry, whatever else they might do, also temper social relations.

or, at the least, serves as a medium through which mortals can communicate with that world. In a word, a pervasive and significant meaning of art is as a "transformer," permitting communication between the sacred and profane levels of existence.

Art and Religion: Compelling Action

Art can not only provide communication with the spiritual realm; it can also *compel* spirits to act. Robert Horton (1965) has described such a process for the Kalabari of southern Nigeria (see also Reichard 1944). Kalabari religious belief includes many spirits—ancestor spirits, water spirits, and the spirits of village heroes. These are all potentially powerful beings, but their strength is contingent upon human intervention. Intensive worship makes a spirit strong, giving it the power either to benefit or harm its devotees; neglect, however, reduces the spirit to insignificance. This is what Kalabari mean when they say, *tomi, ani oru beremara*—"It is men who make the gods important" (Horton 1965:6; cf. also Barbar 1981).

Significantly, the praise given to Kalabari spirits generally takes the form of art—praise song, drama, dance, or sculpture (see **Figure 13–1**). The Kalabari spirits are thus controlled by art. When a man acts arrogantly, Horton observes, he may be asked

> "Are you a spirit without a sculpture?"—meaning, "Do you think we have nothing through which we can control you?" Behind these figures of speech is a serious feeling that sculpture is a necessary instrument for controlling the spirits, and that any spirit without a sculpture to represent it is dangerous because it cannot be adequately controlled.   (Horton 1965:8).

Art's role in compelling Kalabari spirits to action is all the more dramatic in light of the fact that besides the spirits, the Kalabari also believe in a supreme being, *Tamuno,* who is totally independent and who does as he wishes with no concern for human activities. Mortals can only express submission to *Tamuno;* as the Kalabari say in moments of resignation, "*Tamuno* never loses a case" (Horton 1965:7). Consequently, the Kalabari make no art for *Tamuno. Tamuno* cannot be compelled to action, and making art in his name would be futile.

As the Kalabari example illustrates, in addition to art's being a means of religious communication, art can also be used as a means of *controlling* the supernatural. The same is true in several of the cultures discussed in Part One. Through the mechanism of sympathetic magic, Navajo sings, if carried out properly, will guarantee the desired result of creating and maintaining *hózhó;* Shinto annual ceremonies influence the *kami* for human good; Australian Aboriginal ceremonies compel the representatives of the Eternal Dreamtime to renew and sustain the blessings that existed at the

FIGURE 13-1   Carved and painted wooden figure made by the Kalabari in western Ijo, Nigeria. 64.4 cm. high.   *(The Metropolitan Museum of Art, The Michael G. Rockefeller Memorial Collection, Gift of the Matthew T. Mellon Foundation, 1960 [1978.412.404].)*

time of creation; and San healers use the heightened consciousness of *kia* to fend off the invisible but dangerous arrows that harm people.

The claim that art embodies messages about supernatural power should not be dismissed lightly as "mere" superstition. While living with a Navajo family in the summer of 1969, Gary Witherspoon witnessed an interesting series of events centering around an eighty-two-year-old woman. She had suddenly become ill and soon fell into a coma. She was taken to a hospital where doctors believed that she could only be kept alive by intravenous feeding. However, a diviner diagnosed her problem as having a supernatural cause and prescribed the Enemyway rite. Although her doctors said she would die if not given intravenous food, family members took her home and quickly arranged a performance of Enemyway. According to Witherspoon, "When she arrived at home, she seemed to me to be in a deep coma, totally unconscious, and nearly dead. By the conclusion of the rite she was walking around almost normally. Several non-Navajos working at the local school were amazed; most Navajos were not amazed but were gratefully serene. I last saw her, alive and well, in 1973" (Witherspoon 1977:13f).

Before we attribute this and similar cases to "spontaneous remission" (i.e., coincidence) or "merely" the power of suggestion, we should recall the potential power of traditional artistic activity. Art not only conveys meaning but its effects can be quite compelling. Humans live in a world constrained by the laws of the mind no less than the laws of physics. A lifetime of expo-sure to, and implicit belief in, the world of meaning conveyed through art influences an individual's social and psychological well-being as surely as biology influences one's physical health.

A final dimension of art's role in conveying religious meaning should be noted. In some societies, art not only transmits religious meaning, it also carries messages of a particularly deep and obscure nature. When religious concepts are so abstract that even initiates grasp them only with difficulty, art can serve as a means whereby the people at large can gain some grasp of religious principles. Medieval Christianity, with its mysteries and mira-cles, is an example, as is classical India with its concept of *rasa*. Steven J. Lansing has remarked regarding the syncretic religion of contemporary Bali, "For the Balinese, art is not merely ornamental but a way—perhaps the best way—to understand the true nature of reality. . . . The arts provide a way to understand and experience the divine essence" (Lansing 1981:36–37).

The Importance of Meaning in Art

I have claimed that the elusive Calliope thrives in all ten of the societies examined in Part One—that is, that each society produces art, where "art" is defined as being culturally significant meaning that is skillfully encoded in an affecting, sensuous medium. This definition isolates several dimen-sions that are typically present in art; but in any particular cultural context we may find one dimension of art to be emphasized at the expense of the others. Like a mortal, one side of Calliope's personality may be dominant. She may be the beautiful, sensuous Calliope, the belle of the ball, who enter-tains and excites all who meet her; but she can also present a serious side, concerned with matters of deep philosophical import. An examination of meaning in art suggests that this second component of art can rise to such importance that it overshadows all else.

Recall San oracle disks, for example. Little skill is required in creating them, and we find no evidence that the San value them for their sensuous beauty. Yet they convey important *meaning*. They are tools for learning about and influencing that which is otherwise unknown and independent of hu-man control. (Carved amulets probably play a parallel role in traditional Eskimo thought.) Since my definition of art is "open," composed of several traits that constitute a generalized "family resemblance," we cannot authori-tatively determine whether San oracle disks are indeed "art." With regard to meaning and their conformity to a traditional style, they are; but with respect to skill and sensuous appeal, they fall only marginally into the category of art.

Also, although the attribution of sacred meanings to art is widespread, the relative importance of the spiritual dimension of art varies cross-culturally. For example, whereas it was present among all three of the hunting-gathering-fishing groups described in Part One, and granted we are operating in a territory where quantification is impossible, the available information seems to suggest that the sacramental meaning associated with art is greatest in Australian society and least among the San, with the Eskimos falling somewhere between the two.[8]

The use of art for sacramental purposes may vary within individual societies; and this is most apparent in the relatively more heterogeneous complex societies, where fine arts are differentiated from popular arts. The magic of fine art may be most keenly felt, one suspects, because of the rarified and complex meanings it often conveys. In contrast, although popular arts bring satisfactions, they are generally of a more emotionally and intellectually modulated order.

Judeo-Christian ambivalence toward representational art is interesting in this context. Although Western art has produced some of its greatest achievements in service to religious belief, there has also sometimes been a fear of art leading the faithful to worship something other than the one Christian god. The ancient Jews even included in the Ten Commandments a taboo against making and worshiping "graven" images. Jewish scholars have pointed out (cf. Bacon 1971) that the prohibition probably began as a fear that people would worship an idol for its own sake, or that they might come to believe that it held a supernatural spirit other than the Hebrew god, apparently a not-unfounded fear since other Near Eastern groups believed that spirits did control natural phenomena such as rain, health, and human well-being, that they could inhabit inanimate figures, and that worshiping the figures would propitiate the resident spirits.

Symbol and Icon

Humans make meaning. We view the cold and indifferent universe as being alive with spirits and forces that, though not wholly human, are somehow

---

[8]But see also footnote 5, Chapter 12. However, if this claim is correct, it raises another interesting question: When the sacramental function of art is minimal, do other, more unequivocal functions take its place, or does art itself diminish in importance? For the hunter-gatherer societies being discussed here, the latter would seem to be the case inasmuch as Australian art (as I understand it) is the most powerfully polysemous of the three (with the Eskimos ranking second and the San third in this dimension), and art in general may play a more significant role in the lives of Australians—with Eskimos second and San third.

our kin. It is not surprising that we do so. Consider the Eskimo seal hunter standing hour after hour, alone on the windswept, frigid sea ice of an arctic winter, waiting for a sign that a seal has come to breathe through the hole in the ice that he is watching. The seal comes; the hunter strikes. After he has dispatched the seal and pulled it up through the ice, the hunter makes a cut in its body. As he carves out a piece of the seal's liver to eat, both as a memorial and as food, the hunter recognizes his kinship with the seal, the only living thing—the only *warm* thing—in the arctic panorama that surrounds him. He owes his own life to the seal. The seal has spirit; the seal has meaning. The hunter knows these things and expresses them in his carvings of seals, of men, and other living things.

The human penchant for making meaning and investing art with this meaning has implications for several long-standing debates, such as the question of paleolithic art. As far back as 60,000 years ago, *Homo sapiens* were making geometric designs, and the production of sophisticated painting, engraving, and sculpture goes back at least 30,000 years. Animals provided the most common subjects for European artists during the era of the Upper Paleolithic; and although some of the portrayed species were hunted as food, others were not.

Countless explanatory hypotheses have been suggested, but little con-sensus exists among pre-historians regarding the meaning of paleolithic art. Perhaps the motive was "sympathetic magic," whereby artists hoped to gain some measure of control over the beasts they depicted; or maybe the figures reveal a structural interplay between masculine and feminine principles; or the pictures could merely illustrate scenes from their makers' myths. But whatever the case, our present analysis of aesthetics in contemporary socie-ties strongly suggests that the animals must have had a great significance for the communities that produced them. The same must be true for the many pre-historic figures, explicit or stylized, executed in either two or three dimensions, that portray parts of the (usually female) sexual anatomy. Whether they symbolized human reproduction, eroticism, or generalized "fertility magic," we have, I feel, no sure way of knowing. But the drawings surely were vessels of potent meaning, and not meaningless graffiti.

Another old debate concerns the relative ages of representational and non-representational art. In the late nineteenth century and in the early twentieth, some scholars argued that representational art came first and that pictorial subjects sometimes became so stylized that they lost their original meanings and were eventually treated as purely non-representa-tional figures. Others claimed that the instinctive pleasure of design prompted people first to make meaningless patterns, and representational interpretations were read into them at a later time. Like many debates of the day, this one was fought more with polemic and deductive reasoning than with empirical evidence.

Franz Boas was the first to systematically evaluate the cross-cultural and archaeological data bearing on this issue, and he concluded that "it seems futile to discuss the question of whether representative decorative art is older than geometrical decorative art, but that it rather appears that we are dealing here with two different sources of artistic activity, which tend to merge into the development of graphic and plastic arts" (Boas 1940: 236–237).[9]

To consider the question of representationalism cross-culturally, rather than historically, we may start with the end of the continuum at which we find explicitly figurative art. Boas rightly concluded that an absence of realism in most non-Western cultures is not due to a lack of skill. Modern Yoruba carving illustrates well the accuracy with which the human figure can be portrayed; and the pre-historic antecedents of Yoruba art prove that such skill is not limited to the modern era: Benin Bronzes made before the 1700s, Ife bronzes and terra cottas that date before 1200, and Nok terra cottas going back to the fourth century B.C.—all show such consummate artistry in sculptural rendering that the first Europeans to see them believed ethnocentrically (and erroneously, of course) that these art works must have been produced by migrant Caucasians rather than by Africans.

And Westerners have no more of a monopoly on skill of representation than they do on *appreciating* such skill. The Yoruba's neighbors, the Kalabari, may refuse to pay for a commissioned sculpture because it is not true enough to its model. However, the Kalabari case raises an important issue on the subject of representational versus non-representational art. The model for a Kalabari carved figure is not any specific person but an old, often-used cult object that has fallen into disrepair. The carver's success is measured solely by his replication of this model, itself a highly stylized depiction of the human face and form, and all other standards of representational accuracy are irrelevant. Thus, when Robert Horton asked his Kalabari informants which of several masquerade pieces were best, his question evoked puzzlement. "'They are all the same', said one man; 'They are all good'" (Horton 1965:23).

The situation becomes more intriguing when we consider the Fang, who live southeast of the Yoruba and the Kalabari in Equatorial Guinea and Gabon. James Fernandez, who has written extensively on Fang art and aesthetics says, "The Fang often argue that their figures and masks constitute traditional photographs" (Fernandez 1973:204). That Fang informants would identify the mask illustrated in **Figure 13-2** as a portrait of either Franco or DeGaulle reveals the great influence of culture on conceptions of realism. For contemporary Westerners, a photograph shows a particular individual; but for the Fang,

---

[9]This succinct statement of Boas's position, which appeared in *Race, Language and Culture* in 1940 had been discussed and supported at length in Boas's (1927) *Primitive Art* and was extant in his lecture notes many years earlier.

FIGURE 13-2 Fang dance mask, said to depict either Franco or DeGaulle. Made by Mvole Mo Ze in the early 1950s. *(Photo courtesy James Fernandez.)*

what the statue represents is not necessarily the truth, physically speaking, of a human body, but a vital truth about human beings symbolically stated. This symbolic intelligence seems to arise from the way the statue holds opposites in balance—old age and infancy, somber passive inscrutability of visage and muscular tension of torso and legs, etc. What is expressed in these statues, then, is the essence of maturity. (Fernandez 1973:205)

This goal appears in Western art also. The contemporary British painter, Francis Bacon, for example, has said, "Isn't it that one wants a thing to be as factual as possible, and yet at the same time as deeply suggestive or deeply unlocking of areas of sensation other than simple illustrating of the object that you set out to do? Isn't that what art is all about?" (quoted in Berger 1980:112). And classical Chinese aesthetics expresses a comparable belief. Su Tungp'o wrote, "If one criticizes painting by its verisimilitude, one's understanding is similar to that of a child" (quoted in Lin Yutang 1935:309); according to this aesthetic, mature painting should express the subject's *spirit.*

But probably nobody would mistake a Fang mask for an abstract form with no meaningful referent: It clearly represents a human face. However, some art works that appear to be totally abstract turn out, on closer inspection, to actually be representational. The fine rugs woven by women in the Georgian Caucasus appear to be decorated with purely geometric designs.

Research has revealed, however, that these patterns are intended to portray a specific and culturally important subject—namely, one of the four traditional floor plans found in Armenian churches (Sassouni 1981).

We can move one step further in the direction of abstraction by considering mandalas, the seemingly non-representational paintings used by devotees of Tantrism in India and Tibet (see **Figure 13–3**). Although many of the paintings do not portray specific subjects found in the sensible world, they are not meaningless. They represent the highest spiritual principles of Tantric belief. They are meant "to stimulate radiant inner icons, whose bodies and features would be quite unrealistic in any ordinary sense of the word" (Rawson 1973:25).

Body decoration is another notable genre of apparently non-representational art. Among the San, some tattoos do cause their wearers to resemble certain game animals, but do other, less literal body decorations convey meaning? The answer is "yes"—in two different ways. First, specific body decorations that outsiders might assume to be non-representational may turn out to portray a specific figurative subject. Consider the Nuba, a group of farmer-pastoralists who live in Kordofan Province, Democratic Republic of Sudan. James Faris has described in detail several specific ways in which

FIGURE 13–3 Tibetan Mandala representing Par-ka, Mewa, the signs of the zodiac, and the days of the week. *(Courtesy, Field Museum of Natural History, Chicago, neg. no. 100383.)*

Nuba men decorate themselves (Faris 1972). One category of geometric design appears to be devoid of referential meaning—a band of three or more black diamond figures, for example, connected point to point and bordered by two black lines to create a decorative linear figure (see **Figure 13–4**). Although someone unfamiliar with Nuba culture might assume that this is merely a geometric design prompted by the pleasure of pattern, the Nuba call it *ŋōrā* and recognize it as representing cowrie shells on a strip of leather. If the diamonds had not been filled in with black, the design would have been *deŋa-kwa*, a poisonous snake. (Presumably the diamonds correspond to the pattern of scales that characterizes the snake.) Other Nuba body decorations convey different, and more abstract, meanings in a different way. For example, a person's haircut reveals his or her membership in a patrilineal clan.

But Nuba body decoration has a second, and more abstract level of meaning, and this reveals another way in which the art is representational. To shave one's hair, to tattoo oneself, and to apply oil and pigment to the skin is to display one's humanity, one's maturity, one's beauty as a person. Faris notes that in Nuba thought, "It is not language (which monkeys, in Southeastern Nuba myths, once shared with man), but shaving—the *choice* to have or not to have hair—that distinguishes humans from other 'moving species'" (Faris 1972:56). Nuba body decoration is a conscious and explicit

FIGURE 13–4 Nuba man, with painted decorations, hair and neck ornaments. *(Photo courtesy James Faris.)*

recognition of a belief found in many other societies—namely, that body decoration "means" identity of the individual and of the group. Be it the style of fur and leather-work characteristic of a group of Eskimos, the medieval European coat of arms, or the designer clothes of contemporary America, the seemingly non-representational art of body decoration is rich with meaning, especially of membership in an exclusive or bounded group.

Thus all art represents meaning, whether it is figuratively representational or not. The meaning may, following C.S. Peirce, be called iconographic, with the art work resembling the subject it represents, as in the lines, circles, and dots that Aborigines in central and northern Australia often draw to represent the travels of mythic creatures during the Eternal Dreamtime (cf. Munn 1973). Or the meaning may be symbolic, like Tantric paintings and much body decoration.

To return to the debate about whether art was born from a decorative or a symbolic impulse, I would argue that a meaning component (either symbolic or iconographic) is always present, even in most artifacts that appear to be only decorative in nature. The importance of aesthetic playfulness will be considered later, but for now we can see that Boas was probably correct in asserting that a search for the representational versus non-representational origin of art is futile. This is not because separate sources of artistic activity existed but rather because the distinction between representational and non-representational art is in this context spurious. *All* art represents; the only difference is the degree to which an artifact's referent is known to those outside the tradition that produced it and the degree to which the represented subject itself is either concrete or abstract.[10]

Difficult Meanings

That the meaning conveyed by art is not necessarily easily accessible comes as no surprise. Art is often accorded the honor of being the medium through which deep philosophical issues are conveyed. This has been the case historically in Western art and it remains so today. Getzels and Csikszentmihalyi (1976) interviewed a large sample of painting and sculpture students enrolled in American art colleges, asking why they wanted to become artists. The researchers found that

---

[10]I refer here not only to material artifacts but also to such "behavioral artifacts" (or, as Keali'inohomoku has dubbed them, "phenomifacts") as songs, dances, and stories. These also generally convey meanings in ways that are both obvious and obscure. Music, for example, often has a text, and the melody itself may imitate sounds of nature—animal calls, weather noises, and whatnot. And besides these iconographic meanings, music may also symbolically convey messages of group identity. Until recently it was thought that there is much in music that has no referential meaning. However, researchers in mathematics and information theory have now postulated a resemblance between musical structure and the mathematical patterns known as "fractals" that are found in nature (cf. Mandelbrot 1982, M. Gardner 1978).

practically none mentioned the creation of 'beauty,' 'harmony,' 'order,' or any other such aesthetic goal. Most responses centered instead on cognitive goals: the young artists said they painted in order to get a better understanding of reality. The kind of understanding they sought referred to areas of experience that were highly ambiguous, like life and death, or were very personal and complex. They wanted a better understanding of problems for which no rational solution is available. (Csikszentmihalyi 1978:118)

We can only speculate about the psychological basis of this phenomenon. Peckham (1965) has claimed that humans have a natural drive to order and certainty, which is adaptive under many conditions. But we must also have an arena in which we can experience doubt, chaos, and disorientation because only in such a flux can we forge new life ways that allow us to cope with a changing world. Art, in Peckham's view, serves such a need by providing a domain in which chaos and mystery can be experienced without endangering survival.

George Devereux has made a similar proposal, although he turns the matter around by asking psychoanalytically why the significant truths conveyed by art "should have to be beautified, or why the lily gilded. The only reasonable answer to this question is that only painful or upsetting truth needs to be 'varnished'" (Devereux 1961:373). Art can provide an avenue for expressing emotionally and philosophically wrenching ideas because, in the first place, it embodies the idiom of cultural tradition rather than being the proclamation of a lone individual; and in the second place, being symbolic, it is always repudiable.

The societies of Part One provide concrete examples of art conveying difficult and complex messages. But often the problem lies not in the content of the art's subject matter but rather in the art's embodying concepts that are themselves *contradictory*. Yoruba aesthetics provides an excellent example. On a stylistic level, as well as in its manifest meaning, Yoruba sculpture, music, and dance convey a message of "harmonious energy," but, as noted, the goals of harmony and energy ultimately contradict each other.

This capacity for art to encapsulate conflicting messages takes several forms. One possibility is that a particular society may sustain two or more distinctly different art styles, each with its own particular meaning and message. Thompson notes (1973) that the elegant aesthetic criteria which Yoruba art connoisseurs apply to most sculptures are intentionally contravened in art created for satire, social criticism, or psychological harassment. Similarly, among the Bamana (Bambara), McNaughton found that most art reflects such values as "clarity, purity, straightforwardness, and discernibility" (McNaughton 1979:42). However, masks made for use by the powerful *Komo* society of the Bamana purposely contradict these values. For example,

large and small horns may well appear together with the tusks of pigs, the small ones often lashed to the mask with rag or twine so that they wobble slightly when the mask is in motion. . . . This composite imagery is anything but clear (in terms of representation), nor does it produce the impression of economy or harmony. . . . The message is unmistakable. The power of *Komo* is secret; it is unknown and all the more dangerous because of it.   (McNaughton 1979:43f)

A more complex situation occurs when contradictory messages co-exist within a single, unified stylistic tradition. Navajo art, as noted earlier, holds in balance the opposite poles of activity and passivity, of symmetry and asymmetry, of inner and outer aspects, and of masculinity and femininity.

Or consider the conception of art among the central African Fang. Although European collectors highly prize Fang reliquary figures, traditional members of Fang culture are not enthusiastic about the sculptures or the carvers who create them. But because their culture possesses few institutions to insure political integration, the Fang do value highly the artistry of individuals who resolve disputes (*palabras*). These men are masters of the art of oratory. The Fang have a low opinion of the European judge, who is merely interested in distinguishing right from wrong. Instead of artistically "slicing" the *palabra*, he "breaks" it, leaving "jagged edges which will continue to fester" (Fernandez 1973:208). In Fang thought, the artistry of the chief judge of *palabras* outshines that of carvers and troubadours because he "symbolizes in his oratory the vision of a good society, an orderly society, in which men can live in harmony. Through his rhetoric he has power to impose order on his listeners even in this egalitarian culture" (Fernandez 1973:217).

Simon Ottenberg (1982), drawing upon his own field experience among the Afikpo of Nigeria as well as other reports of West African masquerading traditions, has considered at length the ways in which masked dancers simultaneously embody two contradictory messages. As is the case with much art, the masks, costumes, movements, and music of the dancers embody fundamental cultural principles. But Ottenberg points out that on a different level, the dancers also present a counter-reality: After all, the dancers are not mortals but spirits and as such they wear not everyday clothing but extraordinarily beautiful (or grotesque) clothing and masks; their voices, through the use of falsetto or other methods, are made to sound different from normal voices; and by dancing, walking on stilts, or even attacking children and other bystanders, they move their bodies in ways foreign to mundane life.

Although there is no direct evidence to support it, Ottenberg offers the interesting conjecture that the double reality of West African masquerades serves several important psychological functions. For children, the maskers may be larger-than-life embodiments of parents, older siblings, and other authority figures, whom children inevitably see as being alternately wise and funny, entertaining and threatening, and always looking and acting differently from the children themselves. Ottenberg says,

Children may fear these maskers as powerful figures but they also learn that there are limits to how far the maskers (as their parents) will go. Then the children may still be afraid of them, but now it is also a game of play—to run and return, run and return—as in life there is also identification with the father. (Ottenberg 1982:172)

The counter-reality of masquerades also provides opportunities for wish fulfillment for adults. After all, a parent is omnipotent only in the eyes of children, and to be grown up is to feel the inescapable constraints of material and social life. But maskers, as spirits, *are* omnipotent—or, at least, so the spectator is led to believe.

Finally, the contradictions embodied in a masquerade may touch another psychological chord:

The element of secrecy in the masquerades is major; the secret bush, the secret masking societies, the secrecy of the maskers' identities. The masquerade touches on a panhuman illusion. We act toward one another in our roles *as if* we were open and relatively free, yet we are generally guarded, withholding, secretive, having private wishes and fantasies. . . . The performances expose this game, commenting on people's private worlds in a public way. . . . This may be amusing or anxiety producing for those involved, but allows persons to deal with a range of repressed associations. (Ottenberg 1982:176)

Not all art mediates opposing ideas, forces, or groups of people, but the art that *does* accomplish this feat makes an invaluable contribution to its community. It is not surprising that art can do this, since such meanings are, after all, conveyed symbolically. The laws of non-contradiction that we assume to apply to the tangible world are not necessarily required by the subjective world. An electrical charge cannot be both positive and negative, but it is altogether possible to both love and hate someone, to feel dread and relish at the same time, or to experience bafflement and awe while simultaneously feeling comprehension and acceptance. The psychological bases of such phenomena are elusive, but an analysis of the style and symbolic content of art reveals how easily contradictions can be embedded in art objects. The Yoruba statuette *does* represent an individual at the peak of growth, with powerful legs flexed as if ready to spring into action; at the same time, the figure's equipoise reflects its artistic—and cultural—stability.

Conclusion

For all the diverse aspects of meaning in art, the central conclusion remains. In every instance, *art has meaning*—and usually meaning that is of considerable significance in the culture it comes from. Cultures vary in their definition of what is and what is not significant; and there are differences in the overtness with which the meaning is manifest in the art work. But in any case, art does typically convey culturally significant meaning.

14

STYLE, FEELING, AND SKILL

Art is the straining of pure affect against pure. . . discipline.
(Devereux 1961:362)

Part One's survey of ten societies' aesthetic systems revealed that art typically conveys meaning of considerable cultural significance; numerous aspects of that dimension were explored in the preceding chapter. But Calliope has three other widespread and enduring traits: Art everywhere is executed in a style and a medium that is characteristic of its place and time of origin; art usually makes a notable impact on the feelings of those who experience it; and art is typically executed with exceptional skill. This chapter will examine these three final characteristics of Calliope.

Style: The Encodement of Meaning

Information theorists have long known that meaning must be encoded in a medium: The telegrapher's message, for example, is transmitted via the Morse Code; and in a parallel fashion, it is useful to think of artistic style as being the medium through which art's meaning is communicated. It is possible, of course, to discuss style apart from the meaning it conveys. For example, there is a striking contrast between the high level of graphic complexity found in Western Apache art from the American Southwest in comparison to the relatively low level of complexity in Comanche art from the Southern Plains. Visual differences between these two art styles are obvious, and one could limit oneself to describing the exact nature of this stylistic contrast, its historical background as seen in the archaeological record, and the transition in style as one goes from Comanche to Western Apache via intervening groups in the region such as the Puebloans. Or else the stylistic contrast between Western Apache and Comanche art could serve as a starting point for deeper questions regarding the *significance* of this stylistic difference between the two cultures.

But unfortunately, we do not have anything resembling a complete picture of the traditional aesthetics of either of the two groups in question. We do, however, have one clue about the significance of the stylistic differences between Western Apache and Comanche art. Herbert Barry has cross-culturally examined the relationship between art style and several personality variables, and he has found statistically significant data to support his hypothesis that non-literate societies in which child socialization is severe tend to produce graphically complex art whereas societies in which socialization is less severe tend to make art that is less complex in appearance (Barry 1971). And, in fact, ethnographic information indicates that the Western Apache and the Comanche fit this pattern quite well. Of course, this is not really an answer, either, but it can guide research in a direction that may prove profitable— namely, to explore the psychological meaning and consequences of the respective styles of Western Apache and Comanche art. That is, what cultural meanings are conveyed by the two aesthetic traditions, and how are these meanings invested in Western Apache and Comanche art styles?

Style is not a completely independent variable, and practical considerations often restrict the expressive freedom available to artists. Parameters of clay and firing technology, for example, limit the shape of ceramics; and their utilitarian purpose places still further restraints on the shapes of pots (cf. Hendrickson and McDonald 1983).

But within the boundaries set by such factors, style can be thought of as a manifestation of meaning in art. The artistic conventions that characterize the art of a particular place and time convey, at the very least, tacit messages regarding the identity of the makers. Other stylistic conventions convey increasingly narrow and explicit messages. For example, the smooth surface and symmetrical posture of a Yoruba statuette convey (at least to those who can "read" the style) information regarding human beauty and personal demeanor; and even more overtly, Yoruba iconography tells the viewer (or, at least, the informed viewer) which particular orisha cult a given dance mask is made for.

Although artifacts convey information through style, H. Martin Wobst (1977) has asserted that they do this somewhat differently than do other modes of communication, such as language. The foregoing survey of native systems of aesthetics gives us a chance to test—and extend—this claim.

Wobst noted that an artifact "stores" information so that it can be "sent" to people who are temporally and spatially distant. Although all information degrades with the passage of time, the inevitable process of deterioration occurs more slowly in artifacts than it does with other modes of communication. So, according to Wobst's reasoning, although the initial production of the artifact may be "expensive" in energy and matter, sending the message to large numbers of people is inexpensive. For example, the carving of a mask for the Yoruba Gẹlẹdẹ dance requires intensive work by the carver, but during its lifetime the completed mask conveys a potent message to thousands of viewers of Gẹlẹdẹ festivities, year after year, with little further care. Wobst goes on to note the impracticality of encoding highly complex or variable messages in artifacts. The benefits of the stylistic mode rarely justify the effort required to create artifacts with complicated or short-lived messages. Therefore, although any message might in theory be conveyed via artifacts, style is a practical medium only for communicating such simple and recurrent messages as those of emotional state, identification with a particular group, and ownership (Wobst 1977:323; cf. also Rice 1983).

Messages such as these are indeed often communicated by art. Body decoration often conveys information about sexual identity and status, and art used by cults typically objectifies the attributes associated with the group's particular deity. The same is true, however, of many artifacts that by no stretch of the imagination could be considered art. A cult's carvings may be stored in a particular type of building whose construction requires no particular skill and whose visual appeal is considered by its builders to be unimportant. As some future archaeologist might discover, the shed's distinctive style of design means simply, "this is the place were cult objects are stored."

As we saw in the preceding chapter, some things convey meanings that are ambiguous. These artifacts are typically considered to be art, and much of the artist's skill lies in the ability to bind together meanings that contradict each other (as in Yoruba carvings or in Navajo sandpaintings and weaving), that are metaphysically elusive (e.g., the transmuting aesthetics of the Inuit), or that are so complex and subtle that their full meaning may be grasped only after years of study (e.g., the mandalas of Tantrism and of Esoteric Buddhism).[1]

Art that conveys complex and obscure meaning resists simplistic interpretation, especially when its cultural context is unavailable, as is generally the case in archaeology. Consider, for example, Mimbres painted pottery (see **Figure 14–1**). It was made between 1000 and 1200 A.D. in hundreds of small villages scattered along the Mimbres River in what is now southern New Mexico. Geometric and representational designs were used to decorate the inside of many shallow Mimbres bowls. Scratch marks indicate that most of the bowls were used, but many eventually were interred along with other burial items, usually after a hole had been punched in the bowl's bottom. This was almost always the fate of bowls that bore representational drawings, some of which seem to have been used solely for funerary purposes.

---

[1] In his ambitious study of the evolution of art, Pitirim Sorokin did as good a job as any later scholar in characterizing the metaphysical abstractions that are sometimes manifest in art:

The Ideational mentality seeks to find in the universe and in its parts their unchangeable ultimate reality, their Being (*Sein*). . . . This unchangeable Being is thought of as the essence of the reality of a given object or of the whole universe. It lies behind and beyond the appearances perceived by the eye and other organs of sense. (Sorokin 1937:247)

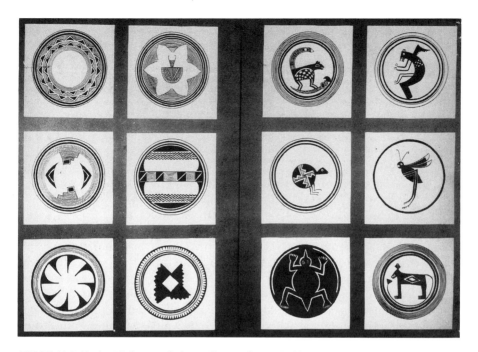

FIGURE 14–1   Twelve Mimbres pot designs.   *(Courtesy Denver Art Museum.)*

What is the meaning of these Mimbres bowls? What information do they convey? In a definitive study, J. J. Brody has argued that the distinctive Mimbres ceramic style must have been a self-conscious symbol of the identity of the Mimbres culture; and beyond that, it may represent an effort to metaphysically "classify the universe" (Brody 1977:212–213).

But we can only speculate about more concrete interpretations of Mimbres designs. Consider for instance the intended meaning of two bowls that seem to clearly portray one individual decapitating another (cf. Brody 1977, Plate 11). The bowls come from different localities, so their message probably was widely known in Mimbres culture. Do they represent a priest sacrificing a man in hopes of bringing an end to a drought, as was done among the Hopi and Zuni as recently as the nineteenth century? Do they portray ritual decapitation, as occurred in Casa Grandes and other cultures to the south? Or might they illustrate "the Mimbres version of a Classic Mayan myth . . . in which one twin culture hero decapitates his brother as part of a scheme to trap and slay the Lords of the Underworld" (Brody 1977:206)? Art style alone is unlikely to reveal which (if any) of these complex messages was vested in the bowls by their makers.

Mimbres pottery, like much of the art discussed in Part One, proves that Wobst's claim to the contrary, those artifacts that are art objects often convey subtle and complex information. What about Wobst's assertion that artifacts, once produced, tend to convey information that is not subject to rapid change?

Clearly this is not true for the "behavioral artifacts" produced in the performing arts; but neither does it hold true for the objects that have been termed "ephemeral art," that is, "visual phenomena created or assembled with the conscious knowledge that they will be destroyed, dismantled, or permitted to decompose within hours, days, or at the most several months" (Ravicz 1976:1). Ephemeral art includes such obvious things as masks that are made for use in a single ceremony but also items that Westerners might tend to overlook, such as fireworks, food decoration, and mud sculpture.

The 155 cross-cultural instances of ephemeral art studied by Ravicz shed new light on Wobst's claim that artifacts tend to convey stable, unchanging messages. Ninety-six percent of the examples, Ravicz found, occur in ritual contexts. Ravicz reasons that although ephemeral art objects are necessarily made from easily accessible materials, they aquire a special, hightened status because aesthetic manipulation raises them above the level of the mundane and common.

Navajo sandpaintings provide an excellent example of ephemeral art, the value of which lies in the very act of creation and in their elevating humble materials to a special, sacred state. Navajo weaving accomplishes the same end, but with the additional factor that the designs themselves are new on each blanket or shawl. But even here the message is not novel because the stylistic and aesthetic principles upon which the new weaving is based are identical to those that informed all previous weaving.

These factors suggest that Wobst draws the right conclusion but for the wrong reasons. It is true that art rarely conveys short-lived and changing information, but this is not because novelty requires extra work; in fact, it takes more effort to doggedly replicate pre-existing designs than to approximate or consciously change them. Instead, innovation is limited by the inertia of tradition, a powerful conservative force in most cultures. The symbolic associations of a given genre and medium cannot easily be exchanged for meanings that are altogether fresh and new.

This being the case, style, as the embodiment of meaning, can be seen as setting limits on creativity in art. Granted, some societies prize innovation, attributing to it a meaning with its own significance. For example, the frequent presence of Changing Woman in Navajo myth indicates the high value placed in Navajo culture upon the creative impulse.[2] Similarly, the basketry of the California Yorok-Karok (cf. O'Neale 1932) and the Mimbres

---

[2]But one must remember that "creativity" in a Navajo context means something quite different from what, say, a Western avant-garde artist might mean by the word. Sandpaintings are actually *re*created; and even in the secular arts of weaving and silversmithing, there are many restraints on innovativeness.

pottery of the pre-historic Southwest both display such exceptional degrees of diversity as to suggest that their makers took positive pride in variety. But such societies are exceptional; more typically, creativity is not sought as an end in itself, and some cultures have an explicit proscription against it. For example, in striving to produce art in accord with *rasa*, the classical artists of India took the ancient Vedas as their law and all art strictly conformed to Vedic principles. Similarly, Australian Aborigines avoid innovation because their art works embody the unchanging Eternal Dreamtime. The Sepik River peoples also avoid artistic innovation because their art products serve as habitations for spirits: If these dwellings are altered, the spirits may not come to live in them—a situation in which mortals would be the losers. Granted, the archaeological record always reveals that as the decades and centuries pass into history, change has indeed occurred. But this is a result of accident and "aesthetic drift" (cf. Anderson 1979:159–162) and takes place despite a reluctance to innovate.

Even in the supposedly dynamic Western tradition, innovation in art has not been as continuous as the developments in twentieth-century art might lead us to believe. Not only have the fine arts been generally conservative, as during the Middle Ages, but the popular arts too have generally resisted change. For example, the history of some Western folk melodies and folktales can be traced back many centuries, and contemporary standards of personal beauty have changed surprisingly little since Roman times.[3]

Whereas from the perspective of cultural history, stylistic conventions limit variation in art objects, for the individual artist they control the extent to which art can serve as a personal, idiosyncratic statement. But again, total conformity is as impossible as total nonconformity. George Devereux summarizes the situation well:

> If mere "expressiveness" and/or "projection" were the criteria whereby one determines whether a given product is art or something else, then the bellowing of an agitated catatonic . . . would be the most genuine of arts. Conversely, were style and other conventions the true criteria of art, then classroom exercises in strict counterpoint would represent the summit of artistic behavior. Ideally, the dynamic criterion of art is the straining of pure affect against pure (culturally structured) discipline.   (Devereux 1961:362)

---

[3]"A fashionable, desirable Roman girl at the beginning of the Christian era would . . . have been tall and blond (rather than brunette), worn a plain robe, and had bright red cheeks and eyes shaded with kohl or painted with saffron. Her brows would have been pencilled, and she would have had a patch or two on her cheek or neck, or, perhaps, even more daringly, on her bare shoulder or arm" (Liggett 1974:61).

This consideration of style brings us close to the position of several contemporary American philosophers of art, notably George Dickie, Howard Becker, and Arthur Danto, who have been credited with developing an "institutional" theory of aesthetics. According to this approach, art objects are those things that are currently recognized as such by members of the "artworld," which is defined as "a loosely organized, but nevertheless related, set of persons including artists . . ., producers, museum directors, museum-goers, theater-goers, reporters for newspapers, critics for publications of all sorts, art historians, art theorists, philosophers of art, and others" (Dickie 1974:35–36). The members of the artworld recognize—indeed, determine—the accepted style of the day, and in so doing define the current meaning of "art." The advantage of the institutional approach lies in its being culturally and historically sensitive, permitting the operational definition of art to evolve as the membership and tastes of the artworld change with the passage of time. It also avoids absolute boundaries, recognizing that since there is a public for, say, work by Frederic Remington, we must accept his "cowboy paintings" as art.

Several writers, including some of the original formulators of institutional aesthetics, have been wary of a theory that hinges on art being that which is accepted by a group of *cognoscenti* since such a theory would include as art not only the recognized masterpieces of the museum but also paintings on black velvet, which are recognized by an avid, and presumably discriminating, audience.

But if the focus is to be upon the social and cultural aspects of art, one should not ignore even black velvet paintings. The real problem with the institutional approach is that it overlooks other dimensions of art such as meaning, skill, and medium. A definition of art based solely on recognition by a group of "experts" does not exclude, say, those things that are approved by Christian theologians, such as daily prayer, or those approved by baseball umpires, such as balls pitched within the strike zone—neither of which is considered to be "art" in the usual meaning of the word. (Obviously, to limit "experts" to "*art* experts" leads to a circular definition.)

Art has meaning, and its messages are conveyed interpersonally via the code that we call style. Far from being simple and redundant, the messages are typically of great cultural consequence (as in art that embodies fundamental metaphysical and religious principles) or else of great individual importance (as with body decorations that convey information about sexual availability, status, and affiliation). But both possibilities lead to two further questions: Are there any pan-cultural bases for the conventions of art style in the canons of art criticism; and what is the basis of the sensuous art object's psychological effect?

Accounting for Taste: The Bases of Stylistic Criticism

Humans can seldom resist passing judgment, not only on people but also on the things people make. One must therefore determine the patterns that can be found in such judgments, especially since standards vary so dramatically from one culture to another. In Western culture we know that even individuals with the most refined of tastes often disagree. Emerson did not like Jane Austen; Carlyle hated Keats; and Turgenev could not abide either Dostoevsky or Tolstoy (cf. Gardner 1983:76). Or, as mentioned in the chapter on aesthetics in the West, George Boas's essay, "Mona Lisa in the History of Taste" (1963/1940) reports the curious evolution of opinions about the Leonardo painting. Even something as supposedly free of cultural associations as the "golden mean," which has been a perennial favorite of Westerners since classical Greece, may not have universal appeal: In one controlled experiment a group of Japanese subjects tended to choose rectangles that were nearly square in preference to ones based on the golden mean (Berlyne 1970; 1980:344).

Information theorists have pointed out that most questions have a limitless number of wrong answers but only a few, or a single, right ones. Applied to the issue at hand, this principle suggests that whereas a system of aesthetics may provide a handful of general principles prescribing what art *should* be, there remains a residual category of infinite size composed of what art *should not* be. There are more ways to be ugly than to be beautiful; discord is unnervingly simple to produce whereas sweet harmony is always elusive; and proper steps are few although the ways to stumble are boundless. Sometimes this situation is reflected in traditional philosophies of art. For example, John and Betty Messenger (1981:35f) report that the Nigerian Anang possess more criteria for personal ugliness than they do for personal beauty; and one's own experience shows that it is far easier to document the flaws in an art work than it is to put accurately into words its qualities of excellence.

Most attempts to uncover cross-cultural similarities of aesthetic judgment have been unproductive.[4] For example, Francés and Tamba (1973) asked Japanese musicology students to rank ten excerpts of Japanese music in order of preference. They then compared these choices to the preferences of three French groups—professional musicians, music students, and non-music students. Not only did the researchers find no tendency for Japanese and French subjects to have similar preferences, but the choices of the

---

[4]This literature has been extensively surveyed and evaluated by Pickford (1972:Chap. 7) and Berlyne (1980). See also Anderson 1979:197–199.

French professional musicians tended to be just the opposite of the Japanese subjects.

If there are universals of artistic taste, they would seem to be manifest in underlying structure rather than in superficial style. For example, Robbins Burling (1966) has found that the rhyme and meter pattern found in the popular English nursery rhyme, "Humpty Dumpty," appears in children's verses in Chinese, Arabic, Serrano (a language indigenous to southern California), Benkula (spoken in Sumatra), Yoruba (Nigeria), and Trukese (South Pacific).

Similar cross-cultural studies have uncovered only the most generalized sorts of agreement in the visual art styles. Rhoda Kellog postulated a series of well-defined developmental stages in children's drawing style (see, e.g., Kellog 1969); but her non-Western data were gathered somewhat haphazardly. When Alexander Alland (1983) carried out a more systematic study of the question, collecting drawings from children in six diverse societies under controlled conditions, he found that after an early stage of "kinetic scribbles," no cross-cultural patterns of development in style or content of drawing were apparent. However, on a deeper level, the drawings Alland collected did seem to support claims by Jacqueline Goodnow that children's drawings conform to certain structural rules such as being thrifty in the use of units and tending to experiment only with a basic vocabulary (cf. Goodnow 1979:141–145).[5]

To extrapolate from these findings about children's drawings to sophisticated art works of adults living in various societies may not be warranted, but the work of Alland (and of other scholars such as the psychologist Howard Gardner [1980] and the art historian E.H. Gombrich [1979]) suggests that although preferences for details of art styles are no more instinctive than are the vocabularies of the world's languages, some formal features may indeed be pan-human.

A similar situation prevails regarding color. Humans have gone to great effort to obtain colored pigments since the most distant antiquity (cf. Wreschner 1976, 1980), but psychological studies of *preferences* of certain colors have often yielded ambiguous results, even with Western subjects. The members of specific societies, however, are often unequivocal in the meanings they attribute to specific colors. The Navajo, for example, associate certain colors with the four cardinal directions; and a convincing illustration of the diffusion of Mesoamerican customs into the Southwest is provided by comparing systems of color symbolism from the two culture areas (cf. Witherspoon 1977:145–146; Nicholson 1976):

---

[5]Interestingly, the two studies of drawings by non-human primates found that chimpanzees also made patterns that are consistent with those postulated by Alland (cf. Shiller 1951; Morris 1962; Whiten 1976.)

DIRECTION	NAVAJO COLOR	TOLTEC COLOR
East	White	White
South	Blue	Blue
West	Red	Yellow
North	Black	Black

That such associations are at least in part arbitrary is illustrated by the color symbolism of the Navajo's neighbors, the Pueblo groups. Ortiz (1972) reports that in the Tewa-speaking Pueblos, blue is associated with north and yellow with the west, although exactly the opposite is true in the Keres-speaking Pueblos. Other areas of the world share this seeming arbitrariness of color symbolism.

But although there is no complete agreement among cultures regarding color symbolism, tentative evidence does suggest that some limited consensus regarding color associations exists cross-culturally. Victor Turner (1966) has argued cogently that red, white, and black play important symbolic roles not only among the East African Ndembu, whom he studied in depth, but also in many other of the world's societies. This, Turner suggests, is because blood is everywhere red, semen and milk white, excreta and rot black.

Using a statistical approach, Eyesenck (1941) surveyed the results of twenty-six early, independently executed studies, of both Western and non-Western subjects and including a total of over 20,000 individuals. He found significant agreement regarding preferences for saturated colors in the following order: blue, red, green, violet, orange, and yellow. Also, Adams and Osgood (1973) used the Semantic Differential test with subjects from twenty-three different countries to study the connotations of color terms; and they found significant cross-cultural agreement on several points, most of which lend support to Turner's conjectures about red, white, and black. As Turner predicted, the subjects had strong feelings about red; and if black's significance derives primarily from its association with excreta, and white with milk and semen, then one would expect black to be viewed as bad and white as good. It would also make sense to expect red, associated with blood, to be strong and active; and black should be passive. And, in fact, Adams and Osgood found these correlations to exist.

A cross-cultural study of philosophies of art (i.e., aesthetics) is not the same as a cross-cultural study of stylistic preferences. This book's major focus is the former; the latter, being discussed at the moment, is highly intriguing but the scarcity of information permits only tentative conclusions at best. At present we have merely clues regarding stylistic preferences derived from the study of aesthetics.

First, it is significant that societies *do* inevitably have stylistic preferences in art objects. This does not necessarily have to be the case: Among flowers, for example, some are "showy" and others "insignificant," but all are generally thought to be beautiful. But artifacts *are* often differentiated according to their quality; and since the distant days of the early paleolithic, individuals have put great effort into obtaining beautiful things (cf. Edwards 1978).

Contemporary cultures, whether complex or small-scale, implicitly differentiate not only art from non-art, but they also distinguish good art from mediocre art. Most Western research on this topic has emphasized the visual qualities of the graphic arts, but this is uncommon cross-culturally. We know that in most of the world's societies the details of a work's superficial appearance are less important than the meaning that lies behind the work.

However, the details *are* inevitably structured according to some principles, and the origin of these principles remains to be accounted for. Near the end of the work that consumed the last two decades of his life, David E. Berlyne wrote of his many psychological experiments on aesthetics that their results

> do not support the view that aesthetic reactions depend entirely on cultural tradition, so that no cross-cultural generalizations about them can be valid. Nor do they encourage the practice of confining psychological aesthetics to experiments with western subjects and neglecting to extend them in cross-cultural directions.   (Berlyne 1976b:54)

The full nature of the stylistic universals has still to be revealed, and we may yet discover a quite elegant model to account for stylistic preferences. For example, linguists assumed for decades that color vocabularies were culture-specific, with each language selecting and naming its own distinctive handful of colors from among millions that can be distinguished by the human eye. But in 1969, Brent Berlin and Paul Kay published their finding that "basic color terms" are not arbitrary, but that they occur cross-culturally according to a relatively simple pattern. For a field as prone to cultural relativism as is contemporary cultural anthropology, the Berlin-Kay hypothesis gave the same admonishment to the discipline that Hamlet gave Horatio: There are more things in heaven and earth than are dreamt of in our philosophy. Time alone will show if a similarly drastic revision of aesthetic relativism is in order.

Art Media

The existence of an art style presupposes the existence of a medium in which art works are executed; and cultures inevitably have something to say, explicitly or (more often) implicitly, about the media that are proper for artistic activities. For example, in early India only poetry, architecture, and music were considered to be appropriate for fine art; dance and the visual arts were secondary; and the senses of touch, taste, and smell were considered to be void of artistic potential. The West, too, has singled out the visual and auditory senses as the media for genuine art. But there is clear evidence that other sensory modes can serve as the basis of art. In Japan, for example, the tea ceremony calls into play the gustatory sense in the participants' appreciation of the flavor of unsweetened tea and the olfactory sense in the smelling of incense.[6] And perhaps it would not be stretching matters to say that Japanese *sumo* wrestling elevates the kinesthetic and tactile senses to the level of art, certainly for the performers and, through identification, for the spectators as well.

Taste and smell are raised to central importance in the artistic activities of women in the United Arab Emirates. Consider, for example, the aesthetic accouterments of the *fualah,* an informal, though highly ritualized, get-together that takes place when a woman entertains morning or afternoon guests (see **Figures 14–2** and **14–3**). The hostess first offers her friends a carefully prepared tray of food that presents a selection of bananas and pomegranates, dark brown sweetmeats, salted pistachios and pumpkin seeds, Danish butter cookies, and imported toffee, an array that fulfills the formal requirement of satisfying sweet, sour, salty, and bitter tastes (Kanafani 1983:1, 21). Coffee follows the food, and then the hostess brings in her *shandug,* a glass-lidded box that holds as many as eight small bottles of perfume oils, several varieties of incense, and one or two bodkins for applying the perfumes. The hostess opens one perfume bottle after another, passing them around the circle of seated women:

> Each woman dips the bodkin in the bottle and depending on the nature of the perfume places it either on her hair, behind her ears, on the neck and nape, on her hair-veil or on her cloak where it covers her chest, shoulders, and armpits. She repeats her gestures several times, dipping and anointing at length.... I have never heard any woman ask her hostess about the kind of perfume offered. Women have developed such a remarkable sensitivity to scents that however different the oil or mixture may be, all are familiar with the basic ingredients and are able to detect them individually. (Kanafani 1983:23, 25)

When everyone has used the oils, the hostess lights perfumed incense or aloewood, and each woman in turn wafts the dense smoke over her hair, lifts her veil a bit to scent her face and inhale the smoke (because incense

---

[6]The Japanese preference for simplicity carries over into their "food arts." Keene reports, "Just as the faint perfume of the plum blossoms is preferred to the heavy odor of the lily, the barely perceptible differences in flavor between different varieties of raw fish are prized extravagantly.... It would be hard to convince a Chinese or European that a lump of cold bean curd dotted with a dash of soy sauce is indeed superior to the supposedly cloying flavors of *haute cuisine*" (Keene 1971:22–23).

FIGURES 14-2 and 14-3   A women's *fualah* in the United Arab Emirates.   *(Photo courtesy Aida Sami Kalafani.)*

dispels tension and aches). Then she places the censor under her dress and, wrapping herself with a cloak, allows the dense fumes to permeate all of her body and clothing. Like most serious aesthetic endeavors, these Arab women practice their gustatory and olfactory arts for several important reasons, some involving purification and compliance with the decrees of the Prophet Mohammed, others prompted by the sensuous (and sensual) pleasures they afford themselves and their husbands.

These scattered ethnographic cases prove that the arts need not be confined to the senses of vision and hearing (cf. Herring 1949). Nevertheless, most societies do emphasize the visual and auditory arts. The only discernable pattern is that the relatively more intricate aesthetic systems of complex societies tend to isolate a few sensory modes for extended consideration while other modes are ignored or else considered only by analogy. By contrast, aesthetics in small-scale societies, being implicit and not generally particularistic, is as applicable to one medium as another.

Not only are some senses favored, but some materials are too. Aztec art is revealing in this regard. All the media that served as bases for artistic activity in the Old World—ceramics, loom weaving, large-scale sculpture, monumental architecture, and metallurgy—had their counterparts in the New World as well.

This is significant in that some contemporary Western theories suggest or assume that any medium can serve as the basis for aesthetic expression. Although there is no logical argument against such propositions, the historical fact is that artists and their art-appreciating publics have had a strong tendency to specialize in a small number of media. By most definitions, art production reflects an especially high degree of skill in the artist, and it is the nature of things that whereas some media lend themselves to high virtuosity, others present little challenge. Thus in far-flung parts of the world where artists are full-time professionals, great craftsmanship has been displayed in subtly carved hard, brittle stone (jade or obsidian rather than the softer sandstone or soapstone); weaving has shown an elaboration of pattern, color, and design; smiths have mastered exacting metallurgical skills; and so on.

This conclusion is difficult to support empirically. Some aesthetic theories downplay manual skill, and the presence of skill may not be easily apparent to outsiders. Further, with a little imagination one may find challenges in *any* medium; perceptual and conceptual skills might be emphasized and the requisite oculomotor skills unexceptional; or the specialness of art may depend less on the rarity of the artist's skills and more on the scarcity of the medium itself—gem stones or precious metals, for example. But although such factors *might* be important (and instances of each are known to exist), the general cross-cultural pattern is toward specialization in a limited repertoire of media. This regularity would seem to derive from the physical properties of the things we find in the world around us.

The Affective Aspects of Art

That art gives *some* form of emotional reward to those who create and experience it can hardly be questioned. Indeed, in each of the societies discussed in Part One, art is appreciated for, among other things, the pleasure it brings to those who perceive it (see Appendix Two). Even the few studies of "art" production by non-human primates suggest that apes apparently enjoy drawing.[7]

What common denominators can be found in the affective response to art cross-culturally? One theme running throughout Part One is that people everywhere savor the beautiful, tastefully adorned human body. As observed earlier, the meaning of personal beauty is not altogether arbitrary. The attractiveness of healthy skin, strong bodies, good teeth, and indications of sexual precocity rest on natural values for survival. And body decorations, besides providing the wearer with protection against the elements, can, and often do, enhance sexual attractiveness.

Although the strong feelings that art evokes typically go far beyond the sensual, they sometimes seem to have evolved from a sexual matrix. For example, the classical Indian concept of *rasa* is an elegant, complex, and subtle theory of aesthetic emotion and although we associate it with Hindu art, the pre-eminent *rasa* theorist, Kasmiri Abhinavagupta, was an initiate in Kula Tantra; and Tantrism, we know, is unusual among religious doctrines for its emphasis on human sexuality. Tantrism equates sexual libido with the essential, beneficial, and creative energy of the universe (cf. Rawson 1973:32). The art of Tantrism is highly charged with sexual and erotic energy, which enhances the vital forces of the universe (see **Figure 14-4**). Hindu aesthetics has a similar impulse, but in a weakened form: Only one of the nine rasas, *kama*, is erotic; the others correspond to a wide variety of other emotions.

A similar situation prevails cross-culturally, where a not insignificant portion of the sensuous and emotional dimension of art can be reduced to sensual delight in the beauty of the human body. But for the remaining (and larger) part of art's affective function, the best we can do is merely catalog the varieties of aesthetic feeling—and here we have progressed little beyond the work of Aristotle two and a half millennia ago, except that now we appreciate that when we widen our domain to include other cultures, the breadth of variation is greater than Westerners had thought possible.

The "Aesthetic Response"

Since the rise of the Western aesthetic theory of formalism (p. 216), some aestheticians have asserted that the definitive feature of art is its capacity to prompt not just an affective reaction but a unique and distinctive "aesthetic

---

[7]Desmond Morris (1962:44) recounts the following anecdote about a chimpanzee named Bella: "The most striking thing about Bella, when she was in a good drawing mood, was her high level of motivation. Miss Hylkema (her caretaker) once made the mistake of interfering when Bella was in the middle of a drawing, with the result that she was bitten by the animal. Bella would never bite when Miss Hylkema interfered with any other activity, not even when taking attractive food away from her."

FIGURE 14-4 Tibetan god, *Hayagriva*, embracing his consort. *(Courtesy, Field Museum of Natural History, Chicago, neg. no. 99646.)*

response," a state of positive, focused attention to the work's *aesthetic* component, as opposed to its subject matter or the artist's technical skill.

This approach prompts us to ask, Do art-attuned audiences in *all* societies experience the refined aesthetic reaction that formalists speak of? Jacques Maquet (1986:64) has answered unequivocally in the affirmative, stating that "many societies—all known societies, I dare say—recognize and actualize the human potentiality for aesthetic perception and appreciation." But as I have shown elsewhere (Anderson 1989), Maquet's argument rests on both flawed logic and dubious readings of the secondary literature.

In fact, when one focuses on societies for which there is ample, intensive, fieldwork-based data, there is virtually no empirical evidence for the existence of the formalist's "affective response" in other societies. Of the ten societies discussed in Part One, only in early Indian aesthetics do we find a non-Western philosophy that attaches significance to a distinctive aesthetic reaction, and in that case there is an important difference between the *rasika's* affective response to an art work and the response specified by Western formalism: The aesthetic response is significantly more personal

and idiosyncratic in comparison to the culturally prescribed emotions specified by *rasa* theory.

Certainly art works everywhere are associated with feelings—with the
delight stimulated by a sensuous medium, with the many emotions engendered by diverse subject matter, with awe in craftsmanship, and so on. But
such feelings vary considerably from one society to another, just as they
differ from one person to another. For example, art inspires feelings, often
quite strong feelings, among the Navajo, who find pleasure in sacred sandpaintings, secular silver jewelry—or the spontaneous singing of a song. But
the deepest and most gratifying feelings for Navajos lie in the act of creation, not in the contemplation of the finished art work, as called for by
formalist dogma.

Art is nothing if it inspires no feeling, but to equate art with a narrowly
defined aesthetic response is to ignore the other powerful sources of art's
impact on the human psyche. Art is seldom the vessel of small feelings, and
art for art's sake alone may be the least important reason for art's existence.

To the contrary, art seems to inspire feeling because of its ability to
encode significant cultural meaning while simultaneously embodying special skill. This is not a contribution to be taken lightly and may well be a
major reason for the universality of art as well as the apparent unity of
Calliope. Art brings together meaning, feeling, and skill to produce a powerful experience, a product that, like kinship and language, has become an
indispensable component of human culture.

Skill in Art

The third trait commonly found in art is the special *skill* with which it is
produced. As with art's meaning and the affective response to art, skill
alone does not define art, and it is futile to seek an unequivocal boundary
between those things that represent special skill and those that do not. But
the skill required to produce art is usually special, raised above the level of
the ordinary in the eyes of the artist's audience.[8]

---

[8]Vida Chenoweth (1979) found that while the New Guinean Usarufa refused to distinguish good from bad music, they did commonly distinguish good from bad *performance* of music;
and McAllester (1954) had a similar experience among Navajos. One might suppose that these
results were to be expected in cultures where songs are produced not by contemporary individuals but are handed down by tradition. Thus they are not the proper object of criticism in the
same way that an individual singer might be. "Criticism" in such a setting might simply take
the form of decreased popularity and eventual extinction of songs that no longer satisfy the
needs of the culture. If this were the case, it would shed considerable light on the question of
the relative explicitness with which aesthetic and critical principles are articulated in a given
culture.

But this argument is thrown into question by Witherspoon's (1977:152) report that some
Navajo songs *are* purposefully written by individuals. Thus, it is interesting to wonder if such
songs (and not just their performance) are indeed the subject of critical appraisal.

Although current thinking in the West does not emphasize skill in art, in fact the English word "art" derives from a Greek term meaning "useful skill," and it originally had a wide application—poetry and sculpture were arts, but so were the heightened skills found among the best practitioners of warfare, medicine, and farming (cf. Munro 1956:227). Only in the modern era have we differentiated the "fine" from the "practical" arts; previously, like other societies, we gave no explicit name to what we now term "art."

The artist's special skill is generally taken for granted in Western society, but how widely is it recognized elsewhere? The other complex societies discussed in Part One all clearly appreciate the uncommon abilities of their artists. Recall, for example, the qualities the Aztecs attributed to true artists: "capable, practicing, skillful; maintains dialogue with his heart, meets things with his mind" (quoted in León-Portilla 1963:168). By contrast, "The carrion artist works at random; sneers at people; makes things opaque; brushes across the surface of the face of things; works without care; defrauds people; is a thief" (León-Portilla 1963:168).

In all three of Part One's horticultural and herding societies, artists are recognized as having special abilities so that the products of their skill are recognized by non-artists. All Sepik men carve wood with a facility that most Westerners would find difficult to match, but only the most accomplished Sepik carver is commissioned to produce the masks and other objects needed for cult activities; and as a reward for his abilities, he receives both goods and prestige. Sepik artists themselves are aware of various criteria of perfection. And there is ample evidence that the Yoruba have equally demanding standards of excellence for statuette carving and the performing arts. For example, Abiodun reports that a sensitivity to the arts is something one acquires only through effort, citing a proverb that says, "Only the wise can dance to [Ògìdìgbo drumming], and only the discerning are able to understand and interpret it" (Abiodun 1987:270).

The Navajo illustrate why a clear demarcation is not possible between activities that embody special skill and those that do not. Given the Navajo concept of hózhǫ́,which attributes beauty, harmony, and positive value to all things as a natural potentiality of their existence, it is not surprising that "nearly all Navajos are artists and spend a large part of their time in artistic creation" (Witherspoon 1977:152). In one sense this is true, but it is also true that those Navajos who possess exceptional skills—Singers, for example—are recognized and rewarded for their abilities. The situation is analogous to Western culture, where most individuals can produce handwriting, a skill whose acquisition requires years of training.[9] But those few people with exceptional handwriting ability are considered to be artists—calligra-

---

[9]Leach (1961:29) has made a similar point regarding carvers among the Borneo Dyak.

phers. Their capabilities are praised, and they may be hired to produce announcements for special occasions. (Of course, calligraphy differs from normal handwriting not only in the level of the skill of the person who creates it but also in the attention to style and attractiveness that are apparent in the result.)

Even small-scale, hunter-gatherer societies, with their distinctively low degree of labor specialization, recognize the singular talents of artists. At least, such was the case in all three of the foraging groups discussed in Part One.[10] Indeed, skill and art seem to go hand in hand in all societies.[11] And the artist's special abilities seem to appear at an early age: Alland's study (1983) of drawings made by children in six diverse cultures revealed that usually one or two children from each group of subjects showed exceptional artistic ability.

The Maroon, a Black African society living in the rain forests of Suriname, South America, are interesting in this regard. Although the Maroon assume that "*all* adults will be active artists and assertive critics," it remains the case that "the work of certain individuals is generally considered especially beautiful.... They are rewarded by the admiration of their fellows, and occasionally asked to help design an object which a friend or kinsman is preparing to execute" (Price and Price 1981:36).

That the most adept of Maroon artists are sometimes asked to "help design" others' objects reveals an important aspect of skill in artistry: The artist's special abilities are more often mental than manual. The technical capacity of the artist may be no greater than that of others, especially in societies where the division of labor is not complex, but the person's con-

---

[10]Thus, Lorna Marshall says that some San "are more talented as musicians than others, and some take more interest in playing and singing well" (Marshall 1976:363; see also Kaufmann 1910:151); and Shostak reports that "a term of respect—the suffix *n!a* attached to a name—acknowledges the attainment of full adulthood. It may occasionally be applied to a younger person to applaud high achievement (in hunting, trancing, or *playing a musical instrument*, for example), but it is usually given to people in their fourties" (Shostak 1981:321, emphasis added). Similarly, Mountford says that although all Australian Aborigines are potential artists, "some are more skilled than others and take more care" (Mountford 1961:7; see also Berndt and Berndt 1964:329; Elkin, Berndt, and Berndt 1950:110; McCarthy 1957a:13–14; and Spencer and Gillan 1938:575). Finally, traditional Eskimos also recognized special abilities, certainly in song, dance, and dress, and probably in carving, although gauging differential skill is difficult because such differences fly in the face of the cooperative ideal that pervades Inuit culture—and the same is true of most other hunting and gathering societies.

[11]For example, Kaeppler (1971) describes the importance of skill in evaluating dance performance among Polynesian Tongans; Bohannan (1971) reports that although the Nigerian Tiv know that most men can carve well enough to make common items, they appreciate exceptional carving and regard as specialists those few carvers who work alone and consciously attempt to excell in their carving. Finally, Harry Silver found that the Ashanti believe that "the gifted are not simply keener of eye or hand; they also possess a facility for concentration which far exceeds their peers. They claim to think deeply about their work, constantly searching for more effective ways to 'tease out' messages from the wood" (Silver 1981:105).

ceptual skills are often outstanding. The ability to innovate, to manipulate visual (or auditory, choreographic, or whatever) images and ideas, to concentrate on a specific task for long periods of time, to recall and play with traditional aesthetic material—these are the hallmarks of the artist. For example, among Navajos it is the skills of the mind, rather than of the hand, that characterize artists. Navajos reserve their highest esteem for Singers, with their prodigious memory of ceremony. By contrast, the execution of the actual sandpaintings may be carried out by any able-bodied man.

The West has recognized the artist's special conceptual skills since at least the time of Plato, who observed that poetic inspiration is "a thing ethereally light-winged and sacred, nor can one compose anything worth calling poetry until he becomes inspired and, as it were, mad" (quoted in Hatterer 1965:17). Such views explain the long-standing tradition of Western master artists assigning to apprentices or technicians those components of their work that require "mere craftsmanship"; and it plays an important role in the rationale of many schools of modern art, from Cubism and Surrealism, through Abstract Expressionism, to Conceptual Art, which attach primary importance to the artist's personal vision. Given the significance of meaning in art, it comes as no surprise that artists' cognitive skills are of vital importance. For most societies, it is in the mind where true artistic genius is found.[12]

Connoisseurship is another special cognitive skill associated with art. Often artists themselves are among the most sophisticated and articulate judges of art, as was shown in Forge's (1967) account of Abelam artists, who discuss carvings more assiduously and incisively than do others. But nonartists may also develop special artistic sensibilities and be considered connoisseurs. Among the many Yoruba critics Thompson interviewed, some were found to be artists but the majority came from a variety of occupations, from village chief, to trader, to farmer. Furthermore, genuine Yoruba art critics are different from those who merely appreciate art: Thompson (1973:23) tells of an occasion on which a young man's efforts at evaluating a statuette were explicitly disparaged by another man of far greater critical ability.

Why do some individuals go to the trouble of mastering the multifarious mental skills required by art? Modern psychology, with its emphasis on behaviors that become habitual as a result of extrinsic rewards, often ig-

---

[12]Thus, the tenth-century Chinese landscape painter Ching Hau distinguished four kinds of painters, ranging from the lowly *ch'iao*, who is merely skillful in imitating nature; through the *ch'i* and the *miao*, or "clever," who "penetrates with his thoughts the nature of everything in heaven and earth"; to the *shen*, the "divine, . . . who makes no effort but achieves the forms spontaneously by following the transformations of Nature" (quoted in Deutsch 1975:39).

nores "autotelic activities"—that is, those that require concentration and energy but provide little in the way of material compensation. In at least some cultural settings art is an autotelic activity, and Csikszentmihalyi (1975) has argued convincingly that individuals may obtain great satisfaction from tasks that are too challenging to be boring yet not so difficult as to produce an unacceptably high level of anxiety. The gratification involved may well account for the fact that some individuals, past and present, have mastered the difficult skills that art media inevitably demand.

Skill alone does not make art, but societies inevitably recognize the exceptional capacities of the artist. The extent to which the artist's heightened abilities are inborn is unknown, but it is clear that art's specialness, its ability to convey potent meaning, and its capacity to affect the emotions of the percipient, must in part result from the artist's exceptional skill.

Conclusion

The available information about aesthetics in the world's societies is still too scant to draw many detailed or certain conclusions. However, a few findings are clear.

First, art is a legitimate and meaningful cultural category. The generalized relativism that informs modern cultural anthropology, as well as the avoidance of stylistic dogmatism that, at least in theory, has been a major tenet of Western thinking about the fine arts in the twentieth century, make this conclusion significant. The assumption that "anything can be art" may lead one to expect that "everything is art" and that nothing distinguishes art from non-art, especially when non-Western societies are included in the picture.

But my conclusion is contrary to this, and I have arrived at it with no semantic sleight-of-hand. Following Weitz, I allowed that only an open definition of art is possible; and I asserted that several traits are the basis of a "family resemblance" among those things and actions we commonly call art. Art generally embodies culturally significant meaning that is encoded in a traditional style and sensuous medium, and this is accomplished with uncommon skill.

After conceding that these traits may be present in different degrees and that an unequivocal dividing line cannot be drawn to separate art from non-art, we nevertheless found that art does exist in all ten of the societies surveyed in Part One. Each culture has principles that account for the fundamental nature and purpose of art. As in the domain of kinship, the principles that a given culture uses to define art's meanings and purposes are unique and may be largely covert. But art is clearly universal; and, as with kinship, the lack of a generic native name for art does not mean that art is a trivial component of culture.

To the contrary, art is usually accorded a vital role in traditional thought, conveying meanings that are fundamental to the culture. The artist's skill may be taken for granted, and stylistic conventions may serve only as a basis of criticism. But meaning is vital; one might even ask, how could so much time and effort be spent in the demanding work that art entails in the absence of a compelling justification for doing so?

The principles for selecting the meaning attributed to art are unclear; in fact, this is one of the most challenging questions in the field of comparative aesthetics. Also important is the way in which aesthetic theory is mapped onto stylistic conventions via the aesthetic socialization of art practitioners and percipients.

A second conclusion is that a knowledge of comparative aesthetics deepens one's capacity for responding to alien art works in ways that their makers intended. There is nothing to prevent a person from treating another society's art works as just so many instances of found art—objects to read one's own interpretations into with no regard for their original meaning. The creator's intentions are not the *only* basis for reacting to art, and indeed art works from other societies provide a very rich storehouse of ideas for stimulating the imagination. The early twentieth century development of Cubism by Western artists who had seen art works from Africa, the Northwest Coast, and Oceania is a testament to how productive such cross-fertilization can be for art (cf. Goldwater 1967).

But if one's aim is to appreciate art of foreign origin (or, indeed, of domestic origin) on its own terms, then obviously an understanding of the philosophical basis of that art is imperative. And clearly the more distant the aesthetic system is from our own, the more such information is necessary. Eliot Deutsch (1975:37–86) has described several levels of meaning that one must possess in order to fully appreciate a given society's art: the world view of the artist's culture, the stylistic and formal options available to the artist, and the symbolic meaning conveyed by the work. The desirability of such knowledge can hardly be questioned; getting it is another matter. (Deutsch's call for an understanding of "cultural-authorial *Weltanschauung* [worldview]," though a mouthful, is nonetheless more easily said than done!)

Although the relative proportions of the factors that are involved in art vary from place to place, they everywhere complement each other to produce something that is vital to human existence—or so art's universality suggests. In *The Picture of Dorian Gray*, Oscar Wilde says, probably facetiously, that "All art is quite useless." The claim is true if one considers only practical usefulness, the sort of instrumentality that puts food in our mouths and roofs over our heads. But when our existence is viewed in humanistic terms and we consider ourselves to be more than just another animal species stalking the land, then Wilde's homily must be replaced by a remark by surgeon Richard Selzer (1979), who, writing on life, death, and the nature of being human, says that art "is necessary only in that without it life would be unbearable." The portrait of Calliope that has emerged in this chapter should prove that art weds sensuousness and intellectuality, play and necessity, shared experience and rare virtuosity, giving us a means to live not as brutes but as human beings.

15

EPILOGUE
Western Aesthetics
in Cross-Cultural
Perspective

No doubt people everywhere have particularly strong feelings about the cultural system that they are a part of; one inevitably has a visceral identification with the art traditions that have constituted one's own milieu since birth. Westerners are no exception to this rule. Western aesthetics necessarily occupies a special place in our thinking about art, and we often assume that our art is *natural*, the standard from which all other possibilities are variants.[1]

And indeed, Western aesthetic traditions are in some respects unique. One of the most distinctive features of the West is our resolute pluralism regarding art, with four theories that emphasize distinctly different qualities in art. (The several Japanese aesthetic themes are, by comparison, far more complementary to each other.) This has meant that although a gradual homogenization has taken place in Western culture as regional and ethnic distinctions become less marked, a Westerner has an exceptionally broad array of possible ways of thinking about art.[2] Not only have there been four aesthetic systems within our own culture, but modern communications and commerce have given us an opportunity to experience art from much of the rest of the world, a situation unique in the history of the human race.

Western culture is distinctive also in its technology, and this too has given our art and aesthetics a distinctive coloration. In many media, even the

---

[1] In referring to the West as "our" culture, I ask the forbearance of readers who are not Westerners. Whether this entire epilogue is "ethnocentric," or merely "reflexive," I leave to those readers to say.

[2] Even though the West is aesthetically pluralistic, the diversity found here is still not proportional to the size of our population. If Western culture is, say, ten times more heterogeneous than a small-scale society, our population is hundreds of thousands of times larger in numbers.

most virtuoso of artists cannot hope to match the skill of technical production easily attained by mechanical devices such as the camera, computer-controlled robot welders, and electronic sound production equipment. As a result, modern Western artists are more often praised for their conceptual and expressive abilities than for their manual skills. Similarly, the ease of mass production has led to a compensatory nurturing of artistic innovation. Since machines can easily turn out duplicates of almost any object *ad nauseam*, artists are expected to produce a never-ending stream of original creations.

The content of some of the Western aesthetic traditions is also unique. The tradition of mimesis, for example, has rarely been carried to such extremes of literalness as in the West. And the glorification of individual expression that characterizes romanticism is developed to a higher level in the West than elsewhere. Granted, the *rasa*-theorists of India talked at length about the percipient's emotional response to art, and the Japanese find delight in the melancholy expression of *mono no aware*, but the individualized and powerful feelings spoken of by the apostles of romanticism find little parallel in other cultures.

Of all Western aesthetic theories, formalism is the most unique. Its assertion that art exists solely for aesthetic satisfaction and its claim that any social, cultural, or even representational message is a distraction from art's higher purpose is, so far as I know, unprecedented in comparative aesthetics. The art-for-art's-sake premise of formalism stands in marked contrast to the various art-for-life's-sake themes found in other aesthetic traditions.

A final question may be asked regarding the comparative standing of Western aesthetics: What is its *merit* as compared to those in other societies' philosophies of art? As in other complex societies, the West has had explicit theories of art for a very long time; and the accumulated body of Western aesthetic thought has examined art from many perspectives and in great detail. So if explicitness and intricateness are thought to be virtues, then Western aesthetics unquestionably gets high marks.

But two other criteria may come to mind when one tries to think qualitatively about aesthetic systems. The first concerns what might be called the *pervasiveness* of the beliefs in the context of the society at large. Thus, Australian Aboriginal and Navajo philosophies of art not only motivate artistic production but inform a very wide range of other activities as well. The fabric of life in these societies seems to be permeated by an aesthetic sensibility. (Again, one hesitates to pass final judgment for lack of exhaustive information; but in, say, Sepik River cultures and in early India, the aesthetic enterprise seems clearly to be demarcated from other endeavors such as subsistence activities, social interaction, and political affairs, except where art objects are called upon as tools, as it were, for carrying out these activities.) Another aspect of the issue of aesthetic pervasiveness is revealed by asking, Does the population at large identify with the aesthetic principles in question, or is aesthetics the domain of specialists who make public pronouncements about art, at some cognitive distance from the mass of people—and even, perhaps, removed from artists themselves?

Besides pervasiveness, another issue one might consider regarding the merit of an aesthetic system is its *depth*. One can plausibly argue, I believe, that the several components of art (that is, its communication of cultural meaning by means of a conventional style through the skillful, affecting manipulation of a sensuous medium) are not of equal value or importance. In my opinion, art reaches its highest purpose when it conveys meanings of significance for a culture's spiritual, philosophical, or ethical traditions. I certainly enjoy the sensuous satisfaction that artistic media can inspire, and I have boundless respect for the consummate skill of the master artist; but all else being equal, I somehow feel that it is a lesser art that embodies primarily sensuousness and skill and has little social or philosophical meaning.[3] If one accepts this premise, then Inuit aesthetics, with its concept of using art to transmute things between the natural, human, and supernatural realms, would score higher than the relatively secular aesthetics of the San.

Also, an aesthetic system that taps several of art's dimensions would seem to be more praiseworthy than one that touches fewer levels. For example, much of the appeal for me of Yoruba aesthetics lies in its amazing capacity simultaneously to challenge the creator's skill, to embody principles of sensuous beauty, to express important social and ethical principles, to mediate the dialectically opposed principles of harmony and dynamism, and to do all this from a compelling metaphysical foundation. By comparison, the Aztec philosophy of immortality via flower and song seems rather one-dimensional.[4]

Using these two standards, pervasiveness and depth, how does Western aesthetics compare to other societies' philosophies of art? Regarding pervasiveness, the picture may at first look unpromising. Aesthetics, after all, is a highly esoteric specialty—indeed, subspecialty— and as such it has been a subject of conscious interest to a small circle of people, usually discussed only in academic monographs and specialized periodicals.

But as the chapter on Western aesthetics noted, although our theories have exclusively addressed the fine arts, the popular arts implicitly accept

---

[3]It is not coincidental that Chapter 13's discussion of meaning in art is longer than Chapter 14's account of the other three dimensions of art—style, feeling, and skill.

[4]Clearly this judgment would be mistaken if we were to somehow learn that, contrary to the picture we receive from the codexes, the *tlamatinime* speculated at length not only about art's ability to prevent the final destruction of the world, but also about issues such as connoisseurship and the secular pleasures of art.

the same assumptions. So Western aesthetics, by influencing both fine and popular art, does pervade all sectors of our population.

Nevertheless, the pervasiveness of Western aesthetics is severely restricted in a different way: It applies only to art and not, generally, to the vast congeries of things and actions that we deem not to be art. Among the Navajos, "one is admonished to walk in beauty, speak in beauty, act in beauty, sing in beauty, and live in beauty" (Witherspoon 1977:153). In contrast, the West makes as firm a distinction between the aesthetic and the (far greater) non-aesthetic world as it does between the realms of the sacred and the secular. Aesthetic considerations play little role in our subsistence activities (i.e., our technology, our industrial production, and our system of commerce). They play an even smaller part in the political arena, formal education, and most components of family life. And in the area of speculative thought, we are admonished merely to seek parsimony (but not, as Whitehead says, to trust it!). Most Westerners do not live particularly aesthetic lives, although the evidence is clear that other peoples such as the Navajo and Australian Aborigines do.[5] Viewed in this way, the West scores low regarding the pervasiveness of its aesthetic system.

The second criterion for evaluating aesthetic systems, depth, concerns the contributions art makes to spiritual, philosophical, or ethical areas of life, and the West hardly excels in this area either. Aesthetics seems to have played a secondary role during most periods of Western intellectual history. Granted, the promulgators of pragmatic theories of aesthetics, whether Christian, neo-classical, or utopian, have seen art as a means to their own desired ends. But even here art has not been as important as it was, say, to Aztec thinkers, who believed that flower and song, the only genuine and enduring things on the face of the earth, were the sole offerings (other than blood sacrifice) that could postpone the final destruction of the world. In Japan and India, as well as in the cultures of the Yoruba, Navajo, and Australian Aborigines, art was thought to be the sole means by which human well-being could be attained or maintained. The Western predilection for mimetic representation, romantic expression, or art for art's sake all pale by comparison to such profound philosophies of art. Other cultures demonstrate unequivocally that art can play a vital role in a people's world view; and Western culture has rarely tapped that potential.

I suspect that this is not the result of an innate insensitivity to art on our part but of other components of Western culture. Since the time of the

---

[5]However, as noted at the beginning of the chapter on Western aesthetics, if one considers not just fine art but also popular art in the West, the extent to which most of us aesthetically enhance our experience is surprising. And it is not just the full-time members of the art world for whom art is an all-pervasive concern. For example, as Keali'inohomoku (personal communication) has rightly pointed out, for some fans of Music Television, MTV is a way of life!

pre-Socratic philosophers, and especially since the Enlightenment, many Westerners have looked to science for answers to the questions of philosophy and religion. Thus, we expect astronomers to provide us with origin stories and biologists and social scientists to explain our basic human nature; and we employ members of the medical profession, rather than shamans, to protect our fertility, health, and peace of mind. For most people, little is left that inspires true awe, and art rarely impinges upon this small preserve of the sacred. Little is left for art to theorize about—except art itself.

Likewise, in such practical matters as subsistence, defense, and communication, we have, especially since the Renaissance, relied on technology; the possible efficacy of art in these areas has been generally ignored. We produce no counterparts to Navajo sandpaintings and songs, Eskimo and Australian Aboriginal amulets, Indian drama, or Aztec architecture—each of which was made for practical and life-sustaining purposes.

Furthermore, the Judeo-Christian religious tradition subsumes ethics, whereas in many other societies art makes a significant contribution to both ethical training and the administration of justice. In the West, bureaucratic governments are expected to enforce ethical codes; no clowns or tricksters, artfully disguised by mask and costume, are seen here—except at Halloween. Finally, much of the human need for sensuous satisfaction also tends to be met in the West by technology, rather than by art.[6]

Thus, although humans seem innately to need larger meanings, in the West we have tended to seek them not in art but in science, technology, government, and so on. In my view, we have some reason to envy the Navajo with their faith in *hózhǫ́* and their belief that the inevitable evils of the world can be held at bay and harmony and that goodness will be restored if artistic activities are properly carried out. We are likewise justified in longing for the certainty of ethical precepts that is condensed in a Yoruba statuette. Some of us might willingly trade a few of the blessings of technology for a grasp of our human past, present, and future comparable to that which is implicit in Australian Aboriginal art's embodiment of the Eternal Dreamtime. Western art does provide an antidote to the highly structured pattern of life in the West; and it encourages a liminal state in which anti-structure and counter-structure are permitted. But beyond that, most Western art, in

---

[6]The foregoing account of contemporary Western culture assumes a minimal importance for popular art, but in the absence of a thoroughgoing analysis of role (and, more importantly, the theoretical underpinnings) of art in popular culture, it must remain *only* an assumption. As Keali'inohomoku (personal communication) has observed, we do live in a world where some individuals mutilate and decorate their physical appearance to a degree that might be the envy of the most ornamented of New Guineans; where pets wear rhinestone collars; where advertisements continually promise to enhance our "sex appeal"; and where politicians and newscasters alike (our tricksters?) commonly put on makeup before appearing in public.

theory and practice, seems to provide little succor for our deeper human needs.

Within some Western subcultures, art does play a meaningful and potent role. For many Western artists themselves, life would be unbearable without the production of art; and this is as true of untutored "folk artists" as it is of fine artists. There are even sectors of Western society in which art has great social and political significance. The ideology of Jamaican Rastafarians is conveyed effectively through their arts such as reggae music. A Rastafarian painter-poet, Ras "T," has said, "Art to me is the integrator of all mankind. . . . My main theme in art is not only the portrayal of oppression in the daily experience of the ghetto-man, but there is also joy. I do not only portray oppression, I try to point the way out" (Barrett 1977:187). Given the ecological, economic, and political impasses the West now faces, one may well applaud Ras "T's" strategy.

APPENDIX

PRÉCIS OF THE AESTHETICS SYSTEMS OF TEN SOCIETIES

The *San* of southwestern Africa love beauty—so much so that they elaborately decorate themselves and many of the things they make. But although the San produce most of their art for the sensuous pleasure it gives, they have other motives too. The performing arts in particular not only give satisfaction; they also embody the spiritual and psychological unity of the San, and they are necessary for sustaining the good health of San individuals.

Art is no frivolous luxury in north-central *Australia*. To the contrary, for the Aborigines who wander from one water-hole to the next, art is crucial for fulfilling human needs. The underlying logic is simple: Through unchanging art, humans can communicate with the eternal realm of the sacred, influencing and ultimately joining with it. As they merge with the spirit world through art, mortals perpetuate the enduring order of all things, including the natural abundance of the environment and human life itself. Even secular art works derive their significance from art's efficacy in religious contexts.

Nomads in another type of wasteland, the arctic *Inuit* think of art as one of life's necessities. Granted, art's beauty gives pleasure and satisfaction, but Inuit art also magically insures future health, security, and prosperity. Art's mystical power comes from its ability to cross the otherwise insuperable barriers between the cold world of nature, the mortal realm of human affairs, and the awesome domain of the supernatural.

For the sedentary farming tribes of New Guinea's *Sepik River* area, religious ceremony and belief provide the context for most art; the scant secular art that they make is valued largely because it resembles the art of cult and ritual. Spirits gave the gift of art to humans in the first place, and they continue to dwell within some art works. Making and using such art insures the continued fertility of the group, as well as victory over its foes. Both Sepik art and ritual are primarily the concerns of men, and both reflect phallic aggression and a prideful male ethos.

In stark contrast is another group of agriculturalists, the *Navajo* herders of the American Southwest. According to their world view, all human experience—indeed the entire sensible world—is filled with both goodness and evil. The creation of art embodies and enhances the positive forces of harmony and beauty, thereby insuring individual life, health, happiness, and safety.

Among a third group of agriculturalists, the West African *Yoruba*, most art serves to propitiate supernatural spirits who, in return, bestow prosperity, fertility, and good health upon mortals. Both sacred and secular art are subjected to explicit criticism, but Yoruba standards of beauty spring from broader beliefs about moral and ethical goodness. The ideal man or woman lives a harmonious and energetic life, and Yoruba aesthetics represents a unification of these potentially conflicting values, harmony and energy. Art's capacity to do this is founded upon the reciprocal link it provides between mortals and supernaturals.

The professional speculative thinkers of the *Aztec* civilization believed art to be a gift that the gods bestowed upon a select, enlightened few. They treasured art's ability to bring transcendent joy and fellowship; but in the considered opinion of Aztec philosophers, art's highest value lay in its encouraging the gods to postpone the impending destruction of the world, providing the possibility of human immortality. As a mystical embodiment of sacred truth, art's beauty was considered to be the only thing genuine and lasting in an otherwise imperfect and transient world.

The philosophers of classical *India* studied the interplay of aesthetic emotions at great length. They assumed that art inevitably portrays the gods in all their supernatural perfection, so to experience art is to touch the divine and be lifted to a higher and holier state.

Art played several roles in traditional *Japan*. It could give pleasure and, via religion, could bring material rewards. But the central axiom of Japanese aesthetics was that art provides a means to spiritual salvation because it portrays and propitiates the spirits and the sacred principles of nature. Therefore, the traditional Japanese sometimes pressed art into duty as a tool for religious recruitment and meditation, believing that art can be a path to higher levels of consciousness. Also, art is a convincing means, perhaps the *only* means, of expressing some religious truths. These aesthetic principles provide a bridge between Japanese ethical and philosophical belief and the stylistic conventions of Japanese art.

Four schools of thought have developed in the *West* regarding the fundamental nature and purpose of the fine arts—and, by extension, the popular arts. One tradition has emphasized art's ability to portray its subject matter, either in superficial appearance or as an idealized essence. A second school has used art to promote the spiritual or social betterment of the individual or the community. Emotions have been the chief interest of a third group of theorists—one that values art for its ability to purge the feelings and stir the passions of artist and audience members alike. A fourth tradition has argued that art's significance lies in its formal qualities, with the artist's skilled use of sensuous media provoking a distinctive response in audience members.

APPENDIX B

THE AFFECTIVE RESPONSE TO ART IN TEN SOCIETIES

A review of the material in Part One demonstrates the wide variations found in the gratifications that art affords those who experience it.

The *San* clearly enjoy the beauty that body decoration provides. Ostrich eggshell beads please them, and the satisfaction they derive from dance and music is well documented.

Evidence about *Australian* Aborigines fails to reveal any effort to make "art for art's sake"; however, Aboriginal artists do evince a genuine pleasure in artistic production, a response that combines a sensuous satisfaction in the "pretty" with an intellectual appreciation of the significant.

Similarly, the *Inuit* enjoy handsomeness of body and the pleasures of the performing arts, and in addition there is some evidence that Eskimo carvers enjoy the act of creation itself.

The aggressive ethos that permeates *Sepik* culture places little apparent emphasis on the emotional gratification of art generally; however, even in the Sepik we find passing references to an appreciation of the beauty of certain physical traits, such as a man's long, narrow nose.

In *Navajo* thought, beauty is a natural condition of the world—beauty that gives satisfaction, security, and well-being. Ecstatic flights of pleasure are neither expected nor sought, but *hózhǫ́* does bring a positively desirable affective state.

The sensual beauty manifest in *Yoruba* body decoration, in graphic and plastic arts, as well as in music and dance is readily apparent. In fact, Yoruba masks that are made to harass the makers' enemies are intentionally repulsive and ugly, thereby showing the keen Yoruba sense of the power of beauty and ugliness.

Although *Aztec* art was made primarily for otherworldly needs, the comments of the *tlamatini* clearly indicate that the supernatural efficacy of "flower and song" lay in their capacity to give pleasure—to the gods *and* to mortals. Thus, there are various references to art serving as the basis for conviviality or, in the extreme, its being "like hallucinating drugs, the best means of intoxicating the heart" (Léon-Portilla 1966:53).

Indian aesthetics, again primarily religious in orientation, did not fail to appreciate the sensuous satisfaction available through art. The "Six Limbs" of Yasodhara called for graphic artists to portray the human form with idealized sensuality. And in any case, the work should reflect the artist's deepest sentiments. The entire concept of *rasa* was based on the refinement of feelings in both the maker and the percipient of art.

The aesthetics of *Japan*, for all its elegance, did not fail to appreciate sensuous beauty. In performing her dance to lure the Sun Goddess out of the Rock Cave of Heaven, Ane-no-uzume exposed her nipples and pudenda, suggestive of not only fertility but also of eroticism. And, like Aztec art, Shinto aesthetics assumes that art will placate the *kami* by giving them pleasure. Similarly, Japanese secular art, as in the tea ceremony, although based on a deeper aesthetic rationale, also tacitly assumes that the arts bring satisfaction to the participants.

Western aesthetics has not been silent on the affective potential of art either. The Romantic Movement has made art's emotional component a central feature of its program; and Formalism is also based on the premise that art should prompt a distinctive response in the percipient. Even mimetic theorists often assume that at least part of the value of representation resides in the delight it gives. Lastly, the popular arts, which are based on these same principles, tacitly assume that art should give pleasure and yield sensuous satisfaction—or at least some type of strong feeling.

REFERENCES

Abiodun, Rowland
　1987　Verbal and Visual Metaphors: Mythical Allusion in Yoruba Ritualistic Art of Orí. Word Image 3(3):252–270.

Abrams, Meyer Howard
　1953　The Mirror and the Lamp. New York: Norton.

Adair, John
　1944　Navajo and Pueblo Silversmiths. Norman: University of Oklahoma Press.

Adams, Francis M. and Charles E. Osgood
　1973　A Cross-cultural Study of the Affective Meanings of Color. Journal of Cross-cultural Psychology 4(2):135–157.

Alland, Alexander
　1983　Playing with Form: Children Draw in Six Cultures. New York: Columbia University Press.

Anderson, Richard L.
　1979　Art in Primitive Societies. Englewood Cliffs, New Jersey: Prentice Hall.
　1989　Art in Small-Scale Societies (second edition of Art in Primitive Societies). Englewood Cliffs, New Jersey: Prentice Hall.

Anesaki, Masaharu
　1915　Buddhist Art: In Its Relation to Buddhist Ideals, with Special Reference to Buddhism in Japan. Boston: Houghton Mifflin.
　1933　Art, Life, and Nature in Japan. Boston: Marshall Jones.
　1963　History of Japanese Religion. Rutland, Vermont: Charles E. Tuttle Company.

Armstrong, Robert Plant
　1971　The Affecting Presence: An Essay in Humanistic Anthropology. Urbana: University of Illinois Press.
　1975　Wellspring: On the Myth and Source of Culture. Berkeley: University of California Press.
　1981　The Powers of Presence: Consciousness, Myth, and the Affecting Presence. Philadelphia: University of Pennsylvania Press.

Bacon, Gershon
　1971　Idolatry. Encyclopaedia Judaica. Vol. 8, pp. 1227–1234. New York: Macmillan.

Balikci, Asen
　1970　The Netsilik Eskimo. Garden City, New York: Natural History Press.

Barbar, Karin
　1981　How Man Makes God in West Africa: Yoruba Attitudes Toward the Oriṣa. Africa 51(3):724–745.

Barrett, Leonard
　1977　The Rastafarians: Sounds of Cultural Dissonance. Boston: Beacon Press.

Barry, Herbert, III
　1971　[orig. 1957] Relationships between Child Training and the Pictorial Arts. In Carol F. Jopling, ed., Art and Aesthetics in Primitive Societies. New York: Dutton. Pp. 64–72. Orig. in Journal of Abnormal and Social Psychology 54:380–383.

Bartlett, Katherine
    1950   Present Trends in Weaving on the Western Navajo Reservation. Plateau 23:1–6.
Bascom, William R.
    1969   The Yoruba of Southwestern Nigeria. Case Studies in Cultural Anthropology. New York: Holt, Rinehart and Winston.
    1973a   A Yoruba Master Carver: Duga of Mẹkọ. In Warren L. D'Azevedo, ed., The Traditional Artist in African Societies. Bloomington: Indiana University Press. Pp. 62–78.
    1973b   African Art in Cultural Perspective. New York: Norton.
Bateson, Gregory
    1946   Arts of the South Seas. Arts Bulletin 2:119–123.
    1958   [orig. 1936] Naven. Second edition. Stanford: Stanford University Press.
    1972   Metalogue: Why a Swan? In Gregory Bateson, Steps to an Ecology of the Mind. New York: Ballantine. Pp. 33–37.
Beardsley, Monroe C.
    1981   [orig. 1958] Aesthetics: Problems in the Philosophy of Criticism. Indianapolis: Hackett Publishing Company.
Becker, Howard S.
    1982   Art World. Berkeley: University of California Press.
Beckwith, Carol
    1983   Niger's Wodaabe: People of the Taboo. National Geographic, October, pp. 483–509.
Bell, Clive
    1958   Art. New York: Putnam.
Bennett, Noel
    1974   The Weaver's Pathway: A Clarification of the Spirit Trail in Navajo Weaving. Flagstaff: Northland Press.
Berger, John
    1980   About Looking. New York: Pantheon.
Berlin, Brent and Paul Kay
    1969   Basic Color Terms. Berkeley: University of California Press.
Berlyne, David E.
    1970   The Golden Section and Hedonic Judgments of Rectangles. Sciences de l'Art/Scientific Aesthetics 7:1–6.
    1976   Similarity and Preference Judgments of Indian and Canadian Subjects Exposed to Western Paintings. International Journal of Psychology 11(1):43–55.
    1980   Psychological Aesthetics. In Harry C. Triandis and Walter Lonner, eds., Handbook of Cross-cultural Psychology. Boston: Allyn & Bacon. Pp. 323–361.
Berndt, Ronald
    1976   Love Songs of Arnhem Land. Chicago: University of Chicago Press.
_____ and Catherine H. Berndt
    1964   The World of the First Australians. Chicago: University of Chicago Press.
    1970   Man, Land and Myth in Northern Australia: The Gunwinggu People. East Lansing: Michigan State University Press.
Biebuyck, Daniel P.
    1969   Introduction. In Daniel P. Biebuyck, ed., Tradition and Creativity in Tribal Art. Berkeley: University of California Press. Pp. 1–23.
    1973   Lega Culture: Art, Initiation, and Moral Philosophy among a Central African People. Berkeley: University of California Press.
Biesele, Megan
    1976   Aspects of !Kung Folklore. In Richard B. Lee and Irven DeVore, eds., Kalahari Hunter-Gatherers. Cambridge: Harvard University Press. Pp. 303–324.
Birket-Smith, Kaj
    1924   Ethnography of the Egedesminde District. Copenhagen: B. Lunos Bogtrykkeri.
    1929   The Caribou Eskimos. Copenhagen: Gyldendal.

1933 The Chugach Eskimo. Copenhagen: Nationalmuseets Skrifter, Etnografisk Raekhe, 6 København, Nationalmuseets Publikationsfond.
1959 The Eskimos. Second edition. London: Methuen.

Bleek, D.F.
1928 The Naron, A Bushman Tribe of the Central Kalahari. Cambridge: Cambridge University Press.

Bleek, Wilhelm H.I. and Lucy C. Lloyd, eds.
1911 Specimens of Bushman Folklore. Cape Town: Struik.

Boas, Franz
1940 [orig. 1916] Representative Art of Primitive People. In Franz Boas, Race, Language, and Culture. New York: The Free Press. Pp. 535–540.
1955 [orig. 1927] Primitive Art. New York: Dover.
1964 [orig. 1888] The Central Eskimo. Lincoln: University of Nebraska Press. Originally published as Report of the Bureau of Ethnology 1884–1885. Washington: Smithsonian Institution, 399–669.

Boas, George
1963 [orig. 1940] The Mona Lisa in the History of Taste. In Marvin Levich, ed., Aesthetics and the Philosophy of Criticism. New York: Random House. Pp. 576–594.

Bohannan, Paul
1971 Artist and Critic in an African Society. In Charlotte M. Otten, ed., Anthropology and Art. Garden City, New York: Natural History Press. Pp. 172–181.

Borgatti, Jean M.
1979 Art and History in West Africa: Two Case Studies. In Justine M. Cordwell, ed., The Visual Arts: Plastic and Graphic. The Hague: Mouton. Pp. 567–592.
1982 Okpella Masks: In Search of the Parameters of the Beautiful and the Grotesque. Studies in Visual Communication 8(3):28–40.

Bowden, Ross
1983 Yena: Art and Ceremony in a Sepik Society. Oxford: Pitt-Rivers Museum, University of Oxford.
1984 Art and Gender Ideology in the Sepik. Man 19(3):445–458.

Brain, Robert
1979 The Decorated Body. New York: Harper & Row.

Brody, J. J.
1977 Mimbres Painted Pottery. Albuquerque: University of New Mexico Press.

Brumfiel, Elizabeth M.
1987 Elite and Utilitarian Crafts in the Aztec State. In Elizabeth M. Brumfiel and Timothy K. Earle, eds., Specialization, Exchange, and Complex Societies. London: Cambridge University Press. Pp. 102–118.

Burling, Robbins
1966 The Metrics of Children's Verse: A Cross-linguistic Study. American Anthropologist 68:1418–1441.

Canaday, John
1981 Mainstreams of Modern Art. Second edition. New York: Holt, Rinehart and Winston.

Carneiro, Robert
1970 Scale Analysis, Evolutionary Sequences, and the Rating of Cultures. In Raoul Naroll and Ronald Cohen, eds., A Handbook of Method in Cultural Anthropology. Garden City, New York: Natural History Press. Pp. 834–871.

Carpenter, Edmund
1973 Eskimo Realities. New York: Holt, Rinehart and Winston.

Chagnon, Napoleon
1983 Yanomamo: The Fierce People. Third edition. New York: Holt, Rinehart and Winston.

Chenoweth, Vida
1979 The Usarufas and Their Music. Dallas: SIL Museum of Anthropology, 5.

Chernoff, John Miller
    1979   African Rhythm and African Sensibility: Aesthetics and African Musical Idioms. Chicago: University of Chicago Press.
Coe, Michael
    1962   Mexico. New York: Praeger.
Cohen, Marshall
    1983   [orig. 1962] Aesthetic Essence. In Earle J. Coleman, ed., Varieties of Aesthetic Experience. Lanham, Maryland: University Press of America. Pp. 235–254. Orig. in Max Black, ed., Philosophy in America. Ithaca, New York: Cornell University Press.
Colby, Benjamin N.
    1973   A Partial Grammar of Eskimo Folktales. American Anthropologist 75(3):645–662.
Comfort, Alexander
    1962   Darwin and the Naked Lady: Discursive Essays on Biology and Art. New York: Braziller.
Coomaraswamy, Ananda
    1924   The Dance of Siva: Fourteen Indian Essays. New York: The Sunwise Turn, Inc.
Cordwell, Justine M.
    1953   Naturalism and Stylization of Yoruba Art. Magazine of Art, pp. 220–225.
Covarrubias, Miguel
    1957   Indian Art of Mexico and Central America. New York: Knopf.
Crowley, Daniel J.
    1971   An African Aesthetic. In Carol F. Jopling, ed., Art and Aesthetics in Primitive Societies. New York: Dutton. Pp. 315–327.
Csikszentmihalyi, Mihaly
    1975   Beyond Boredom and Anxiety: The Experience of Play in Work and Games. San Francisco: Jossey-Bass.
    1978   Phylogenetic and Ontogenetic Functions of Artistic Cognition. In Stanley S. Majeda, ed., The Arts, Cognition, and Basic Skills. St. Louis: Cemrel. Pp. 114–127.
_____ and Eugene Rochberg-Halton
    1981   The Meaning of Things: Domestic Symbols and the Self. New York: Cambridge University Press.
Dart, Raymond A.
    1937   The Physical Characters of the /?auni − ≠khomani Bushmen. In J.D.R. Jones and C.M. Doke, eds., Bushmen of the Southern Kalahari. Johannesburg: University of the Witwaterstrand Press. Pp. 117–188.
deLaguna, Frederika
    1932   Comparison of Eskimo and Palaeolithic Art. American Journal of Archaeology 36:477–454, 37:77–107.
    1933   Comparison of Eskimo and Palaeolithic Art. Ph.D. Dissertation, Columbia University.
Deregowski, J.B., H.D. Ellis, and J.W. Shepherd
    1975   Descriptions of White and Black Faces by White and Black Subjects. International Journal of Psychology 10(2):119–123.
Deutsch, Eliot
    1975   Studies in Comparative Aesthetics. (Monograph of the Society for Asian and Comparative Philosophy, No. 2.) Honolulu: University Press of Hawaii.
Devereux, George
    1961   Art and Mythology. In Bert Kaplan, ed., Studying Personality Cross-culturally. New York: Harper & Row. Pp. 361–404.
Dhayagude, Suresh
    1981   Western and Indian Poetics: A Comparative Study. Pune, India: Bhandarkar Oriental Research Institute Press.

Dickie, George
1974   Art and the Aesthetic. Ithaca: Cornell University Press.

Drewal, Henry John
1973   Ẹfẹ/Gẹlẹdẹ: The Educative Role of the Arts in Traditional Yoruba Culture. Ph.D. Dissertation, Columbia University.

_____ and Margaret Thompson Drewal
1983   Gẹlẹdẹ: Art and Female Power among the Yoruba. Bloomington: Indiana University Press.
1987   Composing Time and Space in Yoruba Art. Word Image 3(3):225–251.

Eber, Dorothy, ed.
1979   Pitseolak: Pictures out of my Life. Seattle: University of Washington Press.

Edwards, Stephen W.
1978   Nonutilitarian Activities in the Lower Paleolithic: A Look at the Two Kinds of Evidence. Current Anthropology 19(1):135–137.

Elkin, A.P.
1938   Foreword to Australian Aboriginal Decorative Art, by Frederick D. McCarthy. Sydney: Australian Museum. Pp. 8–11.
1964   The Australian Aborigines: How to Understand Them. Fourth edition. Sydney: Angus and Robertson.

_____, Ronald M. Berndt, and Catherine H. Berndt
1950   Art in Arnhem Land. Chicago: University of Chicago Press.

Ellis, Catherine J.
1985   Aboriginal Music: Education for Living—Experiences from South Australia. New York: University of Queensland Press.

England, Nicholas
1967   Bushman Counterpoint. Journal of the International Folk Music Council 19:58–66.
1968   Music among the Zhu/wa·si of South West Africa and Botswana. Ph.D. thesis, Department of Music, Harvard University.

Erickson, Edwin E.
1976   Tradition and Evolution in Song Style: A Reanalysis of Cantometric Data. Behavior Science Research 11:277–308.

Evans, David
1982   Big Road Blues. Berkeley: University of California Press.

Everwine, Peter
1970   In the House of Light: Thirty Aztec Poems. Washington, D.C.: Stone Wall Press.

Eyesenck, H.J.
1941   A Critical and Experimental Study of Color Preferences. American Journal of Psychology 54:259–268.

Farb, Peter
1978   Man's Rise to Civilization. New York: Bantam Books.

Farella, John R.
1984   The Main Stalk: A Synthesis of Navajo Philosophy. Phoenix: University of Arizona Press.

Faris, James C.
1972   Nuba Personal Art. Toronto: University of Toronto Press.

Ferguson, George
1954   Signs and Symbols in Christian Art. London: Oxford University Press.

Fernandez, James W.
1971   Principles of Opposition and Vitality in Fang Aesthetics. In Carol F. Jopling, ed., Art and Aesthetics in Primitive Societies. New York: Dutton. Pp. 356–373.
1973   The Exposition and Imposition of Order: Artistic Expression in Fang Culture. In Warren L. d'Azevedo, ed., The Traditional Artist in African Societies. Bloomington: Indiana University Press. Pp. 194–220.

Field, Karen L.
    1982   Artists in Liberia and the United States: A Comparative View. Journal of Modern
            African Studies 20(4):713–730.
Firth, Raymond
    1936   Art and Life in New Guinea. London: The Studio, Limited.
Fischer, John L.
    1971   [orig. 1961] Art Styles as Cultural Cognitive Maps. In Charlotte M. Otten, ed.,
            Anthropology and Art. Garden City, New York: Natural History Press. Pp. 141–
            161. Orig. in American Anthropologist 63(1):79–93.
Forge, J. Anthony W.
    1967   The Abelam Artist. In Maurice Freedman, ed., Social Organization: Essays Pre-
            sented to Raymond Firth. London: Cass. Pp. 65–84.
    1970   Learning to Seè in New Guinea. In Philip Mayer, ed., Socialization: The Ap-
            proach from Social Anthropology. ASA Monograph No. 8. London: Tavistock.
            Pp. 269–291.
    1971a   [orig. 1965] Art and Environment in the Sepik. In Carol F. Jopling, ed., Art and
            Aesthetics in Primitive Societies. New York: Dutton. Pp. 290–314.
    1971b   Marriage and Exchange in the Sepik. In Rodney Needham, ed., Rethinking Kin-
            ship and Marriage. London: Tavistock. Pp. 133–144.
    1974   Style and Meaning in Sepik Art. In Anthony Forge, ed., Primitive Art and Society.
            New York: Oxford University Press. Pp. 169–192.
Fourie, L.
    1960   [orig. 1928] The Bushmen of Southwest Africa. In Simon and Phoebe Ottenberg,
            eds., Cultures and Societies of Africa. New York: Random House. Pp. 87–95. Orig.
            in The Native Tribes of South West Africa. Cape Town: Cape Times, Ltd.
Francés, R. and A. Tamba
    1973   Étude Interculturelle des préférence et musicales. International Journal of Psy-
            chology 8:95–108.
Fraser, Douglas
    1971   The Discovery of Primitive Art. In Charlotte M. Otten, ed., Anthropology and
            Art. New York: Natural History Press. Pp. 20–36.
Frazer, James G.
    1965   [orig. 1890] Excerpt from The Golden Bough: A Study in Magic and Religion, in
            William A. Lessa and Evon Z. Vogt, eds., Reader in Comparative Religion. New
            York: Harper & Row. Pp. 300–315.
Freud, Sigmund
    1956   [orig. 1920] A General Introduction to Psychoanalysis, trans. by Joan Riviere.
            New York: Permabooks.
Frisbie, Charlotte J.
    1980   Ritual Drama in the Navajo House Blessing Ceremony. In Charlotte J. Frisbie,
            ed., Southwestern Ritual Drama. School of American Research Advanced Semi-
            nar Series. Albuquerque: University of New Mexico Press. Pp. 161–199.
Fry, Roger E.
    1910   Bushman Paintings. Burlington Magazine 16:334–338.
Gans, Herbert J.
    1974   Popular Culture and High Culture: An Analysis and Evaluation of Taste. New
            York: Basic Books.
Gardner, Howard
    1980   Artful Scribbles: The Significance of Children's Drawings. New York: Basic
            Books.
Gardner, John
    1978   On Moral Fiction. New York: Basic Books.
Gardner, Martin
    1978   Mathematical Games: White and Brown Music, Fractal Curves and One-over-f
            Fluctuations. Scientific American 238(4):16–31.
    1983   The Whys of a Philosophical Scrivner. New York: Quill.

Geertz, Clifford
    1983   Local Knowledge: Further Essays in Interpretive Anthropology. New York: Basic Books.

Gell, Alfred F.
    1975   Metamorphosis of the Cassowaries. London School of Economics Monographs in Social Anthropology. London: Athlone Press.

Gerbrands, Adrian Alexander
    1957   Art as an Element of Culture, Especially in Negro-Africa. Mededlingen van het Rijksmuseum voor Volkenkunde 12:110–135.
    1967   Wow-Ipits: Eight Asmat Woodcarvers in New Guinea. Trans. by Inez Seeger. The Hague: Mouton.

Getzels, Jacob W. and Mihaly Csikszentmihalyi
    1976   The Creative Vision: A Longitudinal Study of Problem-finding in Art. New York: John Wiley.

Gewertz, Deborah
    1984   The Tchambuli View of Persons: A Critique of Individualism in the Works of Mead and Chodorow. American Anthropologist 86(3):615–629.

Gibson, Charles
    1964   The Aztecs under Spanish Rule. Stanford: Stanford University Press.

Gnoli, Raniero
    1968   The Aesthetic Experience According to Abhinavagupta. Second edition. Varanasi-1, India: Chowkhamba Sanskrit Series Office.

Golde, Peggy
    1963   Aesthetic Values and Art Styles in a Nahua Pottery Producing Village. Unpublished Ph.D. Dissertation, Harvard University.

_____ and Helena C. Kraemer
    1973   Analysis of an Aesthetic Values Test: Detection of the Inter-sub-group Differences within a Pottery Producing Community in Mexico. American Anthropologist 75(5):260–275.

Goldwater, Robert
    1967   Primitivism in Modern Art. New York: Vintage.

Gombrich, E.H.
    1979   The Sense of Order. Ithaca: Cornell University Press.

Goodnow, Jacqueline J.
    1979   Children Drawing. Cambridge: Harvard University Press.

Graburn, Nelson H.H.
    1967   The Eskimo and "Airport Art." Trans-Action 4(10):28–33.
    1974   A Preliminary Analysis of Symbolism in Eskimo Art and Culture. Proceedings of the Fortieth International Congress of Americanists, Rome, 1972.
    1978   "I Like Things to Look More Different than That Stuff Did": An Experiment in Cross-Cultural Art Appreciation. In Michael Greenhalgh and Vincent Megaw, eds., Art in Society. New York: St. Martin's. Pp. 51–70.

Guerin, Wilfred L., E.G. Labor, Lee Morgan, and J.R. Willingham
    1979   A Handbook of Critical Approaches to Literature. Second edition. New York: Harper & Row.

Hall, John Whitney
    1959   The Confucian Teacher in Tokugawa Japan. In David S. Nivison and Arthur F. Wright, eds., Confucianism in Action. Stanford: Stanford University Press. Pp. 268–301.

Hatterer, Lawrence J.
    1965   The Artist in Society: Problems and Treatment of the Creative Individual. New York: Grove Press.

Hayashiya, Tatsusaburo, Masao Nakamura, and Seizo Hayashiya
    1974   Japanese Arts and the Tea Ceremony. Trans. and adapted by Joseph P. Macadam. New York: Weatherhill.

Hendrickson, Elizabeth and Mary M.A. McDonald
    1983   Ceramic Form and Function: An Ethnographic Search and an Archaeological Application. American Anthropologist 85(3):630–643.
Herbert, Jean
    1967   Shinto: At the Fountain-head of Japan. New York: Stein & Day.
Herring, Frances
    1949   Touch: The Neglected Sense. Journal of Aesthetics and Art Criticism 7:199–215.
Herskovits, Melvin J.
    1959   Art and Value. In Aspects of Primitive Art, by Robert Redfield, Melville J. Herskovitz, and George F. Ekhohn. New York: Museum of Modern Art. Pp. 43–60.
Hill, Jane H.
    1987   The Flowery World of Old Uto-Aztecan. Paper read at the 86th Annual Meeting of the American Anthropological Association, November 20, 1987. Chicago, Illinois.
Hill, Willard W.
    1938   The Agricultural and Hunting Methods of the Navajo Indians. Yale University Publications in Anthropology, 18. New Haven: Yale University Press.
Hogbin, Herbert Ian
    1934/35   Native Culture of Wogeo. Oceania 5:308–337.
    1946   Puberty to Marriage: A Study of the Sexual Life of the Natives of Wogeo, New Guinea. Oceania 16:185–209.
    1970   The Island of Menstruating Men: Religion in Wogeo, New Guinea. Scranton: Chandler.
Hori, Ichiro
    1968   Folk Religion in Japan: Continuity and Change. Chicago: University of Chicago Press.
_____, et al.
    1972   Japanese Religion: A Survey by the Agency of Cultural Affairs. Tokyo: Kodansha International.
Horton, Robin
    1965   Kalabari Sculpture. Lagos: Department of Antiquities.
Houlihan, Patrick Thomas
    1972   Art and Social Structure on the Northwest Coast. Ph.D. Dissertation, University of Wisconsin, Milwaukee.
Hrdlicka, Aleŝ
    1975   The Anthropology of Kodiak Island. New York: AMS Press.
Ienaga, Saburo
    1979   Japanese Art: A Cultural Appreciation. New York: Weatherhill.
Izutsu, Toshihiko and Toyo Izutsu
    1981   The Theory of Beauty in the Classical Aesthetics of Japan. The Hague: Martinus Nijhoff Publishers.
Jenness, Diamond
    1928   People of the Twilight. New York: Macmillan.
    1946   Material Culture of the Copper Eskimo. Canadian Arctic Expedition 1913–18, Vol. 16. Ottawa: King's Printer.
Johnston, Thomas F.
    1976   Eskimo Music by Region: A Comparative Circumpolar Study. Ottawa: National Museum of Man.
Jones, Trevor
    1956/7   Arnhem Land Music, Part 2, A Musical Survey. Oceania 26(4):252–339, 28(1):1–30.
Kaberry, Phillis M.
    1941   The Abelam Tribe, Sepik District, New Guinea: A Preliminary Report. Oceania 11:233–258, 345–367.

Kaeppler, Adrienne L.
　1971　Aesthetics of Tongan Dance. Ethnomusicology 15:175–185.
Kanafani, Aida S.
　1983　Aesthetics and Ritual in the United Arab Emirates: The Anthropology of Food and Personal Adornment Among Arabian Women. Syracuse: Syracuse University Press.
Katz, Richard
　1982　Boiling Energy. Cambridge: Harvard University Press.
Kaufmann, Hans
　1910　Die ≠Auin. Ein Beitrag zur Buschmannforshung. Trans. by Richard Neuse. Mitteilungen aus den Deutschen Schutzgebeiten 23:135–160.
Keali'inohomoku, Joann W.
　1985　Music and Dance of the Hawaiian and Hopi Peoples. In David P. McAllester, ed., Becoming Human through Music: The Wesleyan Symposium on the Perspectives of Social Anthropology in the Teaching and Learning of Music. Reston, Virginia: Music Educators National Conference. Pp. 5–22.
Kearney, Michael
　1972　Winds of Ixtepeji. New York: Holt, Rinehart and Winston.
Keene, Donald
　1971　[orig. 1958] Feminine Sensibility in the Heian Era. In D. Keene, ed., Landscapes and Portraits: Appreciations of Japanese Culture. Tokyo: Kodansha. Pp. 26–39.
Keil, Charles
　1979　Tiv Song. Chicago: University of Chicago Press.
Kellog, Rhoda
　1969　Analyzing Children's Art. Palo Alto: National Press Books.
Kirby, P.R.
　1936　The Musical Practice of the ≠ami and ≠khomani Bushmen. Bantu Studies 10:373–431.
Kirk, Malcolm
　1981　Man as Art: New Guinea. Introduction by Andrew Strathern. New York: Viking.
Kishimoto, Hideo
　1967　Some Japanese Cultural Traits and Religions. In Charles A. Moore, ed., The Japanese Mind. Honolulu: University of Hawaii Press. Pp. 110–121.
Kluckhohn, Clyde and Dorothea Leighton
　1946　The Navaho. Cambridge: Harvard University Press.
Kōsaka, Masaaki
　1967　The Statuses and the Role of the Individual in Japanese Society. In Charles A. Moore, ed., The Japanese Mind. Honolulu: University of Hawaii Press. Pp. 245–261.
Kupka, Karel
　1965　Dawn of Art: Painting and Sculpture of Australian Aborigines. Trans. by John Ross. New York: Viking Press.
Ladd, John
　1973　Conceptual Problems Relating to the Comparative Study of Art. In Warren L. d'Azevedo, ed., The Traditional Artist in African Societies. Bloomington: Indiana University Press. Pp. 417–424.
Lansing, J. Stephen
　1981　A Balinese Act of Faith. In Jane E. Aaron, ed., Odyssey: The Human Adventure. Boston: Public Broadcasting Associates. Pp. 35–37.
Lawal, Babatunde
　1974　Some Aspects of Yoruba Aesthetics. British Journal of Aesthetics 14:239–249.
Leach, Edmund R.
　1961　Aesthetics. In E.E. Evans-Pritchard et al., eds., The Institutions of Primitive Society. Glencoe, Illinois: The Free Press. Pp. 25–38.

Lebzelter, Viktor
1934   Eingeborenkulturen in Südwest und Süafrica, Vol. 2. Leipzig: Karl W. Hiersemann.

Lee, Richard Borshay
1979   The !Kung San. New York: Cambridge University Press.

LeFree, Betty
1975   Santa Clara Pottery Today. Albuquerque: University of New Mexico Press.

Leighton, Alexander and Dorothea Leighton
1944   The Navaho Door: An Introduction to Navaho Life. Cambridge: Harvard University Press.

Leiris, Michel and Jacqueline Delange
1968   African Art. Trans. by Michael Ross. New York: Golden Books.

León-Portilla, Miguel
1963   Aztec Thought and Culture: A Study of the Ancient Nahuatl Mind. Trans. by Jack Emory. Norman: University of Oklahoma Press.
1966   Pre-Hispanic Thought. In Mario de la Cueva et al., Major Trends in Mexican Philosophy. Notre Dame: University of Notre Dame Press. Pp. 2-56.
1971   Philosophy in Ancient Mexico. In Robert Wauchope, ed., Handbook of Middle American Indians, Vol. 10. Austin: University of Texas Press. Pp. 447-451.
1983   Three Forms of Thought in Ancient Mexico. In F. Allen Hanson, ed., Studies in Symbolism and Cultural Communication. University of Kansas Publications in Anthropology, Number 14. Lawrence: University of Kansas. Pp. 9-24.

Leroi-Gourhan, André
1982   The Dawn of European Art: An Introduction to Paleolithic Cave Painting. New York: Cambridge University Press.

Lewis-Williams, J. David
1981   Believing and Seeing: Symbolic Meanings in Southern San Rock Paintings. New York: Academic Press.

Liggett, John
1974   The Human Face. New York: Stein & Day.

Lin Yutang
1935   The Artistic Life. In Lin Yutang, My Country and My People. New York: Halcyon. Pp. 287-321.

Linton, Ralph
1941   Primitive Art. Kenyon Review 3(1):34-51.
———— and Paul S. Wingert
1971   Introduction, New Zealand, Sepik River, and New Ireland, from Arts of the South Seas. In Charlotte M. Otten, ed., Anthropology and Art. Garden City, New York: Natural History Press. Pp. 383-404.

Lloyd, Peter C., A.L. Mabogunje, and B. Awe, eds.
1967   The City of Ibadan. London: Cambridge University Press.

Lomax, Alan
1968   Song as a Measure of Culture. In Alan Lomax, ed., Folk Song Style and Culture. Washington, D.C.: American Association for the Advancement of Science. Pp. 170-201.

Luttmann, Gail and Rick Luttmann
1985   Aesthetics of Eskimo Dance: A Comparison Methodology. In Betty True Jones, ed., Dance as Cultural Heritage, Vol. 2. Council on Dance Research: Dance Research Annual XV. Pp. 53-61.

Lutz, Maija M.
1978   The Effects of Acculturation on Eskimo Music of Cumberland Peninsula. Canadian Ethnology Service, Paper No. 41, a Diamond Jenness Memorial Volume. Ottawa: National Museums of Canada.

Madsen, William
1960   The Virgin's Children: Life in an Aztec Village Today. Austin: University of Texas Press.

Mandelbrot, Benoît
1982   The Fractal Geometry of Nature. San Francisco: W.H. Freeman.

Maquet, Jacques
1971   Introduction to Aesthetic Anthropology. Reading, Massachusetts: Addison-Wesley.
1986   The Aesthetic Experience. New Haven: Yale University Press.

Marshall, Lorna
1957a   The Kin Terminology System of the !Kung Bushmen. Africa 27:1–25.
1957b   N!ow. Africa 27:232–240.
1959   Marriage among the !Kung Bushmen. Africa 29:335–364.
1961   Sharing, Talking, and Giving: Relief of Social Tensions among !Kung Bushmen. Africa 31:231–249.
1962   !Kung Bushman Religious Beliefs. Africa 32:221–252.
1965   The !Kung Bushman of the Kalahari Desert. In James L. Gibbs, Jr., ed., Peoples of Africa. New York: Holt, Rinehart and Winston. Pp. 243–278.
1976   The !Kung of Nyae Nyae. Cambridge: Harvard University Press.

Marti, Samuel and Gertrude F. Kurath
1964   Dance of Anáhuac: The Choreography and Music of Precortesian Dancers. Chicago: Aldine.

Martijn, Charles A.
1964   Canadian Eskimo Carving in Historical Perspective. Anthropos 59:546–596.

Mason, J. Alden
1927   Eskimo Pictorial Art. The Museum Journal 18(3):248–283. Philadelphia: Museum of the University of Pennsylvania.

Mason, J.W.T.
1935   The Meaning of Shinto. Port Washington, New York: Kennikat Press.

Masson, Jeffrey L. and M. Patwardhan
1969   Śāntarasa and Abhinavagupta's Philosophy of Aesthetics. Poona: Bhandarkar Oriental Research Institute.
1970   Aesthetic Rapture, Vols. 1 and 2. Poona, India: Deccan College Postgraduate and Research Institute.

McAllester, David
1954   Enemy Way Music. Cambridge, Massachusetts: Peabody Museum.
1980   Shootingway, an Epic Drama of the Navajos. In Charlotte Frisbie, ed., Southwestern Indian Ritual Drama. Albuquerque: University of New Mexico Press. Pp. 199–237.

McCarthy, F.D.
1938   Australian Aboriginal Decorative Art. Sydney: Australian Museum.
1957a   Australia's Aborigines, Their Life and Culture. Melbourne: Colorgravure Publication.
1957b   Theoretical Considerations of Australian Aboriginal Art. Journal and Proceedings of the Royal Society of New South Wales, Vol. 9, part 1.

McGhee, Robert
1976   Differential Artistic Productivity in the Eskimo Cultural Tradition. Current Anthropology 17(2):203–220.

McMahon, A. Philip, trans.
1956   Leonardo Da Vinci, *Treatise on Painting*. Princeton: Princeton University Press.

McNaughton, Patrick R.
1979   Secret Sculptures of Komo: Art and Power in Bamana (Bambara) Initiation Associations. Working Papers in the Traditional Arts, No. 4. Philadelphia: ISHI.

McNeley, James Kale
1981   Holy Wind in Navajo Philosophy. Tucson: University of Arizona Press.

Mead, Margaret
1963   [orig. 1936] Sex and Temperament in Three Primitive Societies. New York: Morrow.
1970   [orig. 1938, 1940] The Mountain Arapesh, Vol. 2. New York. Natural History Press.

Meldgaard, Jorgen
   1960   Eskimo Sculpture. London: Methuen.
Merriam, Alan P.
   1964   The Anthropology of Music. Chicago: Northwestern University Press.
   1973   The Bala Musician. In Warren L. d'Azevedo, ed., The Traditional Artist in African Societies. Bloomington: Indiana University Press. Pp. 255–277.
Messenger, John C. and Betty J. Messenger
   1981   Sexuality in Folklore in a Nigerian Society. Central Issues in Anthropology 3(1):29–50.
Mitchell, William E.
   1978   The Bamboo Fire. New York: Norton.
Moore, Charles A.
   1967   Editor's Supplement: The Enigmatic Japanese Mind. In Charles A. Moore, ed., The Japanese Mind. Honolulu: University of Hawaii Press. Pp. 288–313.
Morris, Desmond
   1962   The Biology of Art. London: Cox and Wyman.
Mountford, Charles Percy
   1954   Aboriginal Paintings from Australia: New York: New American Library.
   1961   The Artist and His Art in an Australian Aboriginal Society. In M.W. Smith, ed., The Artist in Tribal Society. New York: Free Press of Glencoe. Pp. 1–13.
Munn, Nancy
   1973   Walbiri Iconography: Graphic Representation and Cultural Symbolism in a Central Australian Society. Ithaca: Cornell University Press.
Munro, Thomas
   1956   Toward Science in Aesthetics. New York: Liberal Arts Press.
   1963   Evolution in the Arts and Other Theories of Culture History. New York: Abrams.
   1965   Oriental Aesthetics. Cleveland: Press of Western Reserve University.
Murphy, Yolanda and Robert F. Murphy
   1974   Women of the Forest. New York: Columbia University Press.
Nakamura, Hajime
   1967   Basic Features of the Legal, Political, and Economic Thought of Japan. In Charles A. Moore, ed., The Japanese Mind. Honolulu: University of Hawaii Press. Pp. 143–163.
Nelson, Edward
   1899   The Eskimo about Bering Strait. Washington, D.C.: 18th Annual Report—Bureau of American Ethnology.
Newcomb, Franc Johnson
   1940   Navajo Omens and Taboos. Santa Fe: Rydal Press.
Newton, Douglas
   1971   Crocodile and Cassowary: Religious Art of the Upper Sepik River. New York: Museum of Primitive Art.
Nicholson, H.B.
   1976   Late Pre-Hispanic Central Mexican Iconographic Systems. In H.B. Nicholson, ed., Origins of Religious Art and Iconography in Preclassic Mesoamerica. U.C.L.A. Latin American Studies Series, 31. Los Angeles: University of California Latin American Center.
O'Neale, Lila M.
   1932   Yorok-Karok Basket Weavers. University of California Publications in American Archaeology and Ethnology 32(1):1–184.
Olson, Glendin
   1982   Literature in Recreation in the Later Middle Ages. Ithaca: Cornell University Press.
Organ, Troy
   1975   Indian Aesthetics—Its Techniques and Assumptions. Journal of Aesthetic Education 9(1):11–27.

Ortiz, Alfonso
 1972   Ritual Drama and the Pueblo World View. In Alfonso Ortiz, ed., New Perspectives on the Pueblos. Albuquerque: University of New Mexico Press. Pp. 135–161.

Osborne, Harold
 1968   Aesthetics and Art Theory: An Historical Introduction. New York: E.P. Dutton.
 1974   Primitive Art and Society: Review Article. British Journal of Aesthetics 14(4):290–303.

Ottenberg, Simon
 1982   Illusion, Communication, and Psychology in West African Masquerades. Ethos 10(2):149–185.

Oxford English Dictionary
 1971   Compact Edition. New York: Oxford University Press.

Pager, Harold
 1975   Stone Age Myth and Magic as Documented in the Rock Paintings of South Africa. Graz, Austria: Akademische Druck- und Verlagsanslalt.

Pandy, K.C.
 1952   Comparative Aesthetics. Volume I, Indian Aesthetics; Volume II, Western Aesthetics. Varanasi-I, India: Chowkhambra Sanskrit Series Office.

Panofsky, Erwin
 1955   Meaning in the Visual Arts. Chicago: University of Chicago Press.

Parezo, Nancy J.
 1982   Navajo Sandpaintings: The Importance of Sex Roles in Craft Production. American Indian Quarterly 6(1–2):125–148.
 1983   Navajo Sandpainting: From Religious Act to Commercial Art. Tucson: University of Arizona Press.

Park, Edwards
 1986   Around the Mall and Beyond. Smithsonian 17(9):22–24.

Peckham, M.
 1965   Man's Rage for Chaos: Biology, Behavior and the Arts. Philadelphia: Chilton.

Pepper, Steven C.
 1945   The Basis of Criticism in the Arts. Cambridge: Harvard University Press.

Pickford, R.W.
 1972   Psychology and Visual Aesthetics. London: Hutchenson Educational.

Price, Richard and Sally Price
 1981   Afro-American Arts of the Suriname Rain Forest. Berkeley: University of California Press.

Raffé, W.G.
 1952   Ragas and Raginis: A Key to Hindu Aesthetics. Journal of Aesthetics and Art Criticism 11(2):105–117.

Rasmussen, Knut
 1929   Intellectual Culture of the Iglulik Eskimos. Fifth Thule, Vol. 7(1). New York: AMS Press.
 1931   The Netsilik Eskimos: Social Life and Spiritual Culture. Fifth Thule, Vol. 8. New York: AMS Press.
 1932   Intellectual Culture of the Copper Eskimos. Fifth Thule, Vol. 9. New York: AMS Press.

Ravicz, Marilyn Ekdahl
 1976   Ephemeral Art: A Case for the Functions of Aesthetic Stimulus. Paper read at the American Anthropological Association meeting, November 19, 1976. New York City.

Rawson, Philip
 1973   The Art of Tantra. London: Thames and Hudson.

Ray, Dorothy Jean
 1961   Artists of the Tundra and Sea. Seattle: University of Washington Press.
 1977   Eskimo Art: Tradition and Innovation in North Alaska. Seattle: University of Washington Press.

Reichard, Gladys A.
1936 Navajo Shepherd and Weaver. New York: J.J. Augustin.
1944 Prayer: The Compulsive Word. American Ethnological Society Monograph 7. Seattle: University of Washington Press.
1970 [orig. 1950] Navajo Religion: A Study of Symbolism. Princeton: Princeton University Press.
1977 [orig. 1939] Navajo Medicine Man Sandpaintings. New York: Dover.

Rice, Prudence M.
1983 Serpents and Style in Peten Postclassic Pottery. American Anthropologist 85(4):866–880.

Rose, Margaret
1984 Marx's Lost Aesthetics. New York: Cambridge University Press.

Ross, Margaret Clunies and L.R. Hiatt
1978 Sand Sculptures at a Gidjingali Burial Rite. In Peter J. Ucko, ed., Form in Indigenous Art. London: Duckworth.

Russell, Bertrand
1967 The Autobiography of Bertrand Russell, Vol. 1. Toronto: McClelland and Steward.

Ryusaku, Tsunoda, William Theodore de Bary, and Donald Keene, eds.
1958 Sources of Japanese Tradition. New York: Columbia University Press.

Salisbury, Richard P.
1959 A Trobriand Medusa? Man 59(67):50–51.

Saraswati, S.K.
1969 Indian Art: Artist's Point of View. In S.S. Barlingay et al., Indian Aesthetics and Art Activity. Transactions of the Indian Institute of Advanced Study, No. 2. New York: International Publications Service. Pp. 89–91.

Sassouni, Viken
1981 Armenian Church Floor Plans. Hali: The International Journal of Oriental Carpets and Textiles 4(1):24–28.

Schapera, Isaac
1930 The Khoisan Peoples of South Africa. London: Routledge.

Schiller, Paul H.
1961 Figural preferences in the Drawings of a Chimpanzee. Journal of Comparative and Physiological Psychology 44(2):101–111.

Schmitz, Carl August
1963 Wantoat: Art and Religion of the Northeast New Guinea Papuans. Trans. G.E. van Baaren-Pape. The Hague: Mouton.

Schneider, Harold K.
1956 The Interpretation of Pakot Visual Art. Man 56:103–106.
1966 Turu Esthetic Concepts. American Anthropologist 68:156–160.

Selzer, Richard
1979 Confessions of a Knife. New York: Simon & Schuster.

Shostak, Marjorie
1981 Nisa: The Life and Words of a !Kung Woman. Cambridge: Harvard University Press.
1984 The Creative Individual in the World of the !Kung San. Paper read at the Annual Meeting of the American Anthropological Association, November 15, 1984, Denver, Colorado.

Sieber, Roy
1962 Masks as Agents of Social Control. African Studies Bulletin 5(11):8–13.
1971 [orig. 1958] The Aesthetics of Traditional African Art. In Carol F. Jopling, ed., Art and Aesthetics in Primitive Societies. New York: Dutton. Pp. 127–131. Orig. in Froelich Rainey, ed., Seven Metals of Africa. Philadelphia: University Museum, University of Pennsylvania.

Silver, Harry
1981 Calculating Risks: The Socioeconomic Foundations of Aesthetic Innovation in an Ashanti Carving Community. Ethnology 20(2):101–114.

Smith, Bradley
1964 Japan: A History in Art. New York: Simon & Schuster.

Smith, Cyril Stanley
1981 A Search for Structure. Cambridge: MIT Press.

Sorokin, Pitirim A.
1937 Social and Cultural Dynamics. Vol. I: Fluctuations of Forms of Art. New York: American Book Company.

Spencer, Baldwin and F.J. Gillan
1938 The Native Tribes of Central Australia. London: Macmillan.

Stolnitz, Jerome
1960 Aesthetics and Philosophy of Art Criticism: A Critical Introduction. Boston: Houghton-Mifflin.

Stow, George W.
1905 The Native Races of South Africa. London: Sonneschein.

Strathern, Andrew and Marilyn Strathern
1971 Self-decoration in Mount Hagen. Toronto: University of Toronto Press.

Strathern, Marilyn
1979 The Self in Self-Decoration. Oceania 48:241-257.

Suzuki, D.T.
1957 Sengai: Zen and Art. Art News Annual 27 (Part 2):193.
1983 [orig. 1959] Excerpt from Zen and Japanese Culture. In Earle J. Coleman, ed., Varieties of Aesthetic Experience. Lanham, Maryland: University Press of America. Pp. 179-190.

Swinton, George
1978 Touch and the Real: Contemporary Inuit Aesthetics—Theory, Usage, and Relevance. In Michael Greenhalgh and Vincent Megaw, eds., Art in Society. New York: St. Martins. Pp. 71-88.

Taçon, Paul S.C.
1983 Dorset Art in Relation to Prehistoric Culture Stress. Etudes Inuit/Inuit Studies 7(1):41-65.

Tartarkiewicz, Władysław
1970a History of Aesthetics. Vol. I: Ancient Aesthetics, ed. by J. Harrell, trans. by Adam and Ann Czerniawski. Warsaw: Polish Scientific Publishers.
1970b History of Aesthetics, Vol. II: Medieval Aesthetics, ed. by C. Barrett, trans. by R.M. Montgomery. Warsaw: Polish Scientific Publishers.

Tedlock, Barbara
1980 Songs of the Zuni Kachina Society: Composition, Rehearsal and Performance. In Charlotte Frisbie, ed., Southwestern Indian Ritual Drama. Albuquerque: University of New Mexico Press. Pp. 7-36.

Theal, George McCall
1910 The Yellow and Dark-Skinned People of Africa South of the Zambesi. London: Swann Sonneschein.

Thomas, Elizabeth Marshall
1959 The Harmless People. New York: Random House.

Thompson, Robert Farris
1968 Esthetics in Traditional Africa. Art News 66(9):44-45, 63-68.
1971 [orig. 1966] An Aesthetic of the Cool: West African Dance. African Forum 2(2):85-102.
1973 Yoruba Artistic Criticism. In Warren L. d'Azevedo, ed., The Traditional Artist in African Societies. Bloomington: Indiana University Press. Pp. 19-61.
1974 African Art in Motion: Icon and Act. Berkeley: University of California Press.
1976 Black Gods and Kings. Bloomington: Indiana University Press.
1983 Flash of the Spirit: African and Afro-American Art and Philosophy. New York: Random House.

Tobias, Philip V.
1961 New Evidence and New Views on the Evolution of Man in Africa. South African Journal of Science 57(2):25-38.

1964   Bushman Hunter-Gatherers: A Study in Human Ecology. In D.H.S. Davies, ed., Ecological Studies in Southern Africa. Den Haag: Junk.

Tschopik, Harry S., Jr.
1938   Taboo as a Possible Factor Involved in the Obsolescence of Navaho Pottery and Basketry. American Anthropologist 40:257-262.

Turner, Terence S.
1980   The Social Skin. In Jeremy Cherfas and Roger Lewin, eds., Not Work Alone. London: Temple Smith. Pp. 112-140.

Turner, Victor
1966   Colour Classification in Ndembu Ritual: A Problem in Primitive Classification. In Michael Banton, ed., Anthropological Approaches to the Study of Religion. London: Tavistock. ASA Monographs No. 3. Pp. 47-84.

Tuzin, Donald F.
1980   The Voice of Tambaran: Truth and Illusion in Ilahita Arapesh Religion. Berkeley: University of California Press.

Ueda, Makoto
1967   Literary and Art Theories in Japan. Cleveland: The Press of Western Reserve University.

Vaillant, George Clapp
1944   The Aztecs of Mexico. New York: Doubleday.

Van der Post, Laurens
1958   The Lost World of the Kalahari. New York: Harcourt, Brace, Jovanovich.

van Offelen, Marion
1983   Nomads of Niger. Photographs by Carol Beckwith. New York: Morrow.

Vatsyayan, Kapila
1968   Indian Aesthetics and Art Activity. In S.S. Barlingay et al., Indian Aesthetics and Art Activity. Transactions of the Indian Institute of Advanced Study, No. 2. New York: International Publications Service.

Vogel, Susan M.
1979   Baule and Yoruba Art Criticism: A Comparison. In Justine M. Cordwell, ed., The Visual Arts: Plastic and Graphic. The Hague: Mouton. Pp. 309-325.
1980   Beauty in the Eyes of the Baule: Aesthetics and Cultural Values. Working Papers in the Traditional Arts, No. 6. Philadelphia: Institute for the Study of Human Issues.

Warren, D.M. and J. Kweku Andrews
1977   An Ethnoscientific Approach to Akan Arts and Aesthetics. Working Papers in the Traditional Arts, No. 3. Philadelphia: Institute for the Study of Human Issues.

Waterman, Richard A. and Patricia Panyity Waterman
1970   Directions of Culture Change in Aboriginal Arnhem Land. In Arnold R. Pilling and Richard A. Waterman, eds., Diprotodon to Detribalization: Studies of Change among Australian Aborigines. East Lansing: Michigan State University Press. Pp. 101-115.

Weitz, Morris
1967   [orig. 1957] The Role of Theory in Aesthetics. In Monroe C. Beardsley and Herbert M. Schueller, eds., Aesthetic Inquiry. Belmont, California: Dickenson. Pp. 3-11.

Werner, H.
1906   Anthropologische, Ethnologische und Ethnographische Beobachtungen uber die Heihum und Kungbuschleute, nebst einem Anhang uber die Sprachen dieser Buschmannstämme. Zeitschrift für Ethnologie 38:241-268. Trans. in Human Relations Area files by Richard Neuse.

Westheim, Paul
1965   [orig. 1950] The Art of Ancient Mexico. Trans. Ursula Bernard. New York: Doubleday.

White, Lynn, Jr.
1967   The Historical Roots of our Ecological Crisis. Science 155 (3767):1203-1207.

Whiten, Andrew
  1976 Primate Perception and Aesthetics. In D. Brothwell, ed., Beyond Aesthetics. London: Thames and Hudson. Pp. 18–40.

Whiting, John W.M.
  1941 Becoming a Kwoma; Teaching and Learning in a New Guinea Tribe. New Haven: Yale University Press.

Wilde, Oscar
  1891 The Picture of Dorian Gray. London: Oxford University Press.

Willett, Frank
  1971 African Art: An Introduction. New York: Praeger.

Willey, Gordon R.
  1966 An Introduction to American Archaeology, Vol. 1: North and Middle America. Englewood Cliffs, New Jersey: Prentice Hall.

Witherspoon, Gary
  1977 Language and Art in the Navajo Universe. Ann Arbor: University of Michigan Press.
  1980 Language in Culture and Culture in Language. International Journal of American Linguistics 46(1):1–13.
  1981 Self-expression and Self-esteem in Navajo Weaving. Plateau 52(4):29–32.

Wobst, H. Martin
  1977 Stylistic Behavior and Information Exchange. In C.E. Cleland, ed., For the Director: Research Essays in Honor of James B. Griffen. Anthropological Papers No. 61. Ann Arbor: Museum of Anthropology, University of Michigan.

Wolf, Eric
  1959 Sons of the Shaking Earth. Chicago: University of Chicago Press.

Wolfe, Alvin W.
  1969 Social Structural Bases of Art. Current Anthropology 10(1):14–44.

Wolfe, Tom
  1975 The Painted Word. Harpers Magazine, April, 1975. Pp. 57–92.

Wreschner, Ernst E.
  1976 The Red Hunters: Further Thoughts on the Evolution of Speech. Current Anthropology 17(4):717–719.
  1980 Red Ochre and Human Evolution: A Case for Discussion. Current Anthropology 21(5):631–644.

Zantwijk, Rudolf A.M. Van
  1957 Aztec Hymns as the Expression of the Mexican Philosophy of Life. International Archives of Ethnography 48(1):67–118.

Zenkovsky, V.V.
  1962 Dostoevsky's Religious and Philosophical Views. In René Wellekc, ed., Dostoevsky: A Collection of Critical Essays. Englewood Cliffs, New Jersey: Prentice Hall. Pp. 130–145.

Zolbrod, Paul G.
  1983 Diné Bahané: The Navajo Creation Story. Albuquerque: University of New Mexico Press.

INDEX

---

*The letter "n" indicates a footnote.